Praise for *The Monks*

"By Mr. Kiser's own evidence, Muslims in
the West in general, or Christianity in p
quite well is tell the story, at once sad and inspiring, of very good men who took their vocation seriously and died for it."

—*The Wall Street Journal*

"After two years of research and interviews, Kiser chronicles the vision that inspired the monks and the idealism and commitment that kept them in Algeria, despite the increasing violence and approaching danger."

—*Library Journal*

"Kiser's book is an attempt to find an answer to what are perhaps the central questions of our humanity: How to live with our neighbor? What is the meaning of community? The lives of these monks gives thought-provoking answers."

—*East Hampton Star*

"Mr. Kiser's work is beautifully researched, and very, very difficult to put down. It serves a dual purpose, each one worthy of a book on its own. The first is to provide a contrast between the terrorist factions who abuse Islam as a tool, and the people of Tibhirine, who practice Islam as brotherhood."

—*Islamic Horizons Magazine*

"This book is a timely view of an Islam that is not just about hatred and brutality. The book is spiritually uplifting and extremely moving."

—*Roanoke Times*

"Well written and extremely well researched . . . a valuable addition to the literature about modern Algeria. I plan to recommend it to all officers going on assignment there."

—Peter Bechtold, U.S. Foreign Service Institute

"An intellectual and emotional journey through the transcendent themes of faith, hate, war, and reconciliation. *The Monks of Tibhirine* is not only a penetrating account of recent historical events, but of ideas and ideologies driving them."

—Susan Eisenhower, director, Eisenhower Institute

"*The Monks of Tibhirine* is a work of great sensitivity. . . . His insightful prose weaves complex themes from Algeria's history into a single life-affirming whole. It transforms tragedy into hope for the future of Christian-Muslim relations . . . most inspiring!"

—Abdul Aziz Said, director,
Center for Global Peace, American University

"A remarkable book about love, respect, and forgiveness. It should be read by people of all faiths who seek to live in peace. . . . John Kiser makes the monks and the world they inhabit come alive."

—Elizabeth Swenson, executive director,
The Friends of St Benedict

"Kiser reconstructs patiently and impartially the sad story of an Algeria, in which spirituality and violence, peace and war, great hopes, and great contradictions are skillfully interwoven. The book is a testimony to the living pain of a country in search of an identity."

—Marco Impagliazzo, vice president,
Sant' Egidio, Rome

"John Kiser has done a wonderful job in writing about this gem of a story. His telling of it is very convincing . . . the lives of Christian de Cherge and his brothers were a gift of hope."

—Andrea Bartoli, director, Institute of Peace and
Reconciliation, Columbia University

The MONKS *of* TIBHIRINE

Faith, Love, and Terror in Algeria

JOHN W. KISER

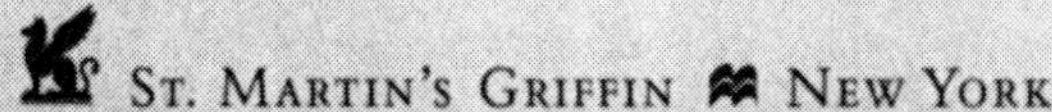

St. Martin's Griffin New York

To the monks of Tibhirine, and to those who loved them

 For information, address St. Martin's Press, 175 Fifth Avenue, New York, N.Y. 10010.

Photographs courtesy of Jacques Guerin

www.stmartins.com

Library of Congress Cataloging-in-Publication Data

Kiser, John W.
The monks of Tibhirine : faith, love, and terror in Algeria / John W. Kiser.—1st St. Martin's Griffin ed.
p. cm.
Includes bibliographical references and index.
ISBN 0-312-25317-6 (hc)
ISBN 0-312-30294-0 (pbk)
ISBN 978-0-312-30294-8

1. Trappists—Algeria—Tibihirine—Biography. 2. Christian martyrs—Algeria—Tibihirine—Biography 3. Victims of terrorism—Algeria—Biography. 4. Notre Dame de l'Atlas (Monastery : Tibihirine, Algeria) 5. Tibihirine (Algeria)—Church history—20th century. I. Title.

BX4155 .K47 2003
271'.1250653—dc21 2002024513

1

Algeria is land and sun. Algeria is a mother, cruel and yet adored, suffering and passionate, hard and nourishing. More than in our temperate zones, she is proof of the mix of good and evil, the inseparable dialectic of love and hate, the fusion of opposites that constitute mankind.

—Albert Camus

CONTENTS

ACKNOWLEDGMENTS

Like Trappist monks, writers do their real work alone, but their efforts are sustained and bear fruit only with the help and support of others. Without the trust and good faith shown by the families and friends of the monks, this book could never have been written. To them, I am especially grateful for letting a stranger share in their memories and sadness.

I would like to thank Bruno Chenu, the former editor of *La Croix,* who, in the spring of 1997, connected me to the right people as I was starting my research. One of those was Marie-Christine Ray, who was extraordinarily generous with her time and sources. She was working on a biography of Christian de Chergé, and her own timely research was of great benefit to me. I am deeply indebted to Bishop Henri Teissier and his colleague Gilles Nicolas for the support they provided during my visit to Algeria in 1999. Others, too numerous to mention, included journalists, friends of the monks within and outside of the Order, diplomats, and scholars.

For moral support in the early stages, I owe much to Ned Chase, Susan Eisenhower, and Carol Edwards, whose interest and preliminary editorial help led me to Michael Denneny, my editor at St. Martin's Press. Michael's wise guidance was invaluable in weaving together the different strands of the story.

I am also indebted to the many friends and acquaintances who took the time to read and comment on the manuscript, often with great care. One of those was Dean Fischer, former *Time* magazine bureau chief for the Middle East, who was struggling with cancer at the time. Mireille Luc-Keith, my good friend and research assistant, read it more often than anyone, possibly even more than I did. I am deeply appreciative of her commitment to this undertaking, enthusiasm, and meticulous attention to the seemingly endless details.

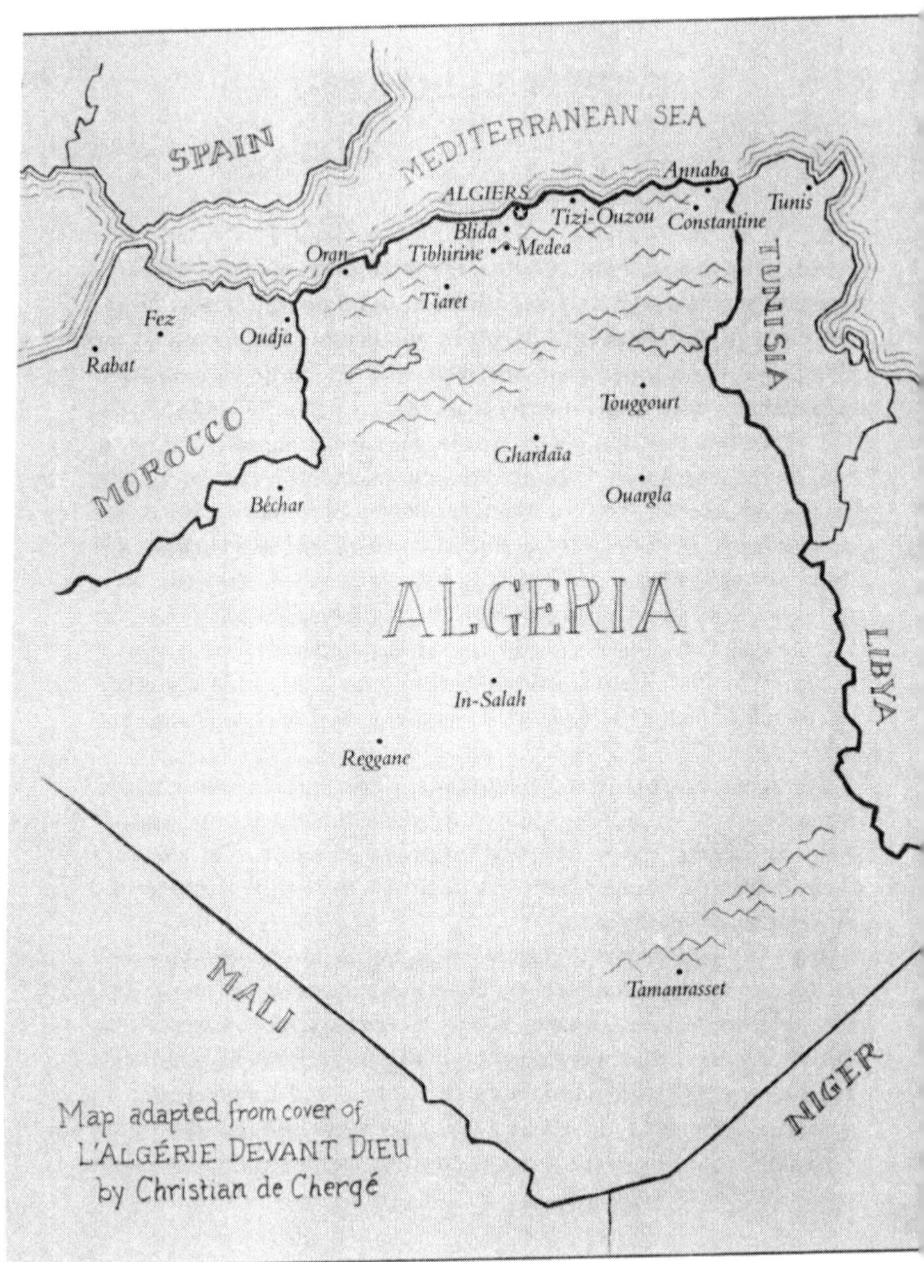

MAP OF ALGERIA

AUTHOR'S NOTE

This is a true story. Yet truth, as we know, is a many-faceted thing. Of one thing I am sure: This is not the whole truth.

Quoted passages represent excerpts from published materials, monastic communications, or interviews. I have accounted for my principal sources in the chapter commentaries at the end of the book, rather than with detailed footnotes. Italics are generally reserved for citations from the Koran, the Bible or the Benedictine Rule, and, in some cases, when I have quoted extensively from articles or documents. Koranic citations are from the Penguin Classics translation by N. J. Dawood, first published in 1956. Biblical quotations are from the New King James Version. Foreign words are defined in the glossary, as are basic Islamic religious terms and concepts.

INTRODUCTION

I first met Robert de Chergé in the lobby of the Grand Hôtel Concorde in Lyons. I had written him of my interest in doing a book about the monks of Tibhirine, whose prior, Christian de Chergé, was his younger brother. He had immediately replied to me in Paris, where I was staying at the time, and invited me to come down to talk. I was somewhat nervous about meeting this retired general from the nuclear artillery branch of the French army who was the designated doorkeeper for screening journalists, writers, and others seeking access to the monks' families.

The story of the kidnapping and murder of seven French Trappist monks in Algeria had been all over the European press during the summer of 1996. Their monastery of Notre-Dame de l'Atlas in Tibhirine was known as a place of friendship between Muslims and Christians. For four years, both the monastery and the village nearby had been spared the violence that raged in the mountains around them. The monks eventually became victims in a struggle among Muslims for a more just society, a struggle that had gone horribly wrong and had cost from 60,000 to 100,000 Algerian lives by 1996. Yet the monks were not martyrs to their faith. They did not die because they were Christians. They died because they wouldn't leave their Muslim friends, who depended on them and who lived in equal danger.

Emotions were still raw one year later, and the monks' families had felt put-upon by the many callers from the media. So it was with some relief when a tall, lanky man with tousled gray hair, *sans cravate,* wearing a half-zippered suede jacket, and an inquisitive smile came up to greet me. At their apartment on the rue Auguste-Comte, his wife, Anne, joined us in the living room where a gentle interrogation began before dinner.

"Are Americans really interested in reading about Algeria? Why are you interested in French monks?"

American interest in Algeria per se, I said, was probably limited to a few academic specialists and oil companies. But there was an interest in understanding the violence done in the name of Islam and in the broader problem of how different kinds of people can live together peacefully. I explained that I had spent a sabbatical year in France in 1994–1995 with my family and, while there, had met Christians and Muslims who were trying to understand one another better. The Muslims I got to know impressed me with their warmth and hospitality, and their respect for Jesus Christ. Five million Muslims live in France, almost 8 percent of the population of a country where I had witnessed growing anxiety about "the Arab," fueled by high unemployment, crime, ignorance, and racism. Every year, more Muslims from around the world are coming to live in the United States, where similar problems of ignorance and acceptance exist. To most non-Muslims, the face of Islam is one of terror and fanaticism. Muslims who love Christians, and Muslims who risk their lives speaking out against terrorism, tell of other Islams.

As to my interest in French monks, I said that the monks were not really "French." To my mind, their country was that of the Gospels. They belonged to everyone, even Americans and Muslims. These men represented my understanding of what Christianity should be. Love God, but love thy neighbor first. The problem is always the neighbor. Theirs was a respectful love that accepted that God speaks to people in different ways. They were practicing their faith without ulterior motives in a Muslim country where spreading the Good News is not permitted.

I also wanted to understand better what it means to be "Christian." Does being baptized make one Christian? Does professing love of Jesus make one a Christian? To lead a Christian life, does one have to be Christian? And why have Christians all too often been bad advertisements for Christianity—dividing and excluding, rather than uniting people—just as certain so-called Muslims are now doing in Algeria? Is the problem with scripture, or with people? I thought the story of these monks and the Muslims whose lives they shared held a clue.

Finally, I told the general, the published writings of his brother had appealed to me. As a young soldier in Algeria during the war of independence, Christian had found in the Muslims a people more devoted to prayer and serving God than in supposedly Christian France. He sought to expand his Christianity, to make a place for Islam, and to seek "the notes that are in harmony." He was a unifier, not a separator. Christian de Chergé's Christianity interested me.

A month later Robert sent me the names and addresses of the relatives of other monks, as well as those of his siblings who were willing to meet with me. Over the next two years, I met with the families of the other monks to learn who these men were and why they had gone to Algeria. But talking with the relatives of the monks was like meeting only half the family, for a Trappist has two—his blood family, from which he is separating himself, and the new family he adopts when he enters the order. He takes on a new first name, symbolic of his new identity in Christ. The abbot becomes his father, and fellow monks, his brothers. He forsakes his worldly wealth for his monk's habit. At death, his few personal possessions—books, papers, and writings—belong to the Order.

The seven monks who died had gone to Algeria from three different Trappist monasteries in France: Notre-Dame d'Aiguebelle, in the Rhône valley near Montélimar; Notre-Dame de Tamié, located in the mountains of Savoy, below Lake Annecy; and Notre-Dame de Bellefontaine, in the flat farm country of Anjou. Staying at each of the monasteries from where they began their calling, I experienced the rhythms and sensibilities of Trappist life and, from their former brothers, I learned more about the men and their lives in the Atlas.

I also began to better understand why my exposure to the Trappist culture had a certain resonance for me. Simplicity is one reason. Doing less, not more, and doing those fewer things more intensely, are values in perpetual struggle for survival in a world that is always offering more—more activities, more choices, more means of communication, things that distract and require decisions. Trappists have stripped their lives down to a simple triad of prayer, study, and manual labor. They have made only one decision: to love and praise God in the Trappist way. Their way is that of obedience, humility, and charity, practiced in a working community of brothers wedded in

Jesus Christ. They are practical, quiet, and frugal as they go about earning a living by making products that come from the land.

The dualities of Trappist life also appeal to me—solitude and community, meditation and action, love and discipline. Trappist monks are both community-disciplined and self-disciplined, though they would say "God-disciplined." They live as a community whose rhythms of work and devotion provide a harness to their daily life. Each monk has freely chosen this discipline in order to excel at love by purging his soul of the dross of envy, malice, anger, ego and other impediments to communal living. It is a discipline that helps him become a receptive vessel for God's spirit to fill. These are a few of the reasons I found their monastic culture to be like that of a rare, easy-to-overlook plant whose medicinal properties are known only to a few but which could benefit many.

The motives for the monks' kidnapping and the cause of their death remain a mystery to this day. It is not my purpose to solve it, but to tell a story of love and reconciliation amid fear and hatred.

PART ONE

Monks in a Muslim Land
1843–1989

1

Mourning

The nearest to the faithful are those who say "We are Christians." That is because there are priests and monks among them and because they are free of pride.

—Koran 5:82

From a certain angle, the Basilica of Notre Dame d'Afrique looks like a giant camel on its haunches, contemplating the Aleppo pine- and eucalyptus-covered hills that form an amphitheater around the port of Algiers. Its tall neck is formed by an elegant Byzantine tower connected to a large redbrick body, surmounted by an enormous gilded cupola that for over a hundred years was a beacon for Christian Europe to come and civilize the land the Arabs called the *maghreb*—"where the sun sets." The newcomers did their work well. Frenchmen sailing into the Bay of Algiers always experienced a sense of homecoming and breathtaking beauty. Algiers was the Nice of North Africa, France's Mediterranean pearl, with promenades along the sea, bustling cafés, beautiful gardens, elegant women, and imperial architecture. La Grande Poste, la rue de la République, la place Delacroix provided a reassuring sense of familiarity.

In the late spring of 1996, Algiers looked like a scabrous bag lady. Once admired for the brilliant snowiness of the whitewashed Casbah rising up the Sahel Hills, "La Blanche," as she was formerly known, now reeked of decay and failure, with crumbling, pockmarked buildings, ubiquitous stray cats, and putrid, garbage-filled streets. Churches that had been mosques before the French arrived were again mosques. Notre-Dame d'Afrique is one of the last citadels of a Christian presence that measures itself in hundreds in a country of 29 million Muslims.

Sunday afternoon, June 2, mourners had gathered on the steps to watch seven coffins being carried into the basilica. There were simple peasants in skullcaps, sunbaked workers in ill-fitting dress jackets, and a scattering of European men and women. Each casket was covered with a blanket of red roses, supported by four military cadets in the traditional ceremonial dress of the French fireman: white spats, gray uniform with red stripes down the pants, topped by a silver helmet of medieval proportions, polished to a mirror finish. Soldiers with Kalashnikovs patrolled the area around the cathedral and kept watch from rooftops. Killing people who came to the funerals of their victims was a favorite tactic of the terrorists.

Inside the massive rotunda, the caskets were placed next to yet one more. Monsignor Léon-Etienne Duval, many would say later, was also a casualty of the massacre. The much-loved ninety-two-year-old cardinal had struggled for fifty years for reconciliation between Europeans and Arabs. The monks were "the lungs" of the Church in Algeria, he liked to say. Their small community in the Atlas Mountains provided spiritual oxygen to Christians and Muslims alike. When he learned that the kidnapped monks had been executed, he told those at his bedside that he felt "crucified," and died a week later.

Behind the altar stood the "black Virgin"—named for the color of her aged bronze skin—gazing down from on top of an azure blue-tiled tabernacle. The words PRAY FOR US AND THE MUSLIMS were painted on the cupola above her head. That day, her prayers were needed more than ever. The Trappist abbot general, Father Bernardo Olivera, was one of many churchmen who addressed the congregation, but his words were the most heartfelt.

> *What can a monk say about his brother monks? I know that our order was founded on our commitment to silence, work, and praise of God. But we know there are times to speak as well as times to be quiet. After fifty years of silence, our seven brothers—Christian, Luc, Christophe, Célestin, Bruno, Michel and Paul—today have become spokesmen for all the stifled voices and anonymous individuals who have given their lives for a more humane world. Our seven monks lend their voices today to me as well. They, and others like them, were living manifestations of the good news of the Gospels: a life freely given in the spirit of love is never a life lost, but one found again in Him who is Life. . . .*
>
> *They showed that we must enter into the world of others, be that "other" a Christian or a Muslim. If "the other" does not exist, there can*

be no love of "the other." Let us learn to go beyond ourselves and to be enriched by those who are different. . . . Our brothers lives were the fruit of this Church in Algeria and of the many Algerians who over the years welcomed them and valued their presence. To the Church of Algeria and to you Algerians, fellow worshippers of one God, I say: A heartfelt thank you for the respect and the love you have shown to our monks."

Other homilies were given by Cardinal Jean-Marie Lustiger, who had come from Paris; Archbishop Henry Teissier of Algiers; and Cardinal Francis Arinze, Pope John Paul's personal envoy. When the service ended, senior officials of the Algerian government, members of the diplomatic corps, and hundreds of ordinary Algerians in the overflowing congregation filed past the photograph set on each monk's coffin. Many who had known them personally embraced their pictures and whispered tearful good-byes to the smiling faces. Outside, one mourner was overheard saying that the ceremony was too grand and pompous for the men who had lived so humbly among simple peasants.

After the service, a reporter from the Parisian weekly *L'Express* had questions for Pierre Claverie, the outspoken square-jawed bishop of the neighboring diocese of Oran. "The French government told its citizens to leave three years ago. What sense is there for the Church to stay in the face of so much danger? Are you being martyrs?" he asked.

"No. There are certain groups here who do not accept us," Bishop Claverie replied, "but the Church is Algerian, not French, and has existed under Algerian law since 1964. The government can cancel our visas anytime it wishes, but it doesn't because Christians are respected here even though we are a tiny community. Anyone who wants is free to leave. Those who stay are committed to the Church's presence here. If we leave, those who want ethnic and religious purification will win. A good shepherd does not abandon his flock when wolves come."

Back in France, memorial services were being held throughout the country. Many questions hung in the air: Why were the monks killed? What kind of Islam murders godly men in God's name? Why were Christians tending a Muslim flock?

2

Two Mohammeds

Righteousness does not consist in whether you face towards the East or the West. The righteous man is he who believes in God and the Last Day; who, though he loves it dearly, gives away his wealth to kinsfolk, to orphans, to the destitute, to the traveller in need and to beggars, and for the redemption of captives. . . .

—Koran 2:176

Where does the story of the monks' death begin? With the expedition in 1830 of the Comte de Bourmont to punish the dey of Algiers for smacking the French consul with a flyswatter, which led willy-nilly to Algeria becoming part of France? Or still further back, to the seventh century, when the Arabs swept through North Africa and converted the Christian Berbers to Islam? Or more recently, in the 1880s, when French anticlericalism drove Trappist monks to seek friendlier climes in Hapsburg Slovenia, and then, fearing Communist anticlericalism fifty years later, they found a new refuge in Algeria?

But those are stories for historians, and this is a story about lovers. Some will die and others kill for their love—of God, of divine law, and justice. But is it possible to love God and hate men? Is Christian love really different from Muslim love? In the summer of 1959, a lean, earnest officer, whose thick tortoiseshell glasses gave him an owlish, pensive air, might well have been wrestling with these questions. He had more reasons for doing so than most French soldiers. Lieutenant Christian de Chergé was a seminary student whose life had been saved by a Muslim.

"The events," as the dirty five-year-old war was known in France, was being won militarily but lost politically. Colonialism was out of phase. In 1956, President Eisenhower had forced Britain and France to recall the troops they had sent to intervene in the Suez crisis, which would leave the canal in Egyptian hands. Leftists in France were comparing the French army in Algeria to the Russians whose tanks had crushed the Hungarian uprising in 1956. Yet, even in an ugly conflict that had divided French and Muslims alike, Christian de Chergé came under Algeria's spell.

He was stationed as a staff officer in the ancient Berber city of Tiaret, famous for its Arab horses and bright ceramic designs. Located three thousand feet above sea level on the southern edge of the Massif Ouarsenis, Christian could see cathedral towers of limestone and marl watching over plains of wheat and alfalfa that descended south into the inland oceans of the Great Erg Desert. To the north of Tiaret, the serene silence of dense cedar forests on the massif had inspired an Arab poet to call the region "the eye of the world."

Algeria had seduced many a Frenchman over the years. For most, it was the seduction of nature, a Wild West four times the size of Texas, full of contrasts, harsh beauty, and exotic adventure. Its immense spaces were unknown in populated Europe, and all this could be reached by a two-hour plane flight on a Douglas DC-3 from Marseilles. Its Mediterranean coast is a twin of the Côte d'Azur. Limestone mountains fall to the sea along a twisting, turning coastline full of intimate bays and indentations. The northern coastal regions get as much rainfall as Paris, and winter snows stay year-round on the mountains of Kabylia. A thousand miles to the south, great sand seas can reach temperatures of 140 degrees Fahrenheit in the shade and tires melt on asphalt roads. Christian de Chergé found everything intoxicating, especially the native Berbers and Arabs, who were uncommonly hospitable by European standards, and uncommonly devoted to prayer and pleasing God.

He had been assigned to a Section Administrative Spéciale, or SAS, one of six hundred rural pacification districts that had been created after thousands of villages were destroyed by bombing attacks. A terrorized and dislocated rural population of over 2.6 million was "regrouped" under French control in order to deprive and protect—to deprive the rebels of support from the population and to protect from retribution the Algerians who were either neutral or friendly to France.

Soldiers in the SAS functioned as administrators, schoolteachers, public-health workers, and engineers who built housing, hospitals, schools, and mosques. The French army organized, armed, and paid

Algerians to protect the harvests, the main roads, and public utilities. The *fellaghas,* or *fells,* as the rebels were called by the soldiers, were boldest at night, when unalert guards risked having their throats slit or their manhood stuffed in their mouths.

Creating trust was the core of the military strategy. To succeed, it required showing trust and developing confidence among the people that France would remain in Algeria. "If you stay and protect us, we will march with you" were words SAS officiers heard often from the Muslims. Many of the Algerians had fought alongside the French in past wars. They showed their combat ribbons and shared recollections of battle-hardened comradeship, whether from World War I, World War II, or Vietnam, as they sat in the local government councils and discussed the future with French officers anxious to counter rebel propaganda.

The tracts of the revolutionary Front de Libération Nationale, or FLN, constantly reminded the population that the French could not be trusted, that they had always broken their promises and always would. To persuade the Muslims otherwise, army units did not rotate assignments. Draftees served their full tour in one SAS to learn the customs of the local population and to create an atmosphere of stability.

More pastor than warrior, the SAS officer was put in a difficult position. He was supposed to make the Muslims "feel French." This meant listening to their problems and making a good-faith effort to help them with tax relief, or health and security concerns. Yet, if he asked the army to compensate villagers whose sheep had been strafed by French airplanes, he would likely be ridiculed as naïve, or labeled a rebel sympathizer.

To learn of these realities, the newly arrived de Chergé had been given temporary duty commanding a platoon of thirty *moghazni.* These Algerian irregulars were assigned to protect him as he made the rounds, cultivating the leaders in the villages, though no self-respecting French officer could act as if he needed protection. As was his custom, Lieutenant de Chergé carried no side arm the day in August 1959 when he was taking one of his regular walks with Mohammed.

It was not Mohammed's importance as the village policeman that drew Christian to him, but their common love of God. Christian had found in Algeria a freedom he did not experience in France. Muslims were infused with a sense of the divine. He could talk unself-consciously with them about God, unlike in France, where God talk made people uncomfortable. Christian wrote to his mother about their long soul-baring walks, and the time Mohammed rankled him when he said, "You Christians don't know how to pray. We never see French soldiers praying. You say you believe in God. How can you not pray if you believe in God?" It was a question Christian had difficulty answering.

The young Frenchman and the older Muslim were lost in conversation during one of their regular rambles in the countryside, when some *fells* appeared from nowhere. It was an unpleasant habit of theirs, made easier by the caves and grottoes that honeycombed the limestone rocks of the massif. Mohammed put himself between Christian and the rifles aimed at his chest. He insisted that the soldier was a godly man and a friend of Muslims. The *fells* withdrew without harming the Frenchman. The next day, Mohammed was found with his throat slit near his home in tiny Aïn Said, where he lived with a wife and ten children.

Mohammed's generosity of spirit contrasted with the anger that Christian found in his parish at Tiaret. The city still radiated an atmosphere of colonial insouciance. Its central square was surrounded by chalky ocre-colored arcades, lined with the government buildings of the prefecture, kiosks, and cafés, where soldiers lounged and flirted. The number of "incidents," as assassinations were delicately called by the French, had been small in Tiaret, compared to other places. But the facade of normality was wearing thin as a growing sense of betrayal was taking hold of the European population.

Every morning, Christian rose joylessly to assist with the morning Mass presided over by the local curé, Ferdinand Lledo, a Catalan by birth. Lledo was full of holy wrath. He refused to read to his clergy the pastoral letters of Bishop Duval of Algiers, whose messages of justice and self-determination for all Algerians were anathema to him. He was enraged at President de Gaulle. "Three departments of France, and he is simply going to give them up!" he thundered at his parishioners on Sundays. He made no secret of his dislike of Arabs or Christians who showed any interest in Islam.

Father Lledo belonged to those in the clergy who believed love of country was a Christian obligation. But the country shared by the Europeans and the Muslims was not Algeria. It was France. France, they argued, had brought reason and order to what had been a nest of pirates, delivered the former Ottoman province from constant internal warfare, and brought modern engineering and medicine to alleviate disease among the *indigènes*.

Fighting to keep Algeria French was to fight for Christian civilization. *Le Petit Bônois,* published by the clergy of Bône, declared that "giving up Algeria to the Marxist-dominated rebels was giving it to the Communists." The champions of Algérie Française were defending Western civilization not only from godless communism but from the equal danger of Muslim fanaticism. "Abandoning Algeria will cause all traces of Christian civilization to disappear from North Africa. This is unacceptable. The church has a missionary role. And it is an outrageous lie to present Islam as a form of morality, or as a civilization that is not inferior to ours." The readers of *Le Petit Bônois* were reminded that "hatred, pillage, and savagery were the qualities of all the primitive races."

Depressed by the spiritual confusion he felt around him, de Chergé took solace in the exceptions. Mohammed had been a light in a morally confused landscape where "war had sterilized both the land and people's hearts," he wrote years later. "He changed my life by liberating my faith in spite of the complexity of daily life and showed me how to live it simply as a response to what is natural and authentic in others."

Of Mohammed, the unlettered policeman and family man, little is known. "Perhaps there is more charm in not knowing much about him. Like those who wrote the Gospels, we know him only by the fruit he bore," reflected Etienne Baudry, Christian's close friend from seminary school days, who later became the abbot of Bellefontaine Abbey. "Mohammed was surely a saint. I don't think Christian ever felt guilty about Mohammed's sacrifice. I think he considered Mohammed's act a gift of love, freely given. But there is no question it profoundly marked his calling."

Christian's commanding officer in Tiaret also offered hope. Colonel André Lalande was a military hero, born in defeat. He had been among the early supporters of de Gaulle's Free French movement, and had participated in the liberation of France in 1944. He had made a name commanding "Isabelle," the last defensive stronghold at the siege of Dien Bien Phu, before surrendering to the Communist-led Vietminh in May 1954. Colonel Lalande was also a committed Christian.

Lalande shared his young lieutenant's respect for the Muslim population. He too was impressed by their piety, as well as by the toughness and loyalty of his contingent of *harkis,* who were among the 250,000 Muslims serving under the French flag, a tradition of collaboration that began with Berber Zouaves who fought with the French in the 1830s. Like Christian, he was drawn to Muslims and had befriended the mufti of Tiaret. One day, Lalande invited Christian to come meet him. The mufti spoke with great politeness of the antagonism between Christianity and Islam, and confirmed Christian's own intuition that the relations between the two religions bore the weight of accumulated centuries of mutual prejudices. "For the mufti, as well as for many of us, man's relationship with God is the seat of all our liberties and source of courage, even the courage to disobey unjust orders," he wrote years later to a wartime friend.

Torture and summary executions were forbidden within Lalande's command. Two years before Christian began his military service in Algeria, these practices had become systematic and widespread. General Jacques Massu's Tenth Paratrooper Division was given a blank check in January of 1957 to restore order in Algiers. Algiers had witnessed an accelerating cycle of violence and reprisal, which began with the execution in June 1956 of two rebels held in Barberousse prison, one of whom was a cripple. In response, the rebel command gave orders to attack Europeans at will. Forty-nine people were killed or wounded in three days. A mysterious Committee of Forty was then formed to retaliate by blowing up a block of Arab houses for each European killed, and so it went, until Massu's arrival. He took on the task of pacification with distaste, calling it "dirty police work."

Stories leaked back to France about the use by special units of electric shock for "accelerated interrogations." To the population back home, the most upsetting accounts were those about Frenchmen—Communists and FLN sympathizers—who also had electrodes attached to their penises and earlobes or inserted in their rectums. After six months of torture, house-to-house searches, and summary executions, Massu's men had demolished the terrorist network. The Battle of Algiers had been won at a cost of only five French lives. But along the way to victory, the army lost the public's support.

With Lalande's backing, de Chergé and other like-minded officers used their rank whenever possible to prevent torture and summary execution of prisoners. They were men who felt as bound to live by the demands of the Gospels as by the Declaration of the Rights of Man. Named "the insolent ones," they were convinced that good cannot come from evil, despite the argument that torture saved innocent lives if it prevented a bomb from exploding. They knew that torture also spawned new terrorists.

"The insolent ones" received strong moral support from another person who tried to live by the Gospels: Bishop Léon-Etienne Duval. Christian first met Duval at Notre-Dame d'Afrique on New Year's Day 1960 soon after a priest had been assassinated and a particularly bloody ambush of FLN partisans had occurred. Duval's desire to keep his heart open to all sides of the conflict made a lasting impression on Christian, as did his views on obedience. He reminded the twenty-two-year-old lieutenant that obedience was the "guardian of all the virtues," provided it was rooted in faith. It was better to obey God than men. Christian obedience required intelligence and discernment; it could not be simply mechanical. It was never permitted a Christian to commit an evil act, even if commanded to do so by a superior. "True obedience assumes a harmony of thought with the one who commands."

During Massu's antiterrorist campaign, Duval outraged the European population. He had publicly condemned the violence on all sides, but singled out the summary executions, the collective punishment and torture practiced by certain units in the French army. Duval's growing number of enemies rechristened him "Mohammed" Duval, which raised his stature further in the eyes of the Muslim population.

Duval was an improbable candidate to become a champion of Muslim dignity in the rough-and-tumble of French Algeria. He was a reserved, some thought icy, cleric from the mountains of Savoy. Too frail for work on the family farm where he was raised, Duval was sent to the Gregorian University in Rome, where he learned an appreciation of Saint Augustine that would underpin his clerical calling. He returned to Savoy to become a professor of philosophy and Catholic dogma at le Grand Séminaire in the provincial capital of Annecy. Under the Nazi occupation, Duval, then the vicar general of the diocese, was responsible for helping the Resistance harbor Jewish families fleeing to Switzerland. Though he had many friends within the Resistance, Duval refused to join. His clerical collar, he reminded them, made him the inheritor of a universal message to serve and respect all men, no matter who they were.

His adherence to the message of universal love soon got Duval into trouble with the European settlers when, in 1947, he was appointed bishop of Constantine in France's eastern-most Algerian diocese. The colonists, or *pieds-noirs,* so named for their characteristic black army boots, were hard-nosed, tough sod-busters who arrived in Algeria usually fleeing some form of political or economic disaster. The first wave were political undesirables coerced to emigrate after the Paris uprising of 1848. Alsace and Lorraine produced a crop of immigrants not wishing to live under German rule after France's humiliation at Sedan in 1870. More came in the 1880s, when phylloxera destroyed the French wine industry.

Throughout Europe, Algeria was advertised by the French as a land of opportunity, but relatively few Frenchmen were tempted by reports of the swampy marshes of the Mitidja Plain, malaria and cholera, periodic rampages by natives whose land had been swindled, and backbreaking work in a country where people could suffocate in the summer and freeze in the winter. In 1917, after eighty-seven years of settlement, colonists of French origin made up only 25 percent of the European population. Spanish, Maltese, Italians, Greeks, English, a few Germans, and people of other nationalities had been lured by the offer of four hectares (ten acres), some farming tools, and a pair of oxen to counterbalance the indigenous Muslim population, which grew rapidly as a result of improved public health introduced by the French. This disproportion of native French within the settler population provoked Anatole France to observe acerbically, "We have despoiled, pursued, and hunted down the Arabs in order to populate Algeria with Italians and Spaniards."

Bishop Duval's first sermon as bishop of the Muslim holy city of Constantine unloaded a bucket of cold water on his European congregation, "You have to be blind not to be terrified at the extent of the social injustice and the consequences it will bring in the future," he warned, appalled at the contrast between the living conditions of Arabs and Europeans. "One day you will reproach me for not having spoken out enough, for not reminding you of your obligations as Christians." Duval spoke about these obligations with the piercing simplicity of a sharp knife.

"Without respect, there can be no love" was Duval's Golden Rule. He repeated it frequently to his parishioners and clergy. Brotherly love, not sentimental love, was the essence of Duval's faith. Love of one's neighbor leads to love of God. To love God is to love all his creatures. But fraternal love comes first, Duval insisted, for "that is the surest and most direct way to loving God." He implemented his Golden Rule in simple, everyday ways. Duval instructed his clergy to apply the rules of grammatical politeness equally. They were to address the Muslims the same way they would Europeans, using the respectful *vous* instead of the informal *tu,* normally reserved for close friends, animals, or children.

Duval was named Archbishop of Algiers in February 1954, which also made him the titular head of the Christian community in French Algeria. He sent shock waves through the European congregation on the occasion of his investiture at the recently built church of Sacré-Coeur, whose oddly modern design resembled a nuclear cooling tower. As if conscious of an impending disaster, Duval warned, "Muslims and Jews know that our Christianity requires us to love them, too. To love God means to love all his children as brothers. Muslims and Jews know that when we don't follow these demands, we betray our ideal as Christians." Duval explained in a subsequent pastoral letter, "A Catholic bishop must be a bishop for all people; otherwise, he is only the head of a sect."

When the struggle for independence was launched by the FLN nine months later, many *pieds-noirs* had roots going back four or five generations, to 1848, when Algeria was divided into departments and administered as an integral part of France, like the Vaucluse or the Loire-Atlantique. They were used to dealing with native uprisings and "incidents," just as they were used to their prejudices toward the "lazy Arab." Thus, when the reports of twelve killings around the country trickled into police commissariats on All Saints' Day, November 1, 1954, few people saw much out of the ordinary. It took a year—and only after the brutal Philippeville massacres, which killed 125 Europeans—for France to notice that this was more than the usual "disturbance."

"Contempt," wrote French author and playwright Jules Roy, "was the essence of the colonial mentality," which ultimately led to Algeria's war for independence. In 1961, his *La Guerre en Algérie* sold 100,000 copies in the first week. A *pied-noir* himself, Roy's *cri du coeur* burned with anger and sorrow. His book revealed the European attitudes that made reconciliation impossible. "Arabs are a filthy breed, good for nothing. . . . Occasionally one turns out to be honest before fanaticism takes over. . . . The Arab God could have nothing in common with the Christian one, we insisted every week. Who was that other God the tattered bastards invoked? . . . Arabs never suffered from swamp fever . . . their happiness was that of cattle."

Civilians were not the only ones who learned to hate Duval for defending the dignity of "the tattered bastards." Many of his own clergy had been baptized in the rivers of colonial prejudice and Algérie Française. "Universal love" and "justice for all," if it was to include Arabs and Muslims, was not in their catechism. As the "events" that had required the deployment of 500,000 soldiers became a bloody snowball rolling out of control, Duval would be called the "Muslims' bishop" because he continued to spread the subversive idea that Christians should be friends with Muslims, sharing equal rights.

Friendship between Muslims and Europeans was at the heart of Duval's calling. But friendship was not possible if one side viewed itself as superior to the other. In the fall of 1956, two and a half years before de Gaulle uttered the once unthinkable words "self-determination," Duval had circulated to his priests a pastoral letter, saying, "The basic problem is one of living together, and to assure equality between individuals without one community overwhelming the other—to create a new relationship between France and Algeria."

Throughout the seven-year conflict, Duval never ceased to stress the apolitical calling of a priest. "There is nothing more pernicious than the linkage of politics and religion" was another statement often heard on Duval's lips. Both suffered. Politics "denatured" religion and religion "confused" politics. Yet, following Pius XI, he also made a distinction between the "politics of parties" and *la grande politique*. His priests were reminded to function as priests only, and to stay out of all party politics. "No party speaks for God," he told them. Their calling, he stressed, was to protect the dignity of all people. But the Church also had to be concerned with the common good, and the problems of living together in the larger sense. It could not preach the Good News of the Gospels and be indifferent to injustice.

But Duval's apolitical message was itself viewed as political by his critics. The Church in Algeria was torn apart. The clergy of Algérie Française considered Duval's sympathy for Muslim rights treasonous in time of war. In their eyes, members of the clergy who harbored FLN sympathizers or gave medical assistance were accomplices of killers, and betraying France. Duval and his clerical allies, in turn, saw the partisans of Algérie Française as betraying the Gospels.

Bishop Duval's daily lot was a devil's brew of contempt from parishoners, vilification, desecrations of his churches, and threats to his life. But trials and hardship only reenergized him. Duval loved the struggle. Tall, pale, dignified, sometimes imperious, this "Mohammed" had the air of a prince of the Church, though of an unusual sort. Duval was profoundly conservative, yet a radical in the way he lived the Gospels.

In matters of ritual, Duval believed the liturgy should have a splendor that reflects upon the grandeur of God. Like the Muslims around him, he thought man should feel small before his Creator. Nor was the liturgy the personal property of the clergy to be tampered with to suit the times or individual preferences. It should be performed as the Church wishes. He liked to cite Saint Augustine, "That which is small is small, but it is a big thing to be faithful in small things." Duval was also a revolutionary who believed in the transforming power of brotherly love. His frequent exhortation to "pay honor to God" formed the hub that unified his radicalism and conservatism. One pays honor to God by honoring God's creation. Duval's Christianity resonated with Muslims.

Duval would remind his clergy that "a priest must have one foot in the street and one in the church." In the street were God's needy and rejected. In the church was the strength of community and God's word. Befitting a prince of the streets, he survived on strong Boyard cigarettes and solidarity. "Without my cigarette each night, I would have ended up in the loony bin," he told a journalist years later. Solidarity with other Christians who shared his loyalty to the Gospels fortified his courage. They included the vast majority of his own clergy within Algiers, as well as the head chaplain of the military, François de L'Espinay, known as "the Baron"; the Poor Clares; the Pères Blancs (White Fathers) of the Casbah; the Soeurs Blanches (White Sisters) of Birmandreis; and the Trappist monks of Tibhirine, whose medical doctor, Brother Luc, took care of everyone who needed attention, no questions asked.

Throughout the seven-year war of independence, the monastery of Notre-Dame de l'Atlas had been in the middle of a rugged, unpacified area, only sixty miles south of Algiers. The nearby town of Medea was occupied by the French army, but the mountains around it were full of small villages and hideouts for the rebels, who had a habit of setting fires to the fields of the Europeans. The army retaliated by dropping napalm in the Tamesguida Mountains.

The *pieds-noirs* were jealous, even suspicious, of the Trappists. Why were their crops never burned? Were these "red" monks like those Red priests who sympathized with the Marxist rebels? The monastery was never touched during the fighting, and Muslim youth groups would sometimes camp near its walls. The bombing in the mountains drove scores of families into the valley. The monks sheltered many of them in their unused buildings, and the Arab men provided them with additional hands to work around the monastery. Thus, from fire was born the village of Tibhirine.

Tibhirine would carry the seeds of hope that were destroyed by the wildfires of rage. Duval had nursed the hope that after independence, French and Algerians could live and work together to build a new country based on mutual respect. But the die-hard believers in Algérie Française had other ideas. The army and *pieds-noirs* had supported de Gaulle in order to keep Algeria French, but he had sold them out.

The bitter fruit of this betrayal was the Organisation Armée Secrète, formed in the winter of 1961. Known as the OAS, this clandestine group of angry French civilians and renegade military men served itself up as a strange pudding of neo-nazism-cum-"save the world" Christian ideology. And if the game could not be won, they would destroy everything. The OAS's distinctive graffiti was: WE KILL WHO WE WANT, WHEN WE WANT, WHERE WE WANT.

During the five months leading up to the referendum on independence, scheduled for July 5 1962, the violence reached its crescendo. The OAS assassins in Algiers were killing one person every six minutes. Their victims included Europeans who didn't pay their levy to the secret organization or were sympathizers of the FLN, French government officials, and Muslims who happened to be in the wrong place at the wrong time. OAS operatives and sympathizers blew up the oil depots near Oran, sabotaged power plants, burned the library of the University of Algiers, and walked into hospitals and randomly shot Arab patients in their beds.

The murder of Arabs had a demonic logic: The OAS wanted to incite reprisals from the Muslim community in order to make the 1.2 million French citizens believe they had only two choices: to leave or to die. "THE SUITCASE OR THE COFFIN" was the OAS's desperate last message scrawled on the walls of Algiers, Oran, and other cities. The goal was not simply to destroy things but to frighten the Europeans into leaving, and deplete Algeria of the human and physical resources that would be needed to rebuild the country after independence. In this, the OAS succeeded.

Despite the terrible legacy of destruction and murder left by the OAS, the French found, to their great surprise, that the Algerians were quick to forgive. They were welcomed back immediately after independence, whether as tourists or to help rebuild the country. Algerians spoke of two Frances. There was a "bad" France and a "good" France. The good France was that of Charles de Gaulle, Bishop Duval, and Joan of Arc. In the years that followed, over fifteen thousand *coopérants* came to Algeria who, like Peace Corps workers, had been recruited from France and other countries by the new government. Engineers, teachers, accountants, planners, adminstrators, doctors, social workers, and even policemen signed on to help the fledgling nation to its feet.

The Algeria of the 1960s was one of hope, high expectations, and tolerance. Algeria's new constitution declared Islam the state religion, but it guaranteed freedom of religious belief. Unlike earlier French policy toward Muslims, Christians did not have to give up their faith to qualify for Algerian citizenship. Duval and other men and women of the church who had supported Algerian independence received Algerian nationality. Christian clerics and Muslim imams alike, were paid a monthly stipend by the Ministry of Religious Affairs. The church had an important place in the new Algeria, so long as it respected Muslim sensibilities. Above all, that meant not trying to convert Muslims. The government broadcast Christmas, Easter, and Pentecost services on the radio each year in Arabic, French, and Berber, and still does today.

The Church of Algeria became a valued partner in the new country's development under Duval's leadership. Yet the number of Christians in Algeria continued to decline. Duval continuously had to remind visitors from France that the Church was not an end in itself. Its mission in a Muslim country was one of presence and sharing. Its men and women were to be living signs of God's love by working together in friendship with Muslims. It was not the Muslims but, rather, the Christians in France who had to be convinced.

Duval could feel his blood pressure rising as Dom Sortais made his announcement at the conciliar meeting of bishops in Rome in 1963. "We no longer see any purpose to be served by our monastic community in the Atlas, which is now without prospects for the future.

Each monastery must be autonomous and recruit from its region. It is a luxury the order cannot afford. Therefore, I have signed the decree today for its closure."

The forceful Trappist abbot general had the prerogative to close one of his monasteries if he thought it best for the order, but Gabriel Sortais hadn't shown the most basic courtesy to a colleague. In his high-handed manner, he had made his decision without consulting Duval, and added insult to injury by making his ex cathedra announcement at a worldwide conciliar meeting of bishops in Rome. Duval was the bishop of the affected diocese and de facto head of the Christian community in Algeria, which had been devastated by the panicky exodus of nearly 900,000 Europeans in the four months following the Evian Accords in March of 1962.

The normally reserved Duval angrily berated the abbot general for abandoning the Church in Algeria, which had just suffered a massive hemorrhage. "The monastery is very important to us. It is our only mission devoted to contemplation. Muslims attach great importance to prayer. The Koran singles out monks as especially worthy of respect and their presence increases the prestige of our Church in their eyes. It is equally important for Christians to have a place of retreat for contemplation, prayer, and rejuvenation. Our community is already demoralized and embattled. Please reconsider."

Gabriel Sortais was not a man used to being challenged, and certainly not in public. "I have made my decision" was his cold reply. That night, an agitated Dom Sortais died from cardiac arrest. With Sortais dead, so was his decree.

A year later, Duval thought he would once again have to battle for the survival of his monastery. Jean de la Croix, the new abbot of Notre-Dame d'Aiguebelle, had come to Algeria to determine the future of this small outpost. There were only four monks left at Tibhirine. What purpose did the monastery serve? Jean de la Croix consulted with local clergymen and -women. He concluded that the monastery was indeed important to the Church in Algeria, which, in order to survive, had to become a church of service to all people. For the Christians, it was a well from which they drew renewed strength. For Muslims, the monks bore witness to the reality of Christian piety. "It would be preferable to close a monastery in

France than to close Tibhirine," Jean de la Croix concluded when he finally met with Duval.

In 1964, Duval's cherished monastery at Tibhirine was more than the lungs of the Church. It was part of a Christian presence that had been replanted on hallowed Church ground. In the fourth century A.D., Algeria was part of the Roman province of Numidia and the home of Saint Augustine, Bishop of Hippo. Duval was guided in his faith by his ancient compatriot Saint Augustine, whom he called "the doctor of love." Duval found in the words of John the touchstone of Augustine's faith, and his own: "God is love, and he who dwells in love, dwells in God, and God in him."

3

Entering the Chain

They say: Accept the Jewish or Christian faith and you shall be rightly guided. . . .
Reply: We believe in God and that which was revealed to us; in what was revealed to Abraham, Ishmael, Isaac, Jacob and the tribes; to Moses and Jesus and the other prophets by their Lord. We make no distinction among any of them and to God we have surrendered ourselves.

—Koran 2: 135

"Read the Gospels again! Read Matthew! You know the parable of the dinars. You're supposed to put your talent to work. You have so much to offer to make the world a better place. Don't go close yourself off from it. Have you gone mad?" General de Chergé had passed from incredulity to fury with his son, who had come to visit his parents at the family château in the Aveyron in 1968.

His mother, Monique, was in tears. Nothing they said made any difference to the son they knew had a natural calling to the church. His outstanding intellect and warm personality would have suited him perfectly to be a Jesuit teacher, a parish priest, or a bishop. But not this. The life of a Trappist monk was like entering a prison. They hadn't realized Christian wanted to be a prisoner of God. And of all places, in godforsaken Algeria, with all its painful memories.

Though others in the family were mystified by "what bug had bitten him," Monique de Chergé alone knew of Christian's other calling, to serve God in Algeria. In his letters home, Christian had revealed his friendship with Mohammed only to his mother. He had written of the feeling he had afterward; that, whenever he heard the muezzin's call to prayer, he too was being called. Painful as it was to lose the child with whom she had the greatest spiritual intimacy, his mother was happy for him. She wore sunglasses for a week to hide her tears, yet Monique knew in her heart that Christian's decision was right. She had always told him there was no higher life than one of prayer, and no greater vocation than to be a monk.

Monique de Chergé was of Lasteyrie stock and related on her mother's side of the family to the Marquis de Lafayette, whose troops had helped George Washington win the Battle of Yorktown. She was also a devout Catholic who suffused her family of six sons, two daughters, and an army officer husband with her powerful faith and piety. Christian's earliest childhood memories were as a four-year-old in Algiers during World War II, reciting the catechism at his mother's knee with his siblings. To most Frenchmen in Algeria, the Arabs occupied a separate world. They often lived side by side and shared buses and trams, but still, Arabs were beings apart, more like oxen than humans.

Yet, even as a child living a closeted military life, Christian had been struck by the fervor and regularity of their prayer. They would drop everything at the muezzin's call, sometimes to pray on the street or in the market. His mother reminded her children that the Arabs should never be mocked and deserved respect. "They are godly people and believe in the same God we do. There is only one God." His father respected them, too. Commander Guy de Chergé led an Algerian artillery unit in the Free French Expeditionary Corps that invaded Italy as part of General Mark Clark's Fifth Army. His tough Algerian units were the first to break through the German Gustav Line and the first to bombard Rome.

Christian, alone of his mother's children, showed unusual piety as a child. His older brother Robert recalled, "Early on, when he was only six years old, Christian would say additional prayers in his room after the nightly family prayers. Sometimes he would kneel at his bed, or he would say them lying in bed. In French we would say he was '*confit en dévotion.*' He took after his mother."

After the war, Commander de Chergé was made director of studies at the War College in Paris and was promoted to general. The family lived in the fashionable neighborhood of the rue Faubourg-Saint-Honoré, where they remained during frequent postings of their father elsewhere in France. Christian and his brothers followed the path of a traditional "good Catholic" upbringing by attending the Marianist boy's school of Sainte-Marie de Monceau. He was remembered by his classics teacher as "intelligent, likable, and possessing a disarming smile." He was also a good negotiator. The professor recalled the day he had proposed that the top fifteen students in the class go on a field trip. Christian objected that it was unfair, and he successfully pleaded the cause of those who would have been left behind. To his father, who gave nicknames to his children that corresponded with the Seven Wonders of the World, Christian was the "Lighthouse of Alexandria." But sometimes, Guy de Chergé called him the "Archduke of Sensitivity." Giving a nickname to his eighth child, Gérard, created a problem. It required a new wonder. So his father solved the problem by making him "the summation" of all the others.

All the de Chergé boys participated in the Catholic Boy Scout movement, in which Christian's troop always finished first or second in the competitions. Singing in the choir was obligatory for the boys, and Christian displayed a voice well suited for praising God. When he was sixteen years old, Christian announced that he would be a priest when he grew up.

But he soon stopped talking about his ambition. His father counseled Christian to keep his priestly ambition a "secret of the heart," to be revealed when he was older and more certain of his vocation. Guy did not want his son to feel trapped later by a youthful profession. He knew Christian well enough to know that his conscience might forgive reneging on being a lawyer or schoolteacher, but the priestly calling, he would take more seriously. Not that Guy de Chergé was against religion or Christianity or belief in a Creator as such, but he doubted that there was any single claimant to the throne of ultimate truth. Skeptical of the certainties that can spring from excessive religious fervor, he spoke tolerantly of all the great traditions and saw them as different ways to reach the same goal. Buddha, Christ, Allah, Yahweh were all fine with him. "Let's just not kill one another over names," he used to tell his children. The general's catechism was good works and showing decency to everyone.

One of the officers who fought in his Third Division in Italy wrote of Commander de Chergé, "He was an officer of great intelligence, physical courage and presence, descended from a military family of artillerists and cavalry officers. He was close to all his men and respected by them. At the front, he was always calm under fire, but he had one peculiarity. No matter where he was, he carried himself as if on a parade ground, and whatever their rank, he always saluted those he passed as if they, too, were generals."

Christian's own physical courage and respectful manner would become important later when he, too, was a leader in a different kind of combat. By the time he was eighteen, Christian had shown his father's sharp intellect and his own intensely competitive nature. He won the top honors at Sainte-Marie de Monceau, even though he did something unusually difficult. Instead of taking the courses that would enable him to graduate with a baccalaureate in either humanities or science, he qualified for both diplomas at the same time.

Christian's "secret" had germinated into firm adult conviction after graduating in 1954. He announced that he wanted to enter the Carms in Paris. Its six-year program, with two years of philosophy and four of theology, gave it the reputation of being the most intellectually demanding of the seminary schools and incubator for a goodly portion of French bishops and Catholic intellectuals.

But first he had to cope with the shock of an unexpected personal failure. Though Christian had distinguished himself academically at the lycée, he failed his state baccalaureate exams required for entering an institution of higher learning in France. "He had physically sprouted in his last year—he had been rather small before—and with the school exams he had already studied for so hard, I think he was just exhausted," explained his brother Robert.

Before retaking the exams, he had to do a postgraduate year at the Lycée Carnot, a secular republican state school dating from the Napoleonic era. Again, he graduated at the head of his class, but he had also gained knowledge that couldn't be measured by grades. The star student had recieved a dose of humility. He also learned the value of exposure to a more diverse world of people and ideas than he had known in his closeted Catholic schooling.

Christian interrupted his six-year course at seminary school after his third year to fulfill the twenty-seven months of military service that hung over all young Frenchmen. In January 1959, after three months of basic training he entered the elite army officer school at Saumur for six months. With the help of his father's connections, he was assured that he would be assigned to work with civilians. Again, Christian graduated at the top of his class. In January 1961, he returned to Paris to finish his last three years of seminary school.

The Carms faces on a quiet, well-planted courtyard within the larger Catholic Institute on the rue d'Assas in the Latin Quarter. The simple stone plaque that had troubled Christian when he first saw it still stands propped in a bed of red impatiens between the pair of winding stairs leading from the garden into the Carms. HIC CECIDERUNT. HERE THEY DIED.

Before the French Revolution, the Carms had been a Carmelite monastery for men. During the Terror, it was converted into a prison, which once held as many as six hundred clerics. On the same steps Christian used daily, 115 priests had been shot and bayoneted for refusing to swear a loyalty oath to the new republican constitution. The inscription on the plaque had bothered him before he did his military service in Algeria, for he saw it as a memorial to the intolerance and anger the Church had aroused in the hearts of France's new rulers. It bothered him even more after he owed his life to Mohammed, an "infidel." Church-hating French radicals had killed more priests in the 1790s than had the Muslims during their seven years of war against France.

As soon as he entered the Carms, Christian impressed peers and teachers alike with his open-mindedness and gentle intelligence. He was one to whom other students confided their doubts, even if he rarely confided in them. "Something emanated from him," remembered Father Jacques Perrier, today the bishop of Lourdes, "there was a depth, a different quality about him hard to describe." Another friend from his days at the Carms called him a "*chevalier* of the spirit" who valued bravery, courtesy, loyalty and the duty to protect the weak.

He was also a conciliator, a man of peace, who told a fellow student that if he had not become a priest, he would have become a diplomat. At the Carms, he found Catholics who were in opposite camps from him on the subject of Algeria, yet he could discuss these differences without hostility. Christian was not one to try to convince others of their errors but to seek higher ground where they could agree.

On October 11, 1962, Pope John XXIII opened the Second Vatican Council in Rome that three years later would lead to changes within the Catholic Church, known collectively as Vatican II. That same day, Christian's sister Ghislaine entered a new Catholic order, the Sisters of Saint Francis Xavier, who lived and worked side by side with the needy and the poor. These avant-garde sisters did not wear traditional habits, but ordinary street clothes. Christian found himself justifying her choice to his mother, who was upset that her daughter had not entered a more traditional order. "He had many of the traits of a conservative," his sister remembered. "He loved Gregorian chants, ceremony, and was fascinated with genealogy. But theologically, he was very modern and open to contemporary thinkers, Christian and non-Christian alike. He was mistrustful of boundaries and limits."

Christian's first job after his ordination in 1964 was at Sacré-Coeur in Montmartre. His dream was to serve in a parish that was both poor and *fraternelle,* living among those who struggled for their daily bread. Instead, he was assigned to serve in a church that was the embodiment of wealth, pomp, and hierarchy, under the domination of the energetic and autocratic Father Maurice Charles. For Christian to work under Father Charles for six years was an act of disciplined obedience. Sacré-Coeur was a place where he learned to suffer and smile.

No occasion was more painful for Christian than the finale of an international convocation of monotheism around the theme "Prayer, the most important activity of our time," organized by Father Charles in 1967. Several thousand people had come from all over the world to attend the conference. The Jewish, Orthodox, and Protestant leaders gave lengthy summations on behalf of their delegations. When Father Charles's turn came, his remarks were embarrassingly short. He spoke of prayer as a communal process in which the Church guides and informs. But his brevity left the unpleasant impression in Christian's mind that he was really saying that Catholics knew best—Come around to Sacré-Coeur and see for yourself. "I don't think it ever occurred to Father Charles to invite Muslims. They were beyond the Pale," reflected Christian's younger brother Hubert, who had also been in the crowd at Saint-Preyel auditorium that had overflowed into the street, blocking traffic on the rue Faubourg-Saint-Honoré.

Father Charles was a passionate Christian crusader against the twin devils of atheism and communism, a sectarian creature of a pre–Vatican II Catholic Church. His twenty-seven-year-old new chaplain was equally passionate about serving a different kind of church, one that would unveil itself officially in December 1965. It would be the church of a big Christianity—ecumenical and universal, one that looked with respect at Islam and other religions.

Christian eagerly embraced the spirit of openness embodied in the Second Vatican Council document, "Gaudium et Spes," popularly formulated as "The Holy Spirit Works Where It Likes," or "The Kingdom of God Is Bigger than the Church." The reexamined Catholic Church was one that welcomed anyone of goodwill. It was to be culture-free and truly universal—neither national, European, nor Occidental. *Dialogue* and *listening* became the new code words of a broader Church, one that respected the different ways in which the Spirit can bring people closer to God, including non-Christians and atheists.

In 1969, a year after telling his family the shattering news of his decision to become a Trappist monk, Christian went to the Drôme, a thumbprint of flat, empty space below the Drôme River in the Rhône Valley, between the French Alps to the northeast and the mountains of the Ardèche to the west. There, he entered the eight-hundred-year-old abbey of Notre-Dame d'Aiguebelle as a novice in God's service.

Aiguebelle. Perhaps one has to arrive in the early spring to experience fully the peaceful tranquillity of this ancient abbey, snuggled in a small wooded valley at the crossroads of Grignan, Allan, Montjoyer, and Roussas, a few miles southeast of Montélimar. The March air is fresh and scented with newly plowed earth. There is a soft gentleness to the land.

Looking north from Roussas, the dark spire on the clock tower of the monastery protrudes upward like a giant woodpecker's beak amid the budding oaks, chestnuts, plane, and locusts trees. Royal purple irises line the access road to the monastery that cleaves off the route to Montjoyer and takes the visitor past the main entrance gate, snakes between the cloister wall and a rock cliff, past the chapel and infirmary, and up and around to the *hôtellerie,* a guest house that surveys the valley from a grassy plateau.

On the edge of this promontory, looking down on the entrance drive, is a large statue of Jesus with outstretched, welcoming arms. A riot of redbud, mimosas, lilacs, wild rosemary, flox, purple irises, and shimmering Russian olives trees engulfs everything in its joyous outburst, softening the martial simplicity and immaculate order of the monastic world. Nearby, a small stream passes near a grotto with a statue of the Virgin Mary inside. *Aiguebelle.* Beautiful water.

Visitors are not allowed inside the cloister. Only the guest house and chapel are open to the public. The chapel has the cavernous feeling of a large wine cellar, its low vaulted ceiling supported by thick Romanesque arches on each side of an elongated nave. I had arrived at the midday Office of Sext. A strong smell of incense pervaded the intimate devotions of men in white cowls and with shorn heads singing in adoration of the Lord.

Tu es la loi, Dieu tout puissant
Du monde et de ses changements
Ornant le matin de splendeur
Offrant à midi ta chaleur.

Eteins le feu des dissensions
Guéris la fièvre des passions
Accorde à nos corps la vigueur
Donne ta paix à tous les coeurs.

"What is the contemplative life?" the brother giving the homily asked rhetorically. "It is a life which each day creates a place for God, in order to receive God each day into our lives."

But why did Christian choose the Trappists, when everyone who knew him thought he was better suited for an order more connected to the world?

"Soon after his announcement, I had a serious car crash that put me in the hospital in Reims for several months," recalled his brother Hubert. "Christian was in Montmartre at the time, but he visited me as often as he could get away from his duties at Sacré-Coeur. We had long heart-to-heart talks and I felt much closer to him afterward. There is no question that his desire to go back to Algeria was behind his choice of orders. If the Trappists hadn't had a monastery down there, he would have joined a different order."

Christian thought being a Jesuit would be too easy, and he thought the Jesuits were too intellectual anyway. He felt the same way about the Benedictines. He wanted dirt under his fingernails, a garden, a place for physical exertion. He hated intellectual blather. The Trappists, he told Hubert, were "more manual." Christian liked that, because he knew he had violent demons inside. As a baby, he had "blue rages," which terrified his parents. If he didn't get what he wanted, he would lie screaming on the floor, become stiff as a plank, and turn blue with anger. When he got older, he had a rage to convince.

"You could see him struggling to control himself when people disagreed with him over questions he thought important," Hubert remembered. "He had a strong sense of the absolute, and he knew that was dangerous. Physical work was important for him in order to keep his emotions in harness. The vow of stability was very important also. He wanted to be part of a community committed to a specific place, living in harmony with his brothers as a way to show love of God. That was the meaning of his faith."

The community of brothers Christian joined in September 1969 had taken vows in accordance with their strict observance of the Rule of Saint Benedict. *Listen my son to the precepts of the Master, and listen with the ear of your heart. Receive willingly and carry out effectively your loving Father's advice that by the labor of obedience you may return to Him from whom you have been separated by the sloth of disobedience.* Thus begins the Rule, one which Saint Benedict called "a little rule for beginners," to set the monk on the right path. The spirit of the Rule reflects the spirit of the man and his era.

Benedict of Nursia was born around 480 A.D., a time when God mattered, belief mattered, and bishops brought princes to their knees with their spiritual power. A hundred years earlier, the Roman emperor Theodosius had submitted himself to the moral authority of the Church. Ambrose, the Bishop of Milan, had ordered him to perform public penance for killing innocent citizens of Salonika in reprisal for the murder there of his governor. "The Emperor is within the church, not above it," he wrote Theodosius after the crime was made known.

The end of the fifth century was also a time of chaos. Rome had been sacked by Visigoths and Vandals. There were plagues and famine. The Arian heresy, which declared Jesus a lesser divinity than the Father, was rampant. A Christianized Roman empire was struggling to replace a decaying temporal order with a new spiritual order. In an end-of-the-world atmosphere of confusion and savagery, a man whom Saint Gregory called the "patriarch of the Western monks" created a religious order whose Rule provided islands of stability, learning, and godliness throughout Europe.

All that is known of Benedict comes from Saint Gregory, who wrote a book about holy men in sixth-century Italy. Benedict was born of a noble family and was sent to Rome to study rhetoric and belles lettres. By the age of twenty, he had tired of his dissolute life in the capital and fled for the solitude of contemplation in a cave near Subiaco, outside of Rome. For three years, Benedict lived there as a hermit, showing himself more desirous to work for God rather than for the favors of this life.

Benedict's desire to "work for God" attracted disciples and led him to establish schools of service to God. His first was built on Monte Cassino, in central Italy. He believed such service was best given by practicing brotherly love in a community of fellow seekers. Such a life was but one form of Christian service, he insisted, no better and no higher than others. Yet it suited his particular soul, which was searching to perfect his love for God through practicing perfect obedience. Through obedience to God, done out of love rather than fear, came freedom from one's servitude to self-absorption and sin. Stripped of external attachments, practicing the disciplines of charity, humility, and obedience within the community, a Benedictine monk could strive to purify his soul in preparation for union with God.

Benedict died in 547. Thirty years later, his school of service to God lay in ruins, destroyed by Lombard invaders. The monks fled, and the monastery at Monte Cassino would lie abandoned for two hundred years. The only source of information about Saint Benedict, aside from Saint Gregory, is the document that makes him live today in the hearts of monks.

The Rule, wrote Benedict, is for the strongest monks—those who want to live in a community in order to be *purified in the crucible of communal discipline* under an abbot's authority. The monks owe obedience to their abbot, just as their abbot owes obedience to Christ, who came into the world to do the will of his Father. The abbot's task is to suffuse their souls gently with his ordinances, so their will to obey rises as naturally as yeast in bread. The behavior of the abbot, disciplining of monks, singing of psalms, the quantity of food and drink to be consumed, the reception of guests, manual work, the maintenance of silence, and other details of daily monastic life are addressed by the Rule's seventy-three chapters. So, too, are the grand themes of humility, good works, obedience, and the disposition of the heart. Benedict's goal was to help guide monks in the path of moral integrity.

He was particularly concerned with two categories of wayward monks. One, he called the "gyrovagues." These vagabond monks were moochers who had no stable community of their own. They went from monastery to monastery, taking advantage of the obligation of hospitality. Such monks, Saint Benedict believed, were given over mainly to pleasure. Their motives were suspect if they stayed more than three days, or if they asked for money. Then there were those who justified their own desires by declaring them "holy," and condemned what displeased them as "forbidden." Benedict called them "sarabites." They were frequently seen in small groups of two or three, without a pastor, and not in normal houses of God. These were the worst monks, for they pretended to act in God's name, but *their tonsures are an affront to God.*

Scholars argue whether or not Benedict wrote the Rule himself, compiled it from others, or had it attributed to him by his followers. The debate is irrelevant to those who practice the Rule. Glory was not a reflection of individual effort and creativity. These qualities were but manifestations of God's grace—gifts from the Creator of all life, for which only the proud and arrogant would dare claim credit. Glory resided in being part of a chain of revelation that would carry men much further than they would ever achieve by their own puny efforts. By living the message of the Gospels, each in his own way, Saint Anthony, Saint Basil, or a Saint Benedict was part of the chain that began with Abraham. It was of little concern to them where in the chain they were. The important thing was to be in the chain, united with Christ.

The order Christian entered in September 1969 had begun to change. Vatican II had concluded three years of deliberation in 1965 that brought in its wake a more egalitarian spirit within the Catholic Church and a new openness toward other religions. For the Cistercians of the Strict Observance, the message of Vatican II was translated as "Unity is not uniformity." Individual abbots were given more autonomy to introduce changes in accordance with guidelines set forth in triannual meetings of the General Chapter, when all the abbots and abbesses gather to discuss the state of their Order. Following Vatican II, authority within the order shifted to the General Chapter from the abbot general, who formerly could veto its decisions. He became more a trustee than a commander in chief, whose charge was to see that the General Chapter's decisions were being carried out, and to play a more pastoral role within the community.

But change came slowly, and with much resistance within the order. At Aiguebelle, there was an argument over reducing the number of psalms sung at Vigils from fifteen to six. The older monks felt that a certain laxity had already been introduced by moving Vigils from 2:00 A.M. to a tardy 4:00 A.M. Prime, which used to follow Lauds, had been eliminated, an Office that was intended to discourage the monks from going back to bed before Terce. Allowing women, even spouses of visitors, in the chapel and *hôtellerie* was controversial.

Nor was the cloister quite the prison people on the outside believed at the time Christian entered Aiguebelle. Before Vatican II, neither death, illness nor marriage in the monks' families was grounds for leaving the monastery. They were allowed to receive only four letters a year. The current abbot at Aiguebelle, Father André Barbeau, gives his monks three visitation days annually, but the families are expected to come to the monastery.

Much rigor still remained when Christian came to the Drôme. There was no central heating. Monks still slept in their habits and in open cubicles, rather than cells; the meatless diet symbolic of the poor was strictly maintained. There was more manual labor then. Virtually all monks did field work, and there were still two classes of monks, though officially Vatican II had abolished the distinction.

The tradition of lay monks, or *conversi,* arose in the Middle Ages to permit men who were uneducated, yet devoted to God, to enter the monastic community. They did not know Latin, the language of the liturgy until 1965, and often had bad voices, unsuited to praising the Lord. They were not required to attend the Divine Offices, except on Sundays, and even then, they were not allowed to sing. The Order recognized that a person can worship God anywhere, in their own way, and *conversi* expressed their devotion through work.

Being unschooled, *conversi* could not be ordained. They lived and ate separately from the choir monks, or *moines au choeur,* who were dedicated to praising God. For the latter, theirs was a marriage of passion, which demanded hymns of love be sung seven times a day. After Vatican II, Latin was no longer required to praise God, and the *conversi* were integrated into the community as "simple" monks, but they still could not sing.

The rule of silence was also relaxed. *He who restrains his lips is wise. . . . Life and death are in the power of the tongue,* Benedict reminds his monks. The pre–Vatican II monks communicated among themselves by sign language and were allowed to talk only with the abbot. The Trappist hallmark of silence became part of a new regimen of strict observance of the Rule following reforms introduced in Normandy by the abbot of Notre-Dame de la Trappe in the 1660s.

Laxness and the corruption of monastic rules had crept into the Cistercian Order since it had been established in 1098 at Cîteaux, in Burgundy. Grants of land and money from nobles seeking to assuage their consciences had produced over the years an unhealthy secular influence on the appointment of abbots, who were often more interested in collecting tithes and pleasing the king than in praising the Lord through a life of poverty and manual labor.

"La Trappe" attracted large numbers of new postulants by restoring prayer, silence, and isolation from the world to their proper place within the monastery. Throughout the following century, a large number of other Cistercian monasteries adopted la Trappe's rigorous example and were reorganized as the Cistercian Order of the Strict Observance. The followers of the stricter interpretation became known simply as Trappists.

Father Jean de la Croix knew Christian was in a hurry to get to Algeria, to enter the chain of revelation. At their first meeting, the bespectacled, tall, ramrod-straight abbot with a Rasputin beard understood that the handsome young priest was no ordinary novice. Jean de la Croix knew of his exceptional intellectual abilities and that he had excelled in his theological studies in Paris. From the moment he arrived at Aiguebelle, Christian made clear to Jean de la Croix that he wanted to take his final vow of stability at Tibhirine.

Notre-Dame d'Aiguebelle was Christian's mother ship, which would take him to Algeria. It was also his "mother" monastery. Aiguebelle had six "daughters," new monastic foundations that had been established in the past by monks from Aiguebelle seeking something different. Four were in France: Notre-Dame des Neiges, Notre-Dame des Dombes, Notre-Dame du Désert, and Notre-Dame de Bonnecombe. Two were in Africa, Notre-Dame de Koutaba, in Cameroon, and Notre-Dame de l'Atlas. The latter had been founded by monks who followed in the footsteps of earlier generations of Trappists who had left Aiguebelle to go to Algeria.

When the first French soldiers landed at Sidi-Ferruch, near Algiers, in 1830, they encountered a Muslim population that was bewildered by their godlessness. Where were their marabouts and their holy places? Why didn't French soldiers ever pray? The natives didn't know that the soldiers were commanded by officers who had once fought with Napoléon to spread a revolution to liberate men from feudal inequalities, clerical influence, and religious superstition.

The French occupiers soon recognized that the absence of priests and visible signs of religious piety was loosing them respect in the eyes of the local population, as well as impeding efforts at pacification. Resistance was organized by the twenty-four-year-old emir Abdelkader, a religious leader, resourceful warrior, and statesman. A cross between a George Washington and Khalil Gibran, Abdelkader was the first Arab leader to bring rival clans together in a disciplined way to defend their land from invaders and form an embryonic Algerian state. At the signing of the Treaty of Tafna in 1837, following the first of many defeats suffered at Abdelkader's hands, the French officers heard him declare, "If you were Christians, as you pretend, you would have churches and priests. We would be the best of friends, for our holy book the Koran tells us to live in peace with Christians."

Six years later, Trappists from Aiguebelle were recruited to apply their well-known agricultural skills to a land the mostly urban settlers from France were taming with difficulty. The monks were known as tireless workers devoted to peace and contemplation, but without the proselytizing instincts of missionaries. Through their piety and hard work, it was thought, they would be excellent ambassadors for carrying out France's civilizing mission.

For their task of impressing the Muslims, the Trappists were granted 2,200 acres on the plain of Staouéli, west of Algiers, where French soldiers had defeated Turkish mercenaries defending Algiers in 1830. The first group of twelve monks arrived in 1843 and were soon joined by ex-soldiers and Arab workers to help them clear the land. The monastery had laid under its cornerstone old cannonballs that had been gathered from the battlefield, making the cross an official partner with the plow and the sword. *La charrue, l'épée, la croix* would become France's motto and strategic triad for the subjugation of its new territory.

The Trappists had an enormous job ahead of them. Their ten-year contract with the government required them to clear the 2,200 acres covered with brush and tenacious dwarf palms, and to plant annually a thousand new trees, after which they would become owners of the land. Within seven months, they had planted 2,500 trees, put sixty acres under cultivation, and were raising livestock, while still praying eight times a day. Their rapid progress came at a price. Seven monks died within two years from dysentery, cholera, or exhaustion.

Over the next thirty years, Aiguebelle would send ninety-five monks to Staouéli. More would come from the Trappist abbeys of Bellefontaine, Melleray, Bonneville, Neiges, and others. The community reached as many as one hundred monks. "La Trappe," as Notre-Dame de Staouéli was called by the local population, gained a reputation as a model agricultural enterprise. Its vineyards were the first of true commercial scale and its wines gained a reputation for excellence. La Trappe also acquired a reputation as a benevolent neighbor to the Muslims, especially during the famines of 1847 and 1867, when the monks supplied food to the starving population in the area.

The Trappists received good marks from agnostic French generals and Muslims alike. Muslims were impressed by their life of prayer, fasting and good works. France's governor-general, General Thomas Bugeaud, noted approvingly "that nothing approaches military organization more than monastic orders." La Trappe became known as a sacred place among Muslims, who were often seen bowing their heads when passing its doors. Years later, after Abdelkader had surrendered to France and been liberated from prison there, he had a chance meeting with Dom François Régis, Staouéli's first abbot. Upon learning his identity Abdelkader remarked, "I had heard about you a long time ago because my men spoke of your monks. You always received them as though they were your own brothers."

The affinity of the Muslims for Christian monks was natural. They were so much alike. An Arab in his long, hooded robe, or *abaya,* was virtually indistinguishable from a monk in his white prayer cowl. Without its black scapular, a monk's rough work tunic was a close cousin of the ordinary *gandoura* worn by peasants. Both monk and Muslim prayed with formalistic, communal regularity. Like the natives, the Trappist monk existed only as part of an extended family; alone, he was nothing. His brothers had survived collectively for fourteen hundred years through the solidarity of monastery, order and church. The architecture of the cloister was one of interiorized space. Like the veil, and the Algerian *gourbi*, an adobe style house with an enclosed courtyard, the Trappist monastery presented to the world a protective exterior that sheltered an inner privacy. Both worlds separated men and women in places of worship and everyday life. And the traditional Muslim, whether Berber or Arab, placed extraordinary importance on the virtue of hospitality. It was more than a virtue. Hospitality was a sacred duty.

On January 15, 1971, sixteen months after entering Notre-Dame d'Aiguebelle, a thirty-three-year-old nomad of God returned to the country he had left as a soldier ten years earlier. But a Trappist monk in Algeria was a special kind of nomad, attached to a single monastic oasis, in a wilderness of poverty, dependence, and adopted exile. "A monk must be a contrarian," Christian wrote a Benedictine friend, "for it is in the insignificance of his life that he leaves his signature." But were the Lord's forty days in the wilderness grounds for leaving the world? His closest friends were as baffled as his family. Christian was being contrary to his own nature, they thought.

Few in his family knew that Christian's great-great-aunt, Marie de Chergé, had fired his imagination. She had joined the Society of Helpers in 1880 as a novice to minister to the needs of the poor and sick. Three years later, Mother Marie Saint Bernard, as she was known, was appointed the superior of a Helper House in the poor working-class district of Montmartre, where Christian would later serve a more well-heeled congregation. In 1892, she and several Helper Sisters were sent to New York City. They founded Helper Houses on lower Seventh Avenue and on East Eighty-sixth Street and became known for their work with poor blacks. "They are so destitute, it defies description," one sister wrote back to Paris. They formed scout troops, taught sewing, cooking, reading, and writing, and organized Thanksgiving and Christmas parties.

In St. Louis, Mother Marie Saint Bernard founded a Helper House to aid white female factory workers. The sisters were mystified by the strange combination of religion and prejudice they found among the whites. "The blacks were not welcome in white churches. They were like sheep without a shepherd, crying, 'O white man, where is my place in the world?' " wrote Mother Marie to her superior in Montmartre. She would go on to do similar works in San

Francisco, help in the chaos caused by the earthquake of 1906, return to France, and go on one final mission to Shanghai, where she died in 1913.

Like his aunt, Christian would push out the frontiers of his church and go beyond the confines of his upbringing to become one of God's nomads. He was exchanging the security and status of a respectable clerical career in France—perhaps that of a bishop, as his father would have wanted—for one of insecurity and obscurity in Algeria. He was adopting a newly independent country, whose culture had been held in contempt by Frenchmen, and now would be a guest, wholly dependent on the goodwill of his hosts. Christian would call himself a *"mendiant de l'amour."*

At Tibhirine, a young, impatient "beggar of love" found everything that was missing at Sacré-Coeur Montmartre—a life of simplicity and poverty. "I have arrived in the Atlas Mountains" Christian wrote a wartime friend, "surrounded by a population that is poor, but smiling, proud, and without bitterness. They are believers and respectful of all religious people, provided that what is in the back room corresponds with what is in the display window."

He also found a monastic community without a sense of purpose. Six temporary superiors had been appointed by Aiguebelle during the nine years since Algeria's independence. Eight monks, whose vow of stability was elsewhere, were on loan from France. Four had come from Timadeuc, in Brittany, and four from Aiguebelle in response to an appeal by Bishop Duval for more monks to supply oxygen for "the lungs" of his church. Only two brothers remained from the period before independence who had taken their Solemn Profession at Tibhirine, committing them to that community for life. With less than the required minimum of six "stabilized" monks needed for a monastery to elect its own superior, there had been a constant flux of *ad nutum* superiors who had been temporarily appointed and served at the discretion of the abbot of Aiguebelle. Most knew nothing of Algeria or Islam.

It had become like a "tossed salad," remembered Jean-Pierre, one of the monks from Timadeuc, "flopping back and forth between traditional, cloistered contemplation and more openness to the surrounding population." Christian also found his new brothers perplexed by his zeal to join hands with Muslims and his obsession with finding "the notes that are in harmony" between the faiths.

A verse in the Koran spoke Christian's language. *God is the light of the heaven and the earth. . . . It is lit from a blessed olive tree, neither eastern nor western. Its very oil would shine forth though no fire touched it. Light upon light; God guides to His light whom He will. . . . His light is found in temples which God has sanctioned to be built in remembrance of His name. In them, morning and evening, His praise is sung by men whom neither trade nor profit can divert from remembering Him.* Christian liked that. He wanted to use local oil in the monastic lamps. But he was far ahead of his brothers. They were older men, educated in a pre–Vatican II world, and were not used to thinking about the meaning of a Christian presence in a Muslim world. The presence of an energetic, self-assured, and impatient young novice was upsetting to many of them. Why, they wondered, did he want to learn Arabic? Theirs was a life of silence. Perhaps he should be a priest in Oran or Algiers, some brothers muttered.

In August 1972, Christian explained to his community in a written statement the reason for his presence in the Atlas, the spiritual impact of Mohammed's act of love, and of his preference, if necessary, to leave the monastery rather than leave Algeria. "In the blood shed by this friend, who was assassinated because he would not practice hatred, I knew that my call to follow Christ would be lived sooner or later in the same country that gave me a tangible sign of the greatest love possible. I also knew that this consecration of mine had to flow through prayer in order to give true witness to the church's presence." The brothers were divided over Christian's suitability for remaining within the community. A sympathetic Jean de la Croix saw Christian's sense of mission as providential for the community. He gave Christian a two-year leave to study at the Papal Institute of Islamic and Arabic Studies in Rome.

The Palazzo di San Apollinare, near Piazza Tre Fontane, would be Christian's new home. He threw himself into an intense program of study under the tutelage of Father Maurice Borrmans, a scholar of both Islam and Arabic. Mornings were devoted to four hours of literary Arabic. Afternoons were for studying Islam for two more hours. Saturday afternoons in the spring, Borrmans and his students had informal seminars in the countryside, where they compared texts in the Koran with those in the Bible. Islam and the Old Testament, they agreed, were pretty much the same.

"Vatican Two," Borrmans explained in his book-stacked office on the via Trastevere, "set the stage for Christian, with its greater emphasis on ecumenicism . . . respecting differences and accepting diversity without proselytizing. Surrounded by Islam, he was in an unusual position to carry out its spirit." His wire-rimmed glasses and strong shock of gray hair gave Borrman's creased, friendly face an air of philosophical weariness, one that comes from thirty years of patient struggle against misunderstanding and willful distortion. His struggle was for clarity and honesty, and just a little humility among the learned representatives of Islam and Christianity in their slow and painful attempts to undo the damage from all the mud balls slung at each other over the centuries.

Christian was in a hurry. He always wanted to know more and to go faster, always looking to open horizons, to reconcile the Gospels and the Koran. "He was a mystical adventurer who was convinced that the Muslims were saved by their Islam and that Islam had something to tell Christians. There are others in the Church who also wonder about Islam's place in God's plan," Borrmans acknowledged. "Some think Mohammed was sent to reunify God and that Islam is God's punishment for Christianity's squabbling and killing over the mystery of the Trinity. Christian was impatient to know how God saw Islam."

Christian wanted to study the writings of pagan, Christian, Jewish and Muslim spiritual figures in Algeria. He entitled his essay, "Algeria Before God," but warned his reader, "This is no religious history of Algeria in the modern Western sense, which carves the sacred out of daily life and gives it a compartment of its own, alongside political, economic, art, and social history." Islam, he explained, refuses to make a distinction between religion and the state, between spiritual life and moral behavior, or between social institutions and confessional communities. Thus, any study of Algeria that neglected the fundamental role of religion was inherently defective. "To proceed in such a way in the name of 'desacralization,' a term that has become common since the death of Christendom, would, in the case of Algeria, ignore the originality of its history."

In the beginning, there was Berber animism. It combined successively with Jewish (second century to the fourth), Christian (fourth century to the seventh), and Islamic monotheism (seventh century to the present). Christian found Algeria's originality in a history lived "continuously under the sign of God." Right up through independence, had there been anything more important than this continuity under God? Christian wondered.

His research was neither "religious sociology" nor an investigation into "the Berber soul." Rather, it was an assemblage of writings from different periods of Algerian history, bearing witness to a people continually imbued with, and looking toward, God. It was a tradition that gave birth to Saint Augustine in the fifth century; Queen Kahena, the Berber Jewess who fought the Arab invaders in the eighth century; Abdelkader, the warrior-statesman and mystic in the nineteenth century; and Ibn Ben Badis in the twentieth century. The latter, a rigorist Islamic reformer, resented the way the French trained its own imams to manipulate local politics, to preach that submission to France was the will of God. He also opposed the corruption of a "pure" Islam and condemned alcohol, smoking, dancing, sports, and especially maraboutism—the veneration of Muslim holy men by simple peasants, who often imputed to them miraculous healing powers. This practice, he feared, bordered on personal cults and the worship of men, not God.

Whether in the pre-Christian Berber period, the early Christian era, or under successive Muslim occupations, there was a divine thread, a worldview that did not disassociate religion from everyday life. "Throughout the ages," he continued, "religion unified their values with an attachment to a specific place, while expressing an instinctive desire for communion with a higher power." Religion also provided the rallying point to resist oppression.

The ninety works Christian read during his time in Rome were mined in search of the spiritual face of Algeria. It took him from Saint Cyprien and Saint Augustine to the great Muslim mystic and twelfth century reformer Abu Madyan of Tlemcen and Emir Abdelkader, whose skillful fifteen-year resistance to successive French armies won him admirers around the world.

Christian liked what Abdelkader had written about God in his *Spiritual Writings.* "If you think God is what the different communities believe—the Muslims, Christians, Jews, Mazdeens, polytheists, and others—He *is* that, but also more. If you think and believe what the prophets, saints, and angels profess—He *is* that, but He is still more. None of His creatures worship Him in His entirety. No one is an infidel in all the ways relating to God. No one knows all God's facets. Each of His creatures worships and knows Him in a certain way and is ignorant of Him in others. Error does not exist in this world except in a relative manner."

Christian was well aware that Algeria had a history marked by conquest and conflict, adaptation and assimilation of different expressions of religious belief: animism, pantheism, Donatism,* maraboutism, and monotheism. But he was a man who sought confluence. Like Abdelkader, his God was big—a unifier, not a separator. The Algerian face that he found was "wrinkled with age, layered with different-colored makeup, and twisted by the realities of everday life." But Christian would look beyond the wrinkles and face tints, for he wanted to know what mattered in God's eyes.

---

*Donatism was a fourth-century heresy that arose out of the persecution of North African Christians by the Emperor Diocletian (ruled A.D. 286–A.D. 305). The Donatists believed that those priests of the African Church who had betrayed their faith under pressure of persecution were not fit to remain priests. This led to a view that the validity of the sacraments depended on the moral worthiness of the priest, a view contested by Saint Augustine and the Church in Rome.

4

Years of Crisis

My house shall be called a house of prayer for all nations.

—Isaiah 56:6–7

Christian returned to the Atlas in the summer of 1974, eager to live his life of monastic prayer in the House of Islam. The superior, Jean-Baptiste, assigned him the job of hotelier, whose responsibility was attending to the guests. God's house has many mansions, and the young Arabic-speaking brother was perfectly suited to usher in Christians and Muslims, the poor and the stranger. Hospitality was at the heart of the Rule. "We will receive guests as if they were Christ Himself, because Christ said 'I was a stranger and you took me in.'"

The abbot himself no longer came to wash the hands and feet of the guests as in former days, but Christian made sure that the *hôtellerie* with its ten beds and small chapel was a place where Muslims, as well as Christians and all people of goodwill would feel welcome. Only tourists looking for cheap lodgings were frowned upon by the new hôtelier.

The visitors to Tibhirine were diverse. They came from all over Algeria. The Sisters of Charity, the Salesians, the Little Sisters of Jesus, and the Protestant Sisters of Grandschamps often came to the monastery for rest and reflection. There were priests and old friends who drove up frequently from Algiers. Especially close to the community was the curé of the nearby city of Medea, Gilles Nicolas, who taught mathematics at the university there and became a good friend of Christian. Jesuits, Pères Blancs, lay missionaries, foreign technicians working on construction projects for the government, and students from sub-Saharan Africa and from Eastern Europe studying in Medea also were frequent guests. So, too, were Muslims. Muslim friends came to take advantage of the tranquil setting and to pray, knowing they would be received as fellow seekers of God. Christian made a point of being sure the Muslims felt at home. He attached a sign on the *hôtellerie* door that read MUSLIMS WELCOME FOR RETREATS HERE.

The *hôtellerie* was detached from the cloister itself, but it was located inside the main entrance gate. Unlike most of the monks who had other jobs to do, Christian was always at the disposal of his guests. Familiar with the Koran and the Bible, sensitive to the Scripture of each faith, Christians and Muslims alike began to look to the young novice as a spiritual guide. Christian soon developed a reputation as a man who could help them understand how the cross and the crescent cohabited in God's house.

One day, a Muslim woman came to him with her intended husband, a Christian. She was torn by the prospect of being viewed as a traitor by her own community. "He received us in his small office, we spoke of our concerns. I didn't want to break with my own faith. I wanted both our religions to be able to walk together. 'As sons of Abraham we are different,' he agreed, 'but we can live our piety together.' He sat motionless, with one hand on the other, and looked at us with great tenderness. He read us passages from the Bible and from the Koran. 'What are you afraid of?' he asked. 'Of being a turncoat.' 'What coat?' he answered. 'We are only an envelope around a soul. Don't worry about your skin. Go a step at a time. Listen to God and let him guide you. The future belongs to God.' Afterward, he escorted us to the entrance gate, loaded down with vegetables and fruit. He helped me to better understand my own faith . . . to trust in God."

Christian kept up an active correspondence with Maurice Borrmans, his old mentor in Rome. "Our way of living places such obvious weight on certain of the pillars of Islam, it causes respect among our neighbors. Often they will say, 'Too bad you are not a Muslim,' but this respect seems to hide another, unspoken question, which is, 'How can they be what they are and not be Muslims?' They also want to know if I believe the Koran comes from God and what Christians think of the Prophet Mohammed."

He wanted the other monks to share his enthusiasm for seeking God with Muslims. But of all the brothers, he was the only one who had come to Algeria to live in spiritual communion with Islam. Jean-

Pierre and Amédée were also interested in Muslims and the Arab world, but as people, not as objects of a unifying intellectual and spiritual quest. Luc had come to care for the sick and poor. Others had come to Tibhirine to serve the spiritual needs of the Christian community in Algeria. Some saw themselves as part of the North African monastic tradition of that went back to Saint Anthony, and there were those who wanted to live their monasticism more simply and humbly. Christian described his brothers to a friend as a "bouquet of flowers, each one in itself not very extraordinary, but together, they were attractive." At the same time, he was aware that he was in danger of being excluded from the bouquet.

Christian went native, too native for the taste of many of the brothers. During Ramadan, which he considered the Muslim Lent, Christian fasted for forty days, drinking and eating nothing from dawn to dusk, while still maintaining his regular work schedule. He followed the Muslim custom of removing one's shoes when entering a mosque, taking off his sandals in the chapel. Then he caused a furor by proposing to have an alternative service with an Arab liturgy, a thought that was firmly rejected by the community as divisive. He recognized his mistake later. "The most beautiful flower has been trampled in the garden of a monk who should have known better and kept quiet," he wrote to a friend from seminary days.

In the fall of 1975, there were other, more disquieting signs outside the monastery. In mid-October, an order came from the gendarmerie to vacate the monastery within eight days. The same order had also been given to the occupants of the Church of Santa Cruz in Oran, the Basilica of Notre-Dame d'Afrique in Algiers, and the Cathedral of Saint Augustine in Annaba. The monks were packing up the books in their library and burning papers when they learned they could stay after all. Archbishop Duval had intervened directly with President Boumediene, whose anticlerical brother-in-law was the head of the gendarmerie and had initiated the action without consulting him. The order was rescinded. Boumediene not only had great respect for Duval but liked having Christians in Algeria.

The following year, on November 19, 1976, a new Algerian constitution officially proclaimed a socialist revolution. Agricultural land was organized into Soviet-style cooperatives. The new constitution was socialist and Islamic. It declared Islam the state religion, while tolerating freedom of worship. The Boumediene government nationalized both Islamic and Christian private schools. Catholic clerics taught 42,000 Muslim students each year in schools that were often favored by Muslim parents for their high teaching standards and good moral instruction. At first, the nationalization of the schools was seen as a massive body blow to the Church. Some members of the clergy returned to France, but for most, nationalization meant continued teaching as salaried employees of the Algerian government.

Nationalization offered the remaining Christians another moment of reflection on the meaning of their faith. Duval viewed it as pushing the Church another step in the direction of gratuitous love, of giving without expecting anything in return. "The Church will be reduced to its essentials," he told the monks during a visit to Tibhirine. The essence of the Church was not in its buildings but in the "spirit of fraternity lived each day." The Church was there not simply to serve the needs of Christians but to be a sign of God's love for all men everywhere. Each Christian community in Algeria would live their faith differently in the years ahead. Some, like the Little Sisters of Jesus, would care for the aged; the Sisters of Saint Augustine worked in hospitals; the Jesuits and Benedictines continued to teach students; and the monks prayed and remembered God.

In July, a mysterious assassination occurred. Monsignor Gaston Jacquier, Duval's vicar general, was walking in central Algiers, when a man came up behind him and plunged a knife into his femoral artery. The incident was officially condemned and treated in the press as the lone action of a wild man, *un fou*. Yet, to those who thought about it, a well-aimed stab to the inner thigh was an unusual way for a crazy person to kill someone. And then the madman escaped into a car that happened to be waiting nearby. Following Jacquier's death, Duval put out the order to the clergy in his diocese not to wear their religious habits in public or ostentatiously display the cross. Later, churches stopped ringing their bells to avoid offending certain extremists.

The year the Church in Algeria seemed to be in the greatest state of insecurity was, oddly, also the year the monastery's own future became more secure. On October 1, 1976, Christian was invited by his brothers to take his final vows, seven years after entering the order. He pronounced his vow of stability in the presence of friends from all over Algeria who had come to Tibhirine for the event. His former abbot at Aiguebelle, Jean de la Croix, came from France for the occasion. Christian committed himself to a lifelong service to God, married to a specific community of brothers, in a specific place. This was the meaning of the vow of stability, which was a hallmark of Trappist culture. He asked his brothers' forgiveness for his willful behavior and for offenses to the community caused by the single-minded pursuit of his special vocation.

Yet Christian did not confuse his willfulness with his commitment to spiritual communion with Islam, a commitment he wanted his brothers to understand. The following day, he presented them with a long written credo of faith, which some found upsetting, even revolutionary. For a monk who had never thought or known much about Islam, it could have been disturbing to read some of Christian's ideas: "The prayer of the monk and that of the Muslim have a common spiritual parentage which must be more celebrated . . . Certain values of Islam are undeniably a stimulus for the monk in his own vocation. These include devotion to the Absolute, regular communal prayer, fasting, submission to the will of God, giving alms to the poor, offering hospitality, self-transformation, trust in divine Providence and spiritual pilgrimage . . . in all this can be recognized the Holy Spirit. No one knows from where it comes or where it goes."

At the request of Abbot Jean de la Croix, four other monks, who were still attached officially to other monasteries in France, took their vows of stability at Tibhirine. This brought to seven the number of brothers who were stabilized at Notre-Dame de l'Atlas. With the minimum of six stabilized brothers secured, the monastery had the right under the Order's constitution to elect its own abbot. This would free it from the carousel of temporary superiors appointed by the mother monastery at Aiguebelle and allow it to become self-governing.

But elections were hardly on Christian's mind. The meaning of the insecurity was. "Personally" he wrote a friend, "I feel the desire to place this surfeit of insecurity we are experiencing under the heading of 'trust' and 'abandon.' " For him, insecurity was "a grace of choice," the constant companion of a Christian, and the "most uncomfortable one for him who wants only to sleep."

In 1978, Christian's father died, unreconciled to his son's calling to abandon himself to God among Muslims in a country that was full of bad war memories. Guy de Chergé's sole visit to Tibhirine at the time Christian took his final vows had convinced him that his son was truly happy there. Yet intellectually, the general believed to the end of his life that Christian's career had become one of wasted promise. Shortly before Christian returned to Paris in the winter of 1978 to preside over his father's funeral, he had applied for Algerian citizenship—a move his father called "idiotic."

Later that spring, Christian wrote to a friend, explaining why he did it. "The calling I feel has made me want to be a stranger who no longer has a home on this earth in order to go there where God intends. But this same calling has consecrated me to live a vow of stability in this monastery, to be a living embodiment with all the inhabitants of this country, this City of God where all the frontiers of country, race, and religion should one day disappear." Christian never received a reply to his application.

There were other disappointments for Christian that same year. His monastic father was sick, too, and going blind from glaucoma. Jean-Baptiste, the appointed superior from Port du Salut, in Normandy, was one of the few who believed in Christian's quest. "If God is the center" he would say, "then as people draw closer to God, they draw closer to one another." Christian greeted Jean-Baptiste's replacement by the abbot at Aiguebelle as a step backward.

In his mind, Jean de la Croix represented traditional French monasticism; the Christianity of wealth and power—the miter, the ring, hierarchy, the Middle Ages. Nevertheless, Jean de la Croix would support Christian in every way over the next six years. He knew that Christian's special calling was needed to give the community a sense of purpose. He also understood Christian's frustration. Jean de la Croix recognized that Mohammed's gift of love had become for Christian a kind of epiphany, and that he wanted to evangelize his brothers with the Good News of Islam. "He was, after all, a military man's son. He had all the discipline and purposefulness of a good officer," Jean de la Croix reflected years later.

His special calling was recognized by all, but few were interested in sharing the light he wanted to spread. Christian was also threatening to many of the older men. His broad intellect, strong education, and knowledge of Arabic and the Koran made him sought after throughout Algeria to talk about the "notes that are in harmony." Jean de la Croix gave Christian his head, seeing in him the monastery's future leader. Once a week he let him present an Islamic point of view on some topic such as death, prayer, Adam and Eve, or the Virgin Mary. Yet the persistent indifference of his brothers produced in Christian a sense of doubt about his place in the community. Could he live this intense vocation alone, without his brothers?

Christian had already established contact with the monastic Fraternities of Jerusalem, a post–Vatican II order, formed in 1975, that was committed to ecumenicism. The fraternities were especially open to the other children of Abraham, the Jews and Muslims. The men and women of the Fraternities of Jerusalem lived in the "desert of the cities"; their monastery was the city itself. During the day, they worked with ordinary people in factories, packinghouses, schools, or markets, while fully connected to the local parish church. Christian was wondering whether he should try to establish a new foundation in Algeria.

In November of 1979, Jean de la Croix gave Christian permission to go on retreat to Assekrem, the hermitage of Charles de Foucauld. He was another of God's nomads who, at the end of the nineteenth century, was also seduced by the people of the Maghreb, with their simple dogma and fervor for God. An eccentric Trappist, Foucauld's commitment to a life of solitary fraternity with the poor in Morocco and Algeria led him to live the Gospel among the poorest of God's children. He found them in Algeria's southern prefecture of Tamanrasset, which was inhabited by nomadic Tuaregs. There, the former agnostic officer from Saumur turned mystic and monk, dispensed medicine and food to all who came to his door. "I desire to live here," de Foucault wrote in his autobiography, "in such a way that all Christians, Muslims and Jewish inhabitants and even idolators regard me as their universal brother. They are beginning to call my hermitage 'the fraternity,' something very sweet to me."

A three-day walk from his fortress-hermitage in Tamanrasset was Assekrem, an isolated seven-thousand-foot plateau of windswept rock and cliffs that surveyed in all directions the surrounding desert, punctuated by giant monoliths of granite and basalt, known as the mountains of Hoggar. In 1911, Foucauld built a small stone hut to pray, meditate, and feel close to God on top of Algeria's highest peak.

There, basking in the same divine solitude as his Trappist predecessor, Christian meditated and prayed for guidance. Should he quit the monastery and start over, or risk all and stay, in the hope that things would change? A thousand miles south of Tibhirine in the Sinai of Algeria, atop a barren mountain of rocks without water or a sprig of vegetation, he penned his lonely anguish in a "Lamentation of Hope" the day before Christmas Eve, 1979.

"[. . .]Nuits de la foi en agonie . . .
Le doute est là, et la folie
d'aimer tout seul un Dieu absent et captivant.
[. . .]Ce que j'espère, je ne le vois . . .
C'est mon tourment, tourné vers Lui.
Toute souffrance y prend son sens,
caché en Dieu comme une naissance,
*ma JOIE déjà, mais c'est la NUIT.**

On January 11, 1980, the entry in the monastery's journal noted that Christian returned "smiling, unshaven, and emaciated." He was also returned confirmed in his vocation as a Trappist monk. His interior peace came with struggle, the struggle, as he wrote a friend, "of a man being pushed and pulled like a mule." Christian counted on the transforming power of prayer. He wanted to be "at least a fountain of sympathy," and, though feeling alone and isolated, to

*Nights of agonizing faith, doubt is there and the madness of loving alone an absent and captivating God. What I hope for I cannot see . . . Such is my torment, as I turn to Him. All suffering finds its meaning there, hidden in God like a child being born. My joy is there but it is night.

have "the courage and patience to place hope in the accomplishment of small things, each and every day."

Soon after Christian's return to the monastery, members of a Sufi brotherhood from Medea came to visit him. They had been brought to the monastery on Christmas day by Jean-Pierre, who had met one of them in Medea weeks earlier. They wished to participate in the new group Jean Pierre had told them about—the Bond of Peace.

The Bond of Peace had not been Christian's idea, but he was an enthusiastic supporter from the day his friend Claude Rault made the suggestion in the spring of 1979. Rault was a Père Blanc and close friend of Christian who had been teaching English in Touggourt, several hundred miles to the south. He had proposed bringing together scattered Christians throughout Algeria who were trying to better understand Islam. Could the One who brought Muslims to their knees five times a day be the same as the more complicated Three-In-One of the Christians? Many of them wondered how a religion whose Scripture seemed so hostile to nonbelievers could produce in the general population the kind, tolerant, and hospitable souls they all knew from daily life.

"We feel called by God to do something together with you," one of the Sufis told Christian when they met. "But we are not interested in theology. Theology raises barriers between people. Let God invent something new between us. Love is what brings people together. And without bonds, there can be no peace." Christian readily agreed, and the Bond of Peace was reborn as the *ribat-es-salaam.* Known in the future simply as the *ribat,* these Christian-Muslim encounters became semiannual meetings, beginning in the fall of 1980. Discussion was organized around a theme agreed upon in advance: the covenant, fraternal love, the Virgin Mary, Jesus, the Holy Spirit, the different names for God. Islam has ninety-nine, the last of which is The Patient One.

Patience was not one of the strongest qualities of the new abbot of Aiguebelle, who came to visit his daughter monastery in the fall of 1981. Jean-Georges Tyszkiewicz was originally from Warsaw, born a Radziwill on his mother's side, scion of one of the great Polish aristocratic families. But when the Russians reoccupied Warsaw toward the end of World War II, he was accused of collaboration with the Nazis and put in Lubyanka prison in Moscow to be shot. As the firing squad was readying itself, a reprieve from the Kremlin arrived. Stalin had saved his life. A kind of divine intervention had been exercised through the influence of his grandmother with Pope Pius XII, who had links with the former Georgian seminary student. After the war, Tyszkiewicz moved to Algiers, where he built a lucrative trading business before experiencing a personal conversion that led him to become a monk. As the abbot of Aiguebelle, he was known as strong-willed, domineering, and a man who liked to give orders.

Tibhirine was not new to him. He had begun his novitiate at Notre-Dame de l'Atlas in 1952, left, and then returned in 1966 as an acting superior. Now he had come back on a routine tour of his monastic family. These were occasions for the abbot of the mother monastery to discuss the concerns of each monk individually and gain a sense of the community's overall health and vigor. Several disgruntled brothers complained to him of Christian's "proselytizing"—their view of his weekly discourses on Islam, given during chapter meetings. Using the chapter meeting to talk about Islam with a captive audience was an imposition, as these occassions, held three times a week, were normally reserved for discussing internal community matters and group reflection.

During a gathering with all the brothers, Abbot Tyszkiewicz expressed surprise to Christian about his wanting Algerian citizenship. Christian's most sensitive nerve was touched by the abbot's implied criticism of his loyalty, causing an exchange that participants remember as "hot." Christian left the room red and angry, and the abbot left orders that there was to be no more Islamology inside the cloister. Henceforth, any communing, discussing, or lecturing on Islam would have to occur in the *hôtellerie* only. Indirectly, Jean de la Croix also had been slapped on the wrist. He had been Christian's ally and had allowed him to hold his weekly seminars, despite grumbling from certain brothers.

Christian did have a novel idea. He believed that all genuine seekers should join hands in their common quest and learn from one another the different spiritual pathways to God. Christian was enchanted by the Sufis' way of looking at the different religions. Each one, they said, was like an individual stone on a divine necklace, reflecting a different aspect of God's nature. For those brothers brought up in a more traditional way, like Roland, the policeman's son from Notre-Dame des Neiges, this constant talk of Islam was nothing less than an irritant, like chalk scratching on a blackboard. They had not come to the monastery to hear about Islam. They were uncertain about where this was all going to lead. Christian was intimidating enough with all his learning, intellect, and youthful energy. Some of the older men feared he would have them wearing a white *kamis* like the Prophet, and would take them off on some wild spiritual adventure. That was the reason several of the brothers were hesitant about Tibhirine becoming autonomous. They feared if Christian were elected superior, there would be nothing left to restrain their wild-eyed Islamophile brother.

Jean de la Croix knew about these anxieties. Nevertheless, he respected Christian's basic good judgment and had faith in his ability to give the community a sense of purpose without imposing his own. The triennial General Chapter meeting of the order was coming up in 1984 and would take place in Holyoke, Massachusetts. He also knew that if the monastery hadn't elected its own superior by then, the General Chapter would inevitably conclude that it needed to appoint a commission to look once again into the future of their odd little place in the Atlas surrounded by Islam. Jean de la Croix could easily imagine the outcome. The commission would be made up of people with no understanding of the situation in Algeria, and they would recommend it be closed.

With that likely result in mind, Jean de la Croix decided to orchestrate an election two months before the meeting of the General Chapter, scheduled for May. Using hints and intimations of closure if an election did not occur beforehand, he coaxed the hesitant community into having an election. But of the eleven monks, only the nine stabilized brothers could vote. Of those nine, three were absent due to bad health.

The electors were Jean de la Croix, the *ad nutum* superior, Jean-Pierre, a calm, well-equilibrated Alsatian from Timadeuc in Brittany who had responded in 1964 to the call for volunteers to go to Algeria following the near closure of the monastery by Abbot General Sortais the previous year; Amédée, a good-natured *pied-noir* priest from Algiers, who had been in the monastery the longest; Luc, the irascible doctor who had come to Tibhirine a month after Amédée, in August 1947 and had little interest in Islam per se (he once told a brother that reading the Koran was like reading a railroad schedule); and Jean-Baptiste, the former *ad nutum* superior from Timadeuc, who had been restabilized at Tibhirine. Christian made six.

On March 31, 1984, with the customary *scrutateurs* present, two monitors from outside the monastery watched as the votes were cast at the large square table in the chapter room. Three times, names had to be written down on little slips of paper, which were then folded neatly into quarters before being given to the *scrutateurs* to count. On the third round, a majority finally agreed. Christian would be the new superior of Notre-Dame de l'Atlas, fulfilling the covert plan of Jean de la Croix. At forty-seven, he was the youngest monk in a community of eleven brothers.

In his tidy, methodical way, Christian drew up a concise inventory of his resources, a kind of résumé of the situation, as a good staff officer might have done for a new commander unfamiliar with the unit.

There were landmark dates to summarize, beginning with March 7, 1934, the day Trappist monks left their monastery in Rahjenburg, Slovenia, for France. Four years later, on precisely the same day, six monks from Slovenia and six from Aiguebelle installed themselves under the patronage of Notre-Dame de l'Atlas at Tibhirine—a Berber word that means "the gardens." The site was selected for its beauty, peaceful isolation, and numerous springs.

When the monastery's population grew to twenty monks, it received the statute of abbey, and in 1947, elected its first abbot, Dom Bernard Barbaroux. He was succeeded by Dom Jean-Marie Frikert, who returned to France after independence in 1962. Frikert was followed by an interregnum of appointed superiors and near closures of the monastery, first by Abbot General Sortais in 1963 and then by the gendarmerie in 1975. Three weeks before Christian's election, and after considerable debate, the brothers voted to change the statute of the monastery from abbey to priory, a more modest but also more appropriate status for a monastery with only fourteen hectares (thirty acres) and eleven brothers.

The brothers' average age was sixty-five. Six of them had been at Tibhirine for more than ten years. The maximum number of monks allowed by the Algerian authorities was twelve. Yet, even with only nine stabilized brothers, the monastery was the largest in the Maghreb. All but two of the monks were ordained.* They lived from the produce of their garden, the sale of honey, and donations from guests staying at the *hôtellerie* or attending the Offices. The budget was in balance, and since 1983, the monastery and its land had belonged officially to the Algerian Association of Religions.

The monastery was part of an Algerian Church whose clergy of more than one thousand was highly dispersed and cosmopolitan. These included Spaniards, Belgians, Americans, Canadians, Italians, Dutch, West Africans, all of whom lived and worked immersed in a Muslim environment. The monks lived their vow of hospitality in different ways. There was a small dispensary open to all, where Luc treated people at no cost and without questions. The *porterie,* or gatehouse, provided a reception area where locals frequently came to use the telephone, ask for water, get a letter written, or sell or barter something. The *hôtellerie* had an average of five guests at any one time. Half of these were laymen, many of them students from other African countries who were studying in Medea. One in ten visitors was Algerian. The *hôtellerie* was also a place of spiritual dialogue between Christians and Muslims.

*There are no theological or educational requirements to become a Trappist; only a commitment to love God in a community of brothers.

5

Ribats

Had God pleased, He could have made of you one community: but it is His wish to test you by that which He has bestowed upon you. Vie with each other in good works, for to God you shall return and He will resolve your differences.

—Koran 5:49

Mohammed's smiling young face was the first to greet the guests as he opened the large blue metal doors that led into the enclosure of the monastery. With a slight bow, hand over his heart, the handsome gatekeeper welcomed the cars that trickled in all day long.

The two-story ocher-colored guest house, which would be the visitors' home for three days, had an air of well-groomed but tired poverty. Pots of marigolds and geraniums lined its front walk. The faded baby blue window trim softened the peeling stucco face of a building stained by dark blotches from a leaky gutter pipe. Opposite the front door, across the dirt driveway, steps descended down an embankment thick with ivy, leading into an outer courtyard shaded with giant cedars and stout Aleppo pines. From here, visitors had access to the chapel, near which stood the Virgin, her hands extended in welcome and her eyes cast diffidently downward.

In May of 1989, Bruno was the hôtelier, the official face of Cistercian hospitality toward strangers. He assigned rooms and explained the house rules. Guests were expected to make up their own beds and clean their rooms when they left. No loud talking. The dining etiquette required silence during meals, though in practice, this was relaxed at Tibhirine. Guests were issued cloth napkins, kept in numbered cubbyholes matching their room numbers. They cleared the table and cleaned the dishes. Each room was equipped with a wooden bed, a wash basin, a chair, and a table. On the table was a schedule of the hours of the Divine Office, when the real work of a Trappist occurs.

Vigils—4:00 A.M.
Lauds—7:30 (7:15 in summer)
Terce—9:15 (summer, in the chapter room)
Sext—12:30 P.M. (includes Eucharist, except Thursdays)
None—2:45 (3:45 in summer)
Vespers—6:00 (Thursdays, includes Eucharist)
Compline—8:00

Unlike for the monks, attendance by the guests at these services was voluntary. Guests could freely wander in the flower gardens behind the *hôtellerie* and around the cemetery, but the vegetable garden was off limits and reserved only for those who worked there. If guests wanted to work in the garden with the brothers, that could be arranged. Guests were asked to make a voluntary contribution to cover expenses. On the bottom of the sheet was a reminder: "We attach great importance to external silence, which allows us to enjoy interior silence." Maximum stay was fifteen days.

The fifteen men and women who drove over the mountain were no strangers to the monastery. It was the tenth anniversary of the *ribat*. Since their first meeting in March of 1979, the group had gathered at the *hôtellerie* twice a year. Little Sisters of Jesus, Augustinian Sisters, Poor Clares, Marists, Pères Blancs, regular clergy, and occasional lay participants trekked every six months to Tibhirine from all over Algeria—three hundred miles from Oran and Arzew, in the west; two hundred miles from Batna, to the east; and still greater distances from the oases of Ghardaïa and Touggourt in the southern desert.

After their meeting with Christian in January of 1980, upon his return from Assekrem, the Sufis became the first Muslims to participate in the *ribat*. But in the mind of some members of the Catholic Church, a dialogue with Sufis is hardly a dialogue with Islam. Sufis, they claim, are not mainstream Islam. They are considered heretics in some parts of the Islamic world because they believe in an accessible God of love with whom a believer can strive to commune. Sincerity of the heart is the hallmark of the Sufi, who is driven by a desire not only to please God but to be reunited with God.

In the eyes of some Muslims, this kind of thinking can lead to the dangerous notion that love of God should be a precondition for praying, giving alms, fasting, or following the other pillars of the faith. This is as foolish as believing one should love one's commanding officer in the army as a condition for following orders. Yes, a soldier may learn to love his commander, and when he does, he will follow orders with more enthusiasm, even anticipate them, but an army can not function on love alone. Nor can society. Obedience to the law is good in itself because it keeps the believer out of trouble. The rules remind believers of their basic obligations to God and to their neighbors. The contentment of inner peace is found through submission. A Muslim is one who submits.*

Worse, the Sufi is a mystic who flirts with a blasphemous notion—that God is somehow "like us," and therefore accessible for spiritual communion. Christians consider Sufis to be those Muslims most like themselves. Sufis also conceive of "knowing God," even if it is without the mediation of the Son. Conscious of this too-comfortable affinity with Sufis, Christian members of the *ribat* asked ordinary Muslims from the neighborhood to join the group.

Ten white tulips decorated the table in the common room of the *hôtellerie*. The men and women sitting around it had come together in the simple belief that God has an immense desire to enter into communion with man, and man with God. The piety, charity, and simple gestures of friendship of their Muslim neighbors represented both a challenge and a confirmation of their own faith. Muslim hospitality toward them had been an invitation to renew their commitment to live the Gospels daily. Wasn't the friendliness of so many of the Muslims with whom they lived a clear sign of the workings of the Holy Spirit, the spirit of fellowship that is at the heart of all men? God's love for man is echoed in His desire for men to love one another. Can't all God's children reveal something of God, each in their own way? How to break out of the horrible errors of the past, when men despised and killed one another in the name of their

*Islam, derived from the Arabic word, *salama,* means "surrender," but also "peace." A Muslim is one who chooses to conform his will to divine will and thereby achieves inner peace.

religion? Isn't the greatest obstacle to peace man's rejection of those who are different? They reflected on the meaning the *ribats* had had for them over the past ten years.

Some in the group had heard Claude Rault, the founder of the *ribats,* tell the story that had brought home to him the power of brotherly love. He had been teaching English for years in Toggourt. He had made a habit of leaving the classroom quickly after his lessons to avoid being caught up in discussions with students that might be interpreted as proselytizing. Once, however, a girl who admired his teaching caught him before he could leave and told him that he should become a Muslim. Rault was flattered, but he explained that he couldn't do that. The student offered to give up her place in heaven for him. The simple but unusual act of a Muslim offering to exchange her place in heaven for a Christian one in hell was, for Rault, a testimonial to the power of love to bridge differences. Others around the table shared their experiences.

Sister M. lived alone in Bir el Ater as a nurse for the aged. She thought the *ribats* had helped her develop a deeper sense of unity with her Muslim brother. "But what is most important is the individual, rather than his Islam." T., a priest from Oran, wanted to reexamine his thinking about Islam. The *ribat* had been for him both "a bond and a thorn." "It causes me a certain anxiety, which is good for my faith—and it helps me not overreact to the current aggressiveness one sees now in the streets." Sister H., who worked in the Casbah of Algiers at a special library for young Algerians, thought she had grown because of the *ribats*. "Before, the muezzin's cry was a form of aggression. Now I feel a part of this prayer; it doesn't bother me anymore. I am at peace."

Sister R. came from Arzew. She found that the *ribats* had helped her return to the essentials of her faith. "It has made me express my faith in a way that doesn't cause harm to the other. One doesn't have the right to appropriate certain aspects of faith, of salvation. . . . Christ, the mystery of salvation, is still unknown. . . . The muezzin's call to prayer recenters me on God."

They had all encountered different Islams: orthodox Islam, mystical Islam, a broad, generous Islam, and a narrow, literalistic Islam. All had experienced the arrogance found most often among the intellectuals and students who used the Koran as if it were Mao's *Little Red Book*. For them, the Koran was a Xerox copy of God's word. It contained no ambiguity, and when they quoted the Koran, they were speaking for God.

F. was a Jesuit priest working at the French Cultural Center in Tlemcen, and not a regular at the *ribats*. He told the group of his experience, confirming theirs:

"I have never been happier than working in Tlemcen. The ordinary people take you into their hearts. The poverty of our church here helps us. Without wealth, hierarchy, security, we can all live close to the people and share in their poverty. My faith has no props, only what is in my heart. In this, I am no different from all of you. I think we are like the Church in the first century before it became a state religion. Frankly, when I go to Rome and see all the pomp, buildings, and wealth, I feel sick. This is not what Christianity is about."

The rigid, intolerant Islam they had all encountered reminded him of Christianity in the sixteenth century. He told the story of his friend Rachid to illustrate what crazy things can happen to people who get drunk on holy righteousness, read Scripture piecemeal, and become self-appointed enforcers of God's word. Rachid had been a friendly, "normal" kid, who had helped F. learn Arabic. Rachid eventually introduced him to his family, where F. felt like one of their own. But after doing his military service, Rachid came back a different person.

"Maybe he got brainwashed by his commanding officer, I don't know. All I know is that afterward, I couldn't talk to him. He was completely rigid. It was simply, 'The Koran says . . .' as if the Koran itself was God.

"Rachid started to badger his sister because she didn't wear a veil. She refused to appease him, saying the Koran was more than just rules. Finally, Rachid became so infuriated with his sister's disobedience, he dowsed her with gasoline and set her on fire. Her whole body was burned. We arranged for her to be flown to a special burn center in France. She is alive today, thanks to French medical treatment."

The aggressiveness and intolerance, they agreed, came mostly from the intellectuals and the younger generation. Their legalistic Islam was like that of the Pharisees, who condemned Jesus for healing the sick on the Sabbath. The Sufis, they thought, represented for Islam what Jesus represented for Judaism—putting the spirit of charity before ritual and formalistic obedience. The Islam of the common man, they thought, was closer in spirit to Sufism. For the simple people who are humble and without pretension, faith is a matter between the individual and God. What matters is a good heart and a generous spirit. Perhaps, the group speculated, Sufism would act as a corrective to legalistic Islam the way Christianity was to legalistic Judaism.

Some in the group thought Islam was close to Protestantism, given its lack of hierarchy, emphasis on a direct relationship between the believer and God, and respect for wealth as a sign of God's favor. Others thought Islam resembled Catholicism, with its emphasis on ritual, recitation, and reverence for saints among the simple people. And in a not-so-distant past, Catholicism had had lots of rules, including the rigid separation of women from men, noted Christian, who had annoyed some of the brothers when he agreed to allow the Little Sisters of Jesus to use one of their empty buildings for summer retreats.

Christian concluded, "One always meets another person at the same level one seeks to know him." His remark, Rault remembered in his minutes, made the group think about where their hearts were in their encounters with Islam, the quality of their listening and their real attitude toward the other person. "In all our encounters, we agreed on the importance of the attitude of the heart, the attentiveness of the spirit."

On the second day, their Muslim friends arrived. As was customary, a topic had been chosen in advance for discussion: humility.

"The *ribat* was born the same year as the revolution in Iran," Rault reminded the new visitors. "The *ribat* dreams of another revolution, one that comes from within ourselves. God has allowed us to meet Muslim brothers who share the same dream. This keeps us from being locked into a view of Islam that does not do justice to how you live with us in the name of your faith. It is good that this anniversary be held under the heading of humility."

Sister M., who lived alone and cared for the aged, felt a sense of humility all around her in Bir el Ater. "The simplicity, serenity, and patience of these people in the face of hardship and their hunger for friendship are for me a kind of divine presence. I have been loved by this population for twenty years . . . have received much from them. I feel blessed." Sister O., who lived in the Kouba neighborhood in Algiers, had witnessed the reactions of extremists since the riots in October 1988. "Humility helps me stay calm, even though I am tempted to react aggressively toward the aggressiveness around me. I cannot wear my crucifix exposed anymore without young men coming up to me and calling me an infidel.

Sister H. was having difficulties in her class. She was the only woman and only foreigner teaching in her school, and she felt isolated and harassed. "How does humility help me to live nonviolently? What does the Koran say about humility toward one's fellow man?" she asked M., a Muslim in the group.

"God is in each of us," he answered. "To be humble toward God means to be humble toward all men. Perhaps, you know the verse in the Koran that says, 'Do not turn away from people in contempt, or go about in an arrogant way. God does not love a conceited boaster. Pursue the right course and lower your voice. There is no noise worse than the braying of asses.' Many of those young men you have trouble with are braying asses. . . . The path toward God is humility. He who thinks about God constantly—in the morning, noon, and evening—can be neither arrogant nor violent. Prostration in prayer is the ultimate sign of humility."

"But I suppose these men pray. They read the Koran. What is wrong with them?"

"Yes, but their hearts are filled with anger and hatred, and they twist the meaning of God's word to suit their own purposes," M. replied. "The Koran says God does not change people's lot unless they change what is in their hearts. False believers profess with their lips but not with their hearts."

Rault reminded Sister H. of the saying of one of the desert fathers: "Souls full of gentleness are worth more than monks full of passion and anger." He added, "Too many 'truths' are wielded by people who are angry and without humility. I think if a truth is not accepted, it is because it is not given humbly. Truth that is wielded like a bludgeon overwhelms and is rejected. Truth should be humble. Jesus said, 'I am gentle and humble of heart.' "

The thought that without humility there can be no attainment of truth brought up the subject of the next meeting. But, they wondered, should it be translated for their Muslim friends as *al haqq, "toward* the truth," meaning truth as an attribute of God, or *al haqiqa, "in* the truth, which expressed more the sense of the mystery of the divine? They settled on *al haqiqa*—"Lead us in truth."

"Yes, God's truth has to be discovered—it is not handed out all cooked," Christophe had jumped in with his usual passion about such things. "The Bible, like the Koran, has to be read and grasped as a whole. Old and New Testament. . . . It's like a set of teeth. You need the uppers and the lowers or you can't chew. We can never be content to read a text in isolation, but only within the total context . . . which is the only hope for understanding the word of God. We need to search for the truth that comes from living, from meeting people, and from love—truths that bring us forward, not those that just titillate the intellect."

Christophe Lebreton had found that the truths of daily life had forced him to confront the meaning of his faith in new ways since his arrival at Tibhirine in 1987. He, too, had been touched by his neighbors' hospitality and had found confirmation of his own faith in their simple God-filled phrases and thoughts. His was a faith unburdened by doctrine, yet deeply rooted in Jesus Christ. Incarnation was God's way of helping his creatures know His love as a friend, parent, spouse, healer, teacher, protector, disturber of complacent souls—a faith that, for Christophe, meant, above all, living in friendship with others. To follow Jesus is to love. To love is to be a friend. In French, the connections are clear: *aimer,* "to love"; *ami,* "friend"; *amitié,* "friendship." *Amour.* Love is the root of all.

"There was something in him from the earliest age. He had a generous nature and was always interested in the needs of other people," remembered Christophe's mother, Jehanne Lebreton. She radiated a gentle, grandmotherly warmth and joyful sorrow as she remembered his youth while sitting in her living room looking at the Ardèche

Mountains, near Montélimar. "But he also had a strong contemplative side. When Christophe had been in Algeria as a *coopérant* in the early 1970s, he had visited the monastery at Tibhirine and was quite smitten by its beauty and simplicity."

The Lebretons came originally from Blois, in the Loire Valley, where Christophe's father was the director of a livestock breeding center. His mother was a devout Catholic, yet Christophe was the only one of her twelve children to enter the church. His heart was never in the law, which he was studying at the University of Tours when thousands of students revolted in the streets of Paris in 1968. Like the Algerian riots that would occur in 1988, the Paris uprising began as a protest against poor conditions at universities and ended with demands for social justice and reform. Christophe joined those in the streets, but then realized that he had no idea what he was really doing there in the faceless crowd. "In the mass psychology I had fallen victim to, I felt a complete void, an emptiness of meaning and direction," Christophe wrote later. It was a turning point that led him to march under a different banner.

Bourgeois-bred, the antibourgeois, rebel son who had flirted with Marxism began spending his summers working with Abbé Pierre. This tenacious Magoo-looking cleric with his trademark black cape and beret, thick glasses, and a limp acquired in the Resistance had become a national folk hero. After World War II, he had single-handedly battled the Parisian bureaucracy on behalf of thousands of homeless who needed roofs over their heads. In a nation that is officially godless, where no government official puts a hand on the Bible or dares invoke the name of God in public, he has been voted the most respected man in France for decades.* Working with the homeless and ex-convicts at the Emmaus camps of Abbé Pierre, Christophe developed the sense that God is with the poor. They are humble, he would tell his parents, and only the humble in spirit can be close to God.

Christophe had selected the Alpine monastery at Tamié over Aig-

*In 2000, Abbé Pierre fell to second place, when the French-born Algerian soccer star "Zizu" Zidane took first place. He is admired by the French for his modesty and simplicity as well as for helping France win the World Cup in 1999. He has become a symbol of successful integration.

uebelle in the Drôme because the latter seemed too grand, and he disapproved of its manufacture of liquors as a way to earn a living. But at Tamié, he was unhappy from the start. There was not enough poverty. Monks are supposed to be following the way of Christ. The monastery was too luxurious. The food was too good. He didn't like the silence, especially at meals. It was not very fraternal. He would not address the abbot with the respectful *vous,* calling him instead by the familiar *tu.* When cordless phones were introduced in the 1980s, he threw his away. They were not monklike. Poor people didn't have them, he insisted. Why should monks? The abbot was so perplexed by Christophe, he sent him to a psychiatrist. The psychiatrist reported that Christophe had nothing wrong with him; the problem, he concluded, was with the monastery.

In 1975, a year after entering Notre-Dame de Tamié, the twenty-five-year-old novice asked to go to Notre-Dame de l'Atlas, where the monks lived closer to his idea of apostolic poverty. But ten months later, he was back at Tamié. The chemistry with the eleven, mostly older men, had not been right. Also, there had been doubts within the order about the purpose of a monastery in a Muslim country. His departure for Tibhirine, he told a friend, was a "false call." It had come only from within: he had been listening to himself, he concluded. When he felt called there ten years later, there was an objective need. The monastery had achieved autonomous status. Christian had been elected superior, but he needed new recruits to augment the aging brothers.

There was a certain attraction, or perhaps shared qualities, between Christophe and Christian. Both had come from large families with devout mothers. Each had shown at an early age a disposition for God's ministry. Both were men of strong emotions and bad tempers that needed to be controlled. And both were well-educated intellectuals who disliked intellectual approaches to life—those that were abstract, doctrinal, and tended toward winning arguments.

Since 1984, detailed minutes of the *ribats* had been piling up on Maurice Borrmans's desk at the Papal Institute of Arabic and Islamic Studies, where many of the Arab-speaking Christians in the group attending the *ribats* had been trained. Christian visited Borrmans whenever he returned to Rome. Their relationship remained close even if his mentor sometimes thought Christian's communing with Islam was with those Muslims with whom it was easiest to get along. With a wave of his hand and the charming smile that was his hallmark, Christian would poke fun at his former professor. "Why do you bother with all these piles of paper and reviews? Live with Muslims and join your heart with theirs"

But how to join hearts, Borrmans would ask him, if the mind is polluted with lies and rubbish? "The brain affects the heart. I am stuck in the mud. I have to teach, edit, and argue with people who say Christianity is polytheism. I have to talk to people with no modesty, with people who have sacralized Islam. 'Islam says this,' 'Islam says that,' as if they were speaking for God. You are up on the mountain with Sufi mystics like yourself. I don't have the luxury of being with fellow seekers as you do."

Borrmans thought the same way about the monks' neighbors around the monastery. He called them "the Biblical poor." "They are people of simple faith, with no pretensions of knowledge. They don't care about theology. Why did God choose the poor and children to bring his message? The rich don't think they need God, and the learned think they know better."

Christian recognized what others in the Algerian Church had discovered, as well. Knowledge puffs up; love edifies. "We never took the initiative. The dialogue came of itself, the fruit of living together with Muslims over a long period of time," Christian wrote in his reflection to Borrmans in the fall of 1989, on the occasion of the biannual Roman Days. The Roman Days had been organized in 1959 to permit Christian clergy serving in Muslim countries throughout the world to meet and exchange experiences. Over the years they had concluded that living among Muslims had been good for their faith. Islam challenged them to be better Christians. They often said it made them practice the Fifth Gospel, meaning the Gospel lived, rather than preached. "We avoid theological discussions," Christian continued in his report to Borrmans, "because they lead to intellectual sparring that gets in the way of getting to know one another. All the little daily gestures of goodwill speak for themselves.

Sharing our water, a piece of bread, a friendly handshake says much more about what we can do together than do theological tomes."

Christian was an intellectual, but he believed the truths of the heart were more sure than those of the head—truths he practiced with his brothers after he became prior. They had finally given him their trust, despite misgivings. Now he had to trust them. Cardinal Duval often said, "He who has only a little trust should give it to someone else, and it will be returned manyfold." The confidence they showed in him by electing him their superior for six years made him more confident in them. He became much more patient and understanding. He slowed down, realizing he couldn't be in a rush to communicate with Muslims while he failed to understand his own brothers. "Mutual osmosis took place," his friend Claude Rault remembered. Christian tried harder to know each monk, to appreciate each individual flower in the bouquet. In turn, his desire to draw closer to God with Muslims and make the neighbors feel part of the extended monastic family gradually took root with the others.

There was a practical side to this growing together. The monks had a tractor, but they needed to borrow a plow. They bartered use of their battery recharger in return for eggs. Their neighbors didn't eat pork, and would give the monks the carcasses of boars they shot. Christian relaxed the rule on meat consumption in order to be gracious with them. Sometimes, the Muslim men were invited to eat in the refectory with the monks. As for the *ribats,* the brothers at first thought they were something of an oddity, but they gradually accepted them as Christian's vocation.

Christian was a radical, but he never tried to impose his beliefs on others. Religion was useless, he would say, if it did not help people to live together.

6

Under the Virgin's Gaze

And of the woman who kept her chastity, We breathed into her of Our spirit, and made her and her son a sign to all mankind.

—Koran 21:91

The noise outside the window of Father Jean Scotto's apartment was deafening. Thousands of the faithful had gathered for midday prayer, spilling onto the street, where loudspeakers carried the imam's words to hundreds more bent in devotion on the pavement. The sheer numbers made an impression on Abbot Jean-Marc Thévenet who had just arrived from France, where the churches were rarely full. Philippe Hémon and Paul Favre-Miville had come with him from Notre-Dame de Tamié in Savoy for the ordination of Christophe. Philippe had been a close friend of Christophe when they were together at Tamié, and Jean-Marc had been their superior. Only Paul had come to stay permanently at Tibhirine, seeking a simpler, poorer monasticism than he had found at Tamié. The three had stopped to have lunch in Algiers with the legendary Scotto before driving the sixty miles up to the monastery at Tibhirine.

The scene below Scotto's kitchen window brought back old memories that filled his eyes with tears as he stood beside his visitors. Scotto had stood firmly with Duval in defending the Arabs' right of self-determination. He had sheltered FLN sympathizers during the war and been considered by the French army as one of the red clergy. Like Duval, Scotto was also given Algerian citizenship after independence.

When the first municipal elections were held in 1967, the residents of Belcourt, once the European working-class neighborhood of Albert Camus's youth, had become predominantly Muslim. Scotto was asked to be their representative to the city council. His campaign workers promoted him with the slogan "This is a man you can vote for. He won't take your money or your women." With 100 percent of the vote, a short, blunt-spoken *pied-noir,* the son of Italian immigrants, who sported a spade beard and had the pugnacious appearance of a boxing coach, became Belcourt's first elected representative on the new postwar city council. Scotto thought this immersion in Muslim society was healthy for the Church. He often said that it prevented self-absorbed "navel gazing."

Nor was he impressed by ecclesiastical status symbols. In 1970, Scotto was named bishop of Constantine. When he was shown the bishop's residence, its grandeur embarrassed him. "I would have needed a bicycle to get around, so I told the Red Cross they could use it," he told a French journalist. "We must get rid of the idea that being a bishop means having a gold ring, a pretty miter, and a Mercedes-Benz. For too long, the Church has acted like an earthly power."

Le pouvoir, as the power structure in Algeria was popularly known, could have benefited from Scotto's example. Love of expensive cars and other status symbols amid growing poverty and the dashed hopes of the younger generation for a brighter future was contributing to the political unrest that the brothers from Tamié saw spilling into the streets of Belcourt.

The signs of economic failure were evident in December of 1989 as the three men were driven in the monastery's battered old brown Renault 4L up the soft yellow sandstone of the Sahel Hills, which form a balcony overlooking the Bay of Algiers. They passed through the shaded neighborhoods of Hydra, Birmandreis, and Birkhadem before descending south into the vineyards and vegetable farms of the Mitidja. This vast alluvial plain was where *pieds-noirs* had transformed mosquito-infested marshlands into a fertile agricultural area producing wines and citrus fruits that were sold throughout Europe. They headed west on the N1, past neglected vineyards and irrigation canals along the northern rim of the plain, past Boufarik, home of the Orangina soft drink, then south toward Blida, the city of roses and French-built prisons, and the gateway to the Atlas Mountains, stretching to Morocco. Everywhere along the route, they saw abandoned construction of housing and mosques. A feeling of stagnation and decay was palpable.

From Blida, they drove though the narrow Chiffa Gorge, traditional home of bandits and Barbary apes, to Medea. This ancient holy city of 100,000 was once Medias, a Roman provincial capital. Today, Medea gives its name to the surrounding high plateau, known as the Medea, which descends into semiarid plateaus and, finally, the oceanic desert extending to Niger and Mali. The FLN's industrial development campaign in the 1970s had transformed Medea's once-agricultural economy into a center for pharmaceuticals, cement plants, and a budding nuclear research program. It was also a city known for its conservatism, where coeducation, or *mixité,* had never been practiced. Girls and boys had always gone to separate schools, women covered their heads and did not leave their homes except to go to the Turkish baths, to market, or to the mosque. "We had no fear at that time," Jean-Marc remembered. "The ferment that was going on in the streets and the mosques had not been directed yet at foreigners. Whenever we went to the market, people were very friendly."

A winter thunderstorm and late-evening arrival had masked the beauty of the scene that greeted them at six o'clock the next morning as they prepared for Lauds. Looking north from the chipped stone terrace off their rooms, they could see the panorama of the rugged pine-covered Tamesguida Mountains across a mist-filled valley. The air had been cleared by the rain of the previous day, revealing dark peaks set in early-morning deep blue.

Suddenly, Philippe heard an unexpected sound interrupt the silence. "*Allahu Akbar, Allahu Akbar; ashadu an la ilaha il l'Allah.* "God is great. There is no god but God. . . . Hurry to prayer. . . . Hurry to salvation." Unbeknown to him, Philippe had found himself in a monastery where church bells and the muezzin's call to prayer inhabited the same enclosure. "The imploring, appeasing, magnificent voice of a muezzin rose into the sky and I thought then, truly God lives in the praise of his children," he wrote later in his diary.

Two years earlier, the government's mosque-building campaign had reached the monastery's front door. The proposed site had been opposite the entrance to the monastery. The monks swallowed this provocation with ironic humor when the construction workers asked to store their equipment within the monastery's enclosure at night as a precaution against theft. When money ran out after the foundation was poured, Christian proposed to the brothers that the unused reception room next to the dispensary be lent to their neighbors for prayer. The building had direct access from the road and local people could come and go as they pleased.

The comingling of Muslim and Christian prayer was a symbol of a reality Christian deeply felt—the call to communion among all God's children that is at the heart of the divine. But it was rumored that some Muslims wondered about the motives of this generosity. Was this a subtle way to undermine their own faithful—with kindness? Some in the Church grumbled about Christian's generosity. Muslims, they complained, were not so inclined to respect diverse expressions of faith in the same God. Christian always had the same response: Christ's love is not an exchange, nor is it limited to a category of people. It is *gratuit*.

So too was the friendship of the many Algerian Muslims who came to Tibhirine on January 1, 1990, to witness Christophe's ordination, presided over by Bishop Henri Teissier of Algiers. It was a time when Islamist extremists were spitting on Christians who were seen publically wearing crucifixes, intimidating licensed bar owners and harassing Muslim women in short skirts. For Muslims to come to the monastery had not been without risk. They joined the twenty-seven members of the Lebreton family in the old wine cellar that Christian had helped convert into a chapel back in the 1970s.

Old familiar faces were gathered in the intimacy of the stone chapel, whose walls were lined with aqua floral tiles left over from the days when it had been used to store wine. Father Carmona had known Christophe when he had come to Algiers as a *coopérant*; he had also played a crucial role in persuading Jean de la Croix, the new abbot of Aiguebelle, to keep the monastery open in 1964. Carmona had told him that he simply couldn't continue in Algeria without the monastery. There was the director of the seminary school Christophe had attended in Blois, and the pipe-smoking Madame Thérèse Brau, who was still doing her prodigious work with orphans in Algiers, and for whom Christophe had worked when he first arrived in the 1970s. Half of those in the chapel were his Muslim friends from Algiers, Medea, and his neighbors and associates in Tibhirine—Mohammed, Musa, Ali, Ben Ali, Salim, and others, all of whom followed the service, which was interspersed with Arabic. And there were the numerous Lebretons, who filled nearly half the seats.

"Do you wish to become a priest, a collaborator of bishops in the priesthood to serve and guide the people of God inspired by the Holy Spirit?" asked the bishop.

"Yes, I do."

At the end of the exchange, Christophe got on his knees and placed his hands between those of Bishop Teissier.

"Do you promise to live in communion with me and my successors respectfully and obediently?"

"Yes, I promise."

"May God complete in you that which He has begun."

The liturgy of saints . . . prosternation, then the laying on of hands by Bishop Teissier was repeated by Father Carmona and the other priests. Wearing their white stoles with bright red geometric Berber designs, each laid their hands on Christophe's head in symbolic transmission of the grace of Jesus Christ, the unique priest and mediator between man and God.

In his homily, Bishop Teissier observed, "There is a certain insanity about celebrating this ordination in a Muslim country. With our priesthood, we are foreign in the eyes of Islam, which does not recognize in principle the mediation between man and God. We will live among ourselves our faith in Jesus Christ as the mediator between men and God. But the Church receives this mediation not only for itself but for the whole world. On the surface, we live a spiritual reality unrelated to Islam. But in actuality, this which Christophe has just received is profoundly connected to the purpose of our Church—to be a Church for Muslims. Christ's mediation is universal. We are priests in the Christian community, but the Christian community is a priesthood for all people."

Teissier concluded with words Christophe had written, "The priest is called to serve this gift of God in order that all people may participate in it. This gift permeates Islam and acts in the hearts of its believers." The bishop then invited Christophe to say some final words: "I am overwhelmed by this gift of God . . . but this is normal, because God is much bigger than our hearts. Happily, you are here. . . . We are one heart, this heart of the Church. It is also the heart of a mother, and the heart of a mother is always very big. It is the heart of Mary . . . and the Church, which is continuously overflowing with the love of Jesus. The only thing I have to say to you is the "I love you" that Jesus said to the Church. This "I love you" is not simply for us [Christians] but for the whole world—for you Mohammed, Ahmed. . . . This "I love you" is for everyone. We all need the love of God to live."

Christian invited Christophe's friend Philippe Hémon to come back the following year, and each year subsequently. He knew his brothers sometimes felt isolated. Contact with someone from France was good for morale. Hémon had used his two-week visit to talk with each of the monks and give them news from the Hexagon, as France is called by its own. Hémon was also a liturgy man.

The heart of the Divine Office is the psalms, and he knew them backward and forward. One problem at Tibhirine in 1989 was the lack of expertise to update the liturgy which had not been modified since the 1960s, when Father Aelred of Tamié was the superior. Célestin was an accomplished organist and cantor with a beautiful voice, but at fifty-six, he was a latecomer to the Order and had little sense for the right liturgical repertoire for the community. Brother Jean-Pierre, a monk for over thirty years, knew the psalms and had a good sense of selection, but he was too modest to decide for the community by himself.

Hémon had first thought simplification of the liturgy was needed to accommodate the more limited vocal range of such a small community. Then he recognized his error. Liturgical prayer was the life of the community. His brothers were supplicants in a land of supplicants, living as their neighbors in a world of utter simplicity. Rather than impoverish the liturgy by simplifying it, Hémon understood that he needed to enrich it. He redrafted by hand some of the psalm sheets that years ago had been run off in blue ink on old duplicating machines and were now barely readable, even though the monks knew most of the psalms by heart.

One hundred and fifty psalms are sung each week by Benedictines throughout the world. If the early church fathers could recite that number in a day, then certainly, Saint Benedict reasoned, the softer, modern monk could sing 150 in a week. The Rule proposes the manner of their recitation, frequency, and order, yet it ultimately leaves the details to the monks themselves. *If the order of the psalms is not to the taste of certain brothers, they are free to change them, as long as the total is one hundred and fifty each week, which begins at Vigils every Sunday.* The Rule does not protect men, men protect the Rule through graciousness, common sense, and a certain flexibility.

Hémon is a short fire plug of a monk, who speaks bluntly about his first experience living among Muslims. In addition to working on the liturgy and having fraternal talks with his monastic brothers, he was taken by Christian to meet some of the local Sufis in Medea who were also members of the *ribat*. "Islam is radical in its faith and piety. Obedience means obedience. Christians can be rather Jesuitical. We are good at rationalizing why we don't have to obey today, or why something is an exception.

"I was very impressed by their deep spirituality and their knowledge of the Gospels. My visit reminded me of something basic. God is one. They forced me to stretch my understanding of Jesus . . . to create a place for Islam. We have many gods in the West—money, power, physical beauty, democracy. But all these things flow from God. Faith is a gift. In Algeria, mosques were being built everywhere . . . so faith was already alive without mosques. Faith existed in their dirt houses—no hierachy, no church, no mediators. Christians get lost too easily in dogma and theology. Every conception imposes a limit. Dogma limits. Doctrine limits. What is important is my relation to the other person."

Abbot Jean-Marc who had accompanied Hemon to Tibhirine was impressed by all the comings and goings around the monastery. Paul loaned out tools and kept a careful record of who got what. There were lots of people hanging around Luc's dispensary and in the outer courtyard. Sometimes women would wander into the cloister and have to be gently escorted out. "The atmosphere was like an extended family. There was a very cozy feeling," remembered Jean-Marc later. "Christian was a radical. He was always pushing out the frontiers. He was ahead of his time in fighting for a truly universal Christianity of the heart that excluded no one . . . a Christianity of friendship, trust, and good works. I came to realize Muslims sing the same song, only in a different key."

Christian could not imagine living his faith without being united with those around him who were also seeking God. A monk is a man of prayer. But how could he, whose life had been saved by the sacrificial love of a Muslim, not associate himself with the prayers of those around him, even if their expressions were different? "I don't believe I have the right to live simply as a cloistered monk here," he told a friend. At times, he spoke of his "surplus" community, one with which he felt as closely bound as with his monastic brothers. Reconciliation in God was not something for the future but something urgent, to be lived today.

Yet sometimes it seemed to those around him that Christian put reconciliation with Muslims ahead of reconciliation with his brothers in the monastery. Some had the feeling of being unloved during Christian's first term as prior. He could be brusque and cold. They always seemed to come last. Christian was becoming the Saint Bernard of Algeria. His opinions and advice were widely sought. He knew all the Christian communities throughout the country and was particularly solicitous of the Little Sisters of Jesus and other female congregations who lived in small communites of two or three, isolated in the *bled.* If he was not traveling, he was preoccupied with the guests, or with his extensive letter writing, or with Muslim visitors. Despite occasional ruffled feelings, in March 1990, the brothers reelected Christian as their superior on the first vote.

Six months later, on October 5, 1990, over 150 people came up to Tibhirine for an all-day celebration of Saint Bernard's nine-hundreth birthday. Throughout the year, a brother had been assigned to read an excerpt from Saint Bernard's celebrated commentary on The Song of Songs in the refectory. In this Old Testament book, God's love for his first spouse, Israel, is likened to the unifying love between man and woman. It is erotic and possessive, and persists inhumanly in the face of repeated infidelity. *"Let him kiss me with the kisses of his mouth—for your love is better than wine."* God is not only passionate but demands of his bride self-knowledge, *"If thou knowest not yourself, go forth . . . get out of my sight.* When man was placed in honor,"

Saint Bernard explains in his great exegesis, "he was delighted with his high estate, but failed to understand that his feet were made of clay. God's grace is only for the humble." And thus, the readings from Saint Bernard had flavored the meals of the monks throughout the year.

Celebrating the nine hundreth birthday of the patron saint of the Cistercian Order was marked by an hour of meditation in the chapel. Each brother commented on a piece of Scripture. An elaborate exposition was set up in the new wing, which had been built in the late 1930s and was known simply as *le nouveau bâtiment*, the new building. There, Christophe gave an audiovisual presentation of the history of Notre-Dame de l'Atlas and of the Cistercian Order to over one hundred guests, mostly Muslims, who had come out of a sense of solidarity and friendship with the monks.

The visitors learned that Saint Bernard was not among the original founders of Cîteaux in 1098. Cîteaux, the eponymous monastery, was founded by disgruntled monks from the Benedictine congregation of Cluny. They had trekked into the marshy wilderness of Burgundy as part of a growing desire of monks throughout Europe to return to a more rigorous practice of the Benedictine Rule. After the death of Saint Benedict in the sixth century, the Rule spread and begat other orders. In the ninth century, Louis the Pious of France declared that all monasteries should follow the Benedictine Rule. In practice, the Rule was often corrupted by the influence of gifts, local customs, and economic necessity. Gradually, monasteries acquired serfs to work in the fields and who paid tithes to work the estates granted the monks by noblemen. Monks increasingly became managers preoccupied with organizing and overseeing others. They found less time to pray, study, copy liturgical texts, and do manual work, departing from the life envisaged by Saint Benedict.

In this atmosphere, dissatisfied monks sought out remote, inhospitable areas to tame and cultivate, believing they were truly monks only when they supported themselves by the sweat of their brow. Manual labor was a reminder of their vow of poverty. The first handful of monks from Molesme, who settled in the boggy, reed-filled lowland that became Cîteaux, wanted to set themselves apart from the black-robed Benedictines. The new Cistercians were optimists who strove for perfection. They wore white cowls to the Divine Office, appropriate to their Holy Mother and to men seeking to purify their hearts and "to be as angels." But when they were working in the fields, a simple undyed woolen robe worn under a black scapular tunic was their distinctive habit.

Cîteaux's third daughter monastery was founded at Clairvaux, in Champagne by the twenty-five-year-old Bernard. His zeal for monastic reform brought an explosive expansion of adherents to the new Cistercians. Clairvaux alone spawned sixty-eight daughter monasteries. By the end of the twelfth century, over 350 Cistercian monasteries stretched from Ireland to the Baltics. Bernard of Clairvaux rose to become a giant figure in Christendom. His campaign for a Second Crusade to free Jerusalem from the infidel, and his championship of papal authority in the face of new Christian heresies that were sweeping through France, made his name synonymous with militant, crusading Christianity.

Christian had mixed emotions about his monastic patron. He was not a fan of Saint Bernard's militant, sectarian Christianity. Two sentences he wrote in a tract for the Knights Templars, an order of fighting monks created to protect pilgrims to the Holy Land, have become anathema to less belligerent Christians. In *Praise of the New Knighthood,* Bernard wrote, "The soldiers of Christ do not know the least fear, neither for sin, when they kill their enemies, nor for danger that they themselves might perish. This is because to kill someone for the sake of Christ, to risk death, is not only completely free of sin, but highly praiseworthy." Such sentiments are difficult to reconcile with a man whose name is associated with an order known for its strict adherence to the teachings of Jesus Christ. Recognizing his own demons, weaknesses, and shortcomings, Bernard fought his greatest battles with himself. Muslims call these inner struggles, "the Greater Jihad." Bernard's humility was declared the winner in 1174, when Pope Alexander III bestowed sainthood upon the great crusader.

Christian would occasionally allude to the blemishes on Saint Bernard's reputation, harkening back to a different time and spirit, when Christendom defined Europe's identity, Muslims and Jews were infidels, and Christian heretics were put on the rack so that they might repent and be saved from the fires of damnation.

On the wall opposite the exhibition honoring Saint Bernard was the permanent one, which, in addition to telling the story of the order, displayed a picture of one of Christian's spiritual heros—Mahatma Gandhi. Next to his photograph was a prickly question from this gentle man of God: "How can he who believes he possesses Absolute Truth truly be fraternal?"

Ora et labora. Prayer and work, it has been said, are the mammary glands that nourish monastic life. In between attending the seven daily Offices, the monks had to maintain the monastery, do housekeeping chores, and earn a living. It was in the garden that the brothers earned their daily bread. During the summers, strong breezes made the one-hundred-degree temperatures just bearable for the men to work in the rows of eggplants, tomatoes, peppers, potatoes, broad beans, zucchini, and other staples of the monks' vegetarian diet. Apples, apricots, and pears from their orchard provided the brothers with their sweets. Grapes from their small vineyard were sent to a local cooperative for pressing. The olive orchard had been neglected since 1979, when the muscle power of the aging monks could no longer turn the presses that had once produced 5,500 liters of oil annually. Lavender was cultivated, then dried and sold at the porterie, along with the honey from their hives.

Four hundred kilos of pure dark honey were produced each season. This "Trappist gold" was highly sought after throughout the region, where people were skilled at distinguishing pure honey from that made from sugar-fed bees. The bees were a favorite occupation of Christian. Bee colonies reminded him of monks. Like a good monk, good honey, he would pun, was *sine cera*—without wax. "Sincere. Pure." *Blessed are the pure in heart, for they shall see God.* And like bees, monks carried out their specialized assignments for the good of the whole community.

Unlike bees, each of the monks at Tibhirine had at least two or three duties, assigned by Christian. Christophe had three. Christian had appointed him master of the novices, but he had only one novice's soul to guide. Philippe Ranc was an ex-army captain graduated from the prestigous Saint Cyr military school. The young soldier turned monk was struggling to decide whether to be a monk or a scholar. "Philippe always wanted to study and travel. A monk is someone who lives to praise God. He is hot or cold, but never lukewarm," recalled one of his brothers. Christophe also helped prepare the weekly liturgy, but his favorite activity was working in the garden, for which he was *le responsable.*

He was responsible for the monastery's main source of revenue. In a good year, this might have amounted to 2 million dinars, about thirty thousand dollars. There, he could dig and sweat with his Muslim associates, forming the bonds of friendship that were the meaning of his faith. *Je t'aime.* Love is friendship, and friendship is love. The garden became his school, his chapel, and a place to learn the wiles and ways of Ali, Musa, Youssef, Ben Ali, Mohammed, Salim, and others.

Like a huge kitchen apron, the vegetable garden unfurled its twelve acres that sloped away from the cloister to the old schoolhouse at the end of the dirt road below. The only road to Tibhirine was from Medea. It snaked over the densely wooded mountain behind the monastery, past the entrance to the *hôtellerie,* the dispensary, and the watchman's house, which had formerly been used for pressing olives and storing farm equipment. Farther down the hill, the road forked. One prong switched back westward into the village itself. The other continued downhill, becoming a dead end below the garden, at the old primary school the monks had built in the 1960s to save the local children a four-mile round-trip hike to Medea each day.

Surrounding the garden was a dilapidated wall. Its western boundary tied into the exterior wall of the watchman's house, and the eastern side hooked around toward the cemetery and the new building. This building was added in 1938, after the second group of Trappists came to Algeria and took possession of a villa built by English colonists who had gone into bankruptcy. The new arrivals from France and Slovenia had been filled with ambition, and they imagined having a hundred monks at Tibhirine someday, as there once had been at Staouéli. But the number never exceeded forty.

There had been plans for a huge chapel on the ground floor of the new building, but they had long since been abandoned. The second floor was used occasionally for large receptions; from here, guests had a panoramic view of the Tamesguida (a Berber word meaning "mountains of fire"), which for centuries had hidden bandits and rebels. Embarrassed by their surplus of real estate, and a certain impression of grandness amid so much poverty, Christian frequently prayed that the new building would somehow disappear. In 1990, its only inhabitant was Ali's cow, which lived under its arcade and had an annoying yen for green vegetables.

Ali was Christophe's second in command in the garden. He had been a salaried worker for the monks since the war and had begun his career as an eighteen-year-old helping Amédée in the laundry room. Ali had liked it that way. So too his son, Musa, or Moses, who worked in the orchard. Neither had been interested when Christian wanted to change their status to "associates," which would have made them more like partners in the cultivation of the garden. He had wanted to eliminate the last whiff of colonialism that lingered around the monastery's custom of using hired labor to work in the garden.

The change carried forward Bishop Duval's wise gesture, made twenty-five-years earlier, when he had persuaded the Order to grant the new Algerian government all but thirty of its eight-hundred acres acquired under French rule. In 1988, four of the former workers had accepted the greater responsibility of being associates. It was a way of achieving through economics the Church's reason for being in Algeria, which Cardinal Duval expressed as *la présence, la prière and le partage.* To presence and prayer at Tibhirine, Christian had added real partnership through sharing the work and rewards of the garden. Each associate was allocated an acre plot to work, which was rotated every few years so he would not confuse a free leasehold with ownership. The monks also provided them with seeds, fertilizer, and water. In return, each associate was required to keep careful accounts of what was sold, and give half the revenue to the monastery.

The harder part of the "sharing" was changing habits that tested Christophe's patience. He continually had to remind his associates that they couldn't simply tell their friends to take whatever they wanted from the garden. It was a habit that died slowly. Not showing up to work was a problem. Jean-Pierre, was responsible for taking the produce to market. He impressed upon them the importance of quality, and of not hiding defective or small tomatoes under the nice big ones. Mohammed became more important when he replaced Ali, who retired in 1990, as Christophe's chief assistant. To help Ali properly enjoy his new assistant leisure status, the brothers gave him an easy chair.

The monks had been advised not to hire Mohammed as *le gardien.* The responsibility of watchman, they were told, would put him in the awkward position of having to say no to friends. He might also be criticized by other Muslims for protecting foreigners. The monks did not regret having ignored the advice. For an Arab, the monks found Mohammed unusually candid. He knew how to say what was on his mind, but always with courtesy and sensitivity. To these good qualities were added his strong sense of responsibility and a diplomatic way of getting others to do things right.

Surveying the monastery from the summit, a few hundred yards higher, was another guardian, on top of Abdelkader Rock. She was the one to whom the monks sang Salve Regina each night, ending Compline before going to bed. To the local Muslims, she was Lalla Mariam, Mother Mary, the Virgin Mother of Jesus, who, by a miraculous birth, gave the world a holy apostle, free of sin.

Over the years, Muslim women from the surrounding villages had worn a path to her feet through the dense cork-oak forest to seek her aid and blessing for sick children or a safe pregnancy. Women having difficulty getting pregnant might well have thought that this particular Lalla Mariam had special powers. This was one of the few statues in existence that depicted her in a family way. Rarer still, both her arms were broken off at the elbow and her stomach had been gouged with a chisel.

When they learned of the attack, the monks felt as if their own mother had been violated.

PART TWO

A Shared Torment
1988–1994

7

Revolution

Men, serve your Lord who has created you . . . so you may guard yourselves against evil . . . Do not knowingly set up other gods beside God.

—Koran 2:20

The colonels who ran Algeria in the 1980s thought Chile was their earthly ideal. They would use General Pinochet's military rule to explain their policies to foreigners. Dictatorship is necessary for creating political stability; economic development will then follow, and, later, democracy. Like the French before them, the ruling class did not think the Algerian people were ready yet for democracy. Chile became an economic success story, but the FLN, *le parti unique,* mismanaged Algeria in every possible way. The leadership favored heavy industry over light industry and agriculture; it trusted too much in its huge oil and gas reserves, which left it unprepared when prices fell; the gap between the privileged elite and the masses grew wider. As if guided by some desperate premonition that the body politic was gravely ill, the president of Algeria, the former Colonel Chadli Bendjedid, visited an antibiotics complex in Medea the day of the outbreak.

At first, it was called the "Couscous Revolt." Later, it became the "October Revolution." The trouble began on the morning of October 4, 1988, when students in the canteen of the University of Algiers created a ruckus about the food. A minor disturbance snowballed into a protest that brought baton-swinging police to the heights of the Ben Akhnoun campus overlooking the sea.

News of the incident flashed across Algiers by word of mouth—the famous "Arab telephone." It was something a clan, a faction, a group could quickly exploit to serve a hidden purpose. Later that afternoon, another crowd, this time teenagers, materialized in the old European blue-collar neighborhood of Bab el Oued, near the port, and began a rampage. Riot police moved in to protect the fashionable Riad el Feth commercial shopping complex, where foreign goods were affordable only to the chi-chi set. The rumor spread that students had been killed. The University of Algiers' four campuses emptied into the streets. Burning and looting soon engulfed the area around boulevard Colonel Amirouche, where government property was destroyed with particular relish—state-owned stores, hotels, the Bank of Algeria, Air Algeria offices, and police stations.

By nightfall, tanks and armored cars were stationed in the center of Algiers. The next day, twelve- and fourteen-year-old, secondary school students, jumped into the fray. They attacked the tanks with Molotov cocktails, stones, and angry fists. Forty of them died. The government of President Chadli Bendjedid declared a state of emergency. The People's Army was given orders to shoot at groups of over ten people on the street and a strict curfew was imposed. The rioters declared a general strike and then, for good measure, set on fire the party headquarters of the FLN and the Ministry of Youth and Sports, famously ineffective at providing activities for the young.

Two days later, the telltale beards, skullcaps, and long, high-collared white *kamis* of the Islamic faithful appeared in the streets, alongside youths screaming "Death to Chadli." By the fourth day, the imams themselves were leading the demonstrators and then, on October 10, after six days of turmoil, the Islamic movement was given its martyrs.

Followers of Imam Ali Benhadj had left the Kabul mosque in Belcourt, named for its popularity with the "Afghans"—the Algerian heroes of Islam who had joined their Afghan brothers in the struggle against communism. Their baggy pantaloons and woolen turbans became *à la mode* for the young militants who adopted the hard gaze of an Islamic warrior. Shouting "God is great," "Down with corruption," "Down with the infidel government," they marched defiantly toward the headquarters of the Sûreté Nationale on the boulevard Amirouche. A barricade was encountered. Shots were fired. In the panic and horror, thirty-six of the faithful died and hundreds were wounded. Afterward, no one could say for sure from where the first shots came.

The government counted 150 dead and 2,000 wounded after six days of mayhem. The Algerian League for the Protection of Human Rights said five hundred had died. Thousands more were arrested summarily. Torture was mentioned and allegations were documented in *Les Cahiers Noirs d'Octobre*, published by the National Committee Against Torture. The Villa Susini, an elegantly moorish tiled former French torture chamber overlooking the Mediterranean, again heard screams echoing in its basement cells. *Le pouvoir* had shown it would kill its own children. The People's Army had done its duty.

Student riots had become regular events throughout the 1980s: Tizi-Ouzou, Algiers, Oran, Sétif, and Constantine had all felt student wrath. The suppression of the Berber language, leftist protests against mosques on campus, police harassment, chronic shortages of textbooks, and bad unchanging food triggered outbreaks that vented much deeper frustrations.

Living conditions were steadily deteriorating. Apartments could have twelve or fifteen people crowded into two or three rooms. Families slept in shifts. Elevators never worked. Garbage was thrown out the back windows of apartments, and left in ever-growing foul-smelling heaps. Finding a time and place for sex was well nigh impossible. Basic products were regularly in short supply at state stores—powdered milk might disappear one month, sugar, butter, or oranges the next. In the fall of 1988, there was no semolina for making couscous. It was being fed to cattle to compensate for feed shortages and to assure export earnings. Only testosterone was in surplus.

Most frustrating of all for the students was the worthlessness of their state-subsidized diplomas. Hopes of a bright future based on oil and free education had turned into a sense of betrayal. Good jobs went to the gilded children of the privileged class or to foreign experts. Ordinary young Algerians, it seemed, could not be trusted with important jobs. The message on a popular men's T-shirt flagged their plight: NO JOB, NO MONEY, NO GIRL.

The university students were lucky, in a manner of speaking, even if they didn't have work. In those years, only 25 percent of the grade school students were accepted into lycées, the final three years of secondary school under the French system. In cities overcrowded because of rural migration, there was simply no space to keep the promise of free education for all.*

The remaining students were put on the street, where they idled time away leaning against buildings. They became known as *hittists. Hittism,* or "supporting walls," was the main career path for young street hustlers, who used their outdoor offices creatively to engage in *trabendo*. Not exactly the black market, not exactly contraband, *trabendo* traffics favors, barter, and contacts to procure everything from cigarettes and baby clothes to dental drills and airplane tickets. There were always careers in ordinary theft and drug dealing, but they were also riskier. The police regularly harassed teenagers on the street, under the pretext of fighting absenteeism or black marketeering.

"If you don't belong to high society, you are undesirable. If you are unemployed and young, you are considered dangerous. You have no rights. You can't go out during the day; you don't have the right to go to discotheques. You have only one right—to go hide and suffocate," a teenager told a French reporter who covered the riots. "I am like a cow. My only function is to eat, sleep, and defecate." Macabre games were played by desperate kids with nothing to do and nowhere to go. Hanging on the back fenders of buses was common, but not to get a free ride. By stuffing a wad of bread in the exhaust pipe, saturating it with the fumes, and eating it, they concocted a carbon monoxide high. Their screaming stomachs told them they were more than cows.

The underclass drank "*zombreto*" cocktails of 7Up, Valium, and methyl alchohol. They howled their pathetic desperation at the soccer matches in the July 5 Stadium, the only place where they could freely sing out their liturgy of pain to the government officials who sat in their box seats. *"Rana daine, rana daine."* Thousands chanted shamelessly, "We are lost. We are lost. You have abandoned us." Their only salvation was "Madame Courage" and other drugs

*Eighteen percent of the population lived in urban areas in 1954, 31 percent in 1966, and 50 percent in 1987.

whose names they sang out for all the world to know: "Six/fifteen, artane, phostan, nausinon . . . or exile."

The paternalistic state had produced the cry of orphans.

The men around President Chadli could not dismiss the October events as yet another riot of whining, ungrateful students or shiftless hooligans who had never lifted a finger for their country's freedom. Leading personalities from the Islamic movement were in the streets. Islam was the state religion, the religion of the people, and its leaders had left the mosques to show sympathy for the students.

And for that reason, Ali Benhadj was a dangerous man. He spoke for the young. He absorbed their anger. That was why, after the riots, he was included in the delegation of imams summoned by the government to act as intermediaries to the people. Chadli had to persuade the imams that there was a peaceful path to change.

Ali Benhadj's Friday sermons in the poor neighborhoods of Kouba, Belcourt, and Bab el Oued had made him the idol of Algiers's disinherited youth. He held them raptured. At thirty-two, he was still one of them. He made them laugh and cry, and think. The performances of the slight, smooth-faced imam were cocktails of righteous anger, sensitive emotion, quiet reasonableness, comedy, and sarcasm. He could speak in street argot or eloquently in classical Arabic. "Imam Ali's" green book of sayings and cassettes were distributed throughout Algeria and North Africa. They found their way into the eighteenth and twentieth arrondissements of Paris, where they were popular with Arab immigrants.

Ali Benhadj was a war baby. Born in Tunis in 1956 to parents originally from Béchar, in the western desert of Algeria, his father was killed fighting the French. At age nine, his mother died. Raised by his maternal uncle in Algiers, he later became a grade school teacher of classical Arabic, the holy language of the Koran revealed to Mohammed by the Angel Gabriel. By the time he was twenty, he had become a popular preacher, known for his passionate tirades against the arbitrariness of the authorities and their politics of "luxury, waste, and self-importance."

Benhadj had spent five years in prison for sympathizing with Moustafa Bouyali, an Islamic revolutionary of the mid-1980s. Bouyali was an old mujahid, a veteran of the war against France, a man of faith but little learning. He was known for his sincerity, love of country and of Islam, but he was disgusted with the arbitrariness and corruption he saw around him. When his brother was assassinated by police, a bitter Bouyali decided to fight back. He fled to the maquis and found himself the center of Islamic discontent for seven years, while he harassed and eluded the security services.

For not reporting to the police a rendezvous he had had with Bouyali, Ali Benhadj was jailed for threatening the security of the state. He refused to accept a presidential pardon offered in the fourth year of his five-year sentence. He would take no favors from corrupt rulers, contemptuous of their own people. Imam Ali had used his time in prison to study the word of God and arm himself to fight *hogra*—that same arrogant, humiliating contempt displayed by Algeria's own rulers that had been shown by the French colonists toward the Arabs.

The Koran had been Ali's passion since he was a twelve-year-old when he was taken under the wing of various sheikhs who had concluded that the malaise affecting the Arab world had a single basic cause. Muslims had departed from the ways of the Koran and the traditions of the Prophet. They had allowed their culture to be invaded by secular and materialistic European values. The victory over France that had cost Ali's father his life was incomplete. Physical expulsion needed to be followed by intellectual and cultural expulsion.

In prison, Ali slept two hours a day, and read voraciously. He devoured the works of Ibn Taymiyya, a strict constructionist reformer whose writings inspired the rigorous Wahhabism practiced today in Saudi Arabia. In the thirteenth century, this Muslim theologian was already advocating a return to a purified Islam to counter the moral corruption that he thought had led to the Mongol victories over Muslims. The writings of the Egyptians Hassan al Banna and Sayyid Qotb, founders of the Muslim Brotherhood,* strongly influ-

*The Muslim Brotherhood preached individual improvement through purification of heart and soul, and the strict application of religious law to both social and political problems. The militancy and popularity of al Banna's movement after World War II led to its repression by Egyptian authorities, and the cycle of violence began and continues

enced Ali. Even in the 1920s and 1930s, these Muslim thinkers were trying to rid Islam of the influence of materialistic and Marxist ideas. Their movement promoted a theocratic alternative to the politics of Muslim leaders enamoured with European secular models of governance.

"Socialism, democracy, dictatorship," Ali would say later to his youthful audiences, were "dung droppings in the garbage of the human spirit." "For Muslims," he wrote in the Islamist newspaper *El Munquid* (*The Deliverer*) a year after his release from prison, "liberty is constrained by the law of God, not by the rights of others . . . rights change and liberty is an illusion that can be trampled by the state. True liberty comes from submission to God."

An Algerian Robespierre, Ali Benhadj was the virtuous one—a model of austerity, humility, and incorruptibility to his admirers. He lived simply. Imam Ali didn't own a TV. He preferred a moped to a car. "You would never see him walking down the street with a pizza in his mouth," a youthful admirer proudly noted. Ali Ben Mohammed Benhadj Habib Ben Salah lived with his mother-in-law, wife, and four children in a two-room apartment in the poor Kouba neighborhood of Algiers. Imam Ali was compassionate. He had time to sit on doorsteps and talk with the poor. Even if he could do nothing for them, he made them feel better.

In February of 1989, four months after the government's meeting with the imams, a new constitution was adopted. Sweeping away the political monopoly held by the FLN since 1962, it introduced rights unknown for twenty-seven years. Freedom of expression and assembly, freedom of conscience, the right to form independent unions and to strike were explicitly granted for the first time since independence. An Algerian perestroika was born.

But was this real change, or just an old whore in a new dress? Many wondered. *Le pouvoir* was clever, especially when it came to keeping control over the flow of oil money. Weren't the diverse political currents inside the FLN simply being exteriorized? And

today. A Muslim Brotherhood splinter group, al jihad, claimed credit for the assassination of President Sadat in 1981.

wouldn't a democracy that had to beat down, with undemocratic means if necessary, a theocratic, backward-looking Islamist movement that frightened Westerners with its antimodern ways and rhetoric be more easily tolerated than continued single-party dictatorship?

In the summer of 1989, "the people" of the People's Republic would finally have their say. A law authorizing new parties opened the door to political competition for the first time since Algeria was governed by the French. The Social Democratic Party, the Party for Algerian Renewal, the National Algerian Party, the Democratic Movement for the Renewal of Algeria, the National Party for Solidarity and Development, the Algerian Democratic Movement, the Algerian Worker Party, the Socialist Organization of Workers were a few of the forty-odd parties that jumped into the fray. The proponents of an Islamic political order jostled with socialists, communists, and liberals of different stripes.

The Islamists had a clear, simple program: the establishment of a theocracy. In a properly run Islamic state, there is also democracy, but it is constrained by God's law, not man's. An Islamist democracy is not about the expression of individual will or rights, but of trust and acceptance by the people of the authority being exercised over them in the name of God. Like the former divine right of kings, exercised by sovereigns whose moral authority was derived from the Church, the Islamic state is based on the responsibility of its governing council, the *majlis ash shoura,* to act as stewards of God's word as revealed in the Koran and practiced by the Prophet. Its power must be exercised justly. The criticisms and opinions of the people are welcomed, but the responses of the *majliss ash shoura* are limited to what is allowed within defensible interpretations of Koranic law, or *sharia.* There are no popular referendums for interpreting the law. It is determined by a "supreme court" of religious savants. The Islamic state is a government of the people ("shouracracy") by the *sharia,* but for God.

Under this broad banner, more than a dozen varieties of political Islam united to form the Islamic Salvation Front, or FIS (Front Islamique du Salut), expressing a common belief that the new republic must be founded on divine guidance, and nothing so feeble as unaided, corruptible human reason. The new constitution was not to the liking of FIS leaders. It was not based on God's law—the *sharia*. Only a society that answered to God could be moral. But the new constitution gave them a way to fight peacefully for their vision of a just society . . . with God's help.

On October 29, 1989, God sent a message to Algeria's rulers. The ancient city of Tipasa, a favorite weekend getaway for rich Algerians, was rocked by an earthquake. Eighty-four people were killed and hundreds were injured. The FIS was the first to arrive with help. Its network of mosques around the country quickly mobilized to collect food, clothing, and blankets. FIS mosques provided up to fifteen thousand dinars about $150 to the families of the dead.

Two weeks later, on Friday, November 10, the Es Sunna mosque in Bab el Oued was overflowing. Ali Benhadj was delivering a jeremiad, telling his listeners exactly what the earthquake meant. The earthquake was divine punishment, and a warning of worse things to come. The gross inequalities of wealth and moral decay—prostitution, alcoholism, drugs, and family disintegration—had sprung from one source: Algeria's corrupt, ungodly elite.

"Our so-called leaders speak of socialism and equality . . . of being 'by the people' and 'for the people.' But they are rich and you are poor. We believe in God and his Apostle, but not their fairy tales and nonsense. Our leaders have governed so long with lies and deception, they don't know anymore where the sun rises, their children's names, or the color of the sky. They are so lost in the vomit of their deceptions they think they have fooled us."

The ruling elites spoke French, used French law and the French police system, lived in the old colonial villas in the cooler, fashionable heights of Algiers—Hydra, El Biar, Birmandreis; they sent their children to French schools and maintained cozy relations with French government authorities.

"They are like the French before them. They believe God can be separated from life, visited perhaps once a week in a mosque. They have adopted the so-called Enlightenment thinking of the French, which is at root Greek, an insolent idea that man is the measure of all things. Everything comes from God. Secular thinking separates man's spirit from God. Islam teaches that it is man's duty to be humble and to serve God in accordance with his commandments."

"The jihad of 1954 must continue," he told his listeners. "Those who died for Islam thirty years ago were betrayed."

In the months following the earthquake, the FIS pursued its jihad peacefully. Its precinct workers went door-to-door distributing clothing and food to the poor in Belcourt, El Harrach, Kouba, Bab el Oued, Hussein Dey, and other overpopulated neighborhoods in Algiers. "It's from Allah. . . . A vote for FIS is a vote for Allah," they repeated in quiet, reverent tones. On the day of the nationwide municipal elections, FIS workers took flashlights to the voting booths in case electricity failed, as it often did. Praise Allah, but tie up your camel, the Prophet said.

Ali Benhadj was right. The destruction of Tipasa had been a sign of worse things ahead. Less than nine months later, a political earthquake stunned the government. The first free, multiparty elections in twenty-eight years were held on June 12, 1990. The results left the FLN in a state of shock. The FIS received 93 percent of the vote in towns with over fifty thousand inhabitants. It controlled twenty-eight of the thirty largest cities, including Algiers, Oran, Constantine, Tlemcen, and Medea. Medea went virtually 100 percent FIS. So too, did tiny Tibhirine. Ali proposed that Medea be the capital of the future Islamic state, only a matter of time.

Imam Ali was in the *minbar* of the Ibn Ben Badis mosque in Kouba three days after the victory. He spoke quietly and modestly. "The elections were won by the grace of God and the people. Your vote has given a slap in the face to those who betrayed the FLN. The road ahead will be hard. Those who have made so many mistakes themselves will not pardon ours. The elections were not a victory for democracy, but for Islam."

In the FIS journal, *El Munquid,* Benhadj railed against democracy. "The word *democracy* is a stranger to the Arab language. It has no precise meaning," he wrote. "It has been used by all the ideologies of the twentieth century. Liberalism, socialism, communism, even fascism, claimed to be democratic. In this confusion, there are no moral criteria. In Islam, God is everything. Everything comes from God, and everything returns to God. Whether socialist or capitalist countries, both put God aside. This is the problem of Algeria's governing class."

But the FIS victory left their leadership disturbed. The results were a disappointment. The party of God had not received the resounding approval they had expected. Over 2 million people had not voted FIS. Many who voted for FIS had done so out of disgust with the FLN. *Fitna,* the scourge of divisiveness within the Muslim community, had raised its ugly head. If the kingdom of Islam can be voted in by believers, can it also be voted out? Islamists were not united on this.

The party had trusted not only in God but in organization. The FIS had been disciplined and backed up by a network of over ten thousand brotherhoods—Islamic associations founded by an imam or layperson that assisted the poor, handicapped, or aged. Brotherhoods had mushroomed after the fall of oil prices in the mid-1980s, which further reduced the ability of the state to provide basic social services. There were 20 million Algerians under the age of thirty, two-thirds of the population, desperate for something to believe in after years of empty promises by the FLN.

The FIS spoke to the disinherited. Party workers provided transportation for the elderly, had cadres of social workers to help the needy, ran schools and hospitals, and provided housing. It had become a state within a state that was failing miserably to look after the welfare of its citizens. Like the powerful American political machines of yesteryear that drew their strength from serving the needs of poor, disoriented immigrants flooding into Boston, New York, and Chicago, the FIS drew its support from the uprooted masses who had migrated from the *bled,* the back country of Algeria, in search of opportunity in the cities.

For eighteen months, the FIS gave Algerians a taste of God's kingdom on earth. It was a mix of old-fashioned New England Puritanism and English Victorianism, with dollops of Francophobia, anti-Semitism, antimasonary, anticommunism, antiliberalism, and other anti-isms. Fallen apostate Muslims were condemned as well, such as the leaders of Tunisia and Egypt. Tunisia's former president Habib Bourguiba had once gone so far as to drink wine on national TV to show that God would not strike him down.

The city of Tipasa banned men from wearing any pants that were less than Bermuda length, and women's dresses had to reach below the knee. In Oran, popular *rai* music was prohibited because its lyrics were laced with sex and drugs. Expired liquor licenses were not renewed in FIS towns. Beauty salons were pressured to close, they were dangerous vanity parlors that served only to arouse the beast in men. *Mixité,* or comingling of the sexes in schools and sports, was banned, though not on public transportation where such segregation was thought too impractical. Rules on women wearing the *hijab*, was left to local discretion. There were cases of individual militants who would take matters into their own hands. Excesses were committed harassing women, though some of the worst incidents, such as throwing acid at short-skirted girls, had occurred before the FIS was founded.

French newspapers disappeared from kiosks. Bending with the political winds, the government declared French-speaking lycées *interdits* to non-Europeans, so that Muslims would not be contaminated by corrupting Western values. Satellite TV dishes in FIS communes were aimed to pick up Arabsat, not French channels, fragmenting families in which the older generation either didn't understand classical Arabic or simply preferred to watch European channels.

FIS-controlled towns, were renamed "Islamic communes." Minutes of town council meetings were posted on government buildings. A new spirit of cleanliness took hold. Garbage was removed from the streets. Neighborhoods called "Paris," "Chicago," or "New York," bywords for crime, drugs, and black markets, were cleaned up too. Corruption was attacked. Bribery was reduced, even for simple things such as getting a birth certificate without endless waiting, and the work ethic improved among the government functionaries in the Islamic communes.

The FIS was for the little guy. It organized open markets supplied with produce from farmers sympathetic to their goals of helping the neediest. Middlemen were bypassed and weights and prices were closely monitored by FIS inspectors. A kilo of meat that normally cost three hundred dinars (five dollars), one-tenth of a month's salary for many, would cost thirty dinars at a FIS market.

To those with a stake in the status quo, thinking about their future under a FIS-dominated government brought on severe indigestion. The FIS was aiming to break the cozy foreign trade monopolies—fiefdoms of the military and its friends, whose high command was known on the street as "General Banana," "General Tire," "General Flour," and their ilk. They controlled the lucrative import licenses necessary to acquire the foreign goods on which Algeria had become so dependent. In 1990, one-third of all its oil and gas revenues went to buy food from abroad.

Honest entrepreneurial activity was encouraged. The Prophet Mohammed himself had been a successful merchant, with the help of his first wife, Khadijah. Wealth was good if acquired honestly and the opportunities for making money were equal. The FIS wanted to tap the energy of the young and create a feeling of inclusion among those classes who had felt excluded. *Hittists* and small businessmen voted overwhelmingly FIS. Whether from pragmatism or conviction, so, too, did many wealthy businessmen. For the Islamic militants, support for the FIS was not about getting water and housing, as it was for many of the pragmatic poor. Their vote was about their new Islamic identity, one that transformed anger and exclusion into righteous wrath.

Two personalities dominated the FIS public image. Ali Benhadj, the FIS vice president, brought to the party a reputation of incorruptibility and the devotion of the disinherited youth. As FIS president, Abassi Madani brought different and more political credentials. Back in February 1989, he had been the one to propose to Benhadj that they join forces to unite the various Islamic movements that had been incubating since the Bouyalist repression of the 1980s.

Madani provided a whiff of respectable decadence wrapped in a *kamis*. Where Ali Benhadj might frighten potential Islamic middle-class supporters by his austere simplicity and a view of Islam that drew inspiration from a thirteenth-century theologian, Madani could reassure them. He had received a doctorate in sociology from the University of London, where he specialized in comparative education. He had a reputation for a certain worldliness—a liking for money, Mercedes-Benz cars, and women. Madani was divorced, had acquired a young second wife, and was distrusted by young Algerians as being "too political." Nevertheless, he was articulate, had a sense of humor, and put a moderate face on the party—which was actually not a party, but a coalition of Islamic movements. But Madani declared otherwise: "There are no alliances in Islam. There is only Islam."

Political religious fundamentalism in Algeria did not appear out of nowhere in 1989, as it seemed to many outside observers. The FIS was the insolent son, born of a marriage of convenience between Islam and socialism, conceived in war, incubated in rejection. In 1956, the FLN Proclamation of Soummam spoke of a future nation that would be "democratic" and "social" within "the framework of Islamic principles." But what are Islamic principles? Who defines a Muslim? Who speaks for Islam? Ibn Ben Badis, who wanted to purify Islam of marabout influences and bring back a grim puritanism while keeping politics and religion separate? Or Emir Abdelkader, the mystic warrior and thorn in the side of the French, who founded a nascent Algerian state on the Islamic principles of religious tolerance and respect for differences? Sunni Muslims have no monolithic clerical hierarchy or single figure with the authority of the Pope to clarify matters of faith.

The Islamists within the FLN had been arguing that Algerians should be able to speak the language of their own holy book. Yet postwar Algerians were ignorant of classical Arabic. Even the educated Francophone elite spoke only the local Arab dialect. There was a bread-and-butter component to the debate, as well. Those who did not speak French were generally excluded from the best positions in the universities, government, military, and industry. Internal FLN power struggles produced a concession to the slighted mujahideen side of the FLN split personality. A policy of Arabization was launched in the late 1960s, beginning in the elementary schools and working its way gradually to the universities by the 1980s.

There was a problem, however. Who would teach Arabic? Bishop Teissier taught Boumediene's sister and the wives of several ministers. He brought in scores of Arabic-speaking nuns from Lebanon to help. They were not enough. The Algerian government sought out Egyptian, Palestinian, Syrian, and other teachers from the Middle East, who often brought along more than knowledge of the language of the Koran. Many carried in their bags a virulent sense of cultural aggression by the Occident, coupled with a belief in the need to renew Islam, not by modernizing Islam but by Islamizing modernity.

In Medea, the Egyptian professors quickly made an impression. They became known as cold and arrogant masters who viewed themselves as teaching backward Algerian pupils. The more schooled Egyptian purists also had come to remind their students of Koranic law. Making statues, they said, is forbidden.* It infringes on God's domain.

The professors wrote the Ministry of Religion in Algiers, telling the authorities that the statue of the Virgin on top of Abdelkader Rock behind the monastery at Tibhirine should come down. The Ministry wrote the *wali* of Medea, the successor to the French prefect, saying the statue should come down. The *wali* wrote back, saying that he would do it after the statue of Abdelkader and all the other ones in Algiers were removed. "The desecration of the Virgin was led by the professors, who egged on the students. But it was not anti-Virgin, but anti-statue," Brother Amédée insists today. The unpopular Egyptians were asked to leave Medea. Afterward, the neighbors built a park around the Virgin and planted flowers at her feet.

Islamization continued, the product of a delicate balancing act within the FLN. The *parti unique* was divided between secularists, whose tastes ran the gamut of socialism, communism, Trotskyism and French-style republicanism, and Muslim traditionalists, who wanted Islamic values more widely taught and respected within society. In the 1970s, President Boumediene began segregating the sexes in universities, closing down bars in the holy city of Constantine, and changing the educational curriculum to require the teaching of Islam in the schools.

The new socialist constitution of 1976 nationalized agricultural

---

*Early Christians were influenced by Judaism's prohibition against making images of God. The iconoclasts were members of the Eastern Orthodox Church who denounced the use of images for worship. Cromwellian Roundheads in the seventeenth century smashed statues in Anglican churches. Differences also exist among Muslims on the subject of images. Iranian Shiites commonly draw and sculpt figures, reflecting a long cultural tradition. Nowhere in the Koran does it say making representations is forbidden, though statues, because they are three-dimensional, are viewed less kindly by strict Muslims.

lands and church property and declared Islam the state religion. The Ministry of Religion built over four thousand mosques and schools for training imams during the next ten years, including the Abdelkader Medersa in Constantine. After years of debate, the National Assembly finally passed the controversial Family Code of 1984, designed to restore Islamic family values. The Family Code reduced women to the status of a minor. After years of debate, its passage gave men the right to forbid wives to work outside the house and the right to divorce on demand, to prohibit daughters to marry without their father's permission and forbid Muslim women to marry non-Muslims.

But official Islam bred its opposite, unofficial Islam. It sprang up in basements, garages, warehouses, morgues, and cheaply constructed buildings thrown together in open spaces without permits. Its preachers were often imams whose qualifications were that they knew a bit more of the Koran than their audiences or were good orators. At least, however, they were not beholden to the state for their wages. Their messages were variations on a single theme: A corrupt, arbitrary state power divorced from God had stolen the revolution from the true mujahideen.

8

A Visit from the General

Just as there is the zeal of bitterness that is evil and separates us from God and leads to hell, so also there is a good zeal which removes vices and leads to God and eternal life.

—THE RULE, CHAPTER 72

June 4, 1991, was a day that tested Christian's negotiating skills. He had driven five hundred miles from Tibhirine to Morocco the previous day in order to escort back to the monastery Bernardo Olivera, the new abbot general, who had been visiting their "annex" in Fez. The Algerian guards at the Oujda checkpoint in Morocco said they couldn't pass through. There had been disturbances in Algiers the day before, they explained.

It was from Oujda, beyond the reach of the French army during the war of independence, that the FLN's army of the exterior, under the command of a Colonel Houari Boumedienne had launched harassing attacks into western Algeria. In a reversal of history, Morocco is now a sanctuary for French monks who are waiting to return to their home in Algeria. The bishop of Rabat had proposed to Christian in 1988 that he take over the monastery in Fez, which would be vacated by a small community of Little Sisters of Jesus. Christian's own community in the Atlas had only eleven brothers, but, seeing an uncertain future, he accepted the bishop's offer. In 1991, Christian had asked Bruno to be the acting superior of the community of three brothers—Roland, Jean-Baptiste, and Jean de la Croix—which functioned as a distant appendage to Tibhirine, and safehouse, if needed.

Father Bernardo Olivera and his aide waited three hours at the border with a mix of concern, amusement, and admiration at Christian's determination to persuade the guards to let them through. Bernardo had been the forty-seven-year-old abbot of Notre Dame of the Angels, near Buenos Aires, when, in 1990, he became the first non-European to be elected head of the Cistercian Order of the

Strict Observance. He and Christian had first met in Holyoke, Massachusetts, in 1984, when all the superiors had gathered to propose modifications to the Order's constitution reflect more closely the spirit of Vatican II. Bernardo had liked the way Christian thought, and he admired his sensitivity to Third World issues.

"It seems not many Argentinians pass through here," Christian said with a big smile after he emerged for the last time from the guardhouse.

"Christian was full of enthusiasm. He was driving, and speaking nonstop the whole way. Several times, I was afraid he would drive off the road. But my French wasn't very good then. I didn't understand that much of what he was saying," Bernardo's thin, angular face and hawklike nose were softened by a gentle, natural manner and easy laugh as he recounted his trip at Trappist headquarters on the Viale Africa in Rome.

"Along the coast between Tlemcen and Oran is a cove that Christian wanted to show me. He called it his 'secret little paradise.' It was a private place he visited to pray and rest during his frequent trips to Fez. He told me it was untouched. 'No one is ever here,' Christian said proudly as we climbed half a kilometer down a steep cliff to the sea. It was there, in his 'paradise,' that Christian revealed a telling characteristic. As we were eating our picnic, I looked around and saw a rock with 'Hassan *aime* Fatima' scratched on it. Later, I saw a Coke bottle off to the side. I pointed these things out to Christian, but he was unfazed. It didn't matter. That was Christian's special place."

Christian would be accused of naïveté in his view of Islam. But in fact, he always chose to see the good in things, to look beyond the irritants and the bad. He did not want to dignify evil by letting it preoccupy him. Nor would he make broad judgments about people or governments. He would merely describe a specific act as good or bad, helpful or unhelpful, according to the situation. He believed people could always change, especially if one addressed their higher nature.

In Algiers, they found roadblocks and armored cars enforcing an uneasy calm. Christian continued straight through the city and drove on that same night to Tibhirine.

The windows of Bernardo's room opened out on the terrace with its view of the Tamesguida Mountains, a sight that always enchanted visitors. When guests expressed surprise that the monks had no TV to watch, Christian would say they had something better—they watched the mountains. Despite the ninety-five-degree summer heat, the air was dry and felt fresh with the scent of eucalyptus. In the midst of the lush, dense shade of the cedars, cypress, and pines with cones the size of pineapples, the grasping wisteria, flowering chestnut and almond trees, Bernardo saw more than sparse, monastic simplicity. He saw real poverty. "It was clear that with their limited number of hands, the emphasis was on the outside."

His small rusted shower stall seemed to be supporting mysterious life-forms in its dark corners. A weak trickle did not invite a long stay. Dim lightbulbs made for a somber atmosphere at night. Everywhere, plaster was peeling. "Water and the garden were their life. That was where their energy went," Bernardo remembered. Water had been a growing problem since the onset of the drought in the 1980s. Keeping an adequate supply flowing to the garden was Paul's responsibility. He had ingeniously cut up the metal fence around the monks' cemetery and welded the bars into conduits for moving water out of the big spring behind the new building and into the fields below. All the monks helped in the garden from time to time, especially during the harvest season.

Bernardo had come to give moral support to the community and to learn more about their life in the Atlas. He talked with each of the brothers individually over the next week. The irascible Luc warmed up once he discovered their common bond. Both had started their monastic lives as lay brothers. Like Luc, Bernardo knew something about medicine, even if his knowledge was only of veterinary medicine. Bernardo asked Luc if he had signed the document on unification, which, in the spirit of Vatican II egalitarianism, would have changed his status from lay brother to simple monk, equal with, but distinguished from, a choir monk. Luc was not interested. He'd been a lay brother for fifty years and didn't want to change. That was what he wanted to be—the humblest of the humble. Stubborn or proud perhaps, even in his humility, Luc would not sign the liberation document making him equal. And no one would try to compel him.

Christophe impressed Bernardo with his enthusiasm for manual work in the garden, which was also his schoolhouse, where he learned about his Muslim neighbors. Christophe was a poet and an artist. His drawings decorated the minutes of the *ribats.* An unexpected challenge made a lasting impression on Christophe. Bernardo asked him one day in the garden how many pull-ups he could do on a hanging bar that was used for drying onions. The brawny Christophe strained his muscles to do ten. He then watched in stunned amazement as the pale, scrawny-looking abbot general bested him by doing fifteen. The new abbot general's stock rose. Christophe did not know Bernardo had flirted with becoming a circus acrobat before entering the Order.

Paul was the most recent arrival from France to take a vow of stability at Tibhirine. He had come from Notre-Dame de Tamié in the winter of 1989, and he was the last of the monks to take his vows at Tibhirine. In Paul, Bernardo found a husky, bald fifty-two-year-old Savoyard whose placid round face masked decisive resolve and dry humor. He was known as a man with "golden hands." His plumber's ingenuity and talent for solving mechanical problems kept the monastery running and the garden watered. Paul's faith had matured slowly. In France, he had been a city council member and the dutiful son of a blacksmith in the tiny village of Bonnevaux. He made clear to Bernardo that he was not enthusiastic about interreligous dialogue—not because he was against other religions, but because he feared blurring his own identity. Paul was a man who liked clarity and precision.

Michel Fleury, Célestin Ringeard, and Bruno Lemarchand would be called by the French press "the three Magi." They had created something of a sensation back in 1984 because of the providential manner in which they came to Tibhirine. One of Christian's first concerns as prior had been to find more monks to come to the Atlas. The three monks had been at Notre-Dame de Bellefontaine when they heard talks by former priests from Algeria who had described the exotic land, the challenges, and the urgent needs of the new Trappist prior. Later, all three had independently confided to their abbot, Etienne Baudry, that they wanted to serve the Order in Algeria. Each monk had gone to Baudry during the course of the same week in April 1984, less than one month after Christian's election.

A hurricane of words descended on Bernardo when he met Célestin. He was called *"l'homme du contact"* by his brothers. He had an incessant need to talk and to be with people. "Please speak slower; I don't understand French very well," Bernardo begged, but to no avail as he listened politely while the fifty-seven-year-old priest poured out his concerns. Célestin had a special fraternal tie to Algeria from his war days as a military medic. After a skirmish near Oran, some soldiers in his unit wanted to finish off a wounded *fell* officer. Célestin told the soldiers they would have to kill him first. He nursed the soldier throughout the night and had him sent to a hospital the next day. Sidi, as the man was called, spent the rest of the war in prison. Almost thirty years later, Sidi sent his son to study in France. The young man wanted to thank the French man who had saved his father's life. After weeks of calling clergymen throughout the country, he spoke to the Bishop of Nantes, who directed Sidi's son to Notre-Dame de Bellefontaine, where Célestin had recently become a novice.

Silent, attentive to others, humble, and obedient, Michel was known as *"l'homme de l'écoute."* Christian said he was the ideal monk. He had been a machinist in Marseilles and active in the Prado, a Catholic lay organization that was founded to serve the needs of the poor and homeless, especially immigrants. In the Prado, he mixed with North Africans and was smitten with their hospitableness, despite their extreme poverty. At Bellefontaine, Michel felt overwhelmed by the size, formality, and grandeur of the monastery. "He was like David in Saul's armor," Baudry remembered. Father Bernardo found that the gentle monk with the hatchet face and modest manner had little to say to him.

Bernardo had already met Bruno, the third of the Magi, in Fez. The introspective former French professor had found Bellefontaine too big, too grand, too hectic. As hotelier there, Bruno had been miserable. He detested his portable phone that never left him in peace. Bruno had found contentment at Tibhirine and wrote to his family that he wanted it to be his final resting place. He was *"l'homme des fleurs,"* happiest when he was in the garden tending flowers.

Amédée had been at the monastery the longest of all the brothers. Like Christian, he wanted to share in Muslim spirituality, but his way was different. He just liked being with Muslims and had no need for a theological approach. Amédée was popular with the women of the village. A visit to father "Ha'mdi" was an outing. It gave them a chance to unburden themselves with a sympathetic and understanding listener. They always brought him little cakes, or presents from Mecca, if they had returned from a pilgrimage. Or they bartered eggs in return for using the monks' battery recharger. Sometimes, they simply needed money. They knew Amédée was the monastery's treasurer.

Some brothers thought Amédée was too much of a traditionalist and lived in the past. Other monks shed their tunics when they went out in public, in order not to invite aggressive remarks from certain types, usually young boys. But Amédée always wore his habit to the local festivals, marriages, and funerals, events to which he was regularly invited. At age seventy, Amédée's hearing was failing. He spent his time with Bernardo tuning both his hearing aids and repeating, *"Je n'ai pas compris."*

After Amédée and Luc, Jean-Pierre had the longest memory of life at the monastery. He had come to Tibhirine in 1964 in response to Bishop Duval's call for monks after he had saved the monastery from Dom Sortais' decree to close it. Jean-Pierre thought as Amédée did about wearing religious habits in public. They should be proud of their uniform. But he stopped wearing his tunic when some teenagers in Algiers murmured *"envahisseur"* as he passed them going to Notre-Dame d'Afrique one day. It made him uncomfortable to be called an invader, even though name-calling was an exceptional occurrence. The cross was still a symbol of colonialism and past humiliations for Algerians. Like Amédée, Jean-Pierre was also a traditionalist, and preferred the way the monks lived when he first arrived from France in the 1960s. At that time, they had dormitories, and each monk slept in a small cubicle, with only a curtain for privacy. Jean-Pierre generally opposed changes that worked against the spirit of community solidarity essential to Cistercian monasticism. He thought the new fashion of sleeping in individual rooms, or *cellules,* eroded this spirit. Rather than read or write in the scriptorium with others, the brothers spent more time alone in their rooms. Bernardo remembered Jean-Pierre as a man of unflappable calm.

Before leaving Tibhirine, Bernardo had a dream, or "a nocturnal visitor," as Christian wrote later. He dreamt that a monk at Tibhirine was being violently lectured to by another monk, who had seized him by the neck, shouting, "First, you are losing face and wasting your time in this Muslim world where you are mocked! There are so many other people who want you, and your community could grow just by its presence. Second, you poor sot, our Order really has no use for your monastery—you're deadweight." Before the gasping monk could reply in the dream, Bernardo woke up. Agitated, he wrote down his responses, which Christian would use later in an address to the Order.

The abbot general left Tibhirine in mid-June. The disturbances that had almost prevented him from entering the country had been caused by the army breaking up a failed general strike that had been called by the FIS.

Emboldened by their party's impressive victory at the municipal level the previous year, Abassi Madani and his allies on the FIS governing council (*majlis ash shoura*) were confident of taking over the National Assembly in the elections scheduled for 1991. But the legislature had gerrymandered districts to favor the rural vote, where the FLN was stronger. It also changed the electoral law to correspond to the French system, requiring a second runoff election between the two top candidates, should no party obtain an absolute majority in the first round.

Though of no consequence to the average voter, who barely understood the electoral process, these political maneuverings by the FLN provided Madani an opportunity for confrontation with the government. His goals in calling a general strike during the last week of May were never clear. At different times, he called for the resignation of President Chadli, for modification of the election law, and for the government to set a date for the elections. The strike was called with no precise demands on behalf of workers; rather, it was a demonstration of political muscle in the streets.

The FIS claimed 100 percent adherence to the strike in Medea. But Algiers was different. Except for a core of militants, much of the population failed to respond to the call for a general strike whose objectives were unclear. Students at the four campuses of the University of Algiers continued to study and take their exams. FIS militants entered examination halls and snatched pens from students at the Babezzour campus. Most businessmen kept their shops open, and the government workers who struck weren't more numerous than usual. Workers were striking all the time in Algeria.

With Islamic fever loose again on the streets, the government's power doctors were divided. Was this an infection, perhaps of Saudi or Iranian etiology, requiring strong antibiotics to wipe it out completely? Or was this an immune system gone haywire, mistaking "self" for "other," requiring not antibiotics but anti-inflammatories and the healing salve of real democracy? Some of the doctors, it was said by cynics, preferred a permanently sick, weakened patient—a populace so distracted by its own ills and fears that it would never be able to fire those in charge of its welfare, who were acting "for the people and by the people."

The doctors were always divided—between military and civilians, between clans, between generations, between FIS sympathizers and FIS opponents, real democrats and phony democrats, sincere Muslims and hypocritical Muslims, Arabophones and Francophones, and those with big bank accounts in Switzerland and those with no bank accounts. They might fight among themselves, but the doctors were united in their desire to remain in charge of treating the patient. In the months to come, these differences would be simplified in the press, becoming a struggle between "eradicators" and "negotiators." The new government slogan was "Change with continuity," which meant same doctors, different medicine, or same medicine, different labels.

The world doctors at the International Monetary Fund always prescribed free markets and democracy. It was their universal cure-all, no matter what the disease. They, too, needed to be kept happy to assure that *le pouvoir*'s financial life-support systems would be kept in place for Algeria's ailing body politic. Whatever the medicine—

bloodletting, purges, isolation, talk therapy, old religion, new religion—the medicine always had to be administered in the name of democracy in the making.

The FIS had been divided as well in the pursuit of a common goal: an Islamic state. "Islam is the solution." They all agreed with the slogan—but whose Islam, and how to get there? There were the traditionalists, who rejected the foray into politics because it would corrupt Islam. They believed that preaching, education, social work, and good example were the best medicine, the way of *da'wa. Da'wa* stimulates and promotes regeneration from within by instructing Islamic morality, respect for Islam, and good behavior. Politics, these argued, promotes the disease of divisiveness, or *fitna.*

Others, the *djaz'arists,* or "legalists," were pursing a national, rather than universal, jihad. They saw the political process that the riots of 1988 opened up as offering the best means to remove the apostates running the country. Eradicating injustice was a sacred duty, but Muslims shouldn't use violence unless forced to by others. *Da'wa* was fine, Madani told the traditionalists, but promoting Islamic culture could not be accomplished if it was disconnected from political and economic realities.

The radicals in the FIS, who rejected participation in the political process, were often *salafists,* or "theocrats." They saw themselves as part of a worldwide revolutionary movement and their loyalty was not to the nation-state but to the *umma,* the original Islamic community which existed before the nation-state was born. Some were either old Bouyalists from the mid-1980s, for whom Ali Benhadj had spent five years in prison, or Afghan veterans who had been schooled in Peshawar and had fought against the Soviet army. Participating in elections, the radicals argued, would only lend legitimacy to an illegitimate government and to a conception of democracy that was Occidental, not Islamic.

The radicals argued that the doctors would never allow the FIS to take over, even if they did win legitimately. They declared the process a sham, another facade for the real power—the military—to hide behind. They accused the legalists of naïveté. The radicals saw the maquis as their solution, just as the martyrs of November 1 had thirty-seven years earlier.

The strike called on May 25 lacked not only support on the street but a consensus within the FIS leadership. Madani was president, but he was only primus inter pares. The future Islamic state had its own form of democracy, which the FIS was supposed to practice. The governing body of the FIS was the forty-member consultative council, the *majlis ash shoura*. By tradition, it was a collegial body, but also a critic and truth sayer, formerly to the *caliph,* but now to the president of the FIS.

Madani was accused by his opponents on the council of taking liberties, of short-circuiting the process of consultation (*shoura*) and consensus (*ijma*). They criticized him for speaking on behalf of the FIS without having the support of the council. There were seventeen dissidents in the *majlis* opposed to a political strategy. Intrigue and suspected contacts between some anti-Madani people on the council and the government led to expulsions from the party.

Ahmed Merrani was one. He had been among the original founders of the FIS in 1989 with Madani at the Es Sunna mosque. He remembered growing up in the Casbah during the war for independence. He spoke fluent French and had always believed the war was about preserving the Muslim religion and moral values of Islam. In the mid-1970s, he had founded an association to care for the needy. Merrani believed that preaching and good works (*da'wa*) was the way to bring people back to Islam. In the 1980s, he did not join with the Bouyalists who had already turned to violence. "You can't sit around with your arms crossed, but *da'wa* is more effective than the Kalashnikov,"

On June 1, Merrani denounced his own party on national TV, saying that the FIS had been taken over by "kids" who lacked "competence and religious knowledge." The rancor within the party and lukewarm support for the strike by the people provided an opening for the generals to put an end to the FIS, and to the "noise, furor, and confusion" in the streets. The night of June 3, the eradicators took charge of the patient. Soldiers with armored cars cleared out demonstrators from the four squares that the prime minister had told Madani the demonstrators could occupy peacefully. Tear gas, rocks, gunfire, ambulances, *you yous, intifada*—the ghost of October 1988 frightened many in the government who did not want a repetition of what had occurred three years earlier.

The "disturbances" of June 3 left 55 dead and 326 wounded. Three thousand had been arrested. Twelve thousand workers who had used the threat of support for the strike to pressure the government for better conditions were fired. Who had given the order to clear the squares on the night of June 3? It came "from above" was the most anyone would ever say later.

Feeling deceived by his own government, Prime Minister Hamrouche resigned on June 5. He had told the demonstrators they could occupy the squares as long as it was peaceful. A new prime minister was appointed, and a state of emergency was declared, which meant a curfew and more arrests.

On June 7, Madani declared the strike over and victory for the FIS. He explained in a press conference the next day that the old election law had been annulled, the FIS was allowed to continue as a political party, and new elections were to be announced for December 21. But with the 1989 constitutional safeguards suspended by the state of emergency, the eradicators could begin to squeeze the Islamic boils afflicting the body politic of the fragile new democracy. And squeeze they did.

It began with the strange case of Roger-Didier Guyon, a Frenchman sympathetic to the Islamists. Known as "Didi" to Ali Benhadj, he was arrested on June 12 for bringing a shipment of weapons into the country. The press implicated Benhadj in the planning of an armed revolt to "destabilize the institutions of government." In an emotional press conference, Benhadj said the fatal words as he denied the charges: "I will take up arms if that is what you accuse me of! . . . The laws? I spit on the laws. I am above the law." The popular daily paper *Horizons* announced in large headlines, ALI BENHADJ ABOVE THE LAW and BENHADJ CRACKS.

The next day, soldiers went into the FIS townships and tore down signs that said ISLAMIC COMMUNE. They were replaced by new ones that read, BY THE PEOPLE, FOR THE PEOPLE. More disturbances, burnings, and riots led Madani to threaten a jihad if the government did not stop its strong-arm tactics.

On June 27, Benhadj ignored a summons to the police commissariat. On the thirtieth, he was arrested as he entered the studios of the national television station to demand the right to respond to his detractors. The same day, Abbassi Madani was arrested at the FIS headquarters on rue Khalifa, only a hundred meters from Bishop Teissier's office. Both Benhadj and Madani were taken to Blida and put in prison for threatening the security of the state.

Many observers thought the FIS leaders had played into the hands of the eradicators by their careless talk and that the emotional Benhadj had been cleverly manipulated. *Le pouvoir* had reason to be in a grumpy mood. It had become a punching bag in 1991. The year had delivered a flurry of woes, beginning with the Gulf War in January. The government had wanted to play its traditional role of conciliator. It had performed the role before by helping France extract a kidnapped journalist from Lebanon in 1986. Algeria had been a vital intermediary in negotiating the release of the American embassy hostages in Iran in 1979. But the war had radicalized many of the young, who hated the fat, smug Saudis and Kuwaitis, causing confusion within both the government and the FIS leadership, which was ready to express solidarity with their Saudi financial backers. The Algerian youth was pro-Saddam Hussein. He was David standing up to the American Goliath. He was an Arab Robin Hood frightening the rich Saudis.

The ideological inspiration for Algeria's left wing, the Soviet Union, was disintegrating before the eyes of the world, confirming the reality of Peter Chaadaev's description of Russia as a country whose fate was to show the world what not to do. Oil prices continued to fall, reducing *le pouvoir*'s gravy, and its ability to serve the country's pressing social needs. New negotiations with the International Monetary Fund were upcoming. Last but not least, there was the Islamist fundamentalist threat which would force them to share power were they to win a significant share of the upcoming vote for the National Assembly. And, an overconfident Madani had carelessly declared that the FIS would not feel bound to honor any past commitments to the IMF, or to anyone else; that these would be the last democratic elections.* The fear of an Iranian revolution was not far from the minds of the generals. They had seen what happened when religion ran amok in politics.

---

*On different occasions, Madani also said he thought the army should be abolished and that women should be paid for their work at home

9

A Country of Orphans

Have we not all one Father? Has not one God created us? Why do we deal treacherously with one another by profaning the covenant of the fathers.

—Malachi 2:9

Hatred and violence in the psalms was becoming a sensitive subject at the weekly meetings of the liturgy committee. They knew that references to Israel and the "enemies of the Lord" found in the psalms were being omitted from the liturgy by certain priests in Algiers who were anxious not to offend Muslims. *"They speak against you wickedly; Your enemies take your name in vain. Do I not hate them, O Lord, who hate you? Do I not loathe those who rise up against you? I hate them with perfect hatred, I count them my enemies. . . ."* Psalm 139 could give the wrong idea. Would Muslims think "enemies" meant them?

Christian understood perfectly well the importance of the violence in the psalms. He called them a cry that says, "God be just, so I don't take justice into my own hands. I know I can't be just when I am angry." The psalms reminded him of the violence in himself, something he believed was at the core of every person. Nevertheless, Christian thought it was insensitive to be singing psalms of violence when violence was increasing all around them.

The brothers were in agreement. Christian was being too sensitive. The liturgy was built around the psalms. They were an ancient patrimony, handed down from the desert fathers, who sang the very same psalms centuries ago. To water them down would be a form of betrayal, a denial of their own identity as monks. Yes, the psalms are violent because they are rooted in real life, full of longing, fear, doubt, and hope of His eternal love and His ultimate justice. But they would not let Christian's zeal to spare hypothetical offenses to Muslims weaken that which was most dear to them. If certain verses offended, they could be explained. But they shouldn't offend. It is clearly written in the Koran that God gave the psalms to David. A greater problem for the brothers was the way they sang to the Lord.

Seven times a day, the monks make love with their hearts, their souls, and, above all, with their voices. Theirs is a physical love of harmonic vibration, of notes and chords, a longing, romantic love of the troubadour for the inaccessible woman of his heart. Like a cherished love letter, the words of the liturgy are inhaled like fine mist into the depths of their being. And the word is made flesh.

Their love is individual, but singing that love together unites them as a community in God. Since Christian's appointment of Célestin as cantor, singing God's praises had become as much a source of discord as unity. Within the committee, Christophe was officially responsible for the liturgy, but Célestin, with his better ear and musical knowledge, was in charge of the singing. Christophe had been a monk for eighteen years. He knew how monks were supposed to sing. Célestin sang like Célestin. He sang too high. He stood out. Monks are supposed to sing in a measured Gregorian monotone, together, and with a passion that burns like a steady flame.

Célestin had been an oddity since the day he entered the order in 1983. Everyone had said then that the square-jawed, white-haired, bustling fifty-year-old was not monklike. He was talkative, excitable, exuberant, and received too much mail for someone who was supposed to be detaching himself from the world. He had led a life of ceaseless activity as a street priest, ministering to people on the margins of society in south Nantes—down-and-out alcoholics, prostitutes, homeless parolees, and homosexuals. Gregarious, committed to helping others, Célestin had been on the verge of exhaustion after eight years of tending his lost sheep all hours of the day. One evening, a suicidal homosexual called him in desperation. Célestin arrived at his apartment building, only to see the man's body land on the cement outside. Soon after, he told his sister, "I've given enough of myself to others; now I am going to give myself only to God."

At Tibhirine, Christian made allowances for Célestin. The Rule doesn't prescribe that all monks be treated the same. A superior is supposed to be like a sensitive parent who recognizes that his children have different needs, according to their age, temperament, and physical constitution. Célestin had spent much of his ordained life in constant motion, as a independent, healing spirit of the church. So Christian turned a blind eye when Célestin began to take long pre-dawn walks outside the cloister following Vigils, when monks are supposed to be doing their *lectio divina,* reading and reflecting on Scripture or some other manifestation of God's word. Furthermore, he would talk freely with whomever he met on the road. He liked people.

Christian may have had a larger view but other monks objected. Jean-Pierre, for one, thought Célestin's early-morning wanderings worked against the spirit of their community. Célestin, he observed in a chapter meeting, had joined a contemplative order, which, unlike the Carthusians, stressed living as a community. If he still needed to grow into this kind of life, then his free-spirited walks would pull him in the wrong direction, and possibly create fissures among the brothers. That was also a delicate way for him to say that, despite Saint Benedict's generosity of spirit, monks have problems when one of their own has a special privilege.

On free days, Célestin took long walks across the Tamesguida valley to visit Robert Fouquez, a Benedictine hermit who lived in the mountains directly across the valley. Normally, a Trappist has no vacation or long weekends "off duty" during his life of service to the Lord. But since Tibhirine was such a small, isolated community, Christian had given the brothers forty-eight hours for themselves each month. The sociable Célestin found in Robert a soul mate who spoke to the individualistic free spirited side of his personality. Robert had rebuilt an abandoned stone shepherd's shelter into a cozy hermitage where he tended flowers and vegetables, and cultivated bees. The locals regarded him as a wise man, and so did Célestin.

In the fall of 1992, Célestin suffered severe chest pains during one of these monthly visits, and he returned early to the monastery, in shaky condition, helped along by Robert's donkey. An examination by a cardiologist in Medea confirmed that he had had a minor heart attack. At the time, he received little sympathy from Christian, who shrugged it off as a case of nerves.

Physical stamina was one of Christian's remarkable qualities, and its absence in others was something he did not always understand, or mistook for something else. He never got sick, ate sparsely, slept little, and wore his sandals, without socks in winter. He could write fifty letters during a single day. Writing was his duty and his passion. Christian was a man of relationships, *l'homme des relations,* as he was known by his brothers.

The annual community bulletin was for keeping friends and relatives abreast of life in the Atlas Mountains. At the end of 1992, Christian looked for signs of hope in a difficult and disquieting year.

"In the name of He who brings us together, peace to you whose names are written in the book of our lives," he greeted his readers. Remembering some of those names, Christian told them that Brother Pierre had died after a struggle with cancer. This "black African and white monk" had come to the Atlas in 1948, when there were no other Cistercian monasteries in North Africa, and left in 1951 to found a new one in his native Cameroon. Before he died, Pierre described his cancer as "his last and blessed calling, for life is given to man so that, little by little, he can get accustomed to God, and at the end feel himself at home, immersed in God."

Christian spoke of Brother Philippe Hémon of Tamié, who had come for Christophe's ordination in 1990 and had since become a regular visitor at the monastery. He had visited for two weeks in 1992 to help Christophe and Célestin find "the notes that are agreeable to the community." As for the Salve Regina, the monks' good-night prayer to the Virgin Mary, sung at Compline, Hémon magnanimously allowed that it could be interpreted in a thousand different ways; only please, he urged the brothers, don't drop the last word. It is a shout, not a sigh. And, yes, he reminded them: What a word: Maria.

Their bishop, Henri Teissier, was also in the book of their lives. Christian reported that the bishop had once again had to tell Christian visitors from France why the Church was still there. "We are asked continuously how many 'baptized' there are left here. It is an irrelevant question. We are not an international corporation trying to win market share. Our priests are here for the whole Algerian community. When a people suffer, it is already something just to be there, to share their suffering. The very simple presence of the

Church speaks volumes at a time when others are trying to leave the country."

Mohammed was another name in the book. He was their versatile watchman, who lived in the building where the old olive press had been located. Mohammed worked in the garden as chief associate to Christophe, following in the footsteps of his uncle Ali, who had retired in 1990 after nearly forty years of service to the monastery. Mohammed was a valued member of the *ribats,* as well. Christian described his Islam as "one of openness." He had taken a trip to France in 1992 with Christophe to visit the monasteries that had sent brothers to Tibhirine. Mohammed was impressed by Trappist piety and striving to obey God's will, and declared to Christian after he returned, "I have seen real Muslims."

Mohammed was also the name of Mohammed Boudiaf, the Algerian president who had been assassinated six months earlier, on June 29. His killing was a reminder of the tensions that had seized the country since the cancellation in January 1992 of the national elections. Boudiaf's simple, straightforward way of talking appealed to people. He had made them believe in his sincerity. "He talked of building a new sense of national unity through honest work and the participation of all classes in opportunities. Again, the youth are at a loss," Christian wrote.

He concluded his bulletin by emphasizing the word *trust.* "It is a name for love of the noblest kind, born from the marriage of faith and hope . . . the best gift a person could give to his neighbor."

By the end of 1992, trust had become a rare commodity in Algeria.

"Those who killed him wanted to kill hope," said Madame Fatiha Boudiaf as she began her official statement to the press the day of her husband's funeral. Millions of Algerians had poured out their grief and shame, leaving little doubt that Mohammed Boudiaf had indeed begun to win the confidence of the people on the street after five months of lonely struggle against old ways.

Mohammed Boudiaf had acquired many nicknames: "Mohammed the Dry," "Ramses II," "the Sphinx," even "Lee Van Cleef," the American actor whose high cheekbones and immovable, hard-lined face bore a marked resemblance to his own. Why he was the choice of the army to succeed President Chadli was easier to understand than why he accepted to head the new extraconstitutional Haut Comité d'Etat. The High Committee of State was made up of four generals. It needed a fifth member, preferably a civilian with stature to mitigate the coup d'état they had engineered in the name of preserving democracy.

Mohammed Boudiaf was a Mr. Clean, unsullied by Algerian politics for the past twenty-seven years. He was an historic figure, one of the original nine who had formed the committee that decided to launch the revolution from a Paris café near the Sorbonne in March of 1954. There, in an act of pure faith and determination, the decison was made to rid Algeria of French rule, even though the future revolutionaries possessed an arms cache of only three hundred rifles and shotguns. When the generals approached Boudiaf after the first-round vote in December of 1991, his name had been expunged from Algerian history books. He was a complete unknown, except to the older generation of mujahideen.

Soon after independence in July 1962, the FLN fell into its natural warring elements once the glue of war-induced cohesion dissolved. A lawyer with socialist leanings, Boudiaf wanted real democracy, not a junta. Others thought Algerians weren't ready yet for democracy. One such person was military strong man Houari Boumediene. He became a champion of Islamic egalitarianism. Some called him "the monk."

The son of a poor Arab farmer, Boumediene was a strict Muslim, known for his unsmiling secretiveness and austerity. After fighting in the maquis around his native city of Tlemcen, he spent the rest of the war rising to the leadership of the army of the exterior, the military reserve based in Tunisia and Morocco. He shunned the pomp of rank or military decorations and despised still more the petty feuding of the ambitious. Boumediene believed only the army was unified enough to transcend the postwar chaos, personal rivalries, and culture of clan warfare that had traditionally divided Algeria. This fractious disease had been briefly surmounted before by only one man, Emir Abdelkader, whose portrait was the sole decoration in Boumediene's stark office. In 1963, Boumediene became allied with the ambitious, if erratic, Ahmed Ben Bella, who had won his sergeant's stripes in the French army and shared Boumediene's belief in the need for single-party politics to bring Algerians together, a belief that suited his oversized ambitions.

Boudiaf had been put in prison briefly by Ben Bella for challenging the single-party political culture that had prevailed over the objections of democrats like himself who wanted genuine pluralism. He had helped create a committee for the defense of the revolution during the year following independence, and after Ben Bella's election as president, Boudiaf formed his own Party of the Socialist Revolution, in spite of the prohibition on alternative political parties. Released a year later, in 1964, Boudiaf went to France, then settled into obscurity with his family to run a brick-making business in Morocco. A year later, Ben Bella himself was deposed by the army and placed under house arrest. In 1980, he, too, went into exile.

When the first round of national elections on December 27, 1991, gave an overwhelming majority to the FIS, the military found itself in the ticklish position of having to choose between the virtually certain likelihood of sharing power with the Islamists or canceling the second-round vote scheduled for January. Boudiaf's name was in play as someone who could get the government out of this impasse. But when he was contacted by journalists to comment on the election results, he said, "*Le pouvoir* has reaped what it has sown. The Islamists have only now to take power."

A few days later, a representative of the government visited him in his small town of Kenitra to tell him that President Chadli would resign and that the military wanted him to head the new temporary governing committee. There was a political void. Only he had untainted prestige and possessed "historic capital," capital that belonged not to him but to Algeria. It was his duty to help his country out of the mess. Again Boudiaf refused. He had been cut off from Algeria for too long, Boudiaf insisted.

What, then, changed his mind about becoming the head of a military government after spending twenty-seven-years in exile because of his opposition to military rule? Had he simply accepted the generals' assertion that they did not want to hold on to power, that they were just doing their duty for Algeria by preserving it from a civil war or a worse form of tyranny? At age seventy-two, perhaps he was thinking about restoring his place in Algerian history. In the end, it may well have been his wife, Fatiha, who made him reconsider. Boudiaf had been agitated and restless after he turned down the job a second time. "Maybe the time has come," she told him. "You have never fled from your responsibilities. You have always said you'd go back to Algeria if the country needed you."

Boudiaf accepted the offer after Chadli resigned on January 11, 1992, the same day the High Committee of State canceled the second round of elections. But he soon became a problem for those who thought he could be controlled. He had no power base that could be pressured by the generals to influence him. Boudiaf floated in the clouds, surrounded by a small group of young émigré professors he imported from Paris, who also had not been in Algeria for years. He was so clean, he was unsteerable. Boudiaf took on the mantle of a severe but just father who spanked all his children.

Putting the lash to the FIS was the first order of business. Its interim president, Abdelkader Hachani, called for insurrection among the voters and for the People's Army to defend the Islamic movement. The eight thousand FIS mosques throughout the country sheltered political harangues against the government every Friday. Boudiaf told his premier, "I don't want Fridays to turn Algiers into a Teheran. There must not be a political Islam." Boudiaf was a practicing Muslim, but one who had been educated in the French republican tradition. A law forbidding mosques to be used for political purposes was strictly enforced. Police cordoned off FIS mosques on Fridays, forbade praying in the streets, and arrested inflammatory FIS imams in the middle of their sermons. Police clashed with FIS supporters and casually shot at minarets from the street. People in the poor neighborhoods were outraged at this insolent blasphemy by the forces of order.

By early February, newspapers reported forty dead and three hundred wounded in confrontations around the country, though most were in Algiers. A state of emergency was declared for 12 months. Toward the end of February, there were mass arrests. The local FIS elected officials and their sympathizers were put into former French detention camps fifteen hundred miles to the south, where temperatures would rise to 130 degrees in the shade. Fifteen thousand people, more or less—teachers, imams, medical doctors, businessmen, professors, eight hundred mayors, and four thousand members of city councils—were held without charge for months in the open-air sand furnaces of Aïn Salah, Reggane, Ouargla, Horm, and others remote places. In early March, the FIS was officially dissolved as a political party. By the end of March, the party's leadership had been arrested or gone into exile.

The FIS weren't the only ones who had to learn to play by the new rules. Boudiaf's slogan was "Algeria first." He began to look into corruption. He started collecting dossiers on those high officers who had valuable foreign trade licenses for the import of such products as antibiotics, sugar, or automobile tires. He probed into customs irregularities. Then came a shock. He put a general in jail. Mohammed Boudiaf was full of rigid rectitude, authoritarian, isolated, and in a hurry. He was waging war, but without consulting the army, without a power base, and, some thought, without humility.

He was determined to bring the country together. Had he lived, Boudiaf would have created a new superparty. His National Patriotic Assembly would have had room for all the other political parties, becoming yet another front, this one for waging a war of national self-renewal. He wanted to reach out to the young and to make them feel Algeria was their country too. "My goal is to create conditions to allow us to give our youth the keys to the prisons." Boudiaf was speaking to them about reconciliation and love of neighbor at the Palace of Culture in Annaba when he heard a hissing sound near his feet. As he turned to see a grenade rolling toward him, a security guard behind the stage curtain fired seven bullets into his back.

On July 1, in scorching heat, a cortege engulfed by crowds of young and old, men and women with faces disfigured by emotion, snaked slowly from the presidential residence along the twisting eight-mile route to the el-Alia cemetery, where Boudiaf would be laid to rest next to Houari Boumediene and Abdelkader.

Army helicopters beat their heavy wings overhead while below women cried haunting, high pitched, ululating *you yous,* their centuries-old dirge for exorcising anguish and pain. There were shouts of "Chadli—assassin," and scenes of young men burning cigarettes into their hands to commemorate forever the man who had become the father they so much needed.

Reporters interviewed people waiting for the cortege to pass. "We are orphans," sobbed two girls. "We have lost our father, the father of all Algerians. The people have a right to know the truth, a trial without lynching, without revenge. . . . Revenge is not Islam." A young man covered in sweat and tears said, "They killed a father. They made use of his dignity and reputation. This was a man of true integrity, not a part of the Mafia. He was the pride of Algeria. . . . The country was boiling with trouble, and they found him to bring calm. Now they've shot him in the back." An old man with tears in his eyes remembered, "They finished off all the old revolutionaries—Krim, Khider, Boumediene . . . and now Boudiaf. . . . Its a bad sign for Algeria. What is happening to us?"

A journalist for the Algerian daily newspaper *La Nation* caught the mood as the cortege crawled along the boulevard Amirouche. "A sense of deep anxiety could be felt moving among the crowd in sad disarray, undone by their mourning. There was a premonition of a descent into hell."

"*They* killed him." The words were repeated by ordinary people who didn't believe for a moment the government's story that this was the act of a lone religious fanatic, an official explanation curiously reminiscent of Anwar Sadat's assassination in 1981. The Egyptian president had also been killed by a member of his security guard, who was said to be a religious fanatic belonging to the Muslim Brotherhood. Seven weeks after Boudiaf's death, an official board of inquiry agreed with the instinctive responses on the street. But the board of inquiry was not capable of saying who "*they*" were. It could only conclude that the chain of circumstances leading to his murder were such as to have been hardly possible for one person to organize.*

---

*French security services did their own investigation and concluded that Boudiaf's assassination was a joint operation of the Algerian gendarmerie, secret services, and former members of Chadli's administration (*Journal du Dimanche,* August 28, 1993).

By midsummer of 1992, the Islamist fever seemed to have broken. In July, Madani and Benhadj were sentenced to twelve years imprisonment by a military court in Blida. FIS elected officials in the municipalities had been removed from office and replaced by new appointed representatives. The call by FIS leaders for mass uprising by the 3 million cheated voters did not occur. They did not revolt after the election was interrupted, or even after the FIS was declared illegal. The security forces had intimidated FIS sympathizers and removed politically inflammatory imams from the mosques. The youth in certain well-known FIS neighborhoods of Algiers were routinely rounded up for interrogations. Much of the FIS intelligentsia were in detention camps or had already left the county. Then, like the raindrops that fall gradually at first and then faster, until becoming a downpour, the violence mutated into new forms, by new actors on whom no police dossiers existed.

On the morning of August 26, a devastating explosion signaled something new. A bomb placed under a seat in the waiting area near the Air France check-in counter at Houari Boumediene Airport killed 9 people and wounded 120. Many of the victims were women and children, though, curiously, no security personnel were injured. Body parts were carried out in plastic garbage bags in a nightmare of carnage that spewed blood and flesh over walls and ceilings. The random killing of innocent civilians, especially of women and children, outraged the public. Total war had been declared, though it was not clear by whom. The prime minister alluded to "a foreign hand" in the matter when he spoke with the press.

A month later, the supposed authors of the attack were caught. Four men were found guilty, even though they insisted in the courtroom that they had confessed only after being tortured. The accused were ex-FIS hard-liners connected to the Mouvement Islamique Armé (MIA) of Abdelkader Chebouti, former captain in the Sécurité Militaire, the intelligence branch of the Algerian army. He had joined the maquis with Emir Mustafa Bouyali in the mid-1980s and had been captured and sentenced to death along with six others. He was the only one to be reprieved.

Chebouti had been one of the *purs et durs*. They were the outspoken diehards in the internal FIS debates over participating in the national elections of December 1991. He protested then that the process was a masquerade. Participating served only to give legitimacy to the apostate neocolonialists who were in cahoots with France. Chebouti's analysis made him a hero to many Islamists when his predictions proved to be accurate. He became the wise combatant. He had foreseen that the elections were not a game that the FIS would be allowed to win.

After the cancellation of the second round of elections, the arguments by FIS leaders against armed revolt were no longer tenable. The peaceful path to theocracy had been blocked. Initially, the MIA was the only armed group in the field ready to fight. His organization was a reincarnation of the Bouyalist jihad that he had joined in 1982.

Many of the MIA's estimated two thousand mujahideen were veterans of the first jihad led by Emir Mustafa Bouyali in the mid-1980s. The names of most of his followers were also in police files—which made hiding in the cities difficult. Chebouti had anticipated the failure of the political strategy of the FIS. He planned his military actions from the maquis and had placed caches of food and arms in the mountains around Blida and in the Medea. Young FIS sympathizers living in the Islamist fiefdoms of southeast Algiers flocked to Chebouti.

But Chebouti was not only wise and farsighted; he was also a seasoned professional who wanted only qualified cadres. Fearing penetration by agents of the Sécurité Militaire, Chebouti employed rigorous recruitment criteria, which prevented him from using the thousands who were ready to fight. His short-lived leadership of the holy war against Taghut, the despotic evil one, gave way to newer, more democratic and less discriminating opposition movements.

The Groupe Islamique Armé was one. Known as the GIA, its new emirs accepted all who were willing to fight. They looked only for zeal and courage. At first, the test of commitment was killing a policeman, just as the FLN had tested its recruits when fighting the French. Later, it was to kill a member of the family.

The teaming population of young men in the Islamist sections of Algiers became a high stakes target for both the army and the Islamist opposition. They were forced to choose. The army could offer them a job, two year contracts, even though the pay was a pittance, and some protection. Later, the army would also promise the possibility of obtaining visas when their service was completed. Yet if a man joined the army, he risked being killed by the GIA when he returned home on leave. If he did not join the army, he risked being suspected by the police of sympathy for the terrorists. In 1992, kids in the crowded neighborhoods of El Harrach, Hussein Dey, Baraki, Kouba, Belcourt, Bab el Oued, Eucalyptus, and others saw greater safety in siding with the emirs. These people, they said, "knew what they were fighting for." On the streets, the mujahideen had a reputation for courage and inspiring fear in the police. In the years ahead, the GIA would dominate the attention of the international community by the savagery and boldness of its attacks.

There was no shortage of motives for the young to fight. Some wanted to avenge the riots of 1988. Others had been brutalized by the police or had had friends or relatives who suffered at the hands of the security forces. There were mundane and practical reasons: to make money, enjoy the booty of war, or to escape the suffocating curfew that kept them inside fetid apartment buildings whose corridors were filled with the stink of urine and feces. Into the ranks of the new mujahideen came a full gamut of recruits. There were unemployed university students, thieves and drug addicts, Afghan veterans from the fight against communism, ex-FIS members and office holders who had been stripped of their elected position, and converts to a cause that offered a sense of higher purpose—to fight for God by opposing tyranny and injustice.

Islamist ideology transformed anger into an instrument of sacrificial zeal. Boudiaf's orphans would find new fathers in the righteous authority of the emirs who were restoring order in the neighborhoods racked by theft and petty crime and social disintegration. They provided money and food for their supporters in the poor neighborhoods, transformed in 1992 and 1993 into "kingdoms," where the forces of order feared to go.

By the end of 1992, a curfew from 9:30 P.M. to 5:00 A.M. had been extended to eight *wilayas,* (or departments,) including Oran, Tlemcen, and Annaba, as well as Algiers and Medea. The age of criminal culpability for terrorist acts had been reduced from eighteen to sixteen. The corpulent general Mohammed Lamari of the Sécurité

Militaire had been put in charge of creating an elite antiterrorist unit of fifteen thousand men drawn from the army, gendarmerie, and national police. They became known as "the Ninjas" and were called into action for one purpose only—to destroy their target.

French researchers in the early 1990s interviewed two dozen families in the pro-FIS neighborhoods of Algiers to understand better the sociology of the violence. They found a youth that felt rudderless and isolated, whose parents had moved from the countryside, where the large extended family had once provided structure, security, and self-sufficiency. In the city, the acid of unemployment had been eroding traditional patriarchal authority. The collective rhythms and values of family life marked by religious celebrations counted for less; contact with other family members became sporadic; fathers were often absent. Urban living had brought on the feeling of breakdown in collective values, replaced by a sense of malignant individualism. "The young are without pity. They are only out for themselves," a twenty-three-year-old shopkeeper explained. Multiparty politics was seen as contributing to the breakdown. "We are all Algerians. Why do we need to have parties that divide us? Democracy is not an Algerian initiative anyway. These things were decided in France", a thirty-year-old *trabendist* told his French interlocutor.

Their heroes were the ascetic leaders, untempted by power and the things of this world. These were men like Ali Benhadj and other imams they considered "disinterested" in power. "The great jihad is for one's own soul." For many, the terrorist had become the defender of the community, fighting against injustice. The true elite were beyond the things of this world. Suffering ennobled. A twenty-eight-year-old produce vendor remarked, "Imprisonment, fear, hunger, deprivation, condemnation—these are the experiences that lead to paradise."

The researchers also found a deep gulf separating the old mujahideen, who had fought the French, and the new mujahideen, who claimed to be continuing the jihad of 1954. In April 1993, the assassination of a woman in the Eucalyptus neighborhood scandalized the "old men," as the veterans of the War of Liberation were sneeringly called by young Islamists. Karima, as she was known in the press, worked for the social and sports directorate of the Police de la Sûreté Nationale. In the local mosque, it was said she was an informer for the Sécurité Militaire and had compromised some young mujahideen. To the older generation, killing a defenseless woman was simply inexcusable. Her family depended on her salary. Killing mothers was ethically beyond the Pale.

The young found such old men laughably sentimental in their views about women. All threats had to be eliminated. Did they think women were incapable of killing? The FLN had used women effectively in their terror campaign during the Battle of Algiers. This was total war, to be fought without mercy. Their fathers conveniently forgot about the violence the government committed against the young Islamists and their suspected sympathizers. Walking on the street with a friend who was wearing a beard could get a young man taken to jail for interrogation. But for the old men, the young were treading a path that would plunge the country into a war worse than the one with France. They knew. They knew from experience that war can mask all kinds of crimes, especially in a society mined with social and economic inequality. Whereas the old men spoke of young kids who killed for money, jealousy, or blood lust, their children saw sincere, committed fighters for justice.

So the old mujahideen became suspects, too. Could they be trusted—even if they were their own parents? The old men had been outspoken. They thought the government had let things get out of control. It had been too lenient with the Islamists, who were guided by foreign ideologies from the Middle East. From the time of the cancellation of the elections in January 1992, the ONM, or the Organisation Nationale des Mujahideen, had consistently supported the government.

Gradually, these old men, heroes of the war of liberation, became suspected of collaboration with the enemy. A young man explained to a French researcher: "You can't trust the old men. They walk into a café say nothing, look at no one, and seem disconnected from the world. In reality, they are listening to everything. Afterward, they tell the police what they have heard. If a stranger comes into a village, they will tell the police. That's why they set one on fire with gasoline in M'sila. It was a warning to others, as well."

More than a source of informers for the police, the old mujahideen were an embarrassment to the Islamists. These old veterans had sacrificed and suffered, too. They had fought the fight. And their support legitimized the regime. The regime could be accused of usurping the revolution, but not the men who had lived in the *bled,* hunted and hungry. Their meager reward was to have free rides on public transportation and to be entitled to import a car without paying a customs tax. Yet these real mujahideen supported the government of apostates and neocolonial Francophiles. One who was interviewed, recalled: "I lived in the mountains for six years. There were days when I ate only leaves. Our revolution was different from today. What is theirs about? They have everything now. They have water piped right into the villages. We fought because we were starving to death. There, you see where the sheep sleep at night? That was our house before."

To the maquisards of the war of 1954–1962, the Islamic revolution had no justification. The Islamists simply wanted power. Their jihad was a jihad for power, not righteousness or defense of the faith. Without the benefit of having read the modern theories of Islamic revolutionaries or knowing what a Muslim apostate was, the whole business was an absurdity to them. "How can Muslims wage a jihad against other Muslims?" they asked.

How indeed can Muslims wage a holy war against other Muslims? By what authority can a Muslim declare another an apostate? Militants belonging to Takfir wal Hijra traced their authority from the Prophet himself. Members of this radical group had strongly condemned as blasphemous the FIS leaders who supported participation in the national elections of 1991. Western-style democracy was shameful, and divorced from God.

Takfir wal Hijra was organized in 1967, a radical offshoot of the Muslim Brotherhood, which was born in Egyptian torture chambers. The Muslim Brotherhood was founded in 1928 to combat through moral teachings and good works the secular influences on Islam coming from Europe. As their influence grew in the 1930s and 1940s, their adherents were persecuted and thrown in jail by King Farouk's security police, further radicalizing the movement. The prisoners told their tormentors they were not real Muslims. Real Muslims didn't torture people, they argued, and certainly not good Muslims, such as founder Hasan el Banna, who was murdered in 1949. Neither, according to Algeria's Takfir wal Hijra, are Muslims who rob the people, promote injustice, and disobey the laws of God. People have a right to overthrow tyranny. It was God's will that men struggle to redress wrongs and fight oppression. But how to wage the struggle?

The Koran is clear. Men should fight against oppression and injustice. But what is oppression? By what means should a good Muslim fight? Every Muslim knows the great jihad is the struggle to conquer oneself—to show forgiveness, rather than vengence, to control one's animal passions and lusts, to be aligned with the will of God in order to avoid the torments of Hell. By comparison, political and social struggles are merely "lesser jihads."

But how does a believer know in what precise form to follow God's will? When should a Muslim resort to violence? How does the believer know whether he is merely listening to himself or if he is listening to God? The Koran is forthright about the difficulty of knowing God's way. It says there are clear and precise parts, and there are ambiguous parts:

> *He has revealed to you the Book. Some of its verses are precise in meaning—they are the foundation of the Book—and others ambiguous. Those whose hearts are infected with disbelief follow the ambiguous part so as to create dissension by seeking to explain it. But no one knows its meaning except God and those steeped in knowledge who affirm—"We believe what is in it is all from God. But only those who have wisdom understand." (Sura 3:7.)*

"Whoever interprets the Koran according to his own meaning will have his place in Gehenna," the Prophet Mohammed said. God's law is not an à la carte menu from which to choose the easy bits, or the agreeable portions. All of it must be consumed, chewed over, and digested. The Koran has a literal meaning and an inner meaning. True understanding, the Prophet said, comes only from grasping both. There are traditional meanings for ordinary people who want simple rules. There are deeper allegorical meanings accessible to saints and thinkers. The meaning of the law presented in the Koran gives only general guidelines. These are explained and illustrated by the life and sayings of the Prophet. He is a living compendium of case history for the interpretation of the law. Thus, the written word (Koran), the recorded sayings (Hadith) and the actions (Sunna) of the Prophet are weighed, using scholarly consensus and inferential reasoning to draw conclusions.* The responsibility for this falls on religious scholars trained at the most prestigious schools of Koranic law—and who have achieved the status of mufti. Only a qualified mufti can issue a valid *fetwa,* the instrument for clarifying points of Islamic law to guide the conscience of believers.

Why, then, would God, man's commander in chief, send an instruction book that was not clear and simple for all His faithful believers to understand? The book was intended to be difficult. If it were as clear and simple as a glass of water, men would too easily rely on it, and become lazy, explained the twelfth-century Persian theologian Ibn Umar az-Zamakhshari. They would neglect that in which they are most lacking; namely, research, meditation, and reflection. The ambiguous parts act as a test. Wrestling with them separates those who are firm in their belief from those who are weak. God, Zamakhshari submitted, has great gifts for those who stimulate one another in their thinking. Through reflection and meditation comes deeper understanding of oneself and one's world. With the help of divine inspiration, a scholar of the law will discover the harmony that exists between the ambiguous and the clear. And this will serve to strengthen his faith further. For it is only through study, reflection, and prayer of the heart that one can attain knowledge of God and His unity. Those whose faith is weak and undisciplined follow the ambiguous parts. This gives them "free rein to innovate without having to harmonize them with the clearly determined verses."

But ambiguity is not necessarily bad, either, Zamakhshari reflected. The existence of verses whose meaning the savants cannot agree on, implies there should be latitude in interpreting the law. Ambiguity can provide room for growth, flexibility, and change.

*For example: "A judge may not judge in anger," the Prophet said. Nor, scholars concluded by inferential reasoning, should he judge when he was hungry or in need of urinating or otherwise distracted from calm, unemotional deliberation. For true savants, a lifetime of study, and proper orientation of the spirit is necessary to interpret the law.

10

Poyo

Whatever your hand finds to do, do it with might.
—Proverbs 9:10

Fittingly, growth and change were the subject of Christian's address in the Spanish village of Poyo in September 1993. Having the prior of a tiny, oddball monastery surrounded by Muslims give one of the keynote speeches at the General Chapter meeting was a bold move by the abbot general. It was as if the president of the International Chemical Manufacturers Association were to ask the head of a scarcely known little specialty company located in the Flathead Indian Reservation of Montana to address the CEOs of Dupont, Bayer, British Petroleum, Rhône Poulenc, and other prestigious corporations. With the help of gentle flattery and persistence, Bernardo Olivera had persuaded Christian to speak to the assembled superiors of much larger and more prestigious monasteries, many of which had been around since the twelfth century.

The Cistercian Order of the Strict Observance numbers 4,400 vocations worldwide in 170 communities throughout forty-three countries. The geographic concentration of the Order has shifted dramatically from the beginning of the century, when 80 percent of its monasteries were in Europe. By the 1990s, only 55 percent were European. Since 1980, twenty-three of twenty-seven new foundations have been outside of Europe, but most of these communities are small, averaging six to twelve men or women. The overall numbers in the Order have been slowly declining, though in 1993, women were entering the Order at a greater rate than men.

Poyo had been selected not only for the beauty of Galicia's emerald green mountains in northwestern Spain, but because there were three monasteries in the area. Together, these provided sufficient facilities to take care of the 170 abbesses and abbots who had come from around the world for their triannual meeting to discuss the state of the Order. Father Bernardo had asked Christian to give the main address. The abbot general recognized his talent for combining deep thought and provocative originality, and he knew Christian was capable of stirring people's thinking.

"I at first viewed the invitation to speak to you as something of a trap. I would have preferred to let the abbot general have the podium. But now I am to talk to you about the 'Cistercian contemplative identity,' an expression which, to be blunt, I don't much like.

"The phrase implies that contemplation yields something stable, an identity. But to my way of thinking, contemplation is either a form of continual searching or it is nothing at all. Here on this earth, it is a journey, a tension, a permanent exodus, the invitation to Abraham, 'Come follow me.' "

Christian reminded his listeners of the wisdom of Muslim mystics: He is not truly a Sufi who says "I am a Sufi." Couldn't the same be said for the contemplative? What would his neighbors in Tibhirine call him? Cistercian? Trappist? Monk? None of these words exist in Arabic. He was, he explained, simply a *roumi*—that is, a Christian. Viewed through his own points of reference, the Muslim neighbor thinks, He prays, he believes in God, fasts, and gives to the poor. He's almost like us!

"I come back now to the idea of letting our Brother Bernardo have a word. I had an ulterior motive in accepting his invitation, for now I can tell you about the dream our abbot general had when he visited us two years ago. In the dream, one monk was throttling another and saying, 'Fool, you're wasting your time in the Muslim world—go where you are needed and can grow. You're a deadweight to the Order.' "

Christian recounted Bernardo's response when he awoke from the dream he had had during his visit to Tibhirine. "You are here so your Cistercian way of life can be enriched by what you gain from the local culture. This process of inculturation does not happen without anxiety over losing one's own monastic identity. To avoid being overcome by this fear, the community must deepen and strengthen its own monastic culture." And that, Christian explained, was what they were trying to do in the Atlas. "We are learning that the trust shown, and the faithfulness demanded by our neighbors is God's gift to us—something to contemplate and which may inspire new forms of communion."

To the more basic charge of the nocturnal aggressor in Bernardo's dream—"you're wasting your time"—the abbot general wrote: "Their mission is one of a living, silent, and vibrant presence—that of Jesus in the Gospels. It is an opening of the heart to their Muslim brother, to help the monk be a better Christian, here and now. It is not a matter of reciprocity. The love of Jesus was gratuitous. It did not wait for a response. The monks have things to learn from the Muslims' own cultural and religious values. And the monks, in turn, can help awaken the contemplative side in the heart of each Muslim."

"The bishops of the Maghreb had posed a question," Christian continued, "in preparing a response to the *lineamenta* proposed for the 1994 synod. They asked. 'Does Algeria help you live out your religious consecration, and if so, how?' The answer is clearly 'Yes,' if *consideratio,* that word so dear to Saint Bernard, means reflection on actual experience lived. We have before us the lives of our neighbors, mostly simple religious people. It would be a scandal if we were not true to our vocation. They know what sharing is. Relationships and hospitality are very important to them. We practice it, too, and often receive lessons from them in how to do so. We live with them in a situation of insecurity and great confusion. This helps us feel connected to the human fabric, yet also separate from it . . . in the world, but not of it. We are insignificant and unknown."

Christian spoke to the question so often posed by visitors from Europe. " 'How can you live in a house so insecure?' they always ask. But how can one really be a contemplative in a house that is too secure and well provided? The order was begun by men of Cluny who left the stable comfort of Molesmes for a place called Cîteaux, a thorny wilderness full of wild animals."

"A few years ago, our bishops of the Maghreb issued a very nice pastoral letter in which they invited Christians 'to welcome something new that was being born in the region.' We should not forget that our Christian identity is always in the process of being born. It is a Paschal identity. Is it not the same for our Cistercian identity? Would we not cease to be contemplative if we were afraid to face new horizons? I mean, of course, modern horizons, but also the search for God beyond the well-worn paths of Christianity. And if Christianity is dying, could it not be to bring forth a new humanity which will need us as midwives?

"Our bishops said in another document: 'Turning toward the future, we foresee a broadening of our vision of man and of Jesus which will give rise to an intense interaction between Christian cultures and the questions posed by those of other traditions.' With this perspective in mind, it is becoming obvious that a monastic community cannot be established with prefabricated beliefs, because the contemplative life requires engaging with the customs, history, religious traditions, and real-life conditions in those lands of which we seek to be a part.

"Faced with the expansion of Islam in the world, it would be good for the monk to become an 'expert in Islam.' He has himself vowed his own submission to God, following the example of the Son's loving obedience to the Father. In this sense, Jesus is the only true 'Muslim.' "

When the General Chapter meeting ended, Bernardo received mixed reactions. People said either "Good" or "It was too much." The latter was a view usually expressed by the abbots of the big European monasteries, though not by the former abbot of Notre-Dame de Tamié. Father François de Sales told Bernardo afterward, "I drank in his words." As for the "It was too much" reactions, Bernardo never did figure out exactly what "it" meant. Was "it" the content of Christian's talk, his brazenness in calling Jesus "a Muslim," or the fact that he ended up being center stage two more times during the three weeks of the General Chapter?

He also had given a homily after Mass on September 14, a day of liturgical celebration: the Triumph of the Cross. Christian repeated a conversation he had had with a Sufi about the meaning of the cross.

"Let's talk about the cross," the Sufi said.

"Which one?" I asked him.

"The cross of Jesus, obviously."

"Yes, but which? When you look at the cross, you see an image of Jesus—but how many crosses do you see?"

"Perhaps three, certainly two," the Sufi replied, thinking a bit. "There is one in front and one behind."

"Which comes from God?" I asked him.

"The one in front," he said.

"Which comes from men?"

"The one behind."

"Which is the oldest?"

"The one in front. . . . God had to create the first one before man could make the second one."

"What is the meaning of the cross in front, of the man with his arms extended?"

"When I extend my arms, he said, "its for embracing, for loving."

"And the other?" I asked.

"The other cross is an instrument of hatred, for disfiguring love."

"My Sufi friend had said, "Perhaps three." This third cross—isn't it perhaps he and I and this common effort we are making to loosen ourselves from the cross of evil and sin behind, so we can bind ourselves to the cross of love in front? Isn't this just what is happening when a Jew, Yitzhak Rabin and a Muslim, Yasir Arafat, yesterday committed themselves by their revolutionary handshake to renounce finally the sword and to plow together in peace the hard soil they share? Isn't that gesture, the struggle of moving from hatred toward love, a third cross?"

Christian alluded to the verses in the Koran that speak of the death of Jesus. He interpreted them in his own particular way. " '*They [the Jews] did not kill him for certain. God lifted him up to Him. God is mighty and wise.*' Yes, by his death, his life was not taken. It was transformed. *'He was not crucified, though they thought they did.'* It was love, not nails, which attached him to the cross we carved for him. And it is love which draws us to Him when he pardons His executioners."

Christian did not tell his listeners that he had already translated this image of Jesus into a new crucifix for the chapel at Tibhirine. He had wanted one that was less offensive to the Muslims. For them, showing Jesus hanging dead and naked on a cross was scandalous. It conveyed a lack of respect for one of God's great apostles. For them, it was part of the incomprehensibility of the Christian faith, this notion of a God who would lower Himself to become a man and then allow His own son to be killed. The Three-in-One God does not fit Muslim ideas of God as one, as unifying all things. God is the integrator and Islam integrates God into all dimensions of life. There is no separate domain for Caesar. There is only one Legislator, and revelation regulates everything from the conduct of war to family life and business. There is no god but God. All else is idol worship.

Christian had commissioned an icon of Jesus on the cross from a hermit monk living near his home in the Aveyron using a new design that respected Muslim sensibilities. The crucifix showed Jesus with his crown of thorns removed, his body covered in a tunic of royal purple, the nails transformed into golden points of light, dignified face looking ahead, without suffering. Above Jesus' head were the words "He has risen" in Arabic.

And finally, to some of those present, the "it" that was "too much" might also have been the "little jihad" against the final summary of the proceedings, waged by Christian and superiors of the "young churches"—those monasteries less than fifty years old. They thought the conference report neglected the realites of the Third World and placed too much emphasis on the preoccupations of the big European abbeys. The emphasis on the problem of aging monks seemed laughable to them compared to the wars, terrorism, and famine in the world they inhabited.

They prepared a strong two-page dissent, placing other issues in the forefront. They described a shared feeling of deracination that came from living outside their own cultures, often amid great insecurity and poverty. They spoke of a continuous need for education aimed at creating a common vision and language within their multicultural monasteries. Most lived in situations of cultural ferment and believed the Western model had too strong an attraction, particularly among the young. The world of the young churches was one where a third of the population was typically under the age of fifteen and had gone directly from illiteracy to TV without learning to read. Local cultures were being eroded, making it difficult for the young to discover the things worth preserving that were theirs.

The young church dissidents emphasized their belief that the order's contemplative dimension must be a transcultural reality. They thought this reality had a prophetic quality, one that pushed them continually to go beyond themselves.

Following this General Chapter session, the Order would make the need to develop a "new anthropology" for the twenty-first century its priority, one that grappled with human diversity in its different cultural expressions, including religion.

While preparing to return to Algiers, Christian received word that two French surveyors had been killed at a fake checkpoint near Sidi-bel-Abbès, former home of the French Foreign Legion. They became the first foreigners to die violently in the eighteen months since the elections had been nullified.

11

God Is Great

There are illiterate men among them who, ignorant of the Scriptures, know nothing but lies and vague fancies. Woe to those that write the scripture with their own hands and then declare: 'This is from God' in order to gain some paltry end.

—Koran 2:77

On October 30, 1993, a month after the Poyo meeting, the GIA officially declared war on foreigners in Algeria. The announcement was made on letterhead with the emblem of the Koran overlaid with crossed swords. "Foreigners have thirty days to leave the country. If they do not, they are responsible for their own death." The signature was curious—"Abu Mariam," the father of Mary. The message had been delivered by three French consular officials who had been kidnapped the previous week by a GIA commando group and held in a suburb of Algiers. They were released near the diocesan residence of Bishop Teissier, with orders to publicize the warning.

The ultimatum expired December 1. The previous day, Christian had driven to Algiers to meet Amédée, who was returning from France. He stayed where he always did when he spent the night in Algiers—at the House of Saint Augustine. The cream-colored Art Deco mansion at the end of Chemin Beauregard, on the heights of El Biar, occupies a top seat in the amphitheater formed by the hills surrounding the harbor. Looking west from his terrace, he could see the Aurassi Hotel, a huge socialist shoe box built by the Egyptians, and the spires of the Mosque of Saint Raphael and the dome of the Mosque of the Jews, as the former church and synagogue were popularly called. Directly below him were the lush tropical gardens of the former St. George Hotel, now the Hôtel El-Djazair, where the allied generals had stayed while preparing the invasion of Italy. Looking east, he could see the Islamist fiefdoms of Mourradia, El-Harrach,

Hussein-Dey, and the great three-hundred-foot, rocket-shaped monument to the martyrs of the revolution.

It was a beautiful spot to think about his death. The *wali* of Medea had tried to convince Christian just two weeks earlier to accept some protection. He had proposed that police occupy one of the monastery's unused buildings. Christian categorically refused. He said that no weapons could be allowed in the monastery. Christian did agree to lock the doors at 7:30 P.M. and to allow no visitors after that hour. But he believed the presence of guards would attract the attention of the terrorists and compromise the monastery's position of siding with neither party to the violence—neither with the "brothers of the mountain," as he called the terrorists, nor with the "brothers of the plain" as he referred to the army. Christian had been reflecting on the writings of Etty Hillesum—a young Jewish mystic who died at Auschwitz. He had been thinking a lot about one passage in her journal: "If there is ever to be peace, it won't be authentic until each individual achieves peace within himself, expels all feelings of hatred for a race or group of people, or better, can dominate hatred and change it into something else, maybe even into love—or is that asking too much? It's the only solution."

Yet despite his insistence on always looking for the good in people, believing as he did that people can always change under the right influence, Christian knew that the GIA announcement increased the probability of his death. That night, he began in his small, neat hand a testament that would be published after his death. "If it should happen one day, and that could be tomorrow, that I am a victim of the terrorism which seems now to be engulfing all the foreigners living in Algeria, I would like my community, my church, and my family to remember that I gave my life for God and this country."

Christian would also have known that December 1 was the day in 1916 when Father Charles de Foucault was murdered in Tamanrasset by a Muslim who thought the Trappist monk was a German spy.

During the following two weeks, the GIA made good its promise. Its escalation to a total war against *le pouvoir* had to include foreigners. To be a foreigner in Algeria meant having a visa, and to have a visa meant the goverment wanted you for some reason. By killing foreigners, the image of Algeria would be further damaged abroad. Foreign investment and foreign aid would be harder to obtain. The GIA had done its moral duty: They had given fair warning.

In quick succession, a Spanish businessman was killed by GIA dressed as police at a checkpoint south of Medea, an Italian coral merchant and the Russian wife of an Algerian were shot in Algiers, and a British employee of Pullman Kellogg was gunned down at a gas station in Arzew, the huge petrochemical complex near Oran. A sixty-seven-year-old French pensioner was killed leaving his apartment in Laarba. Laarba, a town southeast of Algiers, marked one point on the base of the Triangle of Death, the apex of which was Algiers; Boufarik, in the Mitidja Plain, occupied the southwestern corner. The GIA got most of its recruits and did most of its killing in the Triangle.

But the killing of foreigners and other civilians needed to be seen by the new mujahideen as legal. They wanted to know that their killings would lead them to paradise and not to hell, where they would be condemned to drink boiling water and putrid blood. A *fetwa* had to be issued to justify the intentional killing of unarmed civilians. But a legitimate *fetwa* required a qualified mufti, and, if a mufti couldn't be found, then someone whose status as a religious savant was widely recognized.

Sheikh Mohammed Bouslimani seemed to be such a man to GIA supreme emir, Djaffar el-Afghani. Bouslimani was the fifty-seven-year old president of Irshad wal-Islah, a charitable Muslim association meaning Godliness and Reform. He was a respected religious figure who believed in having society governed by Islamic law. He had been a freedom fighter against France, became a proponent of Arabization after independence, and had been put in jail for criticizing the new socialist constitution of 1976. Bouslimani had opposed the FLN's claim to be the sole representative of the people. When competing political parties were made legal in 1989, Bouslimani joined the Hamas* party of his boyhood friend Sheik Mahfoud Nahnah, which was dedicated to building an Islamic state by peaceful means.

*The Algerian Hamas means Movement for Islamic Society (Harakat al Moujtama al-Islami)and is unrelated to the Palestinian Hamas party.

Bouslimani left his position of vice president of Hamas to dedicate himself completely to its social arm, Irshad wal-Islah. It had been originally founded as a clandestine organization and was a form of opposition through good works, to protest the FLN's claim of all inclusiveness. Irshad was known for helping women get out of the home by teaching them literacy and simple trades and by providing day-care services as well as basic parental guidance. Its other activities included giving food, money, or shelter to orphans, the poor, and the elderly and, in 1993, providing aid to victims of terrorism. Irshad was active in forty-five of the forty-eight *wilayas* of Algeria and its work was carried out by 150,000 volunteers. Bouslimani had acquired a national and international reputation as an Islamic thinker and man of faith, one also capable of organizing good works on a large scale. A *fetwa* from the sheikh would give a prestigious stamp of validity to the GIA's killing of civilians as part of its struggle against tyranny.

In the early morning of November 26, four men entered Bouslimani's home on the outskirts of Blida as he was reciting his preparatory prayers for *sobh,* the prayer of first light. Like Christian, he also had been warned by authorities that his life was in danger. They told him to go live somewhere else with a friend, but he chose not, in order to remain with his wife and community of followers.

Bouslimani's nephew came running out of the house when he heard the intruders jumping over the outer wall of their courtyard. In a loud voice, he told the men that his uncle was not home. The intruders entered the house anyway, but did not find Bouslimani, who had squeezed himself into in a small storage place. As the leader of the group was leaving, he had second thoughts, returned for another look, and found Bouslimani in his pajamas, trying to escape into the garden behind his house. Bouslimani's wife begged them not to harm her husband. "Don't worry, it is inconceivable that we would do harm to a sheikh or a religious savant," replied one of the men.

At first, the kidnapping was only for persuasion. Djaffar el-Afghani needed to issue a *fetwa* to legitimize the GIA's campaign of terror. But Bouslimani was adamant. He would not sign a *fetwa* that authorized killing innocent civilians. Police heard the same story several times from GIA prisoners.

Bouslimani's knowledge of the Koran was greater than that of his young kidnappers. His arguments against violence were persuasive and sowed doubt among them. And he was willing to die for his convictions. "I will give you all my blood before I will issue a *fetwa* which will justify the spilling of one drop of innocent Algerian blood" were the words that have become known as Bouslimani's last testament. His body was found in the local cemetery two months later, his throat slit.

If an honored sheikh such as Bouslimani would not read the Koran à la carte to justify civilian assassination, then perhaps a politically sympathetic imam would, one whose specialty was not theology but elocution, or the correct pronounciation of the Koran. That is how the GIA settled on Ikhlef Cherati to issue a *fetwa.* As far as the young and ignorant were concerned, an original FIS founder and professor would know what was legal or not.

Imams have no standing to issue a *fetwa,* not even such a sheikh as Bouslimani. Anyone who knows more than someone else about the Koran can be an imam to the one who knows less, and the GIA had many unlettered recruits. Thus began the destructive process of religious self-justification, using self-proclaimed imams or sheikhs whose authority extended only to those who chose to have their conscience assuaged by such "savants" of Koranic law.

The brothers were in a stupor as they mechanically sang the Office of None on Wednesday, December 15. Total war had struck at their doorstep the previous night. The words of Psalm 44 acquired an awful reality. *It is for You that we are being massacred all day long, that we are counted as sheep for the slaughter. Awake! Why do You sleep, o Lord! Do not cast us off forever.*

Near the village of Tamesguida, two miles from the monastery as the crow flies, was the construction camp of a team of Yugoslav engineers. They had been contracted by the state-run Hydroelectrica company to build a reservoir by drawing water from sources in the mountains opposite the monastery. Fourteen of them were in the common room watching TV after dark when forty men entered, armed with guns and knives. They were told to undress. Their hands were tied behind their backs with wire. The mujahideen knew from experience the superhuman strength that a man full of terror and adrenaline acquires. The Yugoslavs were led into a nearby wadi and told to kneel.

When the bodies were discovered, two men were found alive. Their throats had been imperfectly cut. They recounted how before each of their compatriots were killed, the executioner, as if to gather courage and reassurance, would shout, "God is great." They talked about the four men in the camp who had not been led to the slaughter. They were playing cards in an adjoining room when the terrorists entered and were only discovered after the others had been led away. As they were being tied, one, a Bosnian who spoke Arabic, declared, "I am a Muslim." He was told to recite the Muslim profession of faith. "There is no god but God, and Mohammed is his Messenger," he replied. "These three men are Muslims, too," he said, pointing to his three Catholic friends. The surprised mujahideen left the four men alone. The others were not asked to repeat the shahada.

"This time, the Massacre of the Innocents preceeded the Nativity," remarked Christian's friend Gilles Nicolas, a priest in Medea who had come up to the monastery to preside over the Mass in honor of the twelve dead. The Croats had a special place in the hearts of the monks. One half of the first contingent of twenty monks who came to Tibhirine in 1938 were Croats.

There were also Bosnians, Poles, and Hungarians who had come and gone over the years of construction, first of the tunnel through the Chiffa Mountains and then the hydroelectric project in the Tamesguida Valley. But the Croats had always been the core that stayed. Notre-Dame of the Deliverance in neighboring Slovenia was known to them. Some had even visited the monastery where the French Trappists had established themselves after leaving France in the 1880s.

The Muslim neighbors suffered, too. They felt humiliated at what had been done in the name of their religion. *Ça, c'est pas l'Islam.* Mohammed, Ali, Musa, and the others said repeatedly, "This is not Islam" whenever they saw the brothers. As proof of the folly, they cited a verse in the Koran: "Whoever kills another who has not killed or committed violence shall be seen as having killed all mankind." The insult was double for them—innocents had been killed, and the hospitality due guests had been horribly betrayed. These were family men. Many of the Croatians had not been home for over a year, had stayed on to finish their work despite threats, and had sometimes gone months without pay.

But there was a dark side to the Croat story unknown to the

monks. The "Yugos," as they were known to the locals in the valley, were not all simply lonely, hardworking family men. Among the more educated engineers were rougher characters, former prisoners sent along as manual laborers. There had been incidents that had fouled their reputation in the ultraconservative Medea. Some of them had harassed and insulted local women and gotten into fights that led to bloodshed. Rumors of all kinds circulated. The "Yugos" were perverts who got drunk, trafficked in pornography, and shot the Barbary apes to eat their aphrodisiac brains.

On December 19, Christian was called again to meet with the *wali* in Medea. The *wali* spoke with him about new security measures. He recommended the monks arm themselves and install sirens. He offered to put the brothers up at the Hôtel Grand Imsala in Medea. The government would pay for all expenses. His men would taxi them back and forth each day to the monastery. Otherwise, he told Christian, they should take a long vacation or risk collective suicide. Christian agreed only to have a second phone line installed and to lock the gates even earlier—at 5:30 P.M.

The community agreed with the *wali* on one point: They were not interested in a collective suicide. They did not want to go as sheep to the slaughter. If an alarm was raised by one of the monks, each should try to save himself. The brothers emerged from days of collective reflection and prayer with another consensus. If they left temporarily, or, as the *wali* suggested, took a long vacation, they felt they would probably never return. During their years of living together, they had built up a mutual dependence with the neighbors. The monks were conscious that they bore witness to a Christianity that was open and accepting of differences in the way people worship God. Their neighbors represented an Islam that was also accepting and respected them as they were. In all Algeria, only in the ultra-traditional Medea did church bells still ring without offending people. The monks and their Muslim friends had become like a married couple which, despite their differences, had grown together with time, seeing in "*la différence*" also "*la richesse.*"

12

Father Christmas

My face is flushed from weeping and on my eyelids is the shadow of death; although no violence is in my hands and my prayer is pure.

—Job 16:16–17

Christmas Eve was somber at the monastery as 1993 limped to an end. The murder of the Croats had cast a pall over the annual celebration that brought together local Muslims and a smattering of Christians. The latter were usually African students studying in Medea at the School of Public Administration or technicians who had been contracted to work on a government project. The dozen or more ex-Yugoslavs, as Christian called them after the breakup of their country, had become a regular part of the celebration.

The monks had always given the Croats the job of carrying the incense burners to the Nativity scene, where they would awkwardly wave them about in the role of adoring shepherds. Luc often said they actually looked like shepherds, with their rough faces, gnarly hands, and tender expressions as they approached the crèche. Afterward, they would join the other guests for hot chocolate in the *hôtellerie* and take up the challenge of trying to flirt with the nuns, speaking neither French nor much Arabic. Their numbers had lent a warmth to the celebration, and at the end of the evening, they would leave with a smile and small gifts of lavender, soap, or calendars in hand.

It was 7:15 in the evening. Michel had just rung Angelus the third time, following a late Vespers. Compline would be dropped to allow extra time for a midnight Mass, which was scheduled to begin at 10:45 and would be combined with Vigils. Paul was in the *hôtellerie,* talking about the Croats with Gilles Nicolas and three African students, when three armed men entered the front door wearing army uniforms. "Where is the Pope of the house?" the leader asked. He ordered Paul to go find him.

One of the intruders turned to Nicolas. "Don't you know me? I was one of your students at the university." While Paul went to find Christian, his former student tried to convince Nicolas that the monks should support their fight against the rotten regime. The young montagnard added reassuringly, "You have nothing to fear. You are religious people."

Amédée was going to the kitchen to make himself an herb tea made from linden tree leaves to help him sleep before Mass. On his way there, he saw a man in a khaki uniform and with a gun, leading Célestin and Paul across the inner courtyard. Amédée caught up with Célestin and asked in a whisper what the policeman wanted. "Can't you see, you fool, he's a terrorist!"

"You, everyone to the *hôtellerie,*" said the man, who turned toward Amédée and grabbed his sleeve. Amédée broke away, muttering that he had to close the main entrance gate, as he was circling back to go inside the cloister, he met Christian.

"*They* want to see you."

"I know. I am not in a hurry."

Amédée went in to the cloister and pulled the metal door behind him, leaving open a small crack that he could peer through.

They chose their time well, Christian reflected, as he walked to the *hôtellerie*. It would be quite a publicity coup to kill nine monks on Christmas Eve. But he felt outrage, not fear, when he saw men with weapons inside the building.

"No one has ever come with a weapon into this house of peace," he admonished the man presented to him as *le chef.* Christian turned the law on him. "Both your religion and mine forbid weapons in places of worship. If you want to talk here, you must leave your gun outside the building. Otherwise, we have to go outside."

The man followed Christian into the outer courtyard in front of the chapel, where the Virgin Mary stood with her arms extended in a gesture of welcome. He was thin and tall for an Algerian, made even taller by the Afghan turban covering his head, that complemented his bushy Islamic beard, dagger, and bandoliers. He chopped the air frequently with his hands during the conversation. After fifteen minutes, the two walked back to the *hôtellerie,* where another man joined them. Amédée was astonished to see both of them shake hands with Christian and then leave.

The incident was over by 8:00. Paul called it the visit of Father Christmas. When the montagnards had left, Christian returned to his room with Gilles Nicolas where he repeated the conversation he had just had with Sayah Attia, the executioner of the Croats, and the emir of all the combatants in the central region.

"We are religious, like you. We need your help, and you owe us your help." He had three demands. First, Luc was to go with them to take care of their wounded men.

"No, not that way. Luc is eighty years old. He has a bad heart and asthma. He will die if he goes. Send your wounded to the dispensary. Luc will treat them like everyone else." Attia demanded medical supplies.

"No, you can't take them, but they are available at the dispensary if your men need treatment." He wanted money. "The Church is rich."

"Who told you that? We have no money, and we are poor."

"You have no choice."

"Yes, we do. Anyway, we can't give you what we don't have. Ask the villagers. They know we live simply, only from the produce of the garden. You know the Koran. It is written that monks live modestly. That is why we are close to our neighbors." Surprised by Christian's intransigence, Attia walked with him back to the *hôtellerie,* where two of his men waited.

"I am going to send someone back here. What is your name?"

"Christian."

"Then his password will be 'Monsieur Christian.' Whatever my representative asks of you, you must give."

"Only as we have discussed, no more."

"Yes."

"You know," Christian added, "this is Christmas Eve. This is when we celebrate the birth of Jesus, the son of Mary, whom we call the Prince of Peace."

"Excuse me. I didn't know." Attia was taken aback by the reproach. As Christian reluctantly took their proffered hands, one of

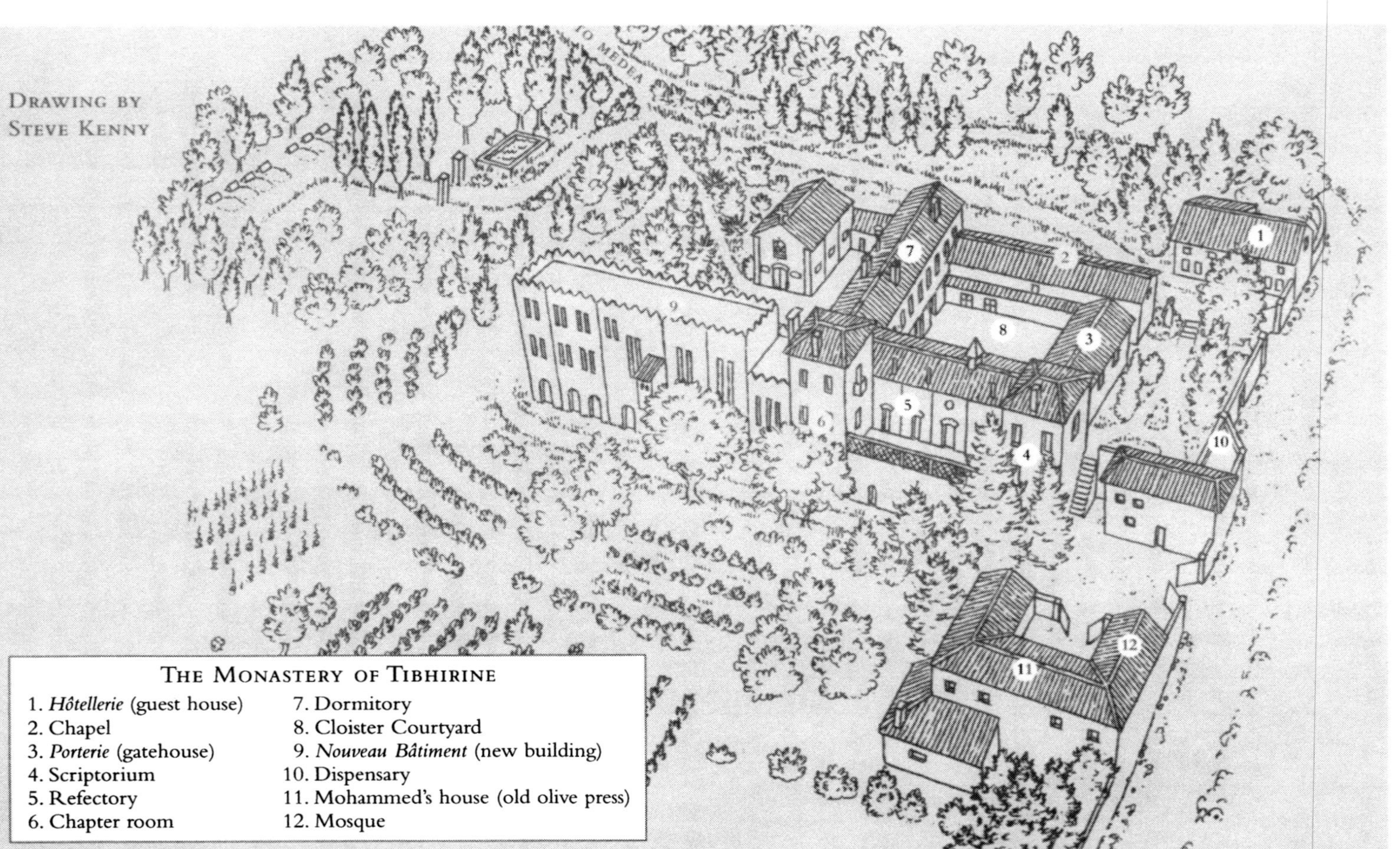
TO MEDEA
1
2
3
4
5
6
7
8
9
10
11
12
Drawing by
Steve Kenny
The Monastery of Tibhirine
1. Hôtellerie (guest house)
2. Chapel
3. Porterie (gatehouse)
4. Scriptorium
5. Refectory
6. Chapter room
7. Dormitory
8. Cloister Courtyard
9. Nouveau Bâtiment (new building)
10. Dispensary
11. Mohammed's house (old olive press)
12. Mosque

his men repeated, "You have nothing to fear. You are religious people. We don't consider you foreigners."

Christian was telling his story to Nicolas when Célestin suddenly burst into the room, completely unraveled. "I thought I was finished. I was in the corridor getting out the song sheets when I heard someone behind me. I shouted from shock. The man had a machine gun. He told me to look for the others. I took him to places where I thought they wouldn't be. Finally, he got mad and made me walk on my knees, with his gun in my neck. My God, I was terrified!"

Jean-Pierre had also thought his time had come. He had been in the sacristy, down the corridor from Célestin, when he heard whispering. He started to investigate, but a man appeared in front of the sacristy holding a Kalashnikov with one hand and Célestin with the other. The montagnard called Jean-Pierre by name, commanding him to come. "What is going on?" Jean-Pierre asked him. The montagnard didn't seem to understand his question or was too preoccupied with Célestin to answer, so Jean-Pierre simply returned to the sacristy to finish his work. He gathered together the chalice, cruets, and altar cloth and walked slowly to the chapel, eyes focused straight ahead, like a horse with blinders. "Jean-Pierre, come here!" he heard the man say again. Jean-Pierre kept walking until he disappeared into the chapel, expecting a bullet in his back at any second.

The only monk who had not been terrified by the evening was Luc, who slept through it all. He simply shrugged when Amédée told him about the incident.

After the intruders left, the ingrained rhythms of monastic life resumed. Mass was celebrated as scheduled. The ringing of bells brought Christophe and Philippe out of the empty wine casks in the basement under Christian's room, where they had hidden when they heard Célestin shouting. They were amazed, and a little ashamed, to find their brothers still alive, attending Mass as though nothing had happened.

Christian did not immediately tell the community of Attia's specific demands. He thought they should at least enjoy Christmas Day without additional worry. Instead, he would tell them at the regular chapter meeting on the twenty-sixth. These took place three times a week in the chapter room in the east tower, facing the mountains. The meetings were the family hour when the brothers talked about problems such as the water shortage, or engaged in communal reflection on some subject, discussed matters of general importance to the community or sought forgiveness from one another for wounds and slights. They sat around a big square table covered with a Berber cloth. A Rubelov reproduction of Abraham and the Three Visitors looked down from a barren wall while Christian presided. Arranged around him, always in the same order, were seated clockwise: Luc Célestin, Christophe, Michel, Paul, Jean-Pierre, and Amédée.

The demand for money was the most worrisome. The monks knew from the conversation with the men in the *hôtellerie* that these were the same men who had assassinated the Croats. They could not let themselves become entangled with assassins. The majority wanted to depart immediately, that night, to avoid being compromised. They expected Attia's representative to return at any moment. Giving medical aid was not the same, by their reasoning, as giving money. One was an act of humanity; the other was an act of collaboration.

"The GIA is not my boss," Jean-Pierre protested stubbornly. He had come to Algeria to follow Jesus Christ. Jesus Christ was his Master, and He did not preach abandoning the flock when there was danger. "If we leave in this manner, we will never come back," Jean-Pierre argued. "We will have broken our bond with the villagers." Christian reminded the brothers that one night had already passed and no one had come.

Bishop Teissier arrived three days later to discuss the situation. Christian had phoned him about the community's vote to leave for a safer place, at least temporarily. Of the four bishops in Algeria, the bishop of the diocese of Algiers was primus inter pares and was recognized by Muslims and Christians alike as the head of the Algerian Church. Teissier was worried about the impact a sudden departure could have on the Christian community in Algeria.

Henri Teissier had been bishop of Algiers since 1980, when Duval became archbishop. He had come from Aix-en-Provence and spoke fluent classical Arabic. Anywhere else, Teissier could have been taken for a banker or an insurance salesman. Sitting in the chapter room, wearing his gray business suit and tie, he spoke quietly and soberly, saying he needed time to explain the situation to the rest of the Christian community. The monks were too well-known throughout the country. If they fled without warning, it might cause the remaining Christians to panic. He wondered about the effect on their neighbors in the village—the ties they had created with them, their good opinion of the monks. Could they just leave them all of a sudden? Poverty, yes, that, too, has different forms. Wouldn't it be a poor showing indeed to leave, but with a little lifeboat in Algiers or Fez, when the neighbors have none? What kind of a lesson in poverty is that . . . to be poor only as long as it's convenient to be poor? he wondered out loud. If they definitely wanted to leave, Teissier wished that it be gradual.

Christian asked his brothers to reflect on what their bishop had said, and to decide according to what gave them the most peace. Each was to meet privately with him that evening to tell him the decision before reconvening in the chapter room the next morning. As each brother talked to Christian after Compline, they all had a similar response: "I am not at peace with the decision to leave."

The next day, Michel, as he usually did when important decisions were to be made, took the candle from in front of the wooden icon of Mary, lit it, and placed it in the center of the table. Christian said nothing to sway the brothers in any direction. Each in his turn expressed a few quiet words of reflection and resolution. Their lives and those of the community around them were at stake. They all sensed that somehow the monastery protected Tibhirine. Violence had struck all around, but not in the village itself. Though they had voted solidly FIS, no villager had ever joined the GIA. If they were to leave, they felt sure the military would take up positions in the monastery. They were certain that an armed presence there would only bring violence into Tibhirine and endanger lives.

Fear wrestled with a sense of responsibility, calling, and the duty of obedience. As each man expressed his view, the vow of stability kept returning as the touchstone of their thinking. Stability meant they were bound not only to a specific place, but to persons—to their neighbors and to one another. One brother recalled Father Scotto's simple explanation of stability: "You stay here with us." A consensus developed against an immediate departure. If necessary, they could all go to Fez, but stability meant staying together.

They decided, however, that Philippe Ranc, still a novice and not yet stabilized, should return to Strasbourg and finish his seminary studies. Paul's mother was ill, and he wanted to return to Savoy for a few weeks' rest. Though outwardly calm, he had been badly shaken by the intrusion. All the horrors of his wartime experience, when he had been a paratrooper, came back to him. Célestin had been terrified to the bone and had a heart condition that needed to be checked.

Cardinal Duval telephoned to give his moral support. "The whole Church of Algeria is with you." Christian asked his advice. "Be steadfast, persevere." And how should they act toward their visitors? "Be firm with those people," Duval answered. The conversation had lasted only two minutes.

Meanwhile, Christian had prepared a letter to be given to Attia's representative should he appear when Christian was absent from the monastery.

Brother

Permit me to address you this way, man to man, believer to believer. You made a point of expressing your peaceful intention. I want to believe you. We would ourselves like our community to be only that: a symbol of peace and in the same manner as our brother, the doctor, who for fifty years has always been at the service of all people day and night and is so, still today, despite his age and bad health.

It is for that same reason that we are unable to take sides in this current conflict which rages in the country. Our position as foreigners forbids it and our status as monks (ruhban) *binds us to the work God has for us, which is prayer, a simple life of manual labor, hospitality, and sharing, especially with the poor. We have no connection to any government or embassy, except for those legal obligations required of all émigrés. Those who know us can testify to this. Each of us chooses to live here of his own free will. We are committed to our calling until death. I don't think it is God's will that this death come from your hand.*

We are conscious of having received much from Algeria and this

Islam which stimulates believers to compete in good works until the day we see God. If one day the Algerians decide we are a burden, we will, with much sadness, respect their wish and leave. I know we will continue to love them all, including you.

How will you get this message? I don't know. I had a need to write you today. Please forgive me for having written in my native language. You understand.

May the one God of all guide us!
Amin.

Christian sent to Gérard, his youngest brother, another letter. It was the one he had begun in Algiers on December 1, when the GIA declared open season on foreigners. His instructions to Gérard were that it not be opened until his death.

As each new day passed with no representative asking for Monsieur Christian, fear seeped slowly into the underground of the monks' subconscious during the day, rising again in the evening. "When it got dark, the fear hung over us like a dark cloud," Jean-Pierre remembers.

They suffered together, exhausted by nervous tension. None of the brothers could sleep soundly at night. For Luc, though, it was asthma that kept him awake and forced him to sleep in a chair, when he slept at all. Like an iron lung, the external rhythms and duties of monastic life pulled them through the darkest aftermath of the crisis. "It's magnificent, this orderliness and regularity," Christian told a group of Belgian sisters months later when retelling the story. "One simply continues to do the things one has to do."

In February, the army reported the death of Sayah Attia, along with several of his men. Attia had been responsible for killing the Croats, who in his eyes had been guilty on two accounts. They were foreigners who had been warned to leave Algeria, and their Christian countrymen in Bosnia were killing Bosnian Muslims. Word circulated that Attia had suffered for nine days from painful wounds after being ambushed by the army. Yet none of his men came to the dispensary for help. Christian felt that some strange bond had been created between them on Christmas Eve. He thought he had disarmed him with brotherly love. But he also understood how to talk to aggressors, to be firm without being aggressive himself. A rumor went out that Attia had given his *aman,* or personal guarantee of protection, to the monastery.

There was plenty of blood on the hands that shook Christian's on Christmas Eve. The newspaper accounts said that he was the emir of the central region from Medea to Tissemsilt and had been responsible for over 200 terrorist attacks and 132 assassinations. These included an assault on an army casern that killed eighteen soldiers, the murder of the police chief of Ksar El Boukhari, the ambush of a gendarme patrol near Medea, and the assassination of the *wali* of Tissemsilt. The day before the intrusion at the monastery, Attia had killed a Spanish businessman on the road to Berrouaghia, south of Medea.

The daily newspaper *El Watan* called the former construction foreman a "bloodthirsty killer without any faith or law." He had been arrested after the strike of 1991 and jailed for three months. A doctor who saw the bodies of Attia and his men said their noses and ears had been cut off, a sign that they were considered sons of *harkis,* Algerians who had fought alongside the French in the war of independence. And even if he wasn't, the army was accustomed to slandering the GIA by saying it was full of sons of *harkis,* an epithet synonymous with traitor in postwar Algeria.

When Christian read about Attia in the Algerian press, he decided to become his intercessor. "I felt I was my brother's keeper, even of the brother in front of me that night. As his keeper, I should be able to find in him more than that which he had become." At a retreat in Algiers, Christian gave three reasons to justify his intervention before the final judge: "He didn't slit our throats; he came outside when I asked him and then didn't return for Luc even when he was wounded; thirdly, he excused himself when I told him he was disturbing our celebration of the birth of the Prince of Peace."

Coping both collectively and individually with fear brought the brothers into profound communion with one another. Like their divine mother, Mary, at the time of her visitation from Gabriel, they also had listened and received. The words they sang and the activities that ordered their lives seemed to guide them, as if telling them what to say and do. "The word has taken this community of flesh and blood, saying, 'Here, today, now,' " wrote Christophe in his journal. "The psalms give us strength in the face of violence, anxiety, and injustice. Yes, we have enemies. And it would be hard for us to say too quickly that we love them without offending the memories of all those who have already died. Oh God, help us!"

Christian understood this difficulty with forgiveness. He and Christophe thought much alike. Yet he was upset when he was told by the *wali* that the bodies of some of the terrorists had been dragged by Jeeps through the streets of Medea. The *wali* defended the exhibition of the bodies. The terrorists were "filthy beasts." Christian reproached him. With that kind of thinking, he said, the cycle of violence would never be broken. The *wali*'s remark was a wound that went to the heart of Christian's faith. All men are created in God's image. God is present in all his children, including killers. It is never too late for his children to come home, to become infants of God. Without gratuitous love, the bloody engine of reciprocal murder would never stop.

He knew that from the war. Without a belief in God's presence in all his creatures, no matter how dim the spark might seem, men lose their humanity. They become mere labels, and abstractions, which are easier to kill—Arab, European, Muslim, Christian, terrorist, racist, fascist, and beast. He knew it as a Christian. If you love only those who love you, what have you accomplished? Even the despised tax collector can do that, the Lord reminded His disciples.

13

In God's Hands

We are hard-pressed on every side, yet not crushed; we are perplexed but not in despair . . . carrying about in the body the dying of the Lord Jesus that the life of Jesus may be manifested in our body.

—2 Corinthians 4:8–10

In their simple, intuitive way, the villagers always knew everything. They knew each monk's weaknesses and foibles, and they knew his fear. They knew giving in to fear was contagious. "If you go away, you will rob us of your hope, and we'll loose ours," Musa told Christian after he learned Célestin and Paul would leave for France.

Mohammed needed consolation. "You have a door to leave from. We have no door, no way out. This was the best corner of the whole *wilaya,* even all Algeria, and now . . ." He remarked on the contrast between the active protesting of French fishermen in Brittany that he had seen on TV and their own passivity. "We are frozen in fear. There is nowhere to turn. We are alone. Children are traumatized. My little twelve-year-old daughter wants to wear a veil now," he told Christophe.

At a chapter meeting, Amédée spoke of "compassion and good humor" as the best response to the gloom of their Algerian friends. Toward the end of January, Jean-Pierre had been assigned the reading at lunch. His subject was taken from an article by Milena Jesenska, a Czech. It was entitled, "The Art of Standing Up." "The essence of anxiety is not being able to stay put. By simply standing still, I face calmly the unknown . . . but in order to do that I need strength. And this strength is possessed by an individual only so long as he doesn't separate his lot from that of the others. He can't loose sight of the essential thing, that he is an intimate part of a community."

Jean-Pierre's reading struck a cord. All the brothers knew, each in his own way, that the strength they found to keep going came from one another; from their neighbors, without whose friendship they couldn't remain; from their bishop, who visited them regularly; from abbots in France who called every Sunday; and from Him, in whose steps they followed. "What holds us here is not our Christian values, but the relationship to Christ," wrote Christophe in the journal he had started in the fall of 1993.

The neighbors were cheered up when Paul returned from the Savoy the day before Luc's eightieth birthday. He brought back strawberry shoots from his mother's house, welding rods, and other things that were impossible to get in Algeria, as well as a hearty cheerfulness. "Something happened while he was away. He made peace with himself," Jean-Pierre recalled.

Christophe was also making peace with himself—seeing his flight into the basement on Christmas Eve as a night of rebirth. The brothers had agreed earlier that day that each should try to save himself if a warning cry went out. Yet Christophe had felt embarrassed, or at least silly, at his cowering in the dark for hours after the terrorists had left, while the others were quietly going about their regular duties. The darkness and silence of the empty cask was "a period of gestation, and an ascent from the abyss." In his "wooden womb," Christophe reflected later, "I was born again on December 24. I have to convert . . . to become an infant. You pulled me out of the grave in order to live by You, with You, and in You. You, Your care, Your anxiety, Your agony—that is now ours."

Christian also began to change. Consultation and consensus replaced his tendency to make decisions alone. He moved his bedroom from upstairs in the dormitory to his office on the ground floor in order to sleep closer to Amédée and Luc, whose bedroom was also the medical supply room. To overcome past feelings of neglect by some of the brothers, he set aside Sundays to be available for individual consultations. He particularly enjoyed talking with Luc, whose age and experience made him something of a father figure. Luc had been one of the bricks holding the community together during the Christmas panic.

Luc had seen it all before. He had told the story more than once in the chapter room, until it had been finally tape-recorded.

It was dusk in August of 1959 and one of the monks had just

Drawing by Brother Christophe

But in the heart of the night, here comes the morning star

rung Compline. In the fading light, Amédée saw a platoon of French soldiers enter the courtyard from behind the chapel. When he went to greet them, he discovered they were rebels in French paratrooper uniforms. "We need to talk with your superior," the commander told him. An imam had been arrested by French soldiers for his inflammatory sermons at the mosque in Medea. On his way to prison in Algiers, the imam was shot while trying to escape. The commander had orders to retaliate by taking the abbot of the monastery prisoner.

Abbot Frikert was firm when he arrived to meet the soldier. "None of my monks go! You will have to shoot me first." The commander was conciliatory, but he was in an impossible position. He had his orders. And he would be shot himself if he didn't carry them out. Someone else would come, he explained, someone less sympathetic to the monks. Frikert asked young Amédée to call the other monks. Matthew arrived first. Matthew was an Italian and was known for his sympathy to the rebel cause. He volunteered to go. Then Luc showed up. He was a doctor and had been making house calls on people throughout the area for years. Luc shrugged phlegmatically and said he, too, would go with Matthew.

The commander of the platoon decided two monks for one abbot would be acceptable to his sector chief. "Don't worry, you will not be hurt," he assured them. When the commander extended his hand in a congratulatory gesture, Luc refused to take it. He and Matthew marched ten to fifteen miles at night through the mountains and hid during the day, making a large circle around the monastery. Their stoicism and humor impressed their captors, who gave them native *abayas,* long cotton robes worn by the peasants. They thought Luc would make a good Muslim. The commander had his men bring the monks fresh fruit from the markets. But the marching all night, hiding during the day in cramped spots, and lack of sleep was slowly ruining their health. Luc's asthma made the trek especially difficult. One day, a new man joined the *fells*. He was astonished to recognize Luc. "You are crazy to have this man. He has cared for people all throughout the area, including myself." The commander didn't know that he had in his midst a doctor who had delivered babies and treated the sick throughout the Medea.

Fifteen days later, the commander gave two weak and emaciated monks a bus ticket, told them to report evidence of the French use of napalm, and left them near a road. The bus ticket wasn't needed. A French military truck picked the two men up and took them in for interrogation. Afterward, Matthew returned to Italy; the asthmatic Luc went to France, where he spent three months recuperating.

Christian knew that the presence of the *toubib,* as the doctor was known locally, gave the monastery practical value to the people in the region. Luc's services were in demand by everyone. Men trusted him, and women were even allowed to visit him alone. He saw at least fifty patients a day, taking care of them in his abrupt, often short-tempered way. The women aggravated him, especially the older ones, who constantly pestered him for clothes and money. Yet Luc had a reputation for caring about women. He helped them with material things, gave advice, and dispensed lots of sugar water for their nonspecific, psychosomatic complaints.

For the women and young girls, Luc had become a confidant, holy man, and healer, and an excuse for women to get out of the confinement of their *gourbis*—simple houses of mud and dung with a walled courtyard. He wore old slippers, a rumpled-looking *taguia* that looked more like a sleeping cap, and a long, grubby gown. His air of poverty and the simplicity of his dispensary made the visitors feel at ease. Luc's rough directness and sweet-and-sour manner was like their own. Everyone knew the *toubib* had a kind heart under his prickly exterior.

But even those who knew him well had been mystified by his decision to become a monk. It was completely unexpected and is still difficult for anyone to explain—except to say that God called him. His family was dumbfounded. His father, a shoe manufacturer in Valence, from whom he had inherited his short temper, was outraged when he learned his son had abandoned a promising medical career.

Tall, lean, and handsome with his King George beard, Luc, then Paul Dochier, was well liked around the new and prestigious La Grange Blanche Medical School in Lyons. He was a good student, gregarious, and had a touch of the bon vivant about him. Although not a libertine by any means, he was a good man to go drinking with, and an amusing storyteller, whose passions ran to rugby, cars, cooking, and Chopin.

Luc was known as an excellent diagnostician, and he had been allowed, along with a few other outstanding students, to start his internship during the last six months of medical school. When his classmates met in April for their last unit assignment before graduating as the class of 1937, Luc was not present, nor did anyone have an idea of his whereabouts. "There were no signs of a tormented soul or internal struggle in Luc. Actually, there was little outward sign that he had any interest in religion," recalled Dr. Paul Grenot, a former classmate living in Lyons who had remained in touch with Luc over the years, and sent him medical supplies regularly. "He surprised us all."

When Luc knocked on the door of the monastery at Aiguebelle, he was told by the abbot to finish his medical studies first. Luc went back to Lyons, where he finished his degree at a different hospital. Afterward, he performed his required military service and was assigned duty as an army doctor in Goulimine, in southern French Morocco. In June 1941, France fell to the Germans, and Luc went back to Aiguebelle to begin his new career as a monk. "Something about Morocco attracted him. The lure of the desert was part of it, but the people of the Maghreb are very seductive, with their open, friendly hospitality, and faith," Grenot mused in the sunny reception room of his pensioner's apartment decades later.

The Vichy government had an agreement with Nazi Germany that allowed an able-bodied man to substitute himself for a prisoner who had dependents at home. In the spring of 1943, Luc had volunteered to work in a German prisoner of war camp, on the condition that he be assigned to OFLAG #7, an officers'camp in the Ruhr, where his brother-in-law was being held, along with thousands of Russian prisoners whom he was assigned to treat. While he was away, his family's house in the Drôme was burned down by the German army. A carbon portrait of Luc drawn by an appreciative Russian soldier is the only picture remaining of the young doctor–novice.

Luc returned to Aiguebelle after the war in order to be the humblest of the humble, a *frère convers*. There were advantages to his love of humility. Father Dominique at Aiguebelle remembered him: "Luc was very independent. He had few needs. His bohemian side didn't like to be bothered by little details like going to the Offices. He couldn't sing, and the services were not so important to him anyway. He preferred to express his faith in his own way, which was being of use to others." Luc wanted to serve the poorest of the poor. In the France of 1946, these were French Muslims in Algeria. In August, Luc began serving the Algerian poor of the Medea from his new home in Tibhirine.

Forty-eight years later, on January 31, Luc entered "the club of eighty." Henri Teissier came up from Algiers for the occassion, as did Gilles Nicolas from Medea. After dinner, Christian toasted Luc as *l'homme des contradictions*: a mystic with his feet on the ground, irritable and yet tender; a learned, voracious reader and a simple *convers,* an asthmatic who spent his days trudging back and forth from the dispensary to his room, where he kept his supplies; a pessimist who saw a bleak future in Algeria, and an optimist who trusted that death was "to bathe in the infinite tenderness of God."

Luc was also a man of pithy thoughts and few wasted words. His greatest regret was not to be able to do more for others; his favorite saint was "the good thief"; the greatest sin for a Christian was not to believe in the Resurrection; to be Christian was to "perfect love," his most fervent prayer was to die without hatred in his heart.

Luc's own remarks that night were practical. He wanted to arrange the manner of his own last rites: In the case of a violent death, there was "nothing to be done." In the case of a slow one, he wanted his friends to gather around his bed and read the parable of the prodigal son, say the Lord's Prayer, and open a bottle of champagne. On the day of his burial, he wanted them to play an Edith Piaf tape he had made: *Non, Je ne Regrette Rien*. Luc had no regrets. After dinner, he went to the *hôtellerie* where the neighbors had prepared an additional celebration in his honor.

That night, Christophe sat in his room with tears in his eyes, listening to Dvořák's *Slavonic Rhapsodies,* thinking about Luc's words at the chapter meeting, about Tibhirine and its mysterious ability to resist war and terrorism. "To resist evil," he wrote in his diary, "is to resist the world, to resist the world is to pursue political solutions when the politicians have given up on them . . . to not give in to the spirit of gloom and pessimism in a world full of mourning. The sole force to rely on, which is inexhaustible, is that of infancy. Only the spirit of the infant, of the new beginning, can renew the world."

In February, Robert, the hermit, started sleeping at the monastery. He had found his hermitage destroyed one day after selling honey at the market in Medea. Some thought the military was responsible; others said the terrorists. Mohammed told Christian that the head of a young boy had been found in the marketplace in Medea. Gilles Nicolas came to celebrate Mass one day, and afterward he told the brothers that two policemen had been killed in Medea and stores pillaged.

Célestin had better luck in France. He would have died had he not had his massive heart attack while undergoing tests at the hospital in Nantes, one that required a sextuple bypass. His brush with death brought forth an avalanche of mail from well-wishers. Stripped of six veins, Célestin's legs had become showpieces, and he displayed them at any opportunity.

Life in Tibhirine, meanwhile, went on as before. The garden continued to be a place of communion with the neighbors. Christophe was touched when four-year-old Amin, the son of Ben Ali had called him "*mon frère*." Mouloud, the wise fool from Medea, who liked to wear a homemade crown of flowers, still came to visit him. He was young, silly, and kindhearted, and the brothers were touched by his way of coming unpredictably to attend the Offices, where he would usually stand beside Christophe and give a military salute before bowing his head in silence. He liked to sing along, too, but he usually held the psalmbook upside down.

All the brothers had heard about Musa's reply when Christian had observed to him that the monks and the villagers were like birds on a tree. "Yes, you are the branch and we are the birds." Amédée and Jean-Pierre continued to be invited to attend the marriages, funerals, and religious celebrations in the villages. They were especially in demand for the rite of circumcision and the popular Festival of Abraham, when a sheep is killed and divided among friends, family, and the poor.

The number of visits to the dispensary increased steadily, reaching a hundred a day. More patients came with ulcers and high blood pressure, in addition to the regular ailments of eye infections and parasites. The lines would form well before the opening hour of 7:30 A.M., even on the Friday Sabbath, since Luc chose to keep instead the Christian Sabbath. All who came to the dispensary were treated, no ID required and no questions asked. "A sick person is neither a terrorist nor a soldier; he is a sick person," he would say if anyone wondered about the wounded men who came from time to time.

In March 1994, a letter from the ministry of foreign affairs was sent to the papal nonce in Algiers demanding that the monastery be closed for security reasons. The *wali* of Medea had washed his hands of responsibility for the monks' safety. He had wanted to post guards at the monastery, and he even sent a detachment of ten soldiers to occupy the new building, from where they could periodically fire their rifles into the air to show their presence. The brothers categorically rejected this. "If you stay here, you will only attract attention that will compromise our position. Anyway, we don't allow arms in the monastery," Christian told the officer in charge. The villagers repeated the same message, telling the soldiers that having weapons in the monastery was *haram*. After camping outside the monastery walls for forty-eight hours, the soldiers departed, but they did leave behind a portable phone, which was installed in the dispensary.

The monks were very appreciative of the *wali*'s goodwill and anxiety about their safety. "He also understood our desire not to desert our neighbors and to maintain our solidarity with them," Jean-Pierre acknowledged much later. Shared risk and shared suffering bound the monks and their Muslim friends together. That bond would be broken if they left. The nonce, a Zairean, finally replied to the foreign ministry, pointing out that the monastery was like a house built on the top of a mountain with cliffs on all sides. Where should they move? he asked.

To help him prepare for an upcoming African Synode, Bishop Teissier had asked Christophe's reaction to its theme, "Mission of the church: to promote evangelical relations with Muslims." Christophe, who was known to be Christian's choice to succeed him as superior, did not like the word *promote*. Promoter of what, he wrote in his journal—of values, products, ideas, moral systems? Such an enterprise was doomed to failure, he thought. Competition in the marketplace of religion is simply too treacherous a territory. Are there not numerous paths to the top of Mount Fuji, paths that cross and can help others arrive at their goal? Yes, God really spoke to man through Jesus Christ, and this message should be heard by all. But "really" isn't the same as "only." Christians can be totally attached to Jesus and yet open to the possible divine messages in the other religions. Or are Christians incapable of that? Christophe wondered.

Were Muslims capable of the same openness that Christophe was asking of his own faithful? The question divided Muslims as well as Christians. Algerians who wanted the answer to be yes had picked May 8 as a day of protest against two years of bloodletting and *mutisme*. *Mutisme*—to say nothing, to hear nothing, and to know nothing—had become the only way to survive. It had become common to see mutilated bodies lining the streets of Algiers like so many dead cats. The incidence of ulcers and heart failures were of epidemic proportions.

The cautious took different routes to work each day. Alert pedestrians crossed over to the other side of the road if they were followed by someone for more than twenty-five yards. A hand reaching in a shirt pocket was a menacing gesture. Girls were killed for not wearing veils; others were killed for wearing them. Parents gave their daughters suicide pills in case they were captured by the GIA and forced into sexual slavery. Kiosk vendors were threatened by local emirs for selling Algerian-brand cigarettes, whose sales tax supported *Taghut*, were threatened by the police if they did not sell them. Many kiosks simply closed. Expressing a desire for peace and reconciliation in an atmosphere of *mutisme* was courageous. Reconciliation and tolerance were sentiments that could be viewed by the "eradicators" on both sides as sympathizing with the enemy.

On the day of the protest, the three-story Turkish mansion on rue Ben Cheneb opened as usual at one o'clock in the afternoon, despite all the commotion and crowds outside. The house had been donated to the diocese by a local businessman and converted into a place for students living in the overcrowded apartments of the Casbah and neighboring Bab el-Oued to work in peace and quiet. The elegantly tiled reading rooms on the main floor were less full than usual that day when Sister Paul-Hélène went to answer the doorbell. The two policemen she greeted wanted to talk with the director. As she led them into his office, one of the men shot Henri Vergès in the face as he rose from his desk. Then he shot Sister Paul-Hélène in the neck.

14

Descent into Hell

Those that make war against God and His apostle and spread disorder in the land shall be put to death or crucified or have their hands and feet cut off on opposite sides, or banished from the country. . . . They shall be sternly punished in the hereafter, except for those who repent . . . for God is forgiving and merciful.

—Koran 5:34

"A brigade of the Armed Islamic Group killed two crusaders who have been spreading evil in Algeria for many years," read the communiqué published on May 13, 1994, in the London-based *El Ansar,* which was the GIA mouthpiece. Rahab Kebir, the FIS spokesman in exile in Germany, issued a statement saying, "The murder of religious men and women is contrary to Islamic law." Many dismissed this disavowal by the FIS as political smoke. A popular imam in the Casbah condemned the assassination and a few days later was himself killed.

The assassination of Father Henri Vergès and Sister Paul-Hélène Saint-Raymond was a shock to Algerians of virtually all stripes. The attack was the first on a representative of the Church since 1976, when Duval's vicar was stabbed in the thigh. Henri Vergès' murder struck Christian especially hard. Henri had been a regular member of the *ribat* and a close friend. The two men even looked alike. Both had high forehead, elongated, pointing-finger nose and lean, bespectacled face. A Marist brother, Vergès had been active in the *ribat* from the earliest days. Understanding Islamic doctrine was difficult for him, but he persisted. He had told Christian that he felt frustrated and "stymied" by the Islamic intellectuals, but thought the "little people" were wonderful. "Like Mary, I don't understand, but I watch and wait," he had told Christian. Henri's and Paul-Hélène's execution confirmed the sense of betrayal and outrage Christian had felt in January 1994 when he had read the article that appeared in *La Vie,* a Catholic magazine published in France.

He had played the gracious host to its author, Annie Laurent, a French political scientist cum journalist who had visited Tibhirine in late 1993 while working on a story she was doing about the Church in Algeria. Her article "Christians on Borrowed Time," published in January of 1994, played to the theme of Muslim persecution of a Christian Church deprived of its real mission of winning souls. Its 170 clergymen and 368 members of religious orders had been reduced, she implied, to a pitiable state of silence, keeping a low profile, "merely being an example," by doing good works among the people.

To Christian, the article gave the impression of an aggrieved Church denied the right to proselytize. This could only feed the prejudices of those Algerians who wanted to see the Church as camouflaged crusaders, lying low, talking "dialogue" and "mutual respect" now that it was weak. The article made no mention of the tremendous strength of the faith among those who stayed, unsupported by the props of power, status, or wealth, or of the challenge of Islam to make them become better Christians, to question their certitudes. The Algerian Church was poor and powerless, so its faith had to be strong. It was persecuted by a few, not as an institution but as part of a bad memory. If some Christians were attacked, so were even more imams. By May of 1994, over fifty imams had been murdered for condemning the killing of civilians.

The word *martyr* was thrown around by certain people back in France. Christian didn't like the term. It implied a sectarian crusade that misrepresented the nature of the violence in Algeria, and the reason for the Church's presence there, one which Duval described as, "presence, prayer, and sharing." Sharing in the suffering of the Algerian people was the Church's most important sign of its love. Christian called Henri and Paul-Hélène "martyrs of love."

He also called martyrs of love the six Algerian military medics whose heads had been left on the pavement in Medea's place du Grand Marché as a warning to those who might care for the terrorists. The Hypocratic Oath and the vow to follow Christ lead down the same path of offering healing help to all who seek it. "Even for the devil," Luc told Christian, who had prepared an article for the influential Catholic daily *La Croix,* in which he explained, "By refusing to take sides, we are not washing our hands in noncommittal neutrality. That is not possible for us. No, we are protecting our freedom to love everyone, because that is our choice. Christians are not the only martyrs of charity. Muslims are, too."

After the murder of Henry and Paul-Hélène, Annie Laurent's article became, in Christian's mind, more than an unwelcome irritant. It might even have lead to their death. Christian thought the article could have been passed along by GIA sympathizers living in France to friends in Algeria. It mentioned "the library of the Little Brothers of Mary in the heart of the Casbah." Nothing could be proven, and some thought Christian overreacted when the article appeared, yet its tone was one that whined about persecution, an attitude that he abhorred and thought dangerous in the existing climate. For those motivated to purify the land of self-defined malignancies and vestiges of cultural imperialism, friendship between French clerics and young Algerian students was potentially subversive. The article gave a road map for easy kills. By assassinating religious men and women, the GIA had brought down the last barrier in a war that the Algerian daily *El Watan* described as having "become like a mad camel ravaging the land."

"The concept of total war is not Islam. Islam says you can kill only those who threaten you. You never kill women, children, or religious people unless they are themselves in combat." Ibrahim Younessi always wears a tie and a jacket. He has a square-jawed, clean-cut look reminiscent of a young 1950s Ivy League professor, or a Mormon. He is a member of the FIS in exile in Paris, an active contributor to French scholarly magazines and the former aide-de-camp of Sheik Sahraoui, one of the original FIS founders. "Islam teaches," Younessi insisted with professorial certainty at the café La Coupole where we met, that "war is waged against men, not peoples and cultures. Members of the FIS even studied the concept of the just war in the writings of Saint Augustine. A Muslim has an obligation to save the helpless, aid the poor, and protect the innocent. What Mohammed did for Christian during the war is not all that unusual. The Koran says whoever kills one person unjustly kills all of humanity and whoever saves an innocent life saves all of humanity."

Others in the FIS thought as Younessi did. The killing done in the name of Islam was discrediting Islam, Islamists, and the FIS. The violence was not serving any identifiable political goal; the GIA slogan "No peace, no truce, no compromise" was a formula for an endless treadmill of killing. FIS sympathizers in the army and within the general population were embarrassed. So, too, were some within the GIA itself. They thought their leaders were not fighting in an Islamic way. Certain emirs required new recruits to kill a parent as proof of their irrevocable commitment to the jihad—something utterly scandalous to true mujahideen. Others did not give money to the widows of their own dead, used *haram,* or forbidden, drug money to buy weapons, raped women for their pleasure, or tortured prisoners.

In July 1994, the FIS in exile created its own armed group, Armée Islamique de Salut, or Islamic Army of Salvation. Known by its French acronym, AIS, this group was consciously modeled after the ALN Armée de Libération Nationale), the armed branch of the FLN in its fight against France forty years earlier. Its "parents" were the old mujahideen, veterans to whom it appealed in its proclamation:

> *Yesterday, you liberated the land. Today, we are liberating our honor and religion. You liberated the plains and the Sahara; we will liberate our spirit and consciousness. . . . Our jihad is a logical consequence of yours. . . . The AIS leads its movement strictly within the framework of the* sharia. *It forbids the killing of innocent people, torture and mutilation of its victims, or to attack those not involved in the conflict, be they men, women, or children, children or adults, Muslims or not, Algerians or foreigners.*
>
> *The apostate regime blames the jihad for certain atrocious acts against defenseless people. The AIS will never attack a woman, burn a hospital or school, or conduct any other operation that is against Islam. . . . The jihad is stubborn adherence to principle, perseverence in spite of great difficulties, sincerity in combat, humane treatment of captives, self-control in the face of the temptations of pleasure and the whisperings of Satan.*

The GIA ideology of violence would cause its self-destruction. The AIS wanted to mobilize the support of people: "They [GIA] are destroying Islam so that oppressed people will have no example to guide them. The victory of the Algerian people in its battle for Islam will be good news [for the people] but its defeat will have severe consequences for those hungry for justice, truth, and liberty. That is why we are condemned to succeed, whatever may be the sacrifices."

By 1994, the GIA was using up the political capital of the FIS. Its atrocities and ever greater economic demands on the population and the businesses on which it depended were alienating its base of support, which was also the FIS base.

Those who read in the Algerian press of the horrors committed by the GIA might have gained the impression that the GIA was a structured, coherent fighting entity. In reality, it was never a single structure or true command system. Rather, it consisted of hundreds of small groups spread over the three regions of Algeria—the west (Oran), the center (Algiers), and the east (Constantine)—just as the FLN had been organized in its struggle. Each region had an emir who, in turn, tried to impose a certain discipline on the many local emirs, who often fought among themselves. The GIA fighting units, or *jamaates,* varied in size, discipline, and duration, behaving like deadly neutrinos that truly existed only when killing. The strong man of any locality could declare himself an emir.

The GIA's lax, open standards of recruitment made it easy to fill with criminals, opportunists, and those who had been detained in the camps, thousands of whom were released in 1993. Prisons everywhere have always provided a source of informers and agents for authorities to use against their enemies. French counterinsurgency in the earlier war had developed to a high level the art of releasing prisoners turned informers, *les oiseaux bleus* "bluebirds," named for the color of their work clothes, into the ranks of the FLN. The Algerian Sécurité Militaire had received its schooling in both Paris and Moscow. By 1994, French intelligence services suspected that 50 percent of the *jamaates* had been infiltrated by Algerian security. The problem was that no one knew which units.

Jamel Zitouni was one of those thousands of FIS sympathizers released from prison in 1992 and 1993. Information published about him is contradictory. Some sources say he was born in 1968; others give 1964. There are reports that in 1992 he was sent to the camps in the Sahara where FIS sympathizers were held, but some say it was not him, but his brother. He had been arrested at least once, in the 1980s for theft, and then again in a police roundup after the national elections were canceled.

Accounts of his youth are more consistant. He was born in Boufarik, where he learned French from the son of his father's employer, a *pied-noir* produce merchant. His father moved to the Birkhadem neighborhood, where both poor and well-to-do families lived on the southeastern heights of Algiers; he had an Islamist brother, but was never particularly religious himself. The nuns who ran the primary school he attended for five years remember him as bright, atheletic, and aggressive with other boys. He led a street life of petty thief and, more than once, his family had been terrorized during police house searches for him.

In the early 1980s, Zitouni went to Afghanistan to fight the Soviets, along with two to three thousand other Algerians. Many of these men had volunteered in order to get military training that could be used at home. Mixed in with the volunteers were agents trained by Algerian security at the behest of the KGB to infiltrate the mujahideen. Police reports say Zitouni returned to Algiers in 1986. He eventually became the head of a group of "Afghans," Algerians who had trained in Pakistan with the Taliban that was then being formed in Pakistani refugee camps. The Katib el-Mout, or Phalanges of Death, was formed to carry forward the revolution begun by Bouyali. Some of its recruits were trained at Qom, the Shiite holy city in Iran, or in Hezbollah camps in Lebanon.

Zitouni's reputation for ruthlessness and organization drew the attention of Cherif Gousmi, a neighborhood friend and emir of Birkhadem, who made him his chief lieutenant in early 1994. Zitouni, along with Gousmi, was credited in the press for a rampage in March that took the lives of a Russian embassy employee, an official in the Algerian Ministry of Foreign Affairs, two ex-Yugoslav technicians strolling in the zoological gardens, and a Frenchman and his twenty-four-year-old son who had started a computer software business in Algiers and were known to be Bible-distributing Jehovah's Witnesses.

Zitouni won the respect of Gousmi by his boldness and ruthlessness, which he exercised personally during the summer of 1994. In July, Zitouni mounted a false police checkpoint and intercepted a bus belonging to the state oil company Sonatrach. Four Russians and a Romanian engineer were summarily shot in the back of the head. A month later, Zitouni struck against France's official presence in Algiers. At seven o'clock on August 3, two police cars approached the apartment complex of Aïn Allah, on the outskirts of town, where French diplomatic personnel lived. Dressed as local police, seven men, led by Zitouni, entered the compound and killed three French security personnel and two embassy employees. They fled, leaving behind a Nissan sedan loaded with forty pounds of explosives, but the timing mechanism failed. The Spanish deputy chief of mission, Louis Calvo, remembered the summer of 1994 as one of sheer terror. "I couldn't sleep at night for four months until our own Guardia Civil came from Spain. The local security police at the embassy told us not to trust them."

In September, Cherif Gousmi was killed in an ambush by the "forces of order," a term used not without irony by the population. He was succeeded by Zitouni, who strangled the man who had betrayed his friend. Jamel Zitouni's eighteen-month reign as supreme emir would be the longest of any up to that time. His disparate army was estimated at between nine and ten thousand mujahideen, with four thousand located around Algiers and the rest distributed in the eastern (Constantine) and western regions (Oran). Zitouni began preparations to export the Islamist revolution to France, putting in place a network of supporters to provide weapons, communications technology, false documents, and medical supplies, all of which could be stashed underground in the extensive caves that honeycombed the massifs.

"Algeria is like a vision from the Apocalypse," Michel wrote his cousin Joseph Crand in late August. He was at his small wooden flip-top desk in the scriptorium as he looked out the window at the

Tamesguida Mountains, where helicopters were beating the air like huge dragonflies. "There is nothing but smoke and fire in the valley, in the hills, in the mountains. . . . How long will this go on? I am fifty years old, and next week, I will have been here for ten years."

Michel had found peace and contentment at Tibhirine working in the kitchen with Luc and preparing with Christian the weekly reading schedule which provided spiritual nourishment during their silent meals. The simplicity of the small community and the poverty of its surroundings suited his gentle personality. He was, along with Christophe and Luc, one of Christian's counselors, known for his attentiveness to others and his desire to please. He was also considered, perhaps uncharitably by some of the monks, as an ink blotter who absorbed faithfully all of Christian's thoughts. Christian called him the "perfect monk," for he was humble, charitable, and perfectly obedient, out of love, not fear.

Michel's letter continued: "We want to live here in solidarity with all the Algerians, who have already paid with their lives . . . in solidarity with all the unknown innocents. . . . It seems that He who helps us to hold on each day is He who calls us here. I remain in a deep state of wonder. . . . At the time of the killing of Henri Vergès and Paul-Hélène, the words of Saint Paul to the Corinthians were read in the liturgy: *Now He who establishes us with you* [the Algerian people] *in Christ and has annointed us is God, who also has sealed us, and given us the Spirit in our hearts as a guarantee. . . .* Words which speak to me still, and are like a force given to me to live today *peacefully* with my brothers. I am not a hero. . . . I am a complete zero. Continue, Joseph, to pray for us and the Christian presence here and for the Algerian people, who suffer the most."

In September, nine brothers met in the chapter room to reconfirm their decision to stay in Tibhirine, something they would do every six months. Célestin had returned from France, where he had become increasingly restless and agitated by gnawing fear. He had a visceral terror of returning to meet a violent death. But his even greater fear was not to be there with his brothers when the time came. "The vote of the community is beautiful, open, without weakness, clairvoyant and benevolent. We are conscious of a maternal responsibility to those we love," Christophe wrote in his journal.

Célestin accepted graciously the loss of his job of cantor, which was taken over by Christophe during his eight-month absence. He suffered from phlebitis and insomnia, and at night, he frequently visited Luc, whose asthma required him to sleep sitting up. This was a convenient inconvenience, since Luc was a voracious reader. He would often read to Célestin, whose nervous restlessness made both reading and sleeping difficult. One night, Luc's asthma became so bad, he asked Célestin to give him the last rites. In fact, they were all suffering in different ways. Mohammed was looking drawn and depressed because his wife cried constantly. Jean-Pierre's face became swollen. Christian's great fear was that the Algerian people he loved would be blamed for his death.

Christophe struggled with his outbursts of anger. He became increasingly annoyed with Luc for borrowing without his knowledge the books his mother would send him. He would flare up over Célestin's habit of leaving a messy desk in the scriptorium. Frustrated with the singing, he had stamped out of an Office more than once. Christophe finally exploded at Ali one day over his cow invading the garden yet again. He told Ali he would have to pay a fine of thirty dinars each time the infraction occurred in the future. Ali kept his word.

The fine was paid each time, but it was Fatima, his niece, who always brought Christophe the money. Curious to know why Ali never came himself, Christophe launched an investigation. Yes, Ali was keeping his agreement. Fatima got the thirty dinars by pressing the three long rings on the small portiers' gate that was Amédée's bell code with the local children. Am—aa—dée, Am—aa—dée. "Father Amédée, I need thirty dinars to give to Father Christophe." Amédée, who was the treasurer, could never refuse her charms. And so, Christophe got angry with Amédée.

"I have been told again this morning by a brother that my tiresome, unseemly temper tantrums will exile me from the community, "Christophe wrote in his journal." I wonder, should I join the really violent ones outside? They have something to say that the government doesn't want to hear. Nothing attracts me to their fight, but am I really like one of them, as a brother said to me, so sure that he was without such emotions? How can I rid myself of this evil humor? Can my bitterness lead me to peace?"

A few weeks later, Christophe found himself in the position of peacemaker.

The monastery maintained a certain détente with both sides to the violence. Luc sometimes treated the wounds of the "brothers of the plain" in the morning, and in the evening, the "brothers of the mountains" might appear, although they were simply called *montagnards*. The local GIA knew everything. They knew they too were called "brothers" by the monks, and that the monks were respected and liked by their neighbors. Christian described the community as "living in a fishbowl." They were under constant observation and could be taken at any time. The local emir knew they weren't going anywhere. But just how accommodating should the monks be to maintain the spirit of fraternity toward all sides? That divisive question broke out again after dinner in early October.

Three men knocked on the door of the new building where Robert was living now that his hermitage had been destroyed. They knew Robert, and had visited him in the mountains many times. Once, they had asked him to go into business with them to sell his popular honey. This time, they wanted to use the telephone. Robert explained that they could not go inside with their weapons, and went to get Christian, who returned with a portable phone. Christian told them the phones were tapped, but they didn't care. Robert pulled out a cigarette while they tried to place a call to an international number.

"That's forbidden" one of the montagnards admonished him.

"What's forbidden is killing people, not smoking," Robert answered after a pause.

Paul arrived on the scene. "That won't do," he almost shouted as he ran up to the men. Paul was belligerent. He didn't like the GIA. They reminded him too much of the *fells* he had fought as a paratrooper during the war. A gun was pointed at Paul's stomach, when Christophe intervened. The "brothers," he told Paul, had no intention of harming the monastery. Unlike Christian, Paul had not mastered the art of being firm without being combative.

Mohammed and Célestin at main entrance to monastery.

Jean-Pierre walking past chapel.

Standing from left to right: Christian, Michel, Jean-Pierre, Jean de la Croix, Bruno, Philippe (in white) Célestin, Christophe, Luc, and Amédée. Sitting: Relatives of Célestin.

Célestin at his ordination, embracing Robert.

Chapel, showing new crucifix designed by Christian.

Inside cloister, from left: Jean-Pierre, Paul, Amédée, Luc, Michel, Philippe, Christophe, and Christian.

Célestin with view of Tamesguida Mountains.

By the chapel entrance: Mohammed, Amédée, Christophe, Célestin, Paul, two unknown, Jean de la Croix, Bruno, and Christian.

Cardinal Duval in his residence.

Vergès, Teissier, Christian, and Bishop Claverie in Algiers.

View of the monastery from bottom of garden.

The monastery's kitchen at the time of author's visit.

Front wall of the monastery, facing garden.

Statue of Cardinal Lavigerie by Notre Dame d'Afrique.

View of the harbor.

After the episode, Christian called a meeting to discuss what to do if they came again to use the phone. The community consensus was simply to discontinue the use of the phones altogether. The GIA would find out from their sympathizers in the police department that the phones were no longer in use. Christian later learned that the call had been placed to Henninge, Sweden, which, unbeknown to him, was the mailing address for the GIA publication *El Ansar,* which was printed in Poland, and distributed in London.

It was customary after dinner for the brothers to gather in the chapter room before Compline. There, they listened to music and did some community task together. According to the time of year, they might be shelling peas, or making a medicinal herb tea from the flowers of their linden trees, or stuffing bags with dried lavender to sell at the *porterie* while Christian would act as a newscaster, reporting on things he had heard during the day. On Monday, October 24, he had more bad news. The previous evening, two Spanish nuns had been shot in the back while entering the chapel of the Little Sisters of Jesus in Bab el-Oued for Vespers.

Details emerged over the following days. Despite pleas by the Spanish ambassador to leave the country, Esther and Caridad, two Augustinian Sisters, had chosen to stay and continue their work as nurses. Algeria, they both said, was where God wanted them. The words of a policeman at the scene were widely repeated. "On behalf of the killers, I ask your forgiveness," he said to the other sisters gathered around the two bodies. Four days later, an editorial by Said Mekbel, a well-known journalist, appeared in the leftist newspaper *Le Matin.*

> *Since last Sunday, people have not stopped talking about the assassination of the two Spanish sisters. How and why could anyone do that? How can anyone shoot two nuns on their way to pray to their Creator? Why? No doubt to thank them for their years of taking care of our people, to have treated a member of our family or comforted a neighbor. Does one ever know what feeds this murderous savagery? Surely as a thank-you for having stayed in this country which we Algerians, in the grip of terror, are leaving.*

The killing of the Spanish sisters prompted Bishop Teissier to urge all his bishops to ask each of their respective religious communities to prepare for the possibility of a rapid departure. He was concerned, though, that a core remain to enable the Church to continue its special calling, to be a presence that shared in the suffering of the Algerian people. Who would make up that core? That could only be an individual decision.

In November, Teissier drove up to the monastery, once a regular habit, now less so, since the Medea was a hot zone. He expressed his gratitude to the monks for staying in the face of so much danger. He told them how much their continued presence meant to the rest of the Christian community, as they were at the most advanced line of fire. "I would like to thank you and our good Lord, who has given you the courage of this loyalty, which has, so far, persuaded the Islamists to respect you."

The monks reevaluated regularly their commitment in debates that included Gilles Nicolas. He had become a virtual member of their community, coming up every Friday to have dinner with the brothers, the day of the week when Luc would prepare his famous *pommes frites*. Nicolas taught engineering at the university in Medea, where he was the only Christian on the faculty. He had even been asked to teach primary school math by his Islamist friends in Medea at the time of the municipal elections in 1990. He had many FIS friends, most of whom he considered decent people. He reproached them for the way they idolized Islam, speaking as if Islam were God, and for stultifying the intellects of their followers. "They teach unquestioning, noncritical thinking. God gave us reason, conscience, and laws of nature to support faith."

Nicolas usually argued that Algiers was really no safer than the Atlas, unless the monks were to lock themselves up and never go out. Security was less a question of location and more a matter of whether the local emir decided it would serve some purpose to kill a monk or religious person. He knew that the killing wasn't really random. As for himself, his hours at the university were regular. Anyone could learn his schedule. Yet Nicolas had never even received a warning to leave, and he had many Muslim friends.

Certain brothers declared themselves ready to remain as a hard core should it come to a precipitous departure. But collectively, they could envisage a hasty exit only if they were overtly threatened—which was usually done with a warning letter, if forced into a form of collaboration that was unacceptable; or, most unlikely, if the neighbors were to ask them to leave.

Following the killing of Henri and Paul-Hélène in May, the shooting of the Spanish sisters made it impossible for the Church not to feel that it had become a target of choice by some of the local emirs. By December, a dozen religious communities in the diocese of Algiers had decided to leave, at least temporarily. The Jesuits, the Little Brothers of Jesus, the Pères Blancs, the Protestant Sisters of Grandschamps, the Poor Clares, and the Trappists were among those in the diocese who recommitted themselves to stay in the face of an estimated one thousand killings a week.

In early December, the monks learned that Said Mekbel had been murdered. His death brought to fifteen the number of journalists who had been assassinated since May 1993. Total war required eliminating apologists for the government, critics of the Islamist movement, and bad influences, such as entertainers who sang pornographic songs or wrote irreverant plays and books. Some of the armed groups specialized. The Mouvement pour l'Etat Islamique (MEI), for example, liked to target anti-Islamist intellectuals. These included professors, doctors, lawyers, judges, writers, and artists. *Le syndrome d'égorgement* or "slit throat syndrome," as it was known on the street, had led ten thousand members of the educated class to emigrate.

Total war also meant killing wives, children, and babies. Nighttime attacks on the enemy was not only safer but Koranic law made moral allowances for mistakes. The soldiers of God had a loophole. At night, visibility was bad and accidents could happen. Damnation might be avoided if innocents were slaughtered in the confusion of darkness. There was both logic and addiction to the massacres of families. Survivors become avengers, so best to kill them all. And the carnage, the bashing, and mutilation become a blood lust, like dogs that have tasted the blood of chickens.

Nineteen ninety-four ended badly. On Christmas Day, the GIA hijacked an Air France plane at Boumediene Airport in Algiers as it was preparing to leave for Paris. The hijackers demanded that the Algerian government release some of their prisoners in exchange for the plane. French lives were at stake, yet Mitterand's Minister of the Interior, Charles Pasqua, agreed to let Algerian security handle the affair directly. A botched attempt was made by the Algerian security services to deceive the hijackers into believing that the government had released Abdelhak Layada, a former emir in prison for murdering an Algerian journalist. When the hijackers discovered that was not the case, they shot an Algerian policeman they had taken prisoner. A Vietnamese diplomat protested and was shot, too. Then for good measure, they killed the cook from the French embassy in order to force the pilots to take off. Once airborne, the pilot convinced the terrorists the plane needed to refuel in Marseilles, where an antiterrorist unit of the Police Nationale was waiting. In a precisely executed rescue, the GIGN (Groupement d'Intervention de la Gendarmerie Nationale) freed the hostages, with no loss of passenger lives. All four of the hijackers were shot and killed, one a close friend of Jamel Zitouni.

Two days later, an unmarked white van pulled up in front of a two-story stucco building with an ornate veranda on the second floor, carved in the distinctive geometric Berber gingerbread style. The house of the Pères Blancs was well-known throughout Kabylia and was a local landmark in the capital of Tizi-Ouzou. Located near the center of town, only five hundred yards from the police station, the three *babas,* as the fathers were known, were constantly receiving visitors. Theirs was the place people came to when they didn't know where else to go with a problem.

Three men in plain clothes left the van and entered the office of Jean Chevillard, but not before first locking in a garage some workers who were preparing an area for the new library. The men flashed police ID cards at Chevillard and said that he and the other fathers were wanted at the commissariat. Chevillard knew the local police. He was suspicious, and he wanted to call first to find out what was going on. When he showed signs of not cooperating, Chevillard was shot in his office. Within minutes, three other men were gunned down in the courtyard of the building as they came to investigate the commotion, or tried to flee. Christian Chessel, Alain Dieulangard, and Charles Deckers were all dead when the police arrived.

Deckers was a Belgian and the chaplain for the Poor Clares in Algiers. He had driven to Tizi-Ouzou to celebrate Saint John's Day, in honor of Jean Chevillard, a sixty-nine-year-old Père Blanc who had been serving there since 1985. An apparent kidnapping attempt had gone awry only ten minutes after Deckers had arrived. The killers were members of a GIA *jamaa* called, "Those Who Fight with Their Blood." Their abandoned van was found a half mile down the road in a heavily wooded area. It was widely believed that the murders were a direct retaliation for the death of the four hijackers. Yet, Charles Deckers was not a Père Blanc, and he would not have been there but for Saint John's Day.

The Pères Blancs were the quintessential Christian presence during the colonial era. They were part of an historical memory that blended the sword and the cross, one that was filled with bittersweet emotions for Algerians. On January 2, that memory was sweet. That these men of God were doing nothing but good for Algerians was clear to the 100,000 inhabitants of Tizi-Ouzou, who showed their shame and grief by closing down the city for two hours the day of the funeral.

Alain Dieulangard had been in Algeria since 1950 and, at seventy-five, was the "grandfather" of the group. During the Algerian war of independence, he had turned the house of the Pères Blancs into a refuge for women in the village who were being harrassed by soldiers on both sides, and had continued to serve the Kabyles in different ways—teaching, catechizing children, looking in on the old and sick, finding jobs for people—in a word, dealing with the daily needs of the population. Jean Chevillard, had helped create professional training centers around the country and had started one for construction engineers in Tizi-Ouzou. He was a social service worker, too. People would go to him for help in getting something from the government, interpreting an official communication, or writing a letter. Christian Chessel, the newest and youngest of the *babas,* had taken an interest in Islam and Berber culture. Chessel had just obtained money and local approvals for the construction of a library, badly needed by the young, who lacked both books and a quiet place to read and study.

"They were buried as heros amid applauds and *you yous,*" reported *Le Matin*. Thousands came from all corners of the *wilaya*. Representatives of the Berber Cultural Movement walked down the streets, reminding shopkeepers to close. The former prime minister, Redha Malek, said some words, as did Bishop Teissier and Christian de Chergé, who noted "the contrast between a few killers and the immense crowd of their compatriots who refuse to let them steal the meaning of these deaths. Those who claimed responsibility for the murder can't take credit for their death. Alain and his brothers knew the risks. They had already given their lives to God and to the people of Kabylia, who have shown their immense gratitude."

Tizi-Ouzou is in a high valley, ringed to the north and east by the Hands of the Jew. The knuckles form the series of broad peaks that give the mountains their name. It is thought by some that the Berbers are descended from Jews who fled Israel after the destruction of the Temple by the Romans in A.D. 70. The Berbers of Kabylia are known for their independent spirit and Kabylia is called the land of *imazighen,* or "free men." Many Kabyles preferred to fight with the first French invaders rather than to submit to the authority of Emir Abdelkader. The famous billowy-panted Zouaves who fought for France in numerous wars were a Kabyle tribe. In the years following the emir's defeat, the Kabyles also led the bloodiest uprisings against France and were prominent among the leaders of the FLN during the war of independence.

They lived in villages perched like eagles' nests on the tops of rocky precipices surrounded by foothills riddled with caves ideal for hiding and valleys that explode in the spring with saffron masses of wild broom or are shaded by groves of blue cedar and Spanish chestnut. Over the centuries, the animist Berbers have pragmatically accepted the religions of newcomers. They have been Jews, Christians, and Muslims, but the few converts to Christianity during the French occupation were mostly Kabyles. They were known by the colonists as being adaptable, entrepreneurial, and as "more European" than the Arabs. Their blood is intermingled with the Arabs now, but the blond, redhead, and fair-skinned Algerians of today are often Kabyles.

The Pères Blancs were preservers of their little-known language, Tamazight. They compiled the first Tamazight dictionary and, over the years, assembled an extensive collection of poems, legends, songs, proverbs, and customs. The fathers became students and stewards of Berber culture.

Today, the Pères Blancs carry a name dripping with anachronism—the White Fathers.* But in 1868, their mission was to go among Muslims—to live with them, dress like them, and to speak their languages. The founder of the Pères Blancs, Father Charles Lavigerie, wanted to harness the religious fervor of the Muslim, so impressive to clerics struggling at home with an increasingly secular society. France in the second half of the nineteenth century was deeply divided over the legacy of its own revolutionary turmoil. When the Ancien Régime had been finally swept away in 1789, so, too, were many of the churchmen who supported it.

The catechism of the French Revolution was liberty, equality, and fraternity for all; its new diety, the goddess of reason. The Declaration of the Rights of Man and Citizen proclaimed men free from the shackles of a feudal caste system in which the Church was embedded. Sure of their path to a better future for mankind, militants of the Revolution shot and bayoneted hundreds of priests and drowned or guillotined thousands of civilians who failed to swear loyalty to the new constitution. "The Church was hated not because its priests claimed to regulate the affairs of the other world, but because they were lords of the manor, tithe owners and played a leading part in secular life" noted Alexis de Tocqueville, who would turn a skeptical eye toward France's Algerian adventure.

Yet, among the common people, faith and the moral authority of the Church did not go away. France restored its monarchy in 1815. The clergy and Catholic orders found the Bourbon restoration hospitable to their return. Catholicism was again declared *la religion d'état*

---

*The name referred to their long white robes, though most of the missonaries were indeed Europeans.

under the restored monarchy of Louis XVIII. During this period, the clergy resumed its traditional role as educator of French youth, reigniting a struggle for the soul of France that would continue into the first decade of the twentieth century.

The outspoken positions of Pope Pius IX against freedom of speech, religious tolerance, divorce, and the cult of reason added fuel to existing suspicions against the Church. An alliance of liberals and socialists launched a counteroffensive in the early 1880s to take the control of young minds away from the antirepublican Church. Primary school became obligatory for girls and boys. Public education would be free and secular. Orders engaged in teaching, such as the Jesuits, Benedictines, and Dominicans, were threatened with closure. Progressively, the clergy was banned from teaching higher educational levels, culminating in the Law Jules Ferry of 1904, which prohibited clerics from teaching in state schools. Displays by students or teachers of symbols of religious affiliation such as crucifixes and yarmulkes were not allowed. France became officially republican and secular.

In this climate, Lavigerie dreamed of lifting up the Arab and rechristianizing France, starting in French Algeria. Appointed Bishop of Algiers in 1867, he saw himself in the chain of church fathers leading back to Saint Augustine. His task, he declared at his investiture ceremony, was to make Algeria again the cradle of a Christian nation "of another France, and to spread the light of civilization of which the Gospels are the source, and the law." Lavigerie was immediately presented with opportunities to demonstrate to Muslims the meaning of Christian charity.

A cholera epidemic broke out the year he arrived, followed by a severe drought and locust infestations. Famine killed an estimated 300,000 Muslims. Thousands of widows and children were taken in by the Church. Lavigerie set up temporary orphanages for eighteen hundred homeless children, the majority of whom were later returned to relatives. The following year, Lavigerie established a new missionary order named for its white robes, which resembled those worn by Muslims.

"Be like the Arabs among the North Africans. Go and love this old people formed from ten different races, mixed with the blood of Christians," Lavigerie told his missionaries, who often departed with guns over their shoulders. To aid in mixing with the population and understanding its ways, Lavigerie established in Tunis a center that later became the Papal School of Arabic and Islamic Studies, which trained missionaries to work in Muslim countries throughout Africa.

The Pères Blancs and Soeurs Blanches were instructed not to seek converts. Instead, they built schools and medical clinics in the forbidden "zone of the saber" administered by the army, an area where the population was predominantly Muslim and was supposed to be protected from proselytizing Christians and land-grabbing colonists. No Muslim child could be baptized without Lavigerie's personal approval, except in the case of infants on the verge of death. There was no need to rush to convert Muslim souls to the light of Christianity. Lavigerie was confident they would see for themselves the light shed by Christian good works.

But Muslims did not see the light, not enough to convert. Aside from a few thousand Kabyle converts whose ancestors had once been Christians before the arrival of the Arabs, Muslims accepted the good works but not the faith. Where was the reciprocity? they often wondered. Muslims accepted the revelations of all the prior apostles, they revered Jesus as an apostle without sin, born miraculously from the Virgin Mary, and who ascended to heaven with Moses and Mohammed. Why didn't Christians accept the revelations of the Koran? They demeaned the Prophet and called him a fraud, a trickster, and a sex pervert. Why? Why didn't Christians really act as Christians should, and follow the teachings of Jesus Christ?

Lavigerie's right forearm was neatly sawed off after Algerian independence. His striding bronze figure, cross thrust triumphantly forward as a battle standard on the plaza surrounding the Basilica of Notre-Dame d'Afrique was hardly a welcome sight to a people who had fought a seven-year-war to be free of the condescending superiority of "Christian" France. Disarmed of his cross, the statue of Lavigerie remains otherwise untouched thirty years later.

15

Déjà Vu

We have rendered Muslim society much more miserable and more barbaric than it was before it became acquainted with us.

—Alexis de Tocqueville, 1847

In 1994, some Frenchmen were calling the events in Algeria "the second Algerian war." The bitter waters of contempt and injustice poured on Muslims by the *pieds-noirs* for over one hundred years had produced the FLN and the rebellion of 1954. Forty years later, continued injustice and *le pouvoir*'s own contempt for fellow Algerians produced the FIS, the political rebellion of 1990, and virtual civil war after the legislative elections of 1991 were canceled. Even François Léotard, the French Minister of Defense, was doubtful in the fall of 1994 about the Algerian government's ability to hang on. He told the French newspaper *Le Monde* in October, "The fundamentalists are on the verge of taking power in Algeria."

As before, this second Algerian war had no frontiers, the enemy was invisible, and the strategy the same—to create a climate of fear and insecurity so as to undermine the population's confidence in the government's ability to govern and protect the citizenry. Again, religion animated and justified the struggle.* Whom the French called *fellaghas,* the FLN called mujahideen. The offical FLN newspaper, *El Mujahid,* still published today, began its career in 1956, when mujahideen caught smoking or drinking alcohol could easily be identified—their lips and noses were cut off.

Few of the horrors were new, only the cast of characters was different, each side struggling to use the vocabulary of the past to condemn its opposition. To its supporters, the FIS was the new FLN,

---

*When the Association of Ulemas joined the FLN in 1956, two years after the outbreak of the war, it took on a more decidedly religious overtone, creating a latent secular-religious schism within the FLN that broke out after independence. Initially, the Ulemas wouldn't join the secular, Marxist revolutionaries.

fighting against injustice and neocolonial oppression; to its enemies, the FIS and its violent offspring were *harkis*, traitors like those who earlier had fought for the French. The GIA shared with the OAS the rage that comes from the marriage of desperation and betrayal; the former, angry children betrayed at the polls by their own government; the latter, honorable soldiers who felt betrayed by a duplicitous de Gaulle. The hiding places, the prisons, the arming of civilians, the atrocities, the paralysis of a population hedging its bets, and the internecine fighting among Muslims were familiar to those who experienced the rebellion of 1954.

Estimates vary widely on how many Algerians died during the war of 1954–1962. The official Algerian numbers are a round 1 million war dead. French figures are predictably lower but are more differentiated: 141,000 male Muslims killed by French forces; 12,000 members of the FLN killed in internal purges, 16,000 Muslim civilians killed by the FLN, and 50,000 abducted and presumed killed. Thousands of *harkis* and other Muslim auxiliaries who fought with the French were massacred in the summer of 1962, well after the armistice was signed in March. Of the 250,000 Muslims who took up arms with France, many became victims of the Evian Accord, which obligated the French army to disarm its Muslim troops. President de Gaulle was for Algerian independence, but he did not want more Algerians in France. De Gaulle gave orders to his Minister of Justice not to allow their former Muslim comrades in arms to seek refuge in France and to punish French soldiers who disobeyed.

French officiers had assured their Muslim allies that France would never leave Algeria and never abandon her friends. Humiliated and ashamed, many French soldiers tried clandestinely to bring them to France. Fewer than fifteen thousand *harkis* made it over, and others were sent back to a certain death.

There were horrible stories about the fate of the *harkis*. Those who were shot summarily or sent to clear mines were lucky compared to those forced to swallow their military decorations before being shot, or made to drink gasoline as a prelude to being set on fire, or who were castrated or cut into pieces and fed to dogs.* Entire *harki* families were

---

*After World War II, Frenchmen also took gruesome revenge against those who had

put to death, including young children. Estimates of Algerians killed in the settling of scores vary wildly from 30,000 to 150,000.

During seven and a half years of war, French security forces lost only 17,465 dead and suffered 64,985 wounded. European civilan casualties were 10,000, of which 2,800 were victims of OAS terrorism aimed at FLN sympathizers and those who refused to pay money to support its cause. By the end of 1994, the European casualties of the new terrorism in Algeria were small compared to the murderous accomplishments of the OAS.

The shootings of the Pères Blancs at Tizi-Ouzou brought to seventy-eight the roll call of foreigners assassinated between September 1993 and the end of 1994. The French daily *Le Figaro* reported twenty-five French, twelve Croatians, eight Russians, eight Italians, three Spanish, two Chinese, two Vietnamese, two Belgians, two ex-Yugoslavs, and one each from Great Britian, Colombia, Peru, Tunisia, South Korea, Bosnia, Belorussia, Romania, the Ukraine, and the Philippines.

At about the same time, the Algerian Committee for the Protection of Human Rights, formed in 1984 with the moral support of Cardinal Duval, issued its *White Book on Repression in Algeria, 1991–94,* prepared by Amnesty International. Hundreds of case histories described victims' accounts of their "accelerated interrogations" at torture centers such as Châteauneuf, Cavaignac, El-Harrach prison, and others. The state-of-emergency law passed after the bomb explosion at Boumediene International Airport in August 1992, allowed suspects to be detained for twelve days without being charged. Many were held for much longer. To the old French standbys of the *"chiffon"* water torture and electroshock, the *White Book* enumerated other practices for producing a confession or bit of information: inserting broken bottles in the anus; ripping of fingernails with a bayonnet; tearing out teeth and facial hair with pliers; beatings and whippings with metal wires; castration and sodomization with clubs and dogs; forcing prisoners to drink their water out of toilet bowls;

---

collaborated with the Nazis—retribution that included stonings and throwing collaborators into the turbine blades of dams.

depriving them of sleep by flooding cells at night; psychological torture by using threats of torture or execution of family members in the presence of the prisoner. "How can Algerians do this to Algerians? How can Muslims do this?" These were questions asked by men whose only crime was to walk down the street with a bearded friend, a beard being considered by authorities an Islamist trademark, and hence an object of suspicion.

Such questions were also being asked by Jacques Vergès. Sadly, this controversial French defense lawyer had seen all this before when the special paratrooper units were torturing Muslims and their French sympathizers whom he had tried to defend or get released from illegal detention. In an impassioned book, *Open Letter to My Algerian Friends Who Have Become Torturers,* published in 1993, Vergès spilled forth bitter incredulity about the role he was now playing—admonishing those friends of his who had been tortured by the French thirty years earlier and who were now using the same rationalizations and same methods to torture other Algerians.

In 1992, the leaders of the FIS had asked Vergès to assist in the defense of Abassi Madani and Ali Benhadj at their trial before a military tribunal in Blida. Algerian authorities told Vergès he could be present as an observer, but on the day he arrived for the hearing, he was denied entrance to the court. "You lied to me," Vergès wrote in his open letter. "Faced with armed police, I realized that our fraternity of yesterday had become transformed into a complicity devoid of principles. The scales fell from my eyes."

Thirty years earlier, Vergès, the defender of the downtrodden, the unpopular, and the reviled,* had denounced the torture practiced by the police and a part of the French army. "If someone had told me then that torture would be used again on Algerians by those who claim to be the inheritors of the revolution, and though I have no illusions about human nature, I would not have believed it. Obviously, I have been naïve. We were all naïve."

To denounce the torture today, he was told by his Algerian friends, would be to betray the ideals that united them at the time of the revolution. It would even put at risk the Rights of Man. "To hear you

---

*In 1988, Vergès defended Nazi war criminal Klaus Barbie.

talk," Vergès responded, "in the universal struggle between modernity and obscurantism, the danger to the dignity of man comes not from those who torture but from the victims of torture." The arguments of *le pouvoir* had a familiar ring. They reminded him of those made by François Mitterand, Minister of Justice at the time of the rebellion, and others. "It was in the name of the Rights of Man—à la Française—that police and soldiers were commiting their acts of torture in the villa Susini in Algiers. Didn't Muslims at that time represent for secularists a return to the past and didn't the coalition of *pied-noirs* and *harkis* represent modernity, this modernity that has become your only, and very weak excuse for your deeds? I am not your enemy, even if you spit on the past and consider me as such. Yet, placed in the same situation as before, I can only act in the same way."

During the war, Jacques Vergès belonged to a legal defense group called, French Lawyers Against Colonialism. This diverse collection of Christians, Communists, and liberals fought to get Algerians and their French sympathizers released from France's guardians of Western civilization. One who benefited from these services is Henri Alleg.

From 1950 to 1955, Alleg had been the publisher of the daily newspaper *Alger Républicain*. It was the sole paper in French Algeria that had been open to all political opinions, including those favoring greater democratic and national rights for Algerian Muslims. For two years, Alleg fought vainly to have the illegal closure of his paper reversed, and in 1956, he went into hiding to avoid the internment that threatened all those who worked on, or collaborated with, his newspaper.

In June 1957, Alleg visited the apartment of a newspaper colleague in Algiers who, unbeknown to him, had been arrested the previous day. He was met instead by a police inspector who handed him over to paratoopers of General Massu's Tenth Division. They held him without charge for a month at a "triage center" in the fashionable suburb of El-Biar.

Alleg lives in Paris today. He is a short, mild-mannered, professorial-looking man. Any hatred toward his tormentors is dormant after forty years, but the memories are seared permanently into his body and spirit. In 1961, the clandestine publication in France of his experience at the hands of the "paras" stoked the outrage in

France that ultimately created an international outcry. His testimonial, *La Question,* written three months after his release from prison, explains the ways in which France mentored its adopted Muslim children and corrupted its own.

Massu's paras had a job to do: to break the terrorism that had gripped Algiers by dismantling its support network. To do that, they had to also penetrate their network of French sympathizers—persons who might provide medical help, money, arms, or hiding places for the FLN. Collectively, such people were called *les porteurs de valises,* bag carriers for the enemy.

The effective use of torture requires asking victims questions they are able to answer. For Muslims, all were required to pay the *zakat,* or Muslim tax, to support the rebellion. So asking to whom a Muslim paid the *zakat* was an effective way to work up the chain leading to the real terrorists. In the case of Henri Alleg, the questions were equally simple: Whom had he been staying with the night before he was arrested and who were the other persons who sheltered him after he went underground?

The paras called him their "client." He was also a vile curiosity, a Frenchman who had chosen to side with the "rats." Electroshock was delivered from a handheld magneto device to metal "crocodiles," pincers attached to whatever parts of the body they wanted to experiment on. His tormentors—Charbonnier, Jacquet, Lorca, Erulin—carried him around naked, strapped to a plank, to different rooms, where the various "séances" were objects of entertainment for his onlookers.

They began by attaching a crocodile to his right ear and right finger. Later on, the crocodiles bit into his buttocks, testicles, and tongue. They tortured him with the ferocious thirst that follows electrical shock, with near drowning by forcing dirty water down his throat, and with the usual beatings. When those techniques failed to make him talk, the paras tried pentathol to coax out his memories, and they finally threatened to get his wife and children and torture them before his eyes.

"He doesn't give a fuck about anything, not his wife, not his children. He loves only the Party," Erulin spat out to Lieutenant Charbonnier, who was mystified by Alleg's determination. "You will talk," screamed Erulin. "This is the Gestapo. You know that? You write articles about torture, you bastard! Well, this is the Tenth Division. We will show you how *it's* done! And we'll do the same to your Mitterand, your Duclos,* and that whore of yours, the Republic."

They never broke him. For a month, Alleg withstood their battery of techniques for prying out the names of his protectors. His refrain was always the same. He would not betray those who had had the courage to shelter him. Toward the end of his stay, a young draftee came into his cell with a big smile. Without embarrassment, he congratulated Alleg, as though he had won a bicycling championship. "I was present at all the séances. My father told me about the Communists in the Resistance. They would die before they would talk. That's good."

More important for Alleg, was the respect he felt from the Muslim prisoners, whose suffering he shared. I read in their eyes a solidarity, a friendship, and a confidence so complete that I felt proud, precisely because I was European, to have a place among them. . . . It is important that the French people know that the Algerians do not confuse their torturers with the people of France, from whom they have learned much and whose friendship is dear to them. But Frenchmen must know what is being done *in their name*."

Luc wrote to his old medical school friend Paul Grenot at the end of 1994: *"Recently, I was rereading Pascal and came upon this, "Men never do evil as thoroughly or as joyfully as when they do it in the name of God."*

We are now 'at risk,' but our community stays on. Fear is the lack of faith. We follow the path of our Lord. He shows us the way—it is one of poverty, failure, and death. The devastating torrential rains of winter have not extinguished at all the violence which seems now to spring from the earth. One side wants to keep power, the other wants to take it. It is a desperate struggle. I have no idea when it will end. Meanwhile, I will do my work, receive the poor and the sick, awaiting the day when I will close my eyes to enter into God's house, whose door is open to all who knock. . . .

Pray for me, my dear friend, that my departure from this world be in the Peace and Joy of Jesus."

---

*Jacques Duclos a leading Communist party member in 1957 and delegate to the National Assembly.

PART THREE

A Light Extinguished?

1995–1996

16

Sorrow and Joy

Therefore take pleasure in infirmities, in needs, in reproaches, in persecutions in distresses for Christ's sake. For when I am weak, then I am strong.

—2 Corinthians 12:10

Paul liked to do things right. He was punctual, thorough, and believed in sticking with something to the end. His strict father had taught him obedience, honesty, and respect for his elders. In short, Paul was a good soldier, which is what he had been during the "rebellion" that he fought to suppress. He finished his military service in 1961 as a second lieutenant in the Eighth Marine Parachute Regiment. Unlike most French soldiers, he was among the small number who had actually fought in the maquis and had been engaged in active pursuit of the *fells* in the back country. But the war was something he never talked about.

After he left the army, Paul continued a life of service in his tiny Alpine village of Bonnevaux, not far from Evian, where the armistice was signed. He was a volunteer fireman, part-time assistant to the mayor, and worked long hours to help his father in the family heating and plumbing business. As the only boy among four siblings, he knew his father depended on him, and though his interests were maturing in another direction, they were deferred until his father's death in 1981.

"His religious life was very discrete," his sister Bernadette remembered. "Paul never discussed theological questions or quoted the Bible. He did acquire a library of religious books and read the Bible regularly with his mother. On Sundays, when he returned from church, he liked to lie on the sofa and listen to sermons broadcast on the radio. Then he would insist that others keep quiet."

Paul's life of quiet competence and civic-mindedness took a new turn in 1984. Though known only to a few people, he had been going as a postulant to visit Notre-Dame de Tamié, near Lake Annecy. As a postulant, a prospective monk could live and work for weeks or months at a time in a monastery without making any commitment. This gave the candidate a chance to look from the inside at a highly disciplined life that would require at least a five-year engagement—two as a novice and three as a Temporary Profession—before making a definitive commitment, or Solemn Profession.

Paul's decision to enter the monastery was not well received by friends and family. Their attitude was based, in part, on a misunderstanding. People didn't know that in 1984 Trappist monasteries were no longer completely cut off from the world.

Decisiveness was one of the qualities people admired in Paul. He was not one to second-guess. He explained in an open letter to his friends and community in September of 1984:

> *Becoming a monk is a choice, like all the other choices one makes in life. . . . It took me ten years to decide to become a monk, the time necessary for me to be certain of the authenticity of my call, to purify my motives, and to submit myself to the test of time. . . . A monk is simply a sinner who joins a community of sinners who are confident in God's mercy and who strive to recognize their weaknesses in the presence of their brothers.*

Five years later, he decided he wanted to leave Tamié and go to the Atlas. He went, he told friends, because he wanted to be among people "who struggled each day to make a living." Yet, monastic life did not change him. His oldest sister, Colette, thought of him as a "bon vivant" at heart. "There was nothing different about him when he returned to visit his family. Perhaps inside there was, but not from the outside." Paul would eat meat when he went home. He liked to sit around and talk for long hours with his friends or go mushroom hunting with them. His sisters would sometimes get upset by his "risk taking." There were occasions when he would urge his young nephews to climb higher up the mountain with him or go a little farther on a hike than their mothers would have liked. But he was never foolhardy.

And he maintained his black humor when friends would ask, "How are things going down there?"

"My head is still on my shoulders" was his stock reply.

Paul revealed a more somber side in a letter written to his former abbot at Tamié in January 1995, following the murder of the Pères Blancs.

Dear Father,

May you have a good, holy, and happy New Year with Him who has come to be among us to reveal the Father, give us His life, His joy, and His peace. After the service at Notre-Dame d'Afrique for Christian Chessel, the youngest of the Pères Blancs, the participants simply wished one another for a "better" New Year. The atmosphere was grave, but serene. No one has any illusions anymore. Each of us knows that tomorrow could be his turn. But each of us has freely chosen to stay.

Our eight martyrs of 1994 were not accidental victims, but part of a process of elimination, necessary purification [of those who are different] by the terrorists. It seems to me reasonable to call them martyrs because they have been authentic witnesses to the Gospels by their love and selfless service to the poorest of the poor. Living the Gospels authentically can only be a radical challenge to all forms of totalitarianism.

The Christian community is riddled with departures now. The small congregations are closing their doors one after another. This month the Sisters of Saint Clare are returning to Nîmes, all twenty-eight of them, after being warned by several of their FIS friends that their names were on the lists circulating in the mosques. The assassination of their chaplain, Charlie Deckers, no doubt played a role in their decision.*

As for us, the terrorist group that rules our sector has obviously judged us, as yet, not sufficiently interesting to bother with. But if raison d'état *requires, other groups can put pressure on our local emir to pluck us away, since we offer such an easy and choice prize to whoever wants us.*

Last Sunday, Christian and Philippe, our young novice, took five

*GIA emirs sometimes posted in FIS mosques the names of people targeted for assassination, in order to give them an opportunity to repent or flee.

hours to come the sixty-miles from Algiers. The bridge over the Chiffa Gorge had been blown up and the temporary pontoon bridges put up by the army were partially submerged by the high water from the heavy rains. They passed a burnt-out bus that was still smoking, one of hundreds that have been destroyed over the past year. More than five hundred schools have been destroyed as well. Our Lord reminds us, Don't fear those who can kill only your body. . . .

How far does one go to save his skin without running the risk of losing his soul? What will remain of the Church in Algeria in a few more months? Little, I fear. Yet, I believe the Good News is spreading; the seed is germinating. How can one doubt it after reading the articles by Said Mekbel, who was himself killed in December? His last words in the article eulogizing the two Spanish sisters were beautiful. "We will miss for a long time the prayers of these sisters who only wanted to tilt the balance toward peace and forgiveness. Toward what kind of world of darkness are we hurtling, we who only dream of light?" His attitude is not unique. The Spirit is at work here in the deep recesses of people's hearts. May we be open to it, that it might also work in us through our prayer and our loving presence toward all our brothers. . . .

Paul's letter expressed something that all the brothers had begun to feel. They talked about it among themselves. It was something real, yet hard to pin down. Yes, nothing had changed. They were still the same individuals, in the same place, doing the same things. Their personalities were still the same, with their charm, quirks, and sharp edges. Yet, something was different. A new quality was developing in their relationships, one of greater harmony and mutual acceptance. The brothers were becoming more attentive to one another, a change brought on by the gravity of the decisions they had to make regularly. They saw that they had to go forward in their faith, together, a step at a time. It was slow, deliberate, and real, this walking together, each bearing alone the reality of his own faith and his own suffering. They developed a powerful sense of inspiration, of not being alone. Yet the awareness of danger was always with them.

A few days after Paul wrote his letter, Christian read excerpts of an article by his friend Christian Chessel during lunch. Chessel was not only the youngest of the three Pères Blancs who had been killed but was considered a rising star in the order. He had arrived in Algeria in 1991 from his home in Nice, in spite of the growing political tensions, and had become the newest member of the *ribat.* Entitled, "In My Weakness, I Find My Strength," the piece was based on a sermon Chessel had given in Rome.

> *Our mission in the Muslim world is marked by weakness. This may seem surprising to say. It is not a fashionable term in the missionary lexicon.* Weakness *is a word with a bad reputation in our world, where strength and vigor—be it physical, psychological, or intellectual—are synonymous with well-being and success. But in his letters, Paul used the word thirty-three times. In the Bible, it is, above all, the weak with whom we are asked to concern ourselves. . . . In Jesus, God becomes man to share in man's inherent weakness. He takes and transforms all human weakness and uses it to demonstrate to all mankind the power of His love. It is the weak who best understand this. I thank you Father, Lord of heaven and earth, that you have hidden these things from the wise and the educated which you have revealed to babes. . . .*
>
> *To accept our lack of power and our poverty is an invitation and an urgent call to create with others relationships that are not based on power; when I recognize my weakness, I can accept that of others, and see a way for me to imitate Christ. This attitude transforms our mission. It invites us to renounce all pretension of superiority in our encounters with others, however weak they are. . . . This attitude of weakness can be misunderstood. Weakness in itself is not a virtue, but, rather, an expression of the essence of our nature, one which must be molded and shaped by faith, hope, and love. To be weak is to be neither passive nor resigned; rather, it supposes courage and pushes us to struggle for justice and truth while resisting the elusive seduction of force and power. . . .*

Chessel's words made a deep impression on the brothers as Christian read from the bright yellow-and-blue *minbar,* the antique Muslim pulpit that occupied a corner of the refectory facing toward the mountains. The monks were weak. They were, as Jean-Pierrre remarked to Christophe one day, completely dependent on the good opinion of the neighbors, "the little people," as he called them.

Barely five two, Jean-Pierre was a tough, quiet little Alsatian, known for his modesty, good humor, and even-tempered spirit. He had thought about giving up his job as the commissaire which required him to go shopping for bread and other staples three times a week. The worm of fear had gotten into him. Since 1993, he had seen with growing frequency the burned shells of cars, lying like rotting carcasses along the route to Medea. The AIS and GIA were divided not only over the right way to fight an Islamic war but also over control of territory. As they did for the medieval barons of a previous age, roads produced booty for those who controlled them. The new barons might be either AIS or GIA *jamaate* looking for enemies of God, but they might also be local defense militia searching for terrorists, or bandits simply looking to take advantage of the general chaos. Roadblocks yielded money, commercial cargoes, identity cards, and the opportunity to settle scores.

Christian was going to find a replacement for Jean-Pierre, when he changed his mind. He decided he would rather take risks than lose contact with the local people, who continued to be as friendly as ever. Unlike Christian's more intellectual approach, Jean-Pierre's Islamology* was that of the street. These personal contacts were his form of dialogue with Islam.

There was Hadj Ben Ali, the ninety-year old kiosk owner on the place du Grand Marché, who let Jean-Pierre use his Xerox machine to make copies of the liturgy and would often press some money in his hand, saying, "For the poor." Stuck in the corner of his kiosk, he kept an ancient magazine cover of Sister Madeline David, a famous French missionary in the days when Algeria was part of a France that stretched from Dunkirk to Tamanrasset. Bachir, the cashier in the *épicerie,* asked Jean-Pierre each year for a new Christian calendar. He wanted the dates of the Christian holy days. Bachir was particularly interested in knowing when they celebrated the Feast of Abraham, as Abraham was the first Muslim and good soldier of God. And then there was Zhohar, from the *boulangerie,* who would come

---

*Term used by monks for the study of Islam.

up to the monastery and deliver cakes and other gastronomic surprises for the monks on their birthdays or for special occasions.

One day, some kids threw rocks at Jean-Pierre's car as he passed through tiny Dakhla, a cluster of houses along the route to Medea, where the GIA was known to be omnipresent. Jean Pierre surprised them when he stopped his car and invited the ringleader to get in. He didn't scold the boy, but instead, offered him a ride to Medea where he helped Jean-Pierre load and unload provisions while making the rounds at the market. On the way back to Tibhirine, Jean-Pierre let the boy off in front of his house and gave him a fresh baguette. "I tried to tame him with gentleness. We became friends," he explained years later in Fez.

Afterward, he never had another problem in Dakhla. "Incidents like that were often connected with some political event in France that was used to stir up hostility. It gave me great pleasure to talk directly with the young people." Eventually, a lay member of the French community in Algiers persuaded Christian to buy a freezer to save Jean-Pierre from having to drive to Medea so frequently.

For Luc, going to the market with Jean-Pierre was an outing and a form of relaxation. Unless, as happened once, street kids tried to grab his scruffy spade beard and taunted him, "Aren't you afraid of loosing your head, too?" They knew what the army did to its medics who treated terrorists. Such things didn't fluster Luc. He would just growl at them, "I don't care. They can have it."

Luc saw people all day long. Mornings at 7:30, his doors would open to the people already waiting outside the small blue gate next to the dispensary. He was now seeing more people than ever, some days as many as one hundred. His closing hour of 5:30 in the afternoon was rarely respected. People came at all hours. One of Mohammed's jobs as watchman was to chase them away at night.

Crowd control had always been something of a problem. Luc was not known for his orderliness. Jean-Pierre and Amédée were supposed to control the flow of people through the little gate next to the dispensary, so too many would not be in the exterior courtyard at one time. But Luc would sometimes appear at the gate himself and call out to those he knew. The women had a tendency to wander off into the inner cloister, and they were not above casual stealing.

Others tended to be overly persistent in demanding more pills or become hysterical about their inability to have children—like the infertile woman who, at age sixty, was still asking Luc if her child had fallen asleep in her stomach. Another went mad after loosing twelve of her fifteen children to disease and accidents.

Two hundred yards down the hill, at the foot of the garden, was a government clinic. When the nationalization program was announced in 1976, the primary school that had been built by the monks for the local children was converted to a medical clinic to compete with Luc. But the state-appointed doctors had been afraid to go to work since the end of 1993, and the clinic was staffed only by nurses, who rarely had adequate supplies. The clinic did have a marabout tree in front, a thousand-year-old live oak, which the villagers considered holy, and thought to possess healing powers. But the people also wanted to see a real doctor supplied with modern medications. In a country known for shortages, being a medically well-stocked, poor Trappist doctor in mountains full of Muslim terrorists was something of a miracle.

Marthe Robin's prediction to Luc had been right. She had told him he would never run out of medical supplies. Luc had once visited this famous mystic in Valence, not far from his house in the Drôme. She was a phenomenon who had perplexed the French scientific and medical establishment for years. The first medical team came from Lyons to examine her in 1942. At that time, Marthe Robin* had had no food or drink for over ten years, except for the host taken at weekly Mass and the application of a moist cloth to her lips before she met with people. "I don't live from nothing" she told the doctors. "I live from Jesus and my nourishment is to do his will."

Marthe Robin died in 1981, at the age of seventy-nine. She had become bedridden in 1928, a result of paralysis thought to have been caused by delayed reactions to the typhoid fever and Spanish influenza she had suffered as a child. In 1930, she started bleeding from her head, eyes, and hands every Friday. By the 1940s, she was attracting pilgrims from all over the world and had developed an ability

**Marthe Robin,* by Jean-Jacques Antier, documents her unusual story.

to see into the future of those others she considered holy. She also had a sixth sense about the people waiting outside her room and would tell her secretary to send away those she believed had come only as sightseers. Luc had successfully passed through her extrasensory screening in the early 1950s.

In the spring of 1995, Luc prayed to Marthe Robin out of desperation. For the first time in forty years, his supplies were on the verge of running out. The day after he had mentioned his concern to Christian, there was news from Algiers. His overdue package had arrived. Luc's supplies came from the donations of friends from all over France, as well as from Switzerland and Germany. Equally important, his friends and admirers in the local administration and in the Ministry of Health had made arrangements with customs officials that packages to Luc were to go through without delay, and untouched.

Luc had been special for years. So special that after Algerian independence, high officials from the FLN would go to Tibhirine to be treated by him. They proposed that he be paid a salary and become a government doctor. It was an offer he was able to refuse.

"When our *frères* of the mountain come to see Luc, it reminds us of the need to continually practice the art of healing among all people, and to force ourselves to see beyond the violence of which each is a part. We, too, have to disarm ourselves of our prejudices," Christian reflected in the bulletin sent to family and friends in April 1995. "Certainly God loves the Algerians. Isn't devoting our lives here evidence of that? But do we love them enough? Our friends here feel loved so little. Slowly, each of us is learning to understand that his death is part of this gift, this ministry of living together, accepting our differences, a ministry that is totally unconditional. On some days," he concluded the bulletin, "this doesn't seem like a very reasonable idea . . . about as reasonable as becoming a monk."

Every few days, the neighbors had new stories to report: twelve mutilated bodies found in the street in Medea, a reprisal, it was said, for a policeman having his throat slit; two female hands lying on the sidewalk, rumored to be a punishment for a fifteen-year-old girl not wearing a veil; heads on benches around the marketplace. Both sides wanted to create as much terror as possible. The eradicators wanted to terrorize the terrorists. The heads of local GIA sympathizers would be recognized by the people, increasing the horror.

The garden was where the monks worked out their frustrations and the violent impulses that simmered below the surface of an outer calm. It was the social club, schoolhouse, and gymnasium. The garden was where they always learned something new about their associates and grew closer to the neighbors who would still wander up and help harvest or weed. Together, they submerged their fears in practical work and easy friendship, which was intensified by the shared danger. "In the garden we were all equal—Mohammed, Musa, Ali, Ben Aissa, and others. It was where we learned about one another. There, and in the marketplace in Medea, was where I felt I was 'on mission,' " Jean-Pierre remembered. Christophe took a particular pleasure in jotting down their observations in his journal: "Why are the generals always fat?" "There is only one who does not seek power, and that is God." "The worst is that these are Muslims who are doing this to Muslims." "You know, it is as if the same blood circulates through us, irrigating us together."

The few visitors who made the trip up to Tibhirine were amazed by the aura of tranquillity that radiated from the monastery as the monks went about their work. There was a contagious calm. Christophe described the process as "detachment." "Something is drawing us away," he wrote. With few overnight guests at the *hôtellerie* now, social life had shifted to the *porterie,* located in the exterior courtyard, where Jean-Pierre, Amédée, and Célestin took turns talking with their neighbors who came to visit and had become the focus of their attention. They came for all kinds of reasons—to borrow tools, have official documents interpreted, or ask for money—but mainly, they came to talk about their woes to patient, sympathetic listeners who tried within their modest means to do what they could.

The neighbors had developed the belief that Lalla Mariam protected them. Mohammed would remind people that the Koran said one must respect the mother of Jesus. Neither during the war of independence nor since the recent fighting began had any of the armed groups ever harmed the Virgin. Despite the violence around them, and the armed opposition in the area, Tibhirine had been spared. No youths from the village had joined the GIA. The few who had joined the army had not returned home, in order to avoid reprisals, even though their families had paid the GIA compensation money. There had been no extortion, theft, or violence. Some people talked of the "monastic effect."

Visits to Fez were becoming more important to the brothers in Algeria. The monastery's annex there had become their decompression chamber. It was also their escape hatch if faced with a direct threat, a warning from an armed group to leave. The brothers went there from time to time to breathe a different air and relax—all except Amédée, who did not like long rides in the car, and Luc. Luc did not want to run the risk of spoiling his good memories of Morocco from the days of his military service at Goulimine, in the southern desert.

The charms of the monastery in Fez were the opposite of those in Tibhirine. It had been originally built by a French railway company as a hotel near the Bab Hadid gate, which led into the old city. The monks' rooms looked out on a small three-acre garden with lemon trees and vineyards that fall toward the valley below, where a highway and railroad line snake westward toward Algeria between tawny hills dotted with olive trees. The pagoda-shaped roof of the monastery gave it a strangely Oriental look, and its walls were covered with a thick blanket of wisteria. Driving from Tibhirine had become too dangerous. So now the monks flew to Casablanca and from there, they took the train to Fez. In May, Christophe, handed over responsibility for the garden to Mohammed while he went to spend time with the Fez four—Jean-Baptiste, Jean de La Croix, Guy, and Bruno.

Bruno had not wanted to go to Fez when Christian asked him in 1991 to take over as *le responsable,* the de facto superior there, though Christian would remain his superior. Bruno had liked Tibhirine's beauty and the simplicity of the life there in contrast to the grandeur of Abbey Bellefontaine in France. This quiet sixty-five-year-old-monk had been drawn to the Church and monastic life as a young man. Sent to a Marist boys school near La Rochelle, he was ordained at age twenty-six, but he never had his own parish. He tried to join the Benedictine monastery of Saint Martin de Ligugé when he was thirty-one, but was rejected. He then settled into a teaching career at a private secondary school, where he eventually served for fifteen years as director. Throughout his twenty-four years at the Collège Saint-Charles in Thouars, he was known by friends as solitary, introspective, and tormented by doubts over his choice of career. In 1981, Bruno gave up the adminstrative work he hated to become a monk at age fifty.

His lonely struggle to express a pent-up interior life was resolved only when he arrived in the Atlas. Bruno had told Christian he wanted to be buried there, but he was a Cistercian monk. Obedience, he knew, was the guardian of all the virtues. Without obedience, there can be no humility, and without humility, no real love of others. So Bruno did what Christian asked.

Bruno was considered rigid and distant, although capable of admitting error. Some brothers thought he gave excessive attention to housekeeping, cleanliness, and order. A bit of dust in a corner, a cobweb, or a spot of chipped plaster was cause for immediate action. He loved flowers, especially geraniums, and was devoted to his cats, which lived outside in the garden but occasionally slipped inside. Cooking was his relaxation. On Sundays and special religious days, he liked to bake cakes. But until a monk dies, his brothers often know little about him, aside from his external behavior. It is not their habit to sit around and chat idly, especially about themselves. Such chatter can lead to gossip and complaining, two poisons that Saint Benedict warned can infect a community. So the monks didn't learn until after his death that Bruno had been born in Vietnam, where his father had been an army commander and that he had spent time as a child in Algeria.

Christophe took long walks with Bruno in Fez. He liked its ancient beauty, narrow, labyrinthine cobblestone alleys, and crowded streets. They discussed the situation in Algeria, their faith, and their future. Christophe remembered the words of the American Trappist Thomas Merton. "He who gives himself freely over to God truly loves Him, and receives back the freedom that belongs to God's children. He will love as the Lord loves, and will be carried away, a captive of the invisible divine freedom."

When Christophe returned to Tibhirine, he found that the army had begun bulldozing the forest that surrounded the Virgin Mary standing on top of Abdelkader Rock. The wooded summit offered the terrorists both a vantage point for observation and a hiding place. It was painful for the brothers to see this massacre of the trees. They knew Merton's famous description of monks: "trees that exist in obscure silence, but by their presence purify the air." Wasn't that what they were doing, keeping the air around them clean, unpolluted by the carnage raging around the monastery?

Friday, November 10, 1995. The brothers were washing the dishes before Terce. That was another communal job. Some cleaned, others rinsed and dried, and still others put the dishes away, though there was an unspoken rivalry for cleaning the dishes, as that was the humblest of the jobs. Then they retired to the chapter room, just down the hall in the tower. After singing the Thirteenth Psalm, Christian announced to his brothers more grim news. Two nuns belonging to the Little Sisters of the Sacred Heart had been shot leaving their home in Kouba, the same neighborhood where Ali Benhadj had stirred the youth with his angry sermons. One of them, Odette Prévost, had been a frequent visitor to Tibhirine and a member of the *ribat.* The brothers sat silently in the chapter room with tears in their eyes, stupefied by the report. Christian read again outloud the bitter lament of the psalm they had just sung. *For how long Lord will you forget me, for how long will you hide your face from me? For how long will my soul be in pain and my heart saddened each day? How long will my enemy be exalted over me?*

Odette was sixty-three when she died. A teacher who spoke fluent Arabic, she had lived for almost thirty years in Algiers. Kouba was a FIS stronghold, yet her relations with the inhabitants had always been friendly. Like the monks, she knew of the dangers but believed that God wanted her to be among Algerians. It was her mission. And any cause that was not worth dying for, she had said, was already dead. Later, it was learned that the other sister, Chantal Galichet, had survived a bullet that entered the back of her neck and exited over her right eye.

Shortly before Christmas, the monks were told by their neighbors that the bodies of two women were found on the street near Aïn el-Ares, not far from the monastery. Amédée was visibly distraught. He received women all the time in the parlor, and, like Luc, he had developed a particular sympathy for Muslim women whose lives seemed especially difficult. Luc didn't speak all that day.

"I am sick, old, and tired" Luc had once written his nephew in Paris. "A man is nothing but a miserable thing unless his soul sings. I ask the Lord to give me joy." Luc's hope in earlier days that the poverty, suffering, and violence in Algeria would diminish had long since turned to pessimism. What kept him going, aside from a natural stoicism, was the pleasure he got from helping people. Luc was like a father to the young, especially to the girls, many of whom were orphans. He would find them clothes, give them a little money, advise them about personal hygiene, matters of the heart, and always encouraged them to get an education.

On Christmas Day, one of Luc's adopted children came to visit him during the Office of Sexte. Mohammed led her into the chapel to find him wheezing and sucking his mentholated bonbons. Normally, Luc did not come to the Offices, except on Sundays. When he did, he didn't sit with the others in a pew near the altar, but on one of the benches for visitors located in a back corner of the nave. On this day, Fatima and her husband had risked the drive to Tibhirine out of gratitude. She was a young lady from the village who, as a girl, had become a burden to her family after her father died. Her mother and brothers wanted to marry her off as soon as possible, and they had selected an older man she didn't like. Luc had persuaded her family to be patient. He gave her a job in the dispensary, got her clothes, and had helped her find another man to marry. After Fatima's visit, Luc's soul sang a little louder.

17

Emptying the Fishbowl

> *. . . when Jesus knew His hour had come that He should depart from this world to the Father, having loved His own who were in this world, He loved them to the end.*
>
> —John 13:1

Sister Chantal was brought back from the brink of death after twenty operations by French doctors. She lost her right eye and her neck was left badly scarred. In 1995, many wondered if Algeria itself was on the verge of death by self-mutilation.

Foreigners had taken an interest in Algeria's fate. Sant'Egidio is a lay Catholic organization in Rome whose members try to live according to the Gospels in the contemporary world, and it has evolved into a third-party force for reconciling conflicts in different parts of the world. During the fall of 1994 and into 1995, representatives of all the main Algerian political parties were meeting in Rome to find a political solution to the conflict. Sitting for the first time around the same table were representatives of the FLN, FIS, FFS, and Hamas, renamed the MSP, or Movement for Society and Peace. The effort failed.

Le pouvoir saw the Sant'Egidio initiative as lending legitimacy to the outlawed FIS. The party line within the Algerian government was that the FIS was a fascist, Nazi-like organization bent on ethnic purification. They wanted nothing to do with a negotiated settlement that included the FIS. If the military dictatorship was seen as bad in some western quarters, *le pouvoir* wanted to make sure the FIS was perceived as worse. Furthermore, the FIS would want its own high-level appointees within the army and other security posts. The government was afraid this could lead to outright civil war within the armed forces, resulting in a "Lebanonization" of Algeria.

More self-interested in the outcome of the Algerian drama than Sant'Egidio were France and the International Monetary Fund. Despite a mild condemnation by President François Mitterand in 1992 of the Algerian government's annulment of their own national elections, his influential Minister of Interior, Charles Pasqua, became deeply concerned that an Islamist victory could produce a tidal wave of immigration to France. France already had 800,0000 Algerian nationals working in France and another 500,000 *beurs,* or second-generation Algerians with French citizenship. The total population of Muslims in France was near 5 million, or 8 percent of its population, and growing faster than the native French. The economy had 11 percent unemployment, which was fueling support for the ultraright party of Jean-Marie Le Pen. His party's appeal was based on economic insecurity, rising crime, and xenophobia mixed with racism.

France had bread-and-butter reasons for its interest in Algeria's future. Thirty percent of Algeria's imports were provided by French firms. A billion dollars in commercial credits were provided by Paris to Algeria in 1994, supplemented by the delivery of helicopters and infrared night-vision equipment to the Algerian military. France's economic stake in Algeria meant it would have a deep interest in the IMF being reasonable in rescheduling Algeria's $26 billion debt.

Le pouvoir had a great interest in the IMF's decisions, as well. It knew that an undifferentiated fear of Islamic fundamentalism was a Western bugaboo, one that crudely and inaccurately equated fundamentalism* with terrorism, an image *le pouvoir* wished to maintain by linking the FIS and the GIA, even if there was no longer a link. Coupled with the requirement to strive for democratic respectability, the presidential election, scheduled for November 16, 1995, was important. After three years of executive rule by the generals, a return to democracy would serve to reestablish the government's legitimacy in the eyes of the world financial community. In order to receive

*The term *fundamentalism* applied to Islam is a misnomer. The term refers to American Protestants who insisted, in the wake of the Scopes trial, that the Bible was the literal word of God. In this sense, virtually all practicing Muslims are fundamentalists. For practicing Muslims, the Koran is indeed the literal word of God, spoken by the Angel Gabriel to the Prophet Mohammed. Muslims revere Jesus as a sinless prophet, born of a virgin, but he is not recognized as the Son of God. Fundamentalists are not necessarily Islamists who are motivated by a political agenda, nor are they by preference violent.

continued financial help, it was also important to give the impression that violence was under control.

The government's democratic charade merely deepened the contempt in which it was held by GIA hard-liners, whose position remained the policy of "no compromise, no truce, no negotiation." All but four of the twenty political parties declined to participate, claiming the results were rigged. As the elections drew nearer, violence increased. Nevertheless, voter participation was high—71 percent, according to government numbers. Some read the large turnout as protest by a population otherwise locked in fear and generally disgusted by the violence and the abuse of their religion for political ends. Through its own excesses, the GIA had eroded support from the "little people" on whom it depended.

Colonel Liamine Zeroual had been the military's candidate to represent the FLN in the elections. Zeroual won 61 percent of the votes in a four-party race. His message to Western observers was that "the threat of general civil war has been avoided; there remained only various local conflicts." In second place was Mahfoud Nahnah of the Hamas, renamed the Movement for Society and Politics, an Islamist party committed to nonviolence. He won 25 percent of the vote, followed by the Assembly for Culture and Democracy (RCD), a militantly democratic and Francophone party that had operated behind the scenes in December 1991 to get the generals to cancel the elections that the FIS were on the verge of winning. These democrats saw a FIS victory bringing down the curtain on democracy, the way the Nazis did in Germany after the elections in 1933. But the RCD itself won only 9 percent of the vote. A distant number four was the PRA, the moderate Islamist Party of Algerian Renewal.

But why was Hamas, as it is still known on the street, in second place, a party which preached theocracy, as did the FIS? With 2,900,000 votes, it won almost as many votes as the FIS had in 1991. Hamas was known for its opposition to violence; it was seen as a preserver of a decent Islam, and it offered a viable alternative to the FLN. Algerians are Muslims. They believe in God's law, and now more than ever, they were for nonviolence. The RCD and others viewed Hamas as a wolf in sheep's clothing. But Hamas had sacrificed blood for this clothing. It believed Islamic law should guide society, and its members were devoted to the cause of God, not by killing, but through reflection, prayer, preaching, and practicing an Islam that balances the heart with the law. The party had never deviated from that doctrine of nonviolence during the seven years of its existence. Even Bishop Teissier tried to persuade leaders of the RCD to withhold judgment on Hamas.

For its consistency, Hamas had been attacked from both sides. At the beginning of the conflict, *le pouvoir* viewed the party as part of the Islamist threat. Hamas wanted an Islamic state, and was viewed simply as more subtle, and thus more dangerous. The FIS leadership distrusted its leader, Sheikh Mahfoud Nahnah. He had long been suspected of betraying Mustafa Bouyali to the army in the 1980s. Had Nahnah simply become a tool of the government, part of a deal to create a new, tamed, state-sanctioned Islamic party? Many wondered. He had refused to join the FIS when it was formed in 1989 or to support it in the municipal elections of 1990. Hamas imams, leaders, and the rank and file had consistently denounced the killing and violence, and they were often murdered for their courage, like Bouslimani. Nahnah was not popular among the FIS, a party he described as run by "religious illiterates."

By the end of 1995, Hamas had lost three hundred party members to violent attacks. As far as Abdelkrim Dahmen, a Hamas/MSP delegate to the national legislature, was concerned, the Algerian newspapers were doing a great injustice to Islam. "They are simply criminals," he said as we were leaving his office at his party headquarters. "I don't know why the papers call them Islamic terrorists. They have nothing to do with Islam." Along the walls of the corridors and down the stairwell hang pencil portraits of dozens of young men, all Hamas members killed by these criminals.

In January 1994, Cherif Gousmi, the friend and mentor of Jamel Zitouni from Birkhadem, gave an interview to the Islamist newspaper *El Wasat,* published in London. At the time, Gousmi was also a member of the GIA's commission on politics and religious legislation. He was asked what qualities were sought in their leaders. "Besides natural qualities of command, they must have taken part in the jihad and have experience in different kinds of military operations. They must also have killed a good number of the enemies of God," Gousmi told the journalist.

Experience at killing provided a career ladder for aspiring emirs. The more spectacular and newsworthy the killing the more laurels to be gained for a neighborhood emir with ambitions to become a more important emir. And the more violence by, or attributed to the GIA, the better for *le pouvoir.* Such publicity only served to undermine GIA support and make the Algerian government look like the lesser evil to the befuddled public at home and abroad, who were trying to understand the butchery.

By 1994–1995, there were always at least four possible suspects for any given horror story: terrorists, government forces, local self-defense militias, which had been armed in 1994, and simple bandits or people with personal grudges to settle. But terrorists fought among themselves, and government clans also had accounts to settle. In the murky netherworld of ambiguity and opaqueness, many suspected the military was not above using the GIA to camouflage its own internal feuding, and thereby avoid open warfare between rival government interests. With four armed segments of the population potentially responsible for an act of violence, and no uniforms that could be trusted, there was a matrix of four by four, or sixteen theoretically possible explanations for each incident. In reality, there were probably only five: (1) GIA and AIS killing its enemies or each other; (2) government security forces killing the GIA or its sympathizers; (3) government clans settling accounts and using infiltrated GIA groups as cover; (4) local militias killing terrorists; and (5) private feuding and robbery done under the cover of war.

Indeed, where were the Algerian press stories about the atrocities commited by government forces—the "commandos of death," which entered the FIS neighborhoods and rounded up anyone who looked under twenty-five-years old, tortured or killed them, and threw their mutilated bodies on piles of garbage. The brother-in-law of Ali Benhadj was kidnapped and found thrown in a cement mixer with his throat cut. Much sympathy was aroused for the Francophone intellectuals and critics of the FIS who were assassinated. But what about the murder of religious intellectuals?

Mohammed Boudjerka, an internationally recognized scholar at the University of Algiers, was kidnapped and tortured to death by the police. Why no outrage at the castration of Mohammed Rouabhi, an accused plotter in the carnage at Boumediene International Airport, or toward the judge who refused to let him show his scars at the trial? The FIS engineers, doctors, and lawyers, most of whom had been trained in the West, had been baking in the desert camps by the thousands, yet their plight brought no outcries from the Western press or intellectual community. Why? Did they not know, or simply not care, like those French intellectuals whose sensitivities became curiously dull when torture was practiced on OAS sympathizers by the paratroopers?

Truth is controlled by those who write about it. In 1995, Western reporting was completely dependent on Algerian sources. The Algerian press had a pluralistic look and was capable of being critical of its own government, and occasionally skewered its own leaders in political cartoons. To the uninformed, it seemed relatively free. But in the Algeria of 1995–96, all Islamist newspapers had been banned and the mainstream Francophone press censored. *La Nation,* well respected, yet sympathetic to the Islamist cause, went out of business in 1994. Nor did it serve the government's version of the truth to encourage front-page headlines or TV stories about the murder of the dozens of imams and hundreds of Hamas members whose refusal to join in or justify the killing muddied the simple picture of Islamists as bloodthirsty fanatics. Unless the event was too spectacular to ignore.

Such an event occurred on July 11, 1995. A man entered the Mosque Khalid Ibn El-Walid on the rue Myrha in Paris's eighteenth arrondissement and shot Sheikh, Abdelbaki Sahraoui. The eighty-seven-year-old Sahraoui was a Francophile Islamist who had been a founding father of the FIS and a respected religious leader. He had been critical of the war declared on foreigners by the GIA, and he had spoken in favor of a political dialogue with the Algerian government. His assassination officially brought the Algerian violence into France's living rooms.

Two weeks later, an explosion in the St. Michel metro station, near the Cathedral of Notre-Dame, injured 117 people and killed 6. On August 19, a letter was delivered to the French embassy in Algiers for new French president, Jacques Chirac. It was an invitation from Supreme Emir Jamel Zitouni to Chirac to convert to Islam and change his policy of support for the Algerian government. Otherwise, there would be continued attacks on French soil. The letter reminded Chirac of a previous warning sent to President Mitterand in October 1994, which had been unheeded. Over the next two months, there would be eight more attacks—7 deaths and 187 wounded, including 14 students at a Jewish school near Lyons.

On September 23, a second letter was sent to President Chirac from Zitouni. It claimed credit for the attacks that had shaken France and put its politicians in a quandary as to how to handle the Algerian hot potato. Publically, France was neutral. "We favor neither the power in place nor the Islamists, but the Algerian people," Chirac announced.

Paris became dirty as a result of new antiterrorist security measures. Public wastebaskets throughout the city were welded shut. Storage lockers in railroad stations were no longer available to the public. The North African immigrant communities were the object of intense pressure from French police. In early November, the head of the GIA network in Paris was arrested. A young Algerian student, Boualem Bensaid, turned out also to be the brain of a European-wide network that spanned England, Belgium, Switzerland, Italy, and Sweden. French police learned that Yahia Riham, nicknamed "the Clove" because of a facial birthmark, had led the attack on the St. Michel metro station and organized the murder of Sheikh Sahraoui. Yahia Riham had also been a member of the Phalanges of Death, along with Jamel Zitouni.

The winter of 1996 saw articles appearing in Algerian and French newspapers that reported not only about feuding between the AIS and GIA but also about the power struggles within the GIA. Dissidents accused Zitouni of being too extreme, of destroying the Islamist movement by killing women, children, and priests. Jamel Zitouni's profession of faith, "Rules of Salafists* and the Duties of

*Salafists are Islamist reformists who see their struggle as pan-Islamic and seek to rebuild an Islamic community that transcends the nation-state, whose demands of allegience are but another form of idolatry, as all authority and legitimacy come from following God's law.

the Mujahideen," declared to his combatants what the GIA was about. "Algeria," he announced, was a "land of war and of Islam, where people would be treated according to how they practiced their Islam or their impiety. . . . The jihad against the disbelievers, the people of the Book, or polytheists is an obligation for all Muslims." The Algerian authorities, its institutions, and its allies were to be brought down. The Algerian government and that of virtually all other Muslim countries were populated with "disbelievers." His "profession" denounced those who fell outside Islam—Communists, nationalists, capitalists, atheists, and Shiites. The AIS, the armed branch of the FIS, were "apostates." Leaving the GIA was punishable by death.

To achieve its goal, his profession declared, "the jihad cannot spare babies, children, and the starving, because the preservation of religion is more important than human lives." Experts agreed that the text sounded like Zitouni, but they doubted he could have written it unaided. Moreover, rumours were circulating that he was "in play" with the Sécurité Militaire, Algeria's military intelligence service.

In early March, mosques in Medea and Blida found their prayer rugs stolen. Grocery store merchants had their stores cleaned out by the two GIA rival groups in the region. The group led by Sidi Ali Benhadjera was known to be highly critical of Zitouni's violent excesses. Benhadjera had been elected a FIS delegate from Medea to the National Assembly in the first-round vote of December 1991. He also had been the director of a primary school in Medea, was a connaisseur of herbal medicine, and liked to discuss botany and astronomy with Brother Robert, the Benedictine hermit who lived in the mountains opposite the monastery. The group of Baghdadi was loyal to Zitouni and had inherited control of the area around Tibhirne, formerly controlled by Sayah Attia. There were those, including Bishop Claverie of Oran, who believed Attia had extended his *aman* or "protection," to the monks following his Christmas visit in 1993. His failure to send his representative to follow up on his demands, as well as the continued, undisturbed functioning of the monastery for over two years were interpreted as evidence of this.

Easter was approaching, and Henri Teissier had persuaded a reluctant Christian to lead a retreat at the diocesan house. The once-itinerant ambassador thought he should remain at Tibhirine with his brothers. However, he knew it was too dangerous to expect people to come to them. "It's easier to move the stool than the piano," Teissier, clinched his argument.

"Christian seemed transparent. He had an incredible serenity about him that day, like a holy man, almost floating, but with his feet still on the ground," recalled one of the participants. Entitled "The Church: the Incarnation Continued," his discourse was later referred to as "the five pillars of peace" by the forty-odd people who had gathered there on March 8. Christian began by remembering the words of his friend Gilles Nicolas:

"Last Christmas, our curé said, 'We must find in the mystery of the Incarnation the true reasons for our staying here despite the threats and torment of the people. Immanuel—that is, God silently present—is also that love which alone is revolutionary, alone transforms the hearts of men and women.' What is true for Christmas is true for Easter. The mystery of the Incarnation. We, too, have to live the mystery of the Incarnation, for that is the deepest of all the reasons why we stay at Tibhirine.

"One must have a broad vision of this Paschal mystery. Everything is Paschal in the life of Jesus. Easter begins from the moment God participates in man's finiteness. This is expressed well in "Gaudium et Spes," the charter for all Christians and for laypeople as well, set forth in the Constitution of the Second Vatican Council. Of all its texts, the one which seems to best address the questions of living together in this world is this: 'GS 22: By his incarnation the Son of God in some way united Himself with all men. He works with the hands of men, He thinks with the intelligence of men, acts with the will of men, He loves with the heart of men. Born of Mary, He truely became human, but for His lack of sin. . . . In effect, Christ died for all mankind so that the last calling of man is truly unique to man. We hold that the Holy Spirit offers not only to Christians but to everyone of goodwill, in a manner only God knows, the possibility to be associated with the mystery of rebirth.'

"Our witness is here in Algeria. The only way for us to give witness is to live where we do, and be what we are in the midst of banal, everyday realities. . . . If redemption is the motive for the coming of Christ, then Incarnation is the method. Intent belongs to the Son. He wanted to save something in us that only He could save. But the method is up to us. In our life, there is always a child ready to enter the world—the child of God that each of us is.

"How do we live this mystery of the Incarnation? St. François de Sales said, 'Accept everything with equanimity, because everything can contribute to the glory of God.' The Incarnation is everywhere. In our rule, Saint Benedict has a small phrase in one of the chapters . . . *in order that in everything, God may be glorified.* That applies even to commerce. The monks at the monastery live by the work of their hands, but they sell their produce a little cheaper than the laymen in order to glorify God. It is as simple as that, the Incarnation. It applies in the kitchen; it is with us in daily life, where we must have a lot of humility and modesty because it is not easy to be heroic every day.

"One way for us to live in accordance with this vocation inaugurated by Jesus is to make sure the words of our faith correspond with our actions."

Christian then described the five pillars of behavior that must be practiced daily to have peace.

He began with patience. Saint Benedict had explained its importance: *Inside the monastic enclosure, persevering in their calling until death, monks participate through their patience in the sufferings of Christ."* "There is no word for *martyr* in the Trappist constitution," Christian elaborated, "nor reference to a bloody death. There is only the demand for patience and endurance in living each day." After the Christmas visit by the montagnards, Cardinal Duval had counseled Christian with one word—*la constance*—"perseverance."

Poverty was the second pillar. "The future belongs to God, not to us. Man does not have the imagination of God, so when we think of the future, we think of it as being like the past." To want to imagine the future is only wishful thinking. Christian reminded his listeners that, in the Old Testament, God provided the Israelites with manna each day. But if they tried to gather more than they needed, storing it up for the next day, they found that it spoiled. "The future is like a tunnel. You can't see anything inside, and only a fool would expect it to look the same upon exiting as upon entering it. When it comes to recruiting for our monastery today, we have no one to approach in Algeria. And among the people, whom are we going to ask? We must simply let the Spirit do its work and fish for souls. That is what I call poverty—to have need only for that which You have always given me."

Christian's third pillar was presence. God is in all his children, and when one kills another, one kills the image of God. In every human being, there is something eternal, something more than a homicidal act. "This is why I cannot kill myself," Christian recalled the words of the Jewish philosopher Emmanuel Levinas, whom he admired. "Morality entered the world by the commandment 'Thou shalt not kill.' The first words a person's face says to another is, respect me. Killing can take different forms, as all who live in a community know. A contemptuous attitude, a wounding word, phrases that assassinate are other ways to kill."

Christian reminded his audience of John's words: *He who hates his brother is a murderer.* "Each person must ask, 'Have I eradicated all forms of hatred from my heart?' We cannot live in this country today, wishing for peace, if we don't go to this extreme of removing hatred from ourselves . . . and no one can say he has done this.

"When I approach my neighbor, I also become his guardian, which means to become his hostage. Justice begins with the other. Take the case of Sayah Attia. I was not only the guardian of my brothers in the monastery but his guardian, too, of this man who stood opposite me and who should have been able to discover within himself something more than what he had become. I think this happened in some small measure, to the degree that he gave way that night, or made an effort to understand me. People say these types are disgusting animals, they are not human, and that you can't deal with them. I say that if we talk like that, there will never be peace."

Prayer is the fourth pillar. "Do we pray enough for one another, for all people without any limits?" Christian asked. "Saint Paul wrote in Romans, *In trying times, persevere in prayer.* . . . We could not keep going if we did not pray and, in our prayers, seek to rid ourselves of the spirit of violence, prejudice, and rejection within us. After the episode with Attia, I wanted to pray for him. What should I pray to God? 'Kill him?' No, but I could pray, 'Disarm him.' But then I asked myself, Do I have the right to ask God to disarm him if I don't begin by asking, 'Disarm me, disarm my brothers.' That was my prayer each day."

Finally, he spoke of that all-important word, forgiveness. "*Forgive us our trespasses as we forgive those who trespass against us.* We must dig into ourselves to follow the path of forgiveness . . . to rid ourselves of the tendency to want to choose one side or the other, to give a prize for good and evil—yes, we monks have this instinct, too. So we called the terrorists the "brothers of the mountain" and the army "the brothers of the plain." The terms are useful for talking on the phone, but it was also a way of maintaining an open, fraternal spirit toward all sides. Coincidentally, Forgiveness is the first name for God in the Muslim litany of ninety-nine names for the divine—*Ar Rahman.* And the last is Patience—*Es Sabur.* But God is also poverty, God is presence, and God is prayer. This is the peace that God gives us. It is not as the world gives it."

On March 11, 1996, Luc received another shipment of medical supplies. He was more depressed than ever by the misery and the killing. A few days later, he wrote to Paul Grenot, his old medical school friend in Lyons: "The violence here has not abated, although the government censors would like to cover it up. How can we get out of this mess? Violence will not cure violence. We can only exist as humans by becoming symbols of love, as manifested in Christ, who, though himself just, submitted himself to injustice."

Bruno arrived from Fez on the nineteenth with several thousand wafers. Manufacturing host wafers for the Christians in the Maghreb was one of the ways the Fez annex supported itself. He came early to visit with his brothers before the election scheduled for Palm Sunday, March 31. It would mark the end of Christian's second term. He had let it be known that he didn't want to be superior again and that he hoped Christophe would succeed him, though some thought Christophe lacked the self-control to be a good prior. Paul returned with a big smile on Monday, the twenty-fifth after a short visit to his sick mother in Bonnevaux, bringing with him a book on Sufism for Christian and a pair of shovels—"to dig our graves," he lightheartedly told inquiring friends before leaving.

On Tuesday, twelve members of the *ribat* trickled in from different corners of the country. It was their first meeting since the visit of "Father Christmas" in 1993. The *hôtellerie* was bustling with activity after being virtually empty for two and a half years. Before going to bed, Jean-Pierre danced in his room as he quietly sang psalms to himself. It was a habit he had confessed to Elisabeth, Christophe's sister. He loved the psalms. They made him joyful even when they were sad. But that night, he had reason to be joyful. The monastery was full of visitors and there was a slightly festive atmosphere. He and his brothers were still alive. Each, in their own way, had made peace with death. The liturgy at midday Mass had spoken directly to Jean-Pierre and his brothers. The reading had been from the Gospel of John, the passage where Jesus speaks to the Pharisees who are demanding His death. *I am going away. . . . He who has sent Me is with Me. The Father has not left Me alone, for I always do those things that please Him.*

Early Wednesday morning, around 1:15, Jean-Pierre was woken by voices outside his gatehouse room, which faced onto the passage way leading from the exterior court into the cloister. At that time of night, he thought the commotion had to do with the montagnards wanting Luc's services. He had not heard the bell ring, so he assumed that they had simply jumped over the walls, as before. From behind the curtains of his glass door, which opened onto the entrance of the cloister, he could see a man with a turban, bandoliers, and a machine gun walking toward the rooms of Christian, Luc, and Amédée in the corridor opposite his room. A few moments later, he heard Christian's voice.

"Who's in charge here?"

"This man here," someone replied. "You must do as he says."

Jean-Pierre could see Christian; Luc, with his medical bag in hand; and Mohammed, who caught a glimpse of his face in the window and gestured for him not to come out. Jean-Pierre stepped back and listened. He could hear someone give the order to open the exterior gates. A few minutes later, there was the sound of footsteps shuffling past his front door. The outside gate clanged shut. A dead silence followed.

Jean-Pierre assumed the past had repeated itself—that Christian had told the montagnards to come back during the day and that Luc's poor health did not permit him to leave. He imagined that the two had simply gone back to bed. He went to the bathroom and saw that all the lights had been turned out. Everything looked to be in order, though he saw one curious thing. Strewn around in the corridor were clothes of the kind Luc would often give to patients. Had they asked for clothes and simply thrown them on the floor because they didn't like them? he wondered. Jean-Pierre had just gone back to bed, when there was a knock on his door. Amédée and Thierry Becker, a priest from Oran, were standing there. "Do you know what has happened? We are alone. All the others have been taken."

After their conversations with the guests and later with Mohammed, they pieced together what had happened. Mohammed had heard men banging on his door at 1:00 A.M., and he told them to go away, saying that the doctor didn't see people at night. The men responded by breaking into his house. They had accents from the east and wore no face masks. Their leader had red hair, and he ordered Mohammed to take them to Luc, who, they said, was needed to care for two wounded men. Mohammed brought them through the entrance that led from the garden into the monastery, then up a staircase under the chapter room. He first went to find Christian, then to Luc's room, which was across from Christian's, off the corridor leading to the scriptorium.

Mohammed was ordered to find the other monks. Paul, Michel, Bruno, Célestin, and Christophe were upstairs in the dormitory. So were six of the male guests who had come for the *ribat*. Their rooms were separated from the monks' quarters only by a door in the middle of the corridor. A guest heard some shuffling of chairs and tables and a protesting voice he thought was Célestin's. Perhaps Célestin was sick, and being taken downstairs to see Luc, since it would not be possible to get to a hospital at night. Thierry Becker opened the door a crack to see the monks and several armed men with Mohammed, who signaled with his head not to come out.

While trooping down the stairwell in the dark with five of the monks, one of the terrorists stumbled in the dark. Mohammed used the few seconds of distraction to break away and run out the door leading to the new building and then disappear in the garden below. In his report to the abbot general afterward, Becker remembered:

"We didn't want to make ourselves noticed or leave by the steps at the back of the dormitory, because they led outside, where there might still have been armed men. We each went back to bed and figured that Christian would come tell us if the disturbance concerned us. I lay in silence, thinking that my time had come. I was cold but calm, asking the Lord to grant me peace but also a little more time. There was so much administrative work for me to take care of back in the diocese. It would be an enormous inconvenience if I were to disappear. I heard some sounds outside but no engine noises. Suddenly, Amédée opened my door, 'Ah, you are there. The monastery is empty. There are no more fathers.' We went to the *porterie* and saw that the main gate was opened and then we knocked on Jean-Pierre's door."

Amédée and Jean-Pierre discovered that the telephone lines had been cut, just as had happened almost forty years earlier when the FLN intruded upon the monastery to kidnap the abbot. Like then, there was also a curfew in place. Practical considerations dictated staying put until daylight. Not only was it dangerous to go out at night during the curfew but even if they arrived at the gendarmerie, it was possible no one would open the door. The gendarmes were scared of nighttime visitors, too. And they were not known for giving hot pursuit to terrorists after dark.

A survey of the damage found Christian's room turned upside down. His typewriter and camera had been stolen, though the book on Sufism that Paul had brought him was still by his bed. His tunics and shoes were thrown in a corner. Luc's room was also a mess. Boxes of medication had been broken into, books strewn on the floor, and his new radio-dispatch equipment had been stolen. Amédée slept a few feet from Luc's room, but he had gotten in the habit of locking his door at night, a precaution that thwarted the curiosity of one of the intruders rifling through the supplies in the room outside and who had tried opening his door. Amédée's and Luc's rooms occupied an area that had once been lined by cubicles with only curtains for privacy. Some of the cubicles had been combined to make two rooms with doors, but Luc, who frequently got up at night to cook, didn't lock his door.

A wheel of cheese that Paul had brought back from Tamié was found in the corridor downstairs. It had been thrown away, Amédée assumed, when one of the terrorists noticed the cross on the wrapping. The rooms in the dormitory upstairs had also been ransacked. The computer in Paul's room was still there, but candy wrappers were strewn all over the floor from the boxes of chocolates he had brought back with him for Easter. Only one box had been left untouched, the one that had alcohol in the bonbons. Thierry Becker took it downstairs and put it in the refrigerator for the brothers when they returned.

It was already three in the morning by the time Thierry Becker and Jean-Pierre had finished reciting the rosary with Amédée. They decided to go back to bed and regroup at five o'clock. Thierry Becker, Jean-Pierre, and Amédée at first thought they should ring Matins to show the neighbors that life at the monastery was going on as usual. Then they changed their minds. Bells would only alert any terrorists in the neighborhood that some monks were still alive.

At the Office of Lauds, they sang the Third Psalm. *Lord, how they have increased who trouble me! Many are they who rise up against me. . . . Many say to me, there is no help for him in God. . . . I lay down and slept; I awoke, for the Lord sustained me. . . . I will not be afraid of ten thousands of people who have set themselves against me. . . .* The visiting priests took the places of the missing brothers, but they had difficulty singing the way monks did. So they stopped trying and simply recited the psalms to themselves. After the Office, they went to the refectory for a hardy breakfast.

By 7:15, Jean-Pierre and Thierry Becker had arrived in Medea after driving through a thick morning fog. Becker spoke fluent Arabic, so he acted as the monks' spokesman with the commandant of the gendarmerie, who expressed little surprise at their story. He then called the general of the gendarmerie in Algiers and told the two visitors they could use the phone to call Bishop Teissier before giving their deposition to one of the officers.

The two men returned to the monastery later that morning and found that the *ribat* guests had already gone back to Algiers. At midday, Jean-Pierre, Amédée, and Thierry Becker celebrated Sext. In his homily, Becker commented on the correspondence between the liturgy for the fifth week of Lent and the events that had just transpired. Like Jesus, they had been living the way of the cross. Was it simply coincidence, or divine plan, that the seven brothers should arrive at their Golgotha as Jesus was preparing for his? The reading was from the Book of Daniel, telling of Shadrach, Meshach, and Abdenago, three men of faith who survived being thrown into a furnace for refusing to worship the false gods demanded by King Nebuchadnezzar.

After Sext, Thierry Becker went to make some lunch for Amédée and Jean-Pierre, who both confessed to not knowing how to cook. He found that Luc had already prepared a large pot of soup and another full of string beans, which were still sitting untouched on the stove. But dining would not be peaceful. The telephone lines had been repaired that morning and the phone began to ring nonstop. The first call was from Luc's cousin, who had heard the news via a relative in the Congo. Another soon came from Monique de Chergé, who was concerned for the safety of Jean-Pierre and Amédée. There were countless pesky journalists, whose calls they wouldn't take. Finally, they decided to take a nap until the Office of None.

Following None, a unit of the gendarmerie arrived to take photographs. Knowing well Christian's admonishing words to Sayah Attia, his old friend Thierry Becker asked the armed escort to withdraw outside the cloister. The gendarmes expressed surprise when they had finished their work. "You live so simply," one of them remarked. The commanding officer asked the remaining monks not to spend the night in the monastery and proposed they sleep instead in the Grand Hotel Msala at the gendarmerie's expense. Shortly before leaving, a neighbor came to the monastery with a white cowl found a quarter of a mile away. It belonged to Michel. Had he left it like a bread crumb to show the trail?

Jean-Pierre, Amédée, and Thierry Becker arrived at the hotel with sheets under their arms, only to recieve royal treatment by the hotel manager, who personally escorted them to their suite. They were asked to join the commandant of the gendarmerie, the head of security for the whole *wilaya,* and the *wali*'s chief of staff, who happened to be having dinner there when the three arrived. Afterward, they went up to their suite and sang Compline together. When they finished, Thierry Becker asked the two monks to forgive him if he did not get up at 4:00 A.M. for Vigils. Guards were posted outside their doors throughout the night.

The next morning, gendarmes drove the three men back to the monastery. Amédée and Jean-Pierre had things to put in order. There were local accounts to pay, money to get from the bank, and certain of the brothers' personal belongings to take with them to Algiers. The gendarmes offered to drive Jean-Pierre into Medea to accomplish his tasks. He thanked them and asked only that they not drive in an ostentatious convoy, as he didn't want to alarm the locals. The monks agreed to leave for Algiers by four o'clock, before it got dark. After lunch, Bishop Teissier, Ambassador Lévêque, and the *wali* arrived and were told about the previous night's events by Amédée and Jean-Pierre. Brother Robert wanted to stay in the monastery, but Thierry Becker insisted that was not possible. He had promised the commandant that no one would sleep in the monastery at night.

As the monks were loading the cars, the commanding officer asked why they were leaving so many things behind—furniture, garden tools, kitchen utensils, pictures. "It's simple. The fathers are going to return," Becker explained.

18

Martyrs of Hope

Faith is the substance of things hoped for, the evidence of things unseen.

—Hebrews 11:1

Ambassador Malarmé received Father Armand Veilleux in his palatial office at Villa Farnese overlooking the piazza. The French diplomat offered perfunctory condolences to the procurer general, who had driven halfway across Rome from Trappist headquarters on the viale Africa. "Well, do you have any news from Algeria?" he asked abruptly.

"But I came here to ask *you* for news, ambassador," Veilleux replied.

"About what?"

"You have not heard of Communiqué 43? It has been all over the newspapers and TV. We are in a new phase."

Veilleux is a soft-spoken, kindly looking French Canadian whose glasses, snow white hair, and matching white beard give him the look of Santa Claus. As procurer general, he was number two in the Order, acting as liaison between the 170 Trappist monasteries around the world and the Papacy, handling their special requests that required papal approval. He had flown to Algiers as soon as he received news of the monks' disappearance. He then returned to Rome after two weeks of hearing the French ambassador there say he knew nothing, or at least nothing he was willing to divulge. For a month, no one claimed credit for the kidnapping. Sant' Egidio, the Catholic Church, and French and Algerian security services turned to their various listening posts. Nothing.

Of course, rumors had been in high season during the thirty days of silence following their abduction. They were being held in the city, they were in the *bled*. Two monks had been killed. Then, two monks had been freed, a report that even reached President Chirac's desk. The appearance in London of a document in the Saudi newspaper *Al Hayat* on April 26 was the first solid information. Communiqué 43 presented religious arguments for kidnapping the monks, as well as the conditions for their release. It was signed by supreme emir of the GIA, Abou abd al-Rahmen Amin, the nom de guerre for Jamel Zitouni.

The ambassador gave a cursory look at the copy of the communiqué Veilleux showed him.

"Yes, so now it is in the hands of the French government and being handled through the proper channels."

"But I am here to ask that we be kept informed of any negotiations. We know that in situations like this, secret talks take place."

"If they are secret, we can't very well talk about them, can we?"

"But we are the monks' family."

Trappist policy, Veilleux assured the ambassador, was to stay out of this sort of thing and leave it to local authorities. He was only asking for privileges customarily granted a family during a hostage crisis. The ambassador reminded Veilleux that France had warned its citizens two years ago to get out of Algeria. Those who stayed behind had to accept the consequences. "In any case," he added, "France has to proceed according to its assessment of its broad political, economic, and moral interests."

On the morning of April 30, a representative of Zitouni, known by his contact as "Abdullah," arrived at the French embassy in the fashionable Hydra neighborhood. By prearrangement, an intelligence officer of the Direction Générale de la Sécurité Extérieure was waiting for him by the side entrance of the security gate and led him inside the huge parklike compound.

Abdullah was known to the local French security officers. His father had been a chauffeur for the French Bank for Economic Cooperation. He was also the brother of Abdullah Yahia, the head of the commando group that hijacked flight Air France 8969 on Christmas Day 1994, and who had been killed during the French rescue operation.

"We are very upset," he told the officer in fluent French after they had gone into the conference room. Abdullah proceeded to show him a letter signed by Abou abd al-Rahmen Amin on now-familiar GIA letterhead, an open Koran framed with two crossed swords. With the letter was an Arab version of Communiqué 43 and a tape recording proving that the monks were alive. A security officer checked the cassette for a hidden explosive device. The ambassador's counselor was then called into the meeting.

They talked with Abdullah for an hour and a half. He wanted the French to help them free the monks. Jean-Charles Marchiani's name was mentioned. He was the prefect from the department of the Var, who had negotiated the release of two French pilots shot down in Bosnia, and was close to the influential Minister of the Interior, Charles Pasqua. Among local French intelligence officers, Zitouni's attitude toward the monks was thought to be neutral. The monks had remained untouched in a region controlled by the Baghdadi family loyal to Zitouni. The tape, the men in the embassy learned, had been given to Zitouni by a rival clan, ostensibly responsible for the kidnapping, a result of internecine GIA feuding.

Before leaving, Abdullah asked for a receipt on embassy letterhead. The letter, addressed to Abou abd al-Rahmen Amin, ended by saying "We wish to maintain contact with you," and it gave two secure numbers to call at any time. The GIA's contact was to be an intelligence officer, code-named "Climau." To avoid Algerian surveillance cameras covering the embassy, Abdullah was driven out in a diplomatic car, accompanied by Climau and the French consul, who left him off in Hussein-Dey, an Islamic neighborhod of Algiers, where he could easily disappear into the crowd.

Bishop Teissier was one of five men at the French embassy listening to the fifteen-minute recording, one that would eventually be replayed hundreds of times for clues. A frequent visitor to the monastery, he knew all the monks personally and could verify the voices. Also present were the ambassador's counselor, the embassy doctor, and two men from intelligence.

"It is the twentieth of April. The time is eleven P.M." The first voice was Christian's. He summarized certain news events of that day reported by Radio Medi I in Morocco, then said, "I am Brother Christian, son of Monique and Guy de Chergé, age fifty-nine, a monk at the monastery of Tibhirine and prior of the community. We are informing you that we are being held as hostages by the mujahideen of the *jamaate el Islamiya* and are alive and in good health."

Christian's voice was followed by that of Christophe and the other five men repeating the same text, "I am . . . son of . . . age . . . a monk at the monastery of Tibhirine. I am in good health." Those listening were struck by the calm tone of their voices. Michel departed from the script and added the word "period" at the end of each sentence. Luc was heard to growl at his captors, "What is this stuff you want me to read?" Only Christian sounded strained, markedly so, as if struggling with himself to pronounce each word. One of the captors was heard to say, "*A toi,* Christian," before he read a second statement. "It is demanded that the French government release a certain number of hostages in exchange for our freedom . . . or we will not return." These were unquestionably the voices of the monks.

The job of finding and freeing them would reveal different psychologies between the two French intelligence services, which, despite their rivalry, could work closely together. The Direction de la Sécurité du Territoire, or DST, was responsible for domestic intelligence. It came under the Ministry of the Interior and had trained many of the senior members of the Algerian security services when Algeria was still part of France and intelligence collection was a matter of internal security. The past director, Yves Bonnet, was the president of a Franco-Algerian Friendship society. Close collaboration with the Algerian security services was an assumed way of thinking to the domestic branch. The Algerians had helped them in 1987 to recover two French journalists taken hostage in Lebanon. They were friends of France.

The domestic intelligence service had a different view of the GIA than did its foreign intelligence rival, the Direction Générale de la Sécurité Extérieure, known as the DGSE. The DST considered the GIA as having no real structure. The GIA was almost fictional, they argued, consisting of only small autonomous groups working for themselves or for someone else. The DGSE, on the other hand, assumed the GIA had real structure and control. It was trying to find an interlocutor with whom to negotiate.

But in the spring of 1996, Algeria was no longer part of France, and security questions at the embassy were officially under the jurisdiction of the foreign intelligence service. The DGSE was part of the army and lacked the DST's history and intimate contacts. Many old *pieds-noirs* filled its rank, and they carried a visceral dislike of the FLN and of the Algerian government, making cooperation less natural. The DSGE was instinctively more distrustful of Algerian security services, which it believed to be thoroughly penetrated by Islamist sympathizers. Not that they weren't, but the Islamist sympathizers in the Algerian security services did not worry the domestic intelligence boys as much as they did the DGSE, where they thought the only good Islamist was a dead one. The DST knew innately that not all Islamists were the same. Experts in Islamic law within the Algerian services often used their superior religious knowledge to persuade those in the maquis to surrender, something the foreign intelligence services knew from radio intercepts and informers.

Knowledge of the Koran became a weapon in this Muslim civil war, in which fighting in an Islamically correct manner was important to many on both sides. Superior learning could sow doubt in the minds of sincere, uneducated mujahideen misled by those with partial knowledge or who followed a personal agenda. The Koran is full of verses warning against its misuse: *Those whose hearts are infected with disbelief follow the ambiguous part, so as to create dissension. . . . You shall not falsely declare, 'This is lawful, that is forbidden,' in order to invent a falsehood about God. . . . He that fights for God's cause fights for himself. God needs no man's help.*

The domestic branch lost the bureaucratic struggle over how best to get back the men who had risked their lives in order to maintain solidarity with their Algerian neighbors. The DGSE sent their Algerian counterparts a copy of the cassette but did not inform them that "they wished to maintain contact" with the kidnappers, as stated in their letter of receipt given to Abdullah, implying a French desire to keep talking. Nor did the DGSE keep their Algerian counterparts informed of the subsequent secret negotiations.

The Algerian security service was divided between the Francophones and Arabophones. The Francophones tended toward cooperation with French security and had persuaded their more skeptical

Arabophone colleagues to go along with DGSE's request not to engage the terrorists if they were located, for fear of accidentally killing the monks.

Communiqué 43 was unsettling to Amédée. It smelled of a death sentence. Just days before the monks were kidnapped, Amédée had spoken to Christian about his scenario for their being plucked from the fishbowl. It was more likely, he thought, that the GIA would want to compromise them, or convince them to join their cause as a moral ally, rather than to kill them. By remaining with their Muslim neighbors and sharing the same risks, the monks had acquired a strong moral influence and an aura of sanctity.

In the communiqué, the GIA seemed to be preparing the justification for an execution. . . . *This announcement, coming now more than twenty days after the abduction of the monks, shows that the infidel junta can neither protect itself nor others. . . . The monks arrogantly presume that sheikh Sayah Attia . . . may God bless his soul, had made a promise to spare their lives . . . There is no evidence of this, and even if he had, such an act would have been wrong because the monks never stopped trying to evangelize the Muslims and to show their religious symbols and celebrate their religious holidays . . . Everyone knows that a monk who withdraws from the world is a hermit. It was the murder of such monks that Abu Bakr* (the Prophet's father-in-law) *prohibited, but monks who leave their hermitage and mix with the people and draw them away from the divine path are proselytizing . . . As it is my duty and that of all Muslims to liberate our prisoners in conformity with the Hadith "free those who suffer." I can imagine freeing our prisoners for yours . . . You have the choice: if you liberate ours we will liberate yours. We have a list, but first free our brother Abdelhak Layada, and then we will give you the names of others, God willing. If you refuse, we will cut their throats. Praise be to God.*

Amédée thought the communiqué meant that the captors had not succeeded in convincing the brothers to join their cause. Now Zitouni was trying a different approach—bargain their lives for some of their own prisoners. That could also explain the long delay before any announcement was made. But the communiqué specifically mentioned only one prisoner, Abdelhak Layada, who had been the subject of the hijacked Airbus negotiation, as well. Layada was the second self-declared supreme emir of the GIA. In 1993, he had expanded the war against the apostate junta by killing outspoken anti-Islamist journalists

But why was the communiqué addressed to President Chirac, if Layada was in an Algerian jail? No other prisoners were mentioned, only that "We have a full list." Many within and outside the Trappist Order saw the communiqué as the GIA's way of insulting the Algerian government. The real power was in France, the communiqué was saying. France can get the Algerian government to do whatever it wants.

Radio Medi I, a Franco-Moroccan station in Tangiers, was widely listened to in Algeria. It had been the only station anywhere to have issued a daily bulletin on the status of the monks during their disappearance. At noon on May 23, the announcer told his listeners "We are going to give you some information even though we have no way of confirming its authenticity. We are always subject to being manipulated. Yesterday, we received a telephone call telling us that the seven monks, kidnapped fifty-six days ago, are now dead. We did not transmit the information yesterday, as we were not able to verify who was the caller. Today, we just received a fax with the seal of the GIA confirming the news. We cannot, however, determine the origin of the phone call or of the fax."

The message was too precise not to be taken seriously. It revealed that there had been contacts and even the beginnings of negotiations with French authorities. It mentioned the cassette that had been taken to the French embassy and the terms for getting the monks back mentioned in Communiqué 43. This latest one, Communiqué 44, added, "We were disposed to negotiate an exchange, citing in particular brother Layada. At first they showed a readiness to negotiate and wrote us a letter signed and stamped that they wanted to proceed. We thought they wanted to save the lives of the monks. Later, the president of France and his foreign minister said they would not negotiate with the GIA, cutting off the dialogue. Therefore, we have cut the throats of the seven monks as we said we would do. It happened this morning. May God be praised." It was dated May 21 and signed by Emir Abou abd al-Rahmen Amin.

In London, the GIA mouthpiece, *El Ansar* (*The Patriot*), published the full text of Communiqué 44 in its May 24 weekly edition, adding that in its next issue it would publish revelations of French "treason." When the May 31 issue appeared, it announced that "the expected information was never obtained." This would be *El Ansar's* last issue.

There were those in Zitouni's entourage in favor of freeing the monks, yet to have done so would have been an admission of failure. Zitouni had already spelled out the consequences of not meeting the terms of Communiqué 43. One fact was certain. The murder of the monks unleashed a fierce internal struggle within the GIA. Even the few supporters of the GIA abroad who financed *El Ansar* accused it of having "violated Islamic law." The Egyptian Jihad, the Libyan Islamic Fighters, and individual Syrian and Palestinian patrons stopped financing the paper.

On Sunday, May 26, forty thousand churches throughout France tolled their bells for the monks. It was the first time since Pope John Paul I died in 1978 that such a countrywide commemoration had occurred. A memorial service was held that day at Notre-Dame Cathedral in Paris, where the seven candles that had been snuffed out three days earlier were relighted. "These candles represented the hope that the seven monks remained alive," Archbishop Jean-Marie Lustiger intoned in his homily. "Let us now pray for all those innocents who have been massacred and for all those whom the monks did not want to abandon. . . . Their death must be a sign of hope, that love is stronger than hatred." After the service, a French Algerian woman who had grown up in the Medea told a journalist, "Everyone loved the monks. They were like our fathers." Etienne Baudry, Christian's boyhood friend from seminary school and the abbot of Bellefontaine, remarked to a reporter, "They had become pawns in a bigger drama being played out, but their death is not an end."

Two days later, a much larger crowd gathered at the Trocadero,* a grand plaza overlooking the Seine, opposite the Eiffel Tower. More then ten thousand people had come to honor the monks, to express solidarity with the Algerian people, and to condemn the barbarism.

*Place du Trocadero was named after Fort Trocadero, near Cadiz, Spain, after it was captured by the French in 1823.

They came in silence, each person holding a white flower—a daisy, a rose, a carnation—accompanied by the doleful strains of Mahler's Fourth Symphony. Like a blacksmith's tongs, the huge curved wings of the Palais de Chaillot's two pavilions hold in their grip the square terrace of the Trocadero. On each wall facing the plaza, a banner was hung bearing the inscription, IF WE ARE SILENT, THE STONES THEMSELVES WILL CRY OUT, words written by Christian de Chergé in an article for *La Croix* after the twelve Croats had been slaughtered in 1993.

The respectful silence was suddenly broken. "Bastards! We will never talk with the terrorists." Someone in the crowd had raised a placard with the hand-scrawled plea: WHY THE CONTEMPT, THE ABSENCE OF DIALOGUE WITH THE GIA? The question was greeted by the crowd with obscenities. "He must be a terrorist," cried a woman. "Maybe he has a bomb!" The placard disappeared in a scuffle of pushing and shoving.

Other messages were floating above the heads of the mass of people crushed around the statue of Marshall Ferdinand Foch on the Place du Trocadero: SALUT, SALAM SHALOM. END ISLAMIST BARBARISM. Someone had remembered Martin Luther King's words—"Let us live together as brothers or we will perish as idiots." A thirteen-year-old Algerian girl was holding a placard with photographs of her brother, sister, and mother, whose throats had been slit in Algiers. Her aunt told a reporter, "I brought her here to show that we Algerians are against the barbarous violence."

Journalists mingled in the crowd. An unemployed Morrocan worker told a reporter, "I came as a Muslim. This is barbarism to kill monks. In our religion, Jews and Christians are protected by a special statute, the *dhimi*." A Catholic lady said, "The God we pray to is the God of everyone. True Islam never says to kill your neighbor." "These people are fanatics, like there are everywhere, and just as we have in Corsica, remarked"* a sister of the Congregation of the Servants of Mary.

A little after 6:30 in the evening notables arrived, signaled by a new dirge. François Bayrou, the Minister of Education, who planned

*The reference was to the Corsican independence movement, which had turned violent.

the event, had selected Samuel Barber's Adagio, played at President Kennedy's funeral, to accompany "the ballet of the VIPs," as the irreverant daily *Libération* described their entrance on the scene. There was Bayrou; Alain Juppé, the prime minister; Lionel Jospin, the secretary of the Socialist party; Cardinal Lustiger; Grand Rabbi Sitruk; Dalil Boubaker, the rector of the Mosque of Paris; and an emotional foreign minister, Hervé de Charette, who told a reporter, "We did everything possible to get them out of the miserable clutches of these savages. For two months, day after day, in secret, I did everything I could."

Ministers and leaders of all political parties came—Communists, Socialists, and Gaullists of different stripes, all save the Greens and the Front National of Jean-Marie le Pen. The Greens didn't come because they saw the event as hypocritical. "A demonstration is too easy and does not absolve France from its responsibilities," such as making it easier for victims of the conflict to obtain the right of political asylum. Le Pen claimed he wasn't invited, and anyway, he told a reporter, "The idea of a peace-seeking Islam is a myth." He and his Christianity and Solidarity Association preferred to join a requiem service organized at the ultraconservative church of St.-Nicolas du Chardonnet, just off the boulevard St.-Germain, where the Mass is in Latin and women cover their heads.

There were also disgruntled Muslim leaders. Cardinal Lustiger had offended the Muslim community by unscripted, emotional remarks made on French TV on May 23, the day he had extinguished the candles at Notre-Dame following the announcement of the monks' execution. He called upon "all Muslims to open their minds and their hearts, to rid themselves of hatred." These words had raised a storm of protest. A representative of the High Council of Muslims in France denounced the cardinal, saying, "At the time when all the religions should come together in denouncing this modern-day barbarism which kills innocents, the cardinal has chosen to throw gasoline on the fire by hurling invective upon seven hundred and eighty million Muslims." The cardinal's public-relations office quickly moved to admit that he had not prepared his remarks well, stating that it was a misunderstanding and that he had really meant to condemn only those Muslims who killed in God's name.

Lustiger's restated meaning was echoed by Muslim religious leaders throughout the Middle East, who also condemned the murder of the monks. The grand imam of al-Azhar Mosque in Cairo denounced the killing as "a criminal act contrary to all divine religions." In Lebanon, the mentor of the pro-Iranian Hezbollah, Sheikh Mohammed Hussein Fadlallah called the act "inhuman." A spokesman for Iran's foreign ministry described the execution as "outside the bounds of humanity."

The National Council of Imams, the highest Muslim theological body in France, issued a *fetwa* stating that the Law obligates its believers to respect and protect non-Muslim religious buildings, to tolerate all religions, especially those of the People of the Book, and monks and priests in particular. It affirmed that Islam "prohibits punishing an innocent person for the sins of another." If the kidnappers thought they were doing something pleasing to God, they were wrong. "The illegality of the act," the *fetwa* concluded, "is evident on the basis of all Koranic texts and prophetic saying."

But where were the bodies? The Algerian government was not officially admitting that the monks were dead until their remains were recovered. On the morning of Thursday, May 30, no hard evidence of their death had been reported. Nine days had passed since May 21, the date of Communiqué 44, which announced the execution. At a time when nothing ever seemed certain, a few people in the Church still clung to the mad hope that the announcement was bogus, an attempt to embarrass the Algerian government or a plot to serve some other hidden purpose. That dream was possible, at least, so long as no bodies were found.

Bishop Teissier received a call little after 8 A.M., saying that Cardinal Duval had passed away that previous evening. Then, shortly after midday, he received another call, this one from the Ministry of Interior. Without any elaboration, the bishop was told that the remains of the seven monks had been discovered.

That afternoon, Bernardo Olivera and Armand Veilleux arrived from Rome to help with preparations for the funeral ceremony on Sunday. They had flown in on an Air Algeria flight scheduled to arrive at 1:15 P.M. Amédée, a Dutch Père Blanc, and nine plain-clothes security police had been waiting two hours by the time the plane finally landed. To avoid a clutch of French journalists waiting out front, the two visitors were whisked out a side entrance and escorted by four police cars to the diocesan house of Bishop Teissier. During the ride, they learned that Duval had died, and that he had made a curious prediction to Father Gonzales, who was at his side when he died. "You will see, one day Algeria will surprise the world."

"Have you heard he news?" were the first words the men heard when they were met at the diocesan house in El-Biar.

"What news?" they all asked at once.

"They have found the monks."

"Alive?"

"Dead."

Inside, they found the widow of former President Boudiaf, the general director of the Algerian newspaper *La Liberté* and his wife, and other people anxious to offer their condolences to the abbot general. Bishop Teissier briefed them on the preparations that were under way. Coffins had arrived from Marseilles and remains would be taken to the Aïn Naadja military hospital.

"But we must see the bodies," Veilleux interjected.

"The military tradition holds that no one can see the bodies until the families do."

"But we are part of their family," Veilleux insisted. "We cannot tell their relatives they are dead without confirming their identification."

"It will be difficult," replied an overwhelmed Teissier, whose phone had not stopped ringing all afternoon and who was not anxious to have new problems. "You can call the ambassador."

Ambasssador Lévêque understood Veilleux's concern and said he thought a visit to the hospital could be arranged.

Teissier talked about the different possibilities for the burial. Rome had been suggested. So, too, had the idea of sending them back to their respective abbeys in France. Again, Veilleux protested. He had spoken with Etienne Baudry at Abbey Bellefontaine early that day. There was a strong consensus among the families that the monks should all be buried together in Algeria, preferably at Tibhirine. That was also the desire of their monastic family. Teissier strongly doubted the government would agree. The authorities were extremely sensitive about security. Veilleux insisted that they pursue every avenue to make this possible. Again, he called Ambassador Lévêque. The authorities certainly would be worried about security, he confirmed, but if things were done with discretion, it might well be possible.

On Friday morning, an interview with French journalists had been organized. Teissier spoke about the testament of Christian de Chergé. The de Chergé family had immediately realized that the testament Christian had mailed to his youngest brother, Gérard, after the visit of "Father Christmas" was not meant only for them. It was a message of love and, above all, forgiveness. The family had sent it to the prestigious Catholic weekly *La Croix,* which had published it on May 29. In his remarks, Bishop Teissier stressed the importance of forgiveness. "Forgiveness is indispensable in a world in which human justice is imperfect." Olivera read a formal statement, in which he also emphasized the need "to harness the power of forgiveness—addressed to the court of a merciful God. Only forgiveness can break the chain of hatred and violence." He asked Veilleux to take questions from the reporters.

"Have you seen the bodies?"

"Not yet," Veilleux replied, "but we have asked the government. I think they will be reasonable.

"Where will they be buried?"

"We have asked the government for them to be buried at Tibhirine. I believe they will be reasonable."

Later that same morning, they were given permission by the ministry to see the bodies. At eleven o'clock, Ambassador Lévêque, his consul general, and the embassy doctor arrived at the diocesan house in an armored van. They drove Amédée, Teissier, Vielleux, and Olivera to Aïn Naadja military hospital on the outskirts of Algiers. Along the way, the French ambassador explained some unpleasant details about the discovery of the bodies and asked that no pictures be taken.

Bernardo Olivera was suspicious. After twenty minutes of polite conversation in the hospital reception lounge, the abbot general whispered to Veilleux, "Thank the colonel for his sympathy, but tell him we did not come for tea and pleasant chitchat. We must see the bodies." As an Argentinian, Olivera remembered the practices of his own countrymen during the dictatorship of the 1970s. It was not unknown for bodies to be recovered by security forces and sealed in coffins before families could identify them. Often the coffins were filled with sand.

The colonel, who was also the general director of the hospital, was surprised by the request to see the bodies. "I thought you came to pray by the coffins. I wasn't told you wanted to see the remains."

"We did come to pray, but also to identify the bodies. The Minister of Interior assured us we could. We cannot tell all the relatives they are dead without confirming this ourselves," Veilleux explained.

"There are only the heads," the colonel confessed, not knowing they had already been informed by the French ambassador of this macabre detail. He assured them the sight would be horrifying, and he expressed concern about the emotional aftereffect this would have on the men. "They are ten-days-old. Have you ever seen a ten-day-old corpse?" Father Olivera assured him that he had, though actually, he had only seen dead animals.

The colonel mentioned another problem. The coffins had already been sealed and the technicians responsible for those matters had left the hospital. They would have to be found and brought back. Olivera agreed to wait. A half hour later, the French consul general, the embassy doctor, Olivera, and Veilleux were led to the Department of Forensic Medicine on the other side of the building, which faced a neglected botanical garden. Amédée had been asked to stay behind with the others to avoid an unseemly crowd around the bodies and to spare him the shock. Reluctantly, he agreed, and used the time to observe the Office of Sext.

After a long walk, the four men entered a bright, naturally lighted morgue, where the seven coffins were placed. Each had a red rose lying on the cover. One by one, two nurses lifted the unsealed lids. The heads had been attached in an upright position to white cotton pads. The monks' desiccated faces, hollow eye sockets, and exposed teeth made them look like mummies, but they were still clearly recognizable. Forensic tests, the colonel explained, showed beyond doubt that the heads had already been in the ground.

If they had been buried, then by whom? And why would they have been dug up later and their heads cut off? This new information added more question marks to an already murky situation. Who had actually found the heads, where, and when? That was not known for sure. There had been a report from a reliable friend of Bishop Teissier that an Algerian businessman had seen three heads in a tree as he was turning off the Blida road to Medea on the morning of May 30. But were they really those of the monks? The man didn't stop to look. Horrified, he had gone in straight to the police. Finding heads strewn about in the countryside was not an unusual event in the Algeria of 1996. Theories about the monks' kidnapping and execution would mushroom over the next weeks and months as more information trickled into the press.

With a look of genuine concern, the colonel bid the men goodbye and reiterated his invitation that they return to the hospital if they should later feel any nausea or experience attacks of vomiting.

Olivera asked Veilleux to go with Teissier that afternoon to talk to the Minister of the Interior about the burial. They returned later with the good news that the monks could be buried at the monastery, as they had wished. The ceremony would be on Tuesday, June 4, but for security reasons, the minister requested that the funeral be "of a private character." There were to be no large crowds, no journalists.

The same evening, Armand Veilleux gave a live interview for French TV. The question of the burial came up. He answered that the government had agreed to have the monks buried at Tibhirine on Tuesday. When Veilleux returned to the diocesan house, he met a dumbfounded Henri Teissier.

"You know, Armand, you committed every diplomatic faux pas possible. You have preempted the Algerian government from making its own announcement. And now it will be neither private nor secret. The whole world knows when and where."

"Well," replied a mildly chastened Veilleux, "that will motivate the government to make sure security is very good."

Security was very good on Sunday for the five o'clock ceremony at Notre-Dame d'Afrique for Cardinal Duval and the seven monks.

The rue Notre-Dame d'Afrique, which snakes up to the basilica from the the old Maillot Hospital, had been blocked off to general traffic since 2:00 P.M. A few Algerians had come on foot over three hours early just to be sure they would not be prohibited from entering the enclosure surrounding the cathedral. Algerian security police were known for being somewhat unpredictable.

Around three o'clock, the embassy van arrived at the diocesan house to drive Olivera, Veilleux, Amédée, and Gilles Nicolas to Aïn Naadja military Hospital. The colonel was expecting them. An honor guard was putting the caskets into four yellow ambulances when they arrived. The procession to the basilica was escorted in presidential style by three motorcycles, three patrol cars, and two armored trucks, which sped across the city, uninterrupted by stoplights.

Three French bishops and Cardinal Jean-Marie Lustiger, along with the Pope's special representative, Cardinal Francis Arinze, were already in the sanctuary of the basilica when the motorcade arrived. They had been joined by Robert and Amédée, as well as Jean-Pierre, who had come from Fez, where he had been made *ad nutum* superior for the monastery, replacing Bruno. When the Algerian ministers arrived ahead of schedule, Bishop Teissier decided to begin the service. The Algerian officials were placed in the first row, followed by the whole diplomatic corps and ordinary Algerians, who had filled the basilica to capacity. Cardinal Arinze read a personal telegram from Pope John Paul and presided over Mass, using the chalice and coral-inlaid paten from the chapel at Tibhirine.

Leaving the two-hour service, Veilleux expressed his appreciation to the Minister of the Interior for agreeing to have the burial at Tibhirine. "It will be an honor to have the monks there," he replied. A member of the honor guard from the Aïn Naadja hospital went up to Olivera and firmly took his hand, "They were our brothers, too." Olivera also ran into Geronimo Cortés-Funes, the Argentinian ambassador and an old family friend, who expressed his deep sympathies, as did dozens of tearful Algerians who went up to the abbot general afterward.

The next morning, Cardinal Lustiger presided over Mass at the basilica, attended by a handful of local clergy. He thanked them for "the faith of this small but vital Algerian Church, which gives support to a declining faith in old Europe." After the Mass, Olivera returned with Amédée and Jean-Pierre to the Diocesan Cultural Center on the rue des Glycines to gather a few of Christophe's personal belongings to give to his family. He also wanted to collect the written accounts of the events of March 27 he had asked from Thierry Becker, Amédée, and Jean-Pierre. They had practical matters to discuss, as well.

There were arrangements to be made for Mohammed and his family. Olivera offered financial help to provide Mohammed with an apartment in Medea. How to preserve a small presence in Algiers for two or three years until the situation permitted them to return to Tibhirine? Amédée could stay in the former quarters of Cardinal Duval at the basilica and maintain contact with their Muslim associates in Tibhirine. There was the matter of Michael, a Polish Dominican who wanted to transfer into the order. He had already spoken with Christian during a past visit to Fez about changing orders because of his interest in a simpler, contemplative life. Michael, too, could be part of a new core. Jean-Pierre would stay at the Fez annex, now the sole address for Notre-Dame de l'Atlas.

When the seven members of the Lebreton family arrived at the Cultural Center, they received three boxes of Christophe's possessions: an envelope with family photos, his certificate of ordination, the New Testament, two Jerusalem Bibles, scores of notes, poems, and drawings, and his personal journal, whose last entry was on March 19, 1996: "I had a good talk in the garden with MS about marriage. I was happy to say the Mass today. It was as if I heard the voice of Joseph inviting me to sing Psalm 101 with him and the Child: 'I sing of justice and mercy. . . . I will behave wisely when You come to me. . . . I will walk in my house with a perfect heart.' "

That Amédée and Jean-Pierre did not have personal belongings to gather for the families of the other monks was the result of an unfortunate misunderstanding, or, more likely, an intentional misrepresentation by the French Foreign Ministry. When the families were informed that the monks were dead, the question of their going to Algiers for the funeral ceremony was presented as a closed matter. Madame Renouard, their contact at the ministry, told them a visa for Algeria was out of the question; for security reasons, it was impossible. Even though the French Foreign Ministry had nothing to do with issuing Algerian visas, nor was security its responsibility, the families took her word at face value—all but the Lebretons, that is.

Christophe's sister, Elisabeth Bonpain, remembers this time with some bitterness: "The local priest in Ancône was barely interested in a memorial service. The death of the monks was no big thing here. They didn't understand why they were down there. I felt wounded by the indifference. A friend with Algerian connections said we should just go to the Algerian consulate in Lyons and try. The people at the consulate were very nice and ashamed at what happened. They made it very easy for us to get our visas."

Without forethought about numbers, seven Lebretons decided to go to Algiers, as if some invisible hand wanted them to act as substitutes for the absent families of the six other monks. Throughout their brief stay, Elisabeth was impressed by the atmosphere of simplicity and sense of solidarity within the Church. "There was no hierarchy, no deference to superior authority. There was a tremendous sense of equality. Everyone pitched in." In his private quarters at the diocesan house, Bishop Teissier was not only the maître d' hôtel but also waiter and busboy. He brought food from his kitchen, cleared the table, poured the coffee.

That deep sense of equality, coupled with love and forgiveness, were the themes that so impressed the Algerians when Christian's testament was published in the local newspapers.

> *If the day comes, and it could be today, that I am a victim of the terrorism that seems to be engulfing all foreigners living in Algeria, I would like my community, my Church, and my family to remember that I have dedicated my life to God and Algeria.*
>
> *That they accept that the Lord of all life was not a stranger to this savage kind of departure; that they pray for me, wondering how I found myself worthy of such a sacrifice; that they link in their memory this*

death of mine with all the other deaths equally violent but forgotten in their anonymity.

My life is not worth more than any other—not less, not more. Nor am I an innocent child. I have lived long enough to know that I, too, am an accomplice of the evil that seems to prevail in the world around, even that which might lash out blindly at me. If the moment comes, I would hope to have the presence of mind, and the time, to ask for God's pardon and for that of my fellowman, and, at the same time, to pardon in all sincerity he who would attack me.

I would not welcome such a death. It is important for me to say this. I do not see how I could rejoice when this people whom I love will be accused, indiscriminately, of my death. The price is too high, this so-called grace of the martyr, if I owe it to an Algerian who kills me in the name of what he thinks is Islam.

I know the contempt that some people have for Algerians as a whole. I also know the caricatures of Islam that a certain (Islamist) ideology promotes. It is too easy for such people to dismiss, in good conscience, this religion as something hateful by associating it with violent extremists. For me, Algeria and Islam are quite different from the commonly held opinion. They are body and soul. I have said enough, I believe, about all the good things I have received here, finding so often the meaning of the Gospels, running like some gold thread through my life, and which began first at my mother's knee, my very first church, here in Algeria, where I learned respect for the Muslims.

Obviously, my death will justify the opinion of all those who dismissed me as naïve or idealistic: "Let him tell us what he thinks now." But such people should know my death will satisfy my most burning curiosity. At last, I will be able—if God pleases—to see the children of Islam as He sees them, illuminated in the glory of Christ, sharing in the gift of God's Passion and of the Spirit, whose secret joy will always be to bring forth our common humanity amidst our differences.

I give thanks to God for this life, completely mine yet completely theirs, too, to God, who wanted it for joy against, and in spite of, all odds. In this Thank You—which says everything about my life—I include you, my friends past and present, and those friends who will be here at the side of my mother and father, of my sisters and brothers—thank you a thousandfold.

And to you, too, my friend of the last moment, who will not know what you are doing. Yes, for you, too, I wish this thank-you, this "A-Dieu," whose image is in you also, that we may meet in heaven, like happy thieves, if it pleases God, our common Father. Amen! Insha Allah!"

"People accused Christian of being naïve," Father Veilleux reflected in Rome a year later. "They said he was dealing only with a small, special group of Muslim mystics like himself, that ordinary Muslims were different. Ever since the Iranian hostage crisis, Muslims have been perceived in the West as crazy fanatics. Maybe Christian wasn't so naïve after all. Thousands of ordinary Muslims responded to their death with letters of condolences and expressions of shame. Yes, Christian did always look for the good in a person. We need people like that."

Bags full of letters poured into Bishop Teissier's office on the rue Khalifa. One signed "An Algerian family, just like so many others affected by this event" expressed the general shame and sense of loss.

Monsignor
. . . It is disgraceful, truly shameful . . . the teachings of Islam are clear as to the sacredness of life, love of one's neighbor, hospitality toward strangers, whatever their religion. These are the true teachings of Islam, which sadly have been trampled upon by this handful of fanatics who daily befoul our reputation as a welcoming and hospitable people. We pray that you, Monsignor, will pass on to our Christian brothers in general, and to the families of the victims in particular, our message of fraternity and friendship. . . ."

A letter, hand-delivered to Teissier's office by a woman doctor who lived in the neighborhood, concluded, "We must water the seeds bequeathed by our monks. Our duty is to pursue peace, love God, and respect people who are different." She told Bishop Teissier that she kept a copy of Christian's testament pinned to the wall in her living room for her whole family to remember.

"Does not God test those he loves?" wrote another. "No matter what has happened, we truly love you. You are part of us. We have failed in our duty—to protect you, to love you, and to love you enough. Forgive us. Your place is with us. Don't listen to the Pharisees. You must accomplish your divine mission with us. I believe it is God's plan."

19

Postmortem

And I saw thrones and they sat on them. . . . Then I saw the souls of those who had been beheaded for their witness to Jesus and for the word of God, who had not worshipped the beast or his image.

—Revelation 20:4

Tuesday morning was gray and drizzling when the van from the French embassy arrived at the diocesan house punctually at 7:30. "You see, God is crying too," Christophe's young friend Ratiba told Elisabeth Bonpain as the group was leaving for the airport. Ambassador Lévêque, Henri Teissier, Amédée, Jean-Pierre, Armand Veilleux, Bernardo Olivera, and three of the seven Lebretons—Elisabeth, Claire, and Xavier—made up the private party that was being flown in a giant Hercules transport plane to the Aïn Oussera military air base south of Medea. From there, they would drive seventy-five miles up to Tibhirine and meet Gilles Nicolas, Robert, and Philippe Ranc, the young scholarly novice who had returned from his studies in Strasbourg for the burial ceremony.

They were sandwiched into four armored Toyota jeeps, each with a complement of two soldiers sitting in the front and back seats. The jeeps were part of a convoy of a dozen military vans filled with soldiers, covered by two helicopters overhead. The decision to fly to an airport south of Medea and then drive north reflected security concerns. Even under heavy guard, driving up the N1 from Blida through the narrow Chiffa Gorge was dangerous. Terrorists could easily hide in the mountains and set off a landslide with explosives that could trap the convoy. Driving from the south, their armed escort could see any movements in the open, rolling hills, which were blanketed by a strangely beautiful almond green grass unfamiliar to the French visitors.

The convoy was greeted in Medea by the *wali* with whom Christian had debated so often the reasons for taking the risks they did.

He joined them on the drive to Tibhirine, whose eight kilometers along a wooded, winding road were lined every few feet with police and soldiers. Seven caskets had already been put in the chapel by the military cadets. They then waited outside the monastery for the service to end, appearing incongruous in their dress grays, white spats, and shiny silver helmets, alongside the simply dressed villagers. Everything moved at a fast pace, too fast for some of the Lebretons, but there was a schedule and security to worry about. The reading during the service was Luke 23:33: *"And when they had come to a place called Calvary . . ."*

There was an awkwardness felt by the Europeans as they left the chapel and followed behind the young soldiers. They were not walking as brothers with the Algerians. The local friends and neighbors of the monks were not with them, as one group. Before the service, they had been kept outside the enclosure by the police. After the service, when the entrance door by the *hôtellerie* was thrown open for the cadets to retrieve the caskets, the villagers were again held back. They followed at an unseemly distance behind the small procession led by Bishop Teissier as it wound through the garden behind the new building, past the large open spring, to the wooded cemetery. Bernardo asked the authorities to close the gap. The gap got smaller, but the neighbors still lagged behind.

The caskets were placed beside their respective graves. Each one had been dug by people from the village, who had swept the dirt and tidied up the area in preparation for receiving their *babas.* In a set sequence, they were lowered—Christian's first, then, according to monastic seniority, beginning with Luc. Jean-Pierre said some words in French, expressing gratitude to the authorities and his hopes for the future. Henri Teissier and Gilles Nicolas spoke in Arabic, drawing the crowd closer to hear their words. Bernardo ended with a brief prayer. Teissier shoveled the first clumps of dirt into Michel's grave, and at that instant, the sun broke dramatically through the overcast sky, as if God himself was giving his blessing. It was 1:15 in the afternoon, the ninth day after Pentecost.

Then the dam of emotion broke. The neighbors from the area, the Sufis from Medea and beyond, local imams and mayors who had come to say good-bye, all plunged forward. The diminutive Jean-

Pierre and Amédée disappeared in a flood of embraces and tears. The two old-timers were the survivors, the two who were always invited to the funerals of the villagers. It was now their turn to be consoled. The monks' friends started shoveling. "There was a mad, almost violent intensity as they threw dirt in the holes, even with their hands. It was as if they were venting anger, shame, and love all at once," Elisabeth remembered. "Luc's grave had the biggest mound of dirt. It was almost funny. Afterward, he looked as if he were pregnant." One of the men throwing dirt on Luc's grave was the commander of the unit that had taken him hostage in 1959. The next day, the women would come to mourn.

After the ceremony, a reception in the new building had been prepared by the *wali*. Bernardo Olivera and the Lebretons went for a quick tour of the monastery with Robert, who took the opportunity to tell them of the scene he had witnessed the previous evening. Against the wishes of the authorities, Robert was still sleeping in the new building. Toward sunset, a detachment of soldiers occupied the monastery to make sure no terrorists would slip into the buildings during the night to prepare an unpleasant surprise. An officer had gone up to the terrace of the new building, from where he could survey the mountains, the gardens, and the positioning of his men. Below, Robert heard him speak in French, as if talking to himself, yet loudly enough for his men to hear.

"If someone told me to become a Christian, I would; yes, I would become a Christian. These men truly loved God. They loved Algeria more than the Algerians themselves." At dawn, Robert went to find the man, to give him a copy of Christian's testament, but the soldiers had already left.

Driving back to Medea, several in the party noticed the graffiti on the wall of a building in tiny Dakhla, the village that gave Jean-Pierre a tight feeling in his stomach when he went to market: CASTRATE THE TERRORISTS.

There were reports in July that the execution of the monks had caused deep splits within the GIA. Sidi Ali Benhadjera, the former FIS deputy from Medea and critic of Zitouni, quit the GIA to form his own Islamic League for Da'wa and Jihad, which stressed fighting by nonviolent means. The legalists, or *djaz'arists,* who advocated a limited national, or "Algerian," approach to the conflict, had been seeking revenge since Zitouni had murdered two of their leaders in the fall of 1995. There were rumors that Zitouni had been disowned even by certain of the *salafists,* his own allies within the governing council, who saw themselves as part of a struggle to return to the Islam of the *umma** and disdained the narrow political goals of the *djaz'arists.*

On July 27, another communiqué was received by Radio Medi I in Tangiers. Jamel Zitouni had been killed in an ambush by "enemies of Islam." But who really ambushed him? Was it the army who killed him with the help of informers within the clans seeking revenge? Or was he killed directly by his opponents at the command of Abou al-Walid, as some reported? Was he really dead? His body was never recovered.

Theories proliferated in the months that followed to explain the motives for the kidnapping. Other theories were needed to explain the monks' death. In a country of civil wars within civil wars, of false identities, disinformation, and manipulation, horror always had many possible authors, both seen and unseen.

Why where they kidnapped? The monks were a threat, according to one widely held line of thinking. But to whom? Zitouni himself said they were a threat in his Communiqué No.43, which accused them of proselytizing by mixing with the people and winning their hearts. Or were they a threat to elements within the Algerian security apparatus who, like some earlier Frenchmen, thought the monks were too friendly with the terrorists? Perhaps they were simply an embarrassment to the eradicator mentality. The monks lived in peace, without weapons or armed guards, protected only by their friendship toward all—something that had gradually transmuted into protection from violence for those living in their shadow.

Another theory, favored by certain journalists, saw the incident as a reply to President Zeroual's claim during the elections of 1995 that terrorism was only "residual," a few brush fires soon to be stamped out. This was a claim the government could directly influence

*The *umma* is the worldwide community of Muslim believers.

through stricter censorship of the press. A highly visible kidnapping of French monks would reveal the hollowness of the image the government was promoting and show the world the GIA was alive and well.

The hypothesis cited most often cast the monks as victims of terrorist rivalries. By their readiness to treat without questions all who came to the dispensary, the monks had become a valued local resource for any emir in control of the area around them. The villagers spoke of their good works and generosity as if the monks were their own fathers. In effect, the monks were loved too much. To hurt the emir controlling the Tamesguida Valley, a rival could take "his" monks.

Could government security forces have manipulated these clan rivalries to get rid of the monks, as some plausibly speculated, because the monks provided medical care to the terrorists? Certainly, and thereby the conspirators would also gain another publicity black eye for the Islamist cause—they would even kill monks. But if so, why were they kidnapped and not simply murdered on the spot, like other clerics?

There is a variant of the clan rivalry explanation: Zitouni did not himself order the kidnapping, but when confronted with a fait accompli, he had to make use of the situation. Amédée's speculation that the motive was to get the monks to declare their moral support for the montagnards may have served a double purpose. The monks represented both valued booty, especially the services of Luc, and a moral force, if they could be turned into sympathizers. This explanation has the advantage of accounting for some intriguing loose pieces of the puzzle.

There were good reasons for the Benhadjera clan and Baghdadi clan to hate each other. Each had murdered members of the other's family. Benhadjera was opposed to Zitouni's excesses. Sidi Ali Benhadjera had a solid religious education and he knew that many things being done by Zitouni in the name of God were wrong. To strike against Zitouni, he could have hatched the idea to kidnap the monks, who lived in an area controlled by Baghdadi, who was loyal to Zitouni. But in a war where "outsiders" from the area were often contracted to do the dirty work, Benhadjera might have brought in another group, who wouldn't fear reprisals if identified. This would explain why the kidnappers didn't wear face masks and why they didn't realize that two of the locally best-known monks, Amédée and Jean-Pierre, were not among the seven taken. The Hattab clan from Jijel, east of Algiers, was often mentioned in the Algerian press as the suspected kidnappers. "They had accents from the east," Mohammed had said in his deposition.

Abdullah, Zitouni's representative, had said to the intelligence officer at the French embassy that they were "very upset" about the kidnapping. Why would they have been "very upset" unless Zitouni had not commanded the action? And why would he have asked for French help to negotiate the monks' release? Accepting the domestic intelligence service's view of the GIA as more accurate than that of the army foreign intelligence—which believed the GIA was composed of loosely controlled autonomous *jamaates*—then it is easy to imagine the action being initiated without Zitouni's knowledge. But once it happened, he had to appear in control and get something that would boost his weakened leadership position. He may have tried getting the monks to cross the line in some public way, as some French clerics had done during the war of independence. When that failed, he bargained for an exchange of prisoners in a way insulting to Algeria's sovereignty. The month-long delay in preparing Communiqué 43 could be explained by internal GIA negotiating over how to capitalize on an event that Zitouni had not planned. Since Zitouni was thought not to have much religious knowledge, or knowledge of literary Arabic, others would have had to have written it.

In the meantime, the monks and their captors were getting to know one another. If history was repeating itself in the manner of Luc and Matthew forty years earlier, the monks may have been winning over their guards by their uncomplaining piety, communal prayer, and perhaps by Christian's knowledge of the Koran. This could explain the widely dismissed "event" reported in the French *Journal du Dimanche* on May 26.

An article appeared in which a monk at Aiguebelle, Father Gérard, talked to a reporter about a conversation he had had with a certain Madame Casanova. She had gone to his monastery in March on a retreat and met him. The story Father Gérard passed on to *Le Journal du Dimanche* was about a French envoy, the husband of Madame Casanova, known for his humanitarian missions. He had told the newspaper that twelve days earlier, Madame Casanova's husband had visited the monks for ten minutes in the maquis. During that short time, he had administered the Eucharist to the monks and given Luc medication for his asthma. The contact had been organized by an intermediary from Doctors Without Borders. The date of the visit would also have corresponded closely with the date of the celebration of the Ascension, Thursday, May 16, a date that would have been important to the monks.

The Quai d'Orsay reacted immediately when the article appeared. Foreign Minister Hervé de Charette denied the existence of any envoy and qualified the report as "unlikely." The next day, Father Gérard's superior, Abbot Yves Brouckner, received a phone call from a high official of the ministry, telling him to call *Le Journal du Dimanche* and deny the reports. Throughout the commotion, Father Gérard maintained the truth of what he had learned. In the weeks after the monks' execution, rumors started circulating that the emissary had taken not only medicine and Communion wafers to the monks but also a small location emitter which was subsequently discovered by the captors. In July, *Algérie Confidentiel,* a bulletin published in Geneva by Algerian émigrés, took up the same theme.

Was this then the "treason" that was alluded to in *El Ansar*'s last edition published in London? But why would the GIA do something so risky as let a French emissary visit the monks? What could they have gained? It would make no sense unless an unusual bond developed (quite possible) between the captors and the monks, and they were willing to take risks to honor a last wish full of deep religious significance for the monks, or, unless the story was fabricated and planted by Algerian intelligence services. Their Sécurité Militaire had reason to be upset with the French for engaging in negotiations behind their back,* negotiations that were admitted by

---

***Si Nous Nous Taisons* (*If We Are Silent*), by René Guitton, published in Paris in the spring of 2001, gives details about the unofficial back channel of Pasqua-Marchiani that had been put to use. Marchiani, according to the author, had succeeded in negotiating the release of the monks during secret talks with Algerian cooperation, but for appear-

Foreign Minister Hervé de Charette when he appeared at the Trocadéro. The escapade seems so absurd, it is hard to know why it would have been made up if it were not true, or else planted to make France appear culpable for the murder.

The mystery of the heads can also be used to support different explanations of the monks' assassination. The colonel at the hospital told Bernardo Olivera that the heads had been buried in the ground. Once Algerian security learned the French had been making contacts with the kidnappers without informing them, then it is likely the Arabophones took over and reversed the decision to cooperate with French security by agreeing not to engage the kidnappers if found. It is plausible to suppose that the army located the group, perhaps in a cave. There was a firefight and the monks were killed by grenades or gunfire. They were then buried, but someone had second thoughts. To make it look as if the terrorists were responsible they cut off their heads and displayed them in public, perhaps in different places for maximum shock effect. *La Croix* had reported on May 26 that seven monks' heads had been found in a field behind a gas station by an old man—four days before the Algerian press made its announcement. Then there was the reported sighting of three heads in a tree alongside the N1 on the morning of May 30, by an Algerian businessman who had been driving south from Blida to Medea. The monks' heads were seen near Tablat, about thirty miles from the monastery, according to another report. All these horror stories would only further alienate public support for the GIA. The worse the better.

Yet, had they been killed accidentally in a shoot-out between the army and the kidnappers, why hadn't any of the seven heads shown signs of wounds? Some in the Church thought it was strange that not one monk received face or head injuries if, indeed, such an event had occurred. Then there is the fact that French intelligence knew on May 23 that they were dead, even though no bodies had been officially recovered. They had informed the Vatican, though not the

---

ances, they were held in Ghadamis, Libya. On May 9, Prime Minister Alain Juppé ordered Marchiani to cease his involvement, and demanded that the regular intelligence services take over, using normal channels.

Trappists. How would intelligence know except by intercepting someone's communications, or by being informed directly by one of the sides involved?

Following Amédée's line of speculation that they were killed in the end for not cooperating as propagandists for the GIA cause, the bodies were buried by the terrorists in some remote area. When their remains were not found in the days immediately following the announcement of their execution, doubts still persisted about their death. The prestige of the GIA would be affected if their act of divine justice was in question. So they dug up the bodies and cut off the heads.

It is still today not in the interest of either the Algerian or French government to reveal the truth if it subtracts from the image of crazy and bloodthirsty *fous de Dieu*. However, the symmetry of Amédée's explanation of the kidnapping with that of fellow spirit, Hamas Sheik Mohammed Bouslimani, is appealing.

Both the monks and Bouslimani had been urged by the *wali* to leave for somewhere more secure. Both decided to accept known risks in order to stay with their "family." For Bouslimani, family was his wife and community work; for the monks, it was their neighbors. Both refused to endorse the killing of innocent people to achieve justice. In each case, their remains went undiscovered for two about months. And both Bouslimani and the monks were willing to die to be true to their families and their faith.

A few weeks after the monks' burial, Sheikh Mahfoud Nahnah, Bouslimani's close childhood friend and the leader of Hamas wanted to pay hommage to the monks at their graves in Tibhirine. He had to leave his bouquet of flowers outside the entrance gate. The local gendarmes guarding the monastery would not allow him inside.

20

A Visit to Algiers

Do not be overcome by evil, but overcome evil with good.

—Romans 12:21

I went to Algeria in the fall of 1999 to sniff the air and to see the monastery I had studied so intensely from videos and photographs. Bales of razor wire and additional security fencing were still on top of the walls surrounding private houses, embassies, and places of work. But laughter on crowded streets, a revived nightlife, and, smiling, if omnipresent, police told a different story. Algiers and Algerians were no longer in the grip of fear.

Six months earlier, in April 1999, a new president had been elected. Abdelaziz Bouteflika was considered by many observers an old-guard apparatchik. He had been a plotter in the coup against Ben Bella in 1965. He was also President Boumediene's minister of foreign affairs and a close friend—so close that when Boumediene died in 1978, Bouteflika left the country for twenty years. Then he was called back to be, it was assumed, *le pouvoir*'s man to replace President Zeroual. Five of Bouteflika's rivals for president quit the race, claiming the election was rigged in his favor. The expectation of many was "more of the same."

Unknown to the electorate, a new page had been turned. The new president's resolve to bring about peace, together with a population out of sympathy with the terror and the growing efficiency of the army, had changed the atmosphere and the amount of violence. Straight talk, breaking taboos, and a determination to heal wounds have been Bouteflika's hallmarks. He speaks French on national TV, despite a law passed in 1998 requiring all government officials to speak Arabic. He talks openly of accepting differences. "Let those who want wear beards or not wear them, but without making judgments about the other," he was quoted recently as saying. The centerpiece of his politics has been national reconciliation. He treats the remaining terrorists as prodigal sons. They are *les égarés,* those who have strayed from the fold. "The strong forgive," Bouteflika reminded his Algerian audiences in his campaign for clemency throughout the previous summer.

So, too, do the weak. Hugh Johnson is an American Methodist pastor and head of a miniscule Protestant presence who, jointly with Bishop Teisssier, represent the Church in its official dealings with the Algerian government. Johnson carries his erudition lightly, spoken with a soft Virginian accent in a jovial exterior. He arrived in Algeria in 1963 with a Ph.D. in international affairs and a knowledge of Hebrew, Greek, and Latin. Since then, he has mastered French, Arabic, and Berber. "I think the killing of the monks was a turning point. Algerians were genuinely revolted by what happened. People were affected not only by the way they lived, but also by the way they died. The testament of Christian made a deep impression. So did the reaction of the Church. There was no spirit of revenge or even ill will toward the killers."

On September 14, Algerians were presented with a referendum on Bouteflika's policy for peace. Eighty-five percent of the eligible voters turned out, 98 percent of whom approved his *concorde civile.* His program offered different degrees of clemency to those in the GIA who surrendered their arms within six months. The program distinguished between sympathizers, who had only provided logistical support, and those who "had blood on their hands." Those who had killed were separated according to whether they had killed only opposing combatants or had murdered unarmed civilians. By the end of October, over a thousand GIA "repentant ones" had given themselves up.

In retrospect, there were many signs that the monks' death had indeed been a turning point. For a country that seemed drunk on violence, their assassination in God's name was, for many Algerians, like hitting rock bottom. It was the final and highly publicized insult to an already-abused Islam.

The outrage over the monks' execution even included members of the GIA. It may well have been the final straw that led to Jamel Zitouni's elimination on July 16, a month and a half later. There were those within the GIA who were trying to fight the jihad decently, as Adbelkader had done over a century earlier. No valid *fetwa* has been issued that permitted the killing of monks or innocent civilians. Furthermore, many within the GIA also had reasons for wanting to kill Zitouni. He had ruthlessly eliminated rivals, and he was suspected in some quarters of being manipulated by the security services. If the aim of government security services had been to use Zitouni to sow dissension within the GIA and discredit Islamic terrorists, they had succeeded.

There was one last horror committed against the Christian community and all the Muslims who loved the Archbishop of Oran, Pierre Claverie. No one has ever claimed credit, though suspicions have been cast in every corner. Late in the afternoon on August 1, 1996, France's foreign minister, Hervé de Charette, was flown with Gilles Nicolas in President Zeroual's private plane to Aïn Oussera military base, south of Medea. From there, they were taken by helicopter to a soccer field in Tibhirine and driven to the monastery for de Charette to pay his respects to the monks.

De Charette had come to Algeria as part of a diplomatic effort to calm the ever-turbulent waters of French-Algerian relations and to encourage the Zeroual government's commitment to democracy. That same day, the minister had met in Algiers with Pierre Claverie and other leaders of the Algerian Church to thank them for their courage in the face of so much danger and for their dedication to a pluralistic Algeria.

Bishop Claverie was a *pied-noir* who had been sympathetic to the FLN during the war. After independence, he was one of a handful of clergy given Algerian citizenship by the new government. Trained as a Dominican monk, Claverie was known as a man who did not mince words—he had been consistently blunt in his criticism of both the FIS and the Algerian government. He was also known respectfully by his Muslim admirers as "Sheikh" Claverie.

The same day of the visit to Tibhirine, Claverie returned to Oran late in the evening, where he was met by his assistant, Mohammed Bouchikhi. As they walked through the door of the Archbishopry, a device exploded. It killed both men instantly, driving their flesh and bone into each other, entangling them forever, even in their separate graves. As of this writing, Claverie was the last Christian cleric to die violently in Algeria.

Zitouni's successors tried but failed to get a *fetwa* pronounced by the Wahhabite sheikhs sympathetic to the tradition of Ibn Taymiyya to justify their killing of civilians and of the monks. The AIS negotiated a truce with the military in 1997 under terms that are still obscure today. Particularly harmful to the morale of the GIA was a *fetwa* signed in December 1998 by Sheikh Nacer-Eddine Albani,* while on his deathbed. Albani was respected among Islamists for his conservative interpretations of the law. Signed by two other sheikhs, the *fetwa* unequivocally denounced Islamic terrorism against unarmed civilians. Some of the repentant ones were put on Algerian TV to explain why they had surrendered. "The Saudis told us,"** they explained during more than one televised confessional.

There is still terrorist violence in Algeria. It occurs in the countryside, on less-traveled roads, usually after dusk. Henri Teissier advised me that there were two ways to go up to the monastery. One was with official protection, or I could simply go privately, which meant at my own risk. My first instinct was to go with protection.

The Ministry of the Interior provides a military escort to the monks who go up to Tibhirine from their temporary base in Cardinal Duval's old residence at Notre-Dame d'Afrique. Every ten days, they drive up to the monastery to stay in touch with the neighbors and to reassure them that the monastery will be reoccupied. At first, only Amédée drove up regularly. Since 1996, four young monks in their thirties and forties have joined him in Algiers as new recruits for the monastery: Michael, from Poland; Ventura, from Spain; Francisco, from Chile; and Jean-Claude, from France, the *ad nutum* superior, pending canonical approval of the restablished monastery. Its

---

*Sheikh Albani was born in Damascus. His father was a religious scholar who had emigrated from Albania and is reputed to have cast his son out of the house when he adopted extreme, conservative Wahabite views.

**The best explanation of the meaning of this response came from an Algerian journalist, Mohammed Bahli. He believes the Saudis, who are now beginning to experience terrorism at home themselves, are afraid that the radical, puritanical Wahabite Islam which they promote around the world is going to come back and haunt them.

new name will be Notre-Dame de Tibhirine, leaving the old name, Notre-Dame de l'Atlas, to be carried on by the annex in Fez.

Jean-Claude had never given a moment's thought to Algeria or Islam when he saw his friend André Barbeau, the abbot of Aiguebelle, who had come to Cîteaux to ask him personally to consider leading the revived community. At fifty-seven, he had experience in both spiritual and secular realms. Jean-Claude was an ordained priest. He also occupied the important position of *cellérier,* combining responsibilities of business management and administration of the order's nine-hundred-year-old monastery. For Jean-Claude, Barbeau's request was a "call from God." There was also the vow of obedience to consider. Barbeau asked Jean-Claude to reflect on the proposal. But Cistercian thinking is never wholly individual; it is communal as well. His call was first debated within the abbot's council of seven. Jean-Claude had a responsible position and a bright future at Cîteaux. Barbeau had to explain to the brothers the exceptional nature of the situation in Algeria, which merited an exceptional appointment, one which normally would have meant choosing a monk from Aiguebelle, the mother monastery. Another lengthy discussion followed with the whole community of thirty brothers. Both sessions finally came to the same unanimous conclusion: Follow the call.

The choice of a monk from Cîteaux to maintain a tiny, impoverished monastery surrounded by Muslims was not lost on the Order. Cîteaux had been founded back in the eleventh century because its location invited hard labor, "a marshy wilderness full of thorns," which would remind the monks of their vow of poverty. André Barbeau knew that for Christians serving in the House of Islam, the Muslims were important "thorns." These fellow seekers of God had challenged and stimulated the monks in ways that made them better Christians, simplifying, rejuvenating, and expanding their faith.

"For us, returning to Tibhirine is the best way to pay respect to our brothers. There was never a question of abandoning the place," Jean-Claude told a journalist from *El Watan*. "The most important thing for us is knowing that the population wants us after what happened." All five monks went to Tibhirine for the first time in April 1999 to celebrate Easter. No one had been told that they were coming, yet upon their arrival in the morning, the "Arab telephone" had shown its mysterious power. Fifty villagers were waiting to greet them, holding candles. After the ceremony of the lighting of the candle, a practice that Christian had initiated, the monks went into the chapel for Mass. Unlike in the past, the villagers did not linger outside, but pressed into the interior to listen to the service.

"He has learned nothing, nothing! He has interiorized the rules of the ministry as if they were the Rule of Saint Benedict." Bishop Teissier shouted with exasperation in the hall of the bishopry when I told him of my conversation with Amédée. I had asked Amédée if I could go up with him on his next trip to the monastery. He said I should notify the Ministry of the Interior in advance. "The ministry will take forever. You just have to go." The next day, Bishop Teissier told me his librarian, Jean-Pierre Henry, was driving up to the monastery on Saturday. I could go with him if I wanted.

I figured the librarian was not suicidal, and was further reassured when I learned that Brother Jean-Claude wanted to join us. Nevertheless, danger was present. The previous week, a bus had been blown up while going through the Chiffa Gorge, killing a dozen people. "Don't follow close to buses. They are preferred targets, since they are bigger than cars," was Teissier's off handed recommendation, as well as "to get home by dark."

I did experience terror. But it came not from the maquis. Rather, it came from Jean-Pierre Henry's jerky, high-speed Le Mans style driving on the autoroute to Blida which he practiced while turning around to talk with Jean-Claude in the backseat! The only other remarkable thing about the sixty-minute trip was the large number of police at intersections and the heavy military presence in the Chiffa Gorge. Otherwise, I could have been in Southern California as we drove through the Mitidja Plain, or northern Utah as we climbed south into the mountains from Blida toward Medea. Concrete watchtowers dot hilltops throughout the Medea, and one overlooked the monastery and valley below. We descended toward Tibhirine, past the entrance to the park with the statue of the Virgin.

It is the Virgin Mary who continues to protect the village. Amédée is convinced of that, and so are many of the Muslims. The monastery had been empty for three years, yet there had been no vandalism or theft. Not one stick of furniture, one picture, or one utensil had been stolen, in stark contrast to experience in Mokoto, Zaire, where the local Christian converts killed two monks and pillaged a Cistercian monastery in the early spring of 1996, a result of warfare between Tutsis and Hutus in the region.

Nor has the army occupied the monastery as a convenient lookout post. Only one unusual event has been reported: A bicycle was stolen in the village. But for that incident, the local families in Tibhirine remain today untouched by violence, and none of its children have joined the GIA. And those who left their homes after the report of the massacre went back when they heard the monks also intended to return.

Yet, there were some small changes. *Sobh*, the prayer of first light, had been canceled. There is now a local civil guard that patrols the area at night. The first shift is relieved at 3:00 A.M. and doesn't want to be disturbed by the muezzin's call. The monastery has the eerie feeling of being almost occupied. But whose presence is it? The old or the new? Perhap both. White cowls hang on hooks near the sacristy, but there are five not seven. Some of the rooms have personal belongings in them. The kitchen is fully equipped. Supplies are in the cupboard. Musa and Ben Ali work in the garden. I am introduced to Salim, who kisses me three times. The atmosphere is pregnant with expectation.

But one big cloud hung over everything: the fate of Mohammed. Since the summer of 1996, Mohammed had been watching over the monastery, but as a commuter. Living at the monastery was considered too dangerous after the kidnapping, so the Order bought him a car and rented an apartment for him and his family in Medea. In the spring of 1999, he was arrested and put in preventative detention by the local *juge d' instruction,* the French equivalent to a grand jury judge and state prosecutor. The charge against him was complicity in the kidnapping.

Personal pleas by Bishop Teissier, Gilles Nicolas, and dozens of character witnesses notwithstanding, the judge has not been swayed to release Mohammed on bail. He remains, as of this writing, in jail in Medea, where his wife and six children can see him once every two weeks.

The judge's reasoning was simple. He concluded that Mohammed must have been an accomplice to the abduction by virtue of the simple fact that he was still alive. As the sole person to get a close look at the kidnappers, who were not wearing masks, it was inconceivable to him that Mohammed would not have been killed. Mohammed had drawn the same conclusion while leading the men around the monastery, so he took the chance to run when one of the terrorists stumbled down the stairs. The fact that he actually escaped and was not hunted down gave further credence to Mohammed's culpability as a collaborator. Pressure to accuse someone can produce strange results, especially in a society where trust has been shredded and families divided to the point of murdering one another. Who belongs to whom?

With plenty of daylight still ahead after seeing the monastery, we drove to the town of Staouéli, where the French won their first victory in 1830. The old cloister, built by the first generation of Trappists, has been turned into apartments and is now engulfed in a busy suburb of Algiers. Its vast agricultural lands are now a public recreation park. All that remains as a reminder of the past is the concrete pedestal that supported a colossal, conquering cross which was pulled down after independence. The plain of Staouéli produced the famous Trappist wines in the nineteenth century, and an especially fine muscat. But inert symbols of the past are one thing. People and wine are another. Not only in the hearts of Muslims will the memory of the monks live on. Today, a new label is being used in Algeria to sell premium red wines. They are called vin de la Trappe. It is a name for quality.

There is another name in Algeria that means quality. Abdelkader. Emir Abdelkader. The mystic warrior embodied the generous and open spirit of Islam that Christian de Chergé feared was being overshadowed by the Islam of violent extremists, and being obliterated in the consciousness of dubious Western observers. Abdelkader's was a big Islam which matched Christian's big Christianity, and fittingly, their faiths found both real and symbolic fraternity at Tibhirine.

The monks lived in his shadow. A bald cliff face in the mountain behind the monastery, Abdelkader Rock, was the site of an encampment during the emir's running battle with the French. From the top of the cliff, Abdelkader's men had a panoramic view of any movement of enemy troops coming from the west. Today, the Algerians at Tibhirine pray for the return of their French monks, though to them they are not really French. They are men of God.

When the monks first took possession of the monastery in 1938, they put their statue of the Virgin Mary on the summit behind them, a few hundred yards above Abdelkader Rock. Abdelkader would have liked that, for his Islam was respectful of all religions. His generous spirit was that of the monks. Like Christian, he was imbued with a sense of chivalry, a broad view of God's ways, and a keen intelligence, coupled with wide learning and a hospitable spirit toward all people of goodwill. Abdelkader even looked like a Trappist monk, with his expressionless, bearded face covered in his white hooded *abaya*. The calling would have suited him. Had he lived his life the way he wanted, it would have been devoted to study, prayer, and meditation, much like that of Christian.

But it was not to be. He became a nation-builder, statesman, and tenacious Islamic resistance fighter. His green-and-white battle colors became the flag of the new Algerian nation in 1962. A poet, Sufi mystic, religious leader, and holy warrior, Abdelkader would be honored over the years by tens of thousands of Algerians who took his name, one which has been abused and insulted by the new mujahideen for an Islam he would not have recognized. Abelkader's fifteen-year struggle to hold together independent-minded clans to harass, discourage, and defeat successive French armies was followed closely in England and even in the United States. Today, Abdelkader's name can be found on a map of the Midwest, shortened to something pronounceable for the American tongue. He is the namesake of the town of Elkader, population two thousand, the county seat of Clayton County, Iowa.

The man whose name was given to this new frontier town in the Missouri Territory in 1845 was born in 1808 in a small village near Tlemcen in the western *beylek* of a loosely governed Ottoman territory. Like Christian, Abdelkader first learned Scripture from his mother. By the time he was five, she had taught him to read and write. His father, Abdelkader Mahdi el Din, was considered a wise man and was the head of the Qadiriyyah Brotherhood, one of the oldest Sufi brotherhoods in Islam.

From him, Abdelkader acquired a respect for science and learning, and became accomplished in the practical arts of hunting, riding, agriculture, and animal husbandry. He excelled in everything he did. He learned quickly. Everything interested him. He studied astronomy, mathematics, read widely, and admired the writings of Plato and Aristotle. "Knowledge has the value of fasting, and teaching, the value of prayer" was one saying of the Prophet that he heard often from his father. By the age of fourteen, Abdelkader knew the entire Koran by heart. It would guide his conduct in war and peace.

Following two years of educational travel to Cairo, Mecca, Jerusalem, Damascus, and other religious centers in the Middle East with his father, Abdelkader was ready to settle into the life of a "married monk."* But events changed his calling.

The French occupation of Algiers in 1830 was initially paid scant attention by the native population. Invaders had come and gone many times before. But two years later, the tribes began to see that this was turning into a new occupation, and not a liberation from the Turks, as the French had claimed. When the tribes came to Abdelkader senior for advice, the father realized that his son was quicker than he to understand the situation. He also saw that he was a natural leader. Abdelkader Mahdi el Din wisely stepped back to give his son the room he needed. In 1832, the tribes proclaimed the twenty-four-year-old Abdelkader their sultan, but he preferred the title of emir.

"Paradise," the Prophet said, "is found in the shadow of the sword." Emir Abdelkader established firmly that his authority rested only in the shadow of God. He was neither hot-blooded nor eager for war, but the Koran was written for life in this world. *Permission to take up arms is hereby given to those who are attacked, because they have been wronged,* "My goal is to drive out the infidels from the land of our fathers," he told his followers. Injustice that cannot be corrected by peaceful means may be transformed into a holy war, but within

*This is an expression used by Sufis to describe themselves. See Seyyed Hossien Nasr, *Ideals and Realities of Islam*.

limits prescribed by the Koran. The declaration of a holy war gave him the authority to begin to impose an unaccustomed discipline and unity on tribes not used to giving up their independence.

Abdelkader understood that the tribes had to unite and form an embryonic state. They needed a capital, a unified army, a tax levy and a system of justice that was independent of clan ties. He required his military chiefs, or caliphs, to have both skills in warfare and religious knowledge. His discipline was just but severe, especially toward tribes that betrayed him or fought with the French.

Tobacco, drink, and gambling were forbidden. Prostitution and displays of ostentatious living were suppressed. Each clan was held responsible for crimes committed on its territory. "Order reigned such that a woman could go out at night without risk of being insulted," Abdelkader noted proudly.

Every soldier under his command was held accountable for the treatment of his prisoners and faced punishment for any harm that came to them. In the last years of the fighting, a European woman with a young child went to visit the Bishop of Algiers, Monsignor Antoine-Adolph Dupuch, to ask a favor. Her husband was in the hands of Abdelkader. Could he intervene to obtain his release? Dupuch wrote to the emir:

> *You don't know me, but my calling is to serve God. If I could ride a horse, I would not fear either the blackness of night or the howling of storms. . . . I would deliver myself to the door of your tent and say—I don't think you would object—give me one of my brothers who has fallen into your hands. Let me send one of my servants to you. I have neither money nor gold to offer, only the prayers of a sincere soul.*

The emir proposed in return that the bishop improve upon his claim to act as a servant of God and friend of men. Why free only one prisoner? Why didn't the bishop ask for the release of all of the French prisoners? And moreover, the bishop could have doubled the value of his mission had he offered to release a corresponding number of Arabs in French prisons. Thus began the inauguration of prisoner exchanges between the emir and the French, as well as a long friendship between Bishop Dupuch and Abdelkader.

The emir also surrounded himself with a brain trust, composed of the best minds he could attract. He had Christians from Spain and England advising him on procurement of weapons and technology for weapon making. The number of Jews advising him were so numerous, they were called his "Jewish court." They handled diplomatic and business negotiations abroad.

Abdelkader was both a man of faith and an intellectual. He valued education and learning highly, as did the Prophet himself, who reminded the faithful with the Hadith. "A man of knowledge who can be of use to the people is of greater value than a thousand worshipers of Allah." Anyone with useful expertise was to be paid a small wage. Students were sent abroad to copy valuable manuscripts, and he was continuously adding books to his library. Anyone caught damaging or even dirtying a book was severely punished.

As 1847 came to an end, Abdelkader realized there was no purpose in continuing the killing and suffering. His troops and people were slowly starving. The French had turned his Moroccan allies against him and the countryside had been devastated by their scorched-earth tactics. On a rainy December 24, a cold, thin Abdelkader surrendered his favorite stallion to the Duc d'Aumale, looking like a Benedictine "black friar" with his black burnous on the outside overlaying his two white ones. From the Duc d' Aumale, the son of King Louis-Philippe, Abdelkader received the promise of safe passage to the Middle East in return for his pledge never again to return to Algeria.

The word of the Duc d'Aumale was not good enough. Instead of going on to the Middle East as expected, Abdelkader found himself and his entourage of eighty family members and servants detained indefinitely in Toulon. The king's position was weak, and many influential men in Paris did not trust the emir. In February 1848, Louis-Philippe would abdicate his throne, a victim of the democratic movements that were sweeping through Europe. When Abdelkader heard of the revolution and installation of the new republic, he wrote to the new government:

Praise to God, whose empire alone is eternal. . . . I rejoice over the news because I have read that this form of government is intended to get rid of injustice and to prevent the strong from preying on the weak. . . . Your actions are supposed to be dictated by the spirit of justice. God has made you protectors of the poor and afflicted. Therefore, I hold you as my natural protectors. Remove the veil of grief you have thrown on me. I ask only for justice from you. . . .

No one ever responded to his appeal.

Thus began a five-year period of captivity, marked by the death of twenty-five of his retinue from living in cold, damp castles. He lost a daughter, a son, nieces and nephews, and various of his retainers and their young children.

Always addressing himself to the noble side of the French spirit, Abdelkader continued tirelessly to seek justice. He expressed astonishment that a "a nation so rich and so great could lack the generosity toward those who have placed themselves in its trust." To cope with his depression and thoughts of suicide, Abdelkader read and meditated regularly upon the Koran and the mystery of God's ways that would lead him to such a state. He taught the Koran to his children, read Scripture to his entourage, took care of his mother, and received visitors. One of his most faithful visitors and correspondents was Bishop Dupuch. They had long theological discussions while he was in prison; Dupuch would help the emir get through his darkest days.

At Château d'Amboise in the Loire Valley, Abdelkader held a veritable salon. Churchmen, generals, and intellectuals came and were astonished by his active curiosity about France, broad-ranging mind, generosity of spirit, and lack of bitterness toward the country that had broken its word. He addressed himself always to the good France, and would not judge France at its worst.

In 1852, the Second Republic gave way to the Second Empire. With the help of advocates in high places, among them Bishop Dupuch, Abdelkader's case was brought before the emperor, Louis-Napoleon, who signed his release on October 16.

Abdelkader

I have just announced your liberation. . . . For a long time you should know that your imprisonment has troubled me because it has been a constant reminder that the goverment that preceeded me did not keep

> *its commitment toward an ill-starred enemy. Nothing in my view is more humiliating for the government of a great nation than to misuse its power by breaking its word. Generosity is always the better counsel, and I am convinced that your stay in Turkey will not harm the tranquillity of our possessions in North Africa.*
>
> *Your religion, like ours, teaches submission to the decrees of Providence. If France is master of Algeria, it is God who wants it so, and the French nation will never renounce it.*
>
> *You have been the enemy of France, but I do not pay any less hommage to your courage, your character, and your resignation in your misery; that is why I have the honor of ending your captivity with complete confidence in your word.*

In exile, Adbelkader's stature continued to grow. He settled in Damascus, surrounded by students, Algerian refugees, and a steady stream of visitors. He valued above all other activities reading, prayer, and reflection, yet he was not one simply to withdraw from the world. Again, outside events changed his life. In the spring of 1860, fighting broke out between Druze Muslims and Maronite Christians in neighboring Lebanon, creating tensions throughout the region. Abdelkader saw the danger of the conflict spreading to Syria and wrote to the Turkish govenor in Damascus, as well as to Druze leaders, urging them to calm things down. But the Turks did nothing.

The spark that ignited the tinder in July of 1860 was the punishment by local authorities of some young Muslims who publically insulted the cross. For their crime, the disrespectful youths were forced to sweep the streets of Damascus in chains. The spectacle triggered outrage among the Muslim population and led to an invasion of the Christian quarter. During the first three days of what became a weeklong rampage, five hundred Christians were massacred, churches, convents, and consulates burned, young women dragged off to harams. The Dutch consul was hacked to pieces and the American consul wounded. The French, Russian, and Greek diplomats, along with over a thousand other Europeans, were given refuge in Abdelkader's family residence. Together with other Muslim residents living in the vicinity of the Christians, Abdelkader organized a defense of strategic streets leading into the Christian neighborhood.

In all, it was estimated that eight thousand men, women, and children were killed. Diplomatic reports after the events pointed to Muslims from outside of Damascus and irregular militias as the provocateurs. Muslims living near the Christian quarter were among those who helped save Christian lives. When his spacious residence filled up with refugees, Abdelkader's men would escort under armed guard groups of fifty or sixty to the citadel, where the Turkish governor and his retinue were waiting out the storm. He reminded them of their duty as Muslims and obliged them to take the Christians under their protection.

Abdelkader explained afterward that he was simply doing his duty as a Muslim, though many Frenchmen did not believe him. They thought he must have done it out of a sense of indebtedness for his generous release from prison by Napoleon III. Why else would France's former enemy save French lives? they wondered, unaware that Abdelkader was only applying words of the Prophet he knew by heart: "If you see evil, intervene to change the situation, if you cannot, then condemn it with words, and if you cannot even do that, then disapprove it in your heart, which is the least you can do for the faith."

Despite the mutterings of the cynics and the incomprehension of the faithless, Abdelkader was credited with saving the lives of some ten to twelve thousand people of diverse nationalities. France awarded him the Legion of Honor. Abraham Lincoln sent him a pair of pistols inlaid with silver and gold, presented in a fine wood box of birds'eye maple, inscribed "From the President of the United States, to His Excellency, Lord Abdelkader, 1860." The governments of England, Spain, Greece, Prussia, Russia, and the Vatican all expressed their gratitude to the emir with gifts and decorations. The French Masonic lodge Henry IV sent the emir a letter, declaring, "French masonry, which believes in the existence of God and the immortality of the soul and bases its actions on the love of humanity, tolerance, and universal fraternity, is deeply moved by the great example you have given the world. We recognize, and claim as one of its own, the man who so unostentatiously applied its sublime motto,

'One for all.' " But the letter that touched him most was from a fellow Muslim, one whose fate was similar to his own. Mohammed Chamyl, exiled in Russia after years of defending his Chechen homeland in the Caucasus, wrote, "When I heard of the recent events in Damascus between Christians and Muslims, in which the latter showed a behavior unworthy of Islam, conduct which can only lead to the worst excesses, a veil fell over my soul. . . . May God be praised for having clothed his Servant with strength and faith! We speak of our sincere and true friend, Abdelkader, the just. I salute you!"

Five years later, in 1865, France was considering the creation of the post of viceroy for its Syrian protectorate. Napoléon III wanted to know if Abdelkader would consider the position. The proposal was controversial. Many of Napoléon's advisers were against any move that would raise the prestige of Islam. Under Abdelkader, Islam could be reinvigorated. His personal interpreter, in France, M. Bullad, had heard him say often, "The religion of Islam is dying because of the lack of Muslims, real Muslims." But Napoléon's advisers had nothing to fear. Abdelkader told an emissary sent to probe his interest, "I consider my political life over. I want to devote my remaining days to prayer, study, and meditation."

His devotion to meditation and reflection had already produced a document addressed to France in 1858 that was embarrassing to its men of letters. It said things Frenchmen didn't want to hear, especially from a defeated Arab, even one who had impressed, titillated, and amused the salons of Paris. This was the France of *enrichissez vous*. "Get rich" was the best advice Prime Minister Guizot could offer the French public in midcentury. France was a society Balzac described as "red in tooth and claw." It was materialistic, this liberated post-Napoleonic bourgeois grabfest. Positivism ruled. Science and technology held the keys to human progress and enlightenment, powered by money. Above all, it was about money.

Abdelkader knew he was held in contempt by his detractors and thought of as a "sheepherder." Nevertheless, he wrote a letter of love and concern about the condition of France's soul and, by extension, that of the Occident, a letter he called rather cumbersomely

"Brief notes to those with understanding, in order to draw attention to essential questions." In the preface of this forty-page letter, he wrote:

> *First realize, that it is necessary for an intelligent person to reflect on the words that are spoken, not the person who says them. If the words are true, he will accept them whether he who says them is known as a truth teller or a liar. One can extract gold from a clump of dirt, a beautiful narcissus comes from an ordinary bulb, medication from the venom of a snake. . . .*
>
> *An intelligent man gets to know others through what is trustworthy and authentic in him, not through words. For an intelligent person, wisdom is like a lost sheep which is to be sought, and can be found anywhere and in any individual.*

A student of Plato, Abdelkader knew truth had an independent reality, in but not of the material world. He hoped in vain that his words would find an audience in France, but they were discreetly put in oblivion's drawer. His letter was not written as an argument. It offered up no ideology in the modern sense. It was written the way a wise, kindly uncle would.

In Abdelkader's view of the world, politics, religion, and science should all work together to serve the same end of glorifying God. Politics is the art of leading people to live in harmony with one another. Religion provides a moral base of shared values to aid in living together and recognition of our common origin in God. Knowledge, if it probes beyond the material world, will lead us to grasp the basic unity of mankind.

Abdelkader was overwhelmed by the modern technology he saw in France. The French "savants" possessed an impressive spirit of "practical application." Yet, he wondered, where was their "spirit of metaphysical speculation," which would allow them to go beyond the narrow confines of objective reality to reach a science truly worthy of the name, one that served man's most intimate needs, the needs of his soul? "If the spirit is healthy, it can only take pleasure in knowledge. If it is sick as a result of bad habits, it will take pleasure in other things than knowledge, just as certain people take pleasure in eating mud or a sick person can't taste the sweetness of honey."

If the West wanted to rule the world, and it seemed to have the material means to do so, did it have the wisdom necessary to succeed? It might profit from opportunities granted by its power at the moment, but did it have the ability to foresee the consequences that might come to haunt it and the rest of the world if it did not proceed humbly and prudently? These questions were tactfully raised in his "brief note."

Abdelkader was not against progress. He embraced modernity, provided that this modernity—be it "technology," "democracy," "capitalism"—not be elevated to a divine principle and turned into an idol, demanding loyalty from cultures that chose to be different. *La richesse, c'est la différence.* We learn about ourselves by taking note of the other.

His letter discussed relations between Christians and Muslims, too. "If Muslims and Christians had wanted to listen to me, I could have ended the quarreling. . . . They would have become true brothers in God." Abdelkader believed the only bond that ties a community together is one that unites both their material and spiritual interests. In 1840, Christians and Muslims had a chance to build something together. "They didn't pay attention to my words. Divine wisdom decided that they were not to be united in a single faith. Only when the Messiah comes will their differences cease. But He will not reunite by the Word, even though He raised the dead and healed the blind and the lepers. He will unite them only by the sword and a fight to the death."

He sounded pessimistic, indicating that men must first butcher one another before they can come together. Only from the ashes and slaughter of World War I and its continuation, World War II, did Europe finally see the light and agree to corset and gird itself against future fratricidal conflict. Was it a coincidence that the leading personalities who helped create the European Coal and Steel Union, which led to the European Community, were deeply religious men bent on reconciliation—Jean Monnet and Robert Schuman of France, and the Belgian Paul-Henri Spaak whose joint efforts were brought to fruition with the crucial support of Konrad Adenauer and Charles de Gaulle.

However, Abdelkader offered, "If anyone wishes to know the way of the truth and comes to me, I will lead him without difficulty to the way of truth without promoting my own ideas, but rather by helping him see the truth with his own eyes in such a way that he cannot but see it." Each society, he continued, must evolve according to its own inner rhythms. Like the great Anglo-Irish political thinker Edmund Burke, he believed the way of truth could be none other than the way of prudence.

"Just as a man cannot see the things that come into view around him without continually moving his eyes back and forth, in the same way, a mind that does not move continuously from one concept to another will not understand the truth of things at their deepest level," he wrote. Is not the emir talking about a process of ceaseless questioning in order not to become stagnant in a fixed definition of oneself, or one's faith? Sufis talk of Islam as a river. Rivers are like life, dynamic, cutting and changing the land, picking up new elements and dropping others.

What is it to be a Christian or a Muslim? Christian de Chergé believed the contemplative life meant constantly pushing out frontiers, redefining and questioning, being willing to depart, like Abraham, for new lands. Abdelkader called this same spirit "a continual moving of the mind's eye" to different ideas and concepts to find the deeper truths that both unsettle and unite.

The remains of Abdelkader were moved from Damascus to Algeria in 1963, one year after independence. France could no longer object to his return.

El-Alia cemetery is several miles east of the center of Algiers and had been on my list of places to see during my visit. Abdelkader rests there. In 1992, the cemetery also had been the last stop for grief-stricken Algerians who, in the suffocating July heat, had been following the funeral cortege with the body of President Boudiaf.

My driver, Mohammed, was told by a guard at the entrance that we had to park the car and walk into the grounds down a tree-lined allée. Mohammed had been recommended to me by Bishop Teissier as a reliable driver, and he spoke fluent French. He was probably in his fifties, had gray tufts on the side of a bald pate, and wore reading glasses that gave him a rumpled, professorial air. This was Mohammed's first visit to the cemetery.

We walked into a small esplanade where there were three large headstones, two of which were identical, five feet high, the tapered stones resembling giant spatulas. Mohammed asked a passerby whose monument belonged to whom. At that moment, I understood why he had a preference for perusing French-language newspapers while he waited for me in his aged Russian Lada during my house calls in Algiers. He could not read Arabic.

Boudiaf's grave was the far left, his headstone an identical twin to that of Houari Boumediene. Set slightly apart from the two former presidents was the plain marble sarcophagus of Abdelkader. It was lying in front of a similarly shaped stone, though his was distinguished from the other two by being wider at the top and narrower at the bottom, like the torso of a Greco-Roman wrestler. Their section of the cemetery was well maintained and the burial sites were in orderly rows, evidently a section reserved for notables.

The rest of the cemetery was a disordered mishmash of neglected grave sites—stone tombs pointing in every direction lay on the dusty, weedy ground. A cross or a star identified the tomb as Christian or Jewish. In another part of El-Alia was a tidy plot for British Commonwealth soldiers killed during World War II, and beyond them, in an area that was being encroached upon by new housing and garbage, were more Muslim graves. Compared to the Christians and Jews, the Muslims had smaller, shorter tombs, with double headstones, like the head and footboards on a cradle.

The cemetery seemed to represent Algeria, a jumbled, confused home to many peoples over the centuries. Whose home will it be in the future? The monks' death and those of 100,000 Algerians was part of a larger, ongoing conflict over inheritance. It is a house full of ghosts, suppressed memories, and ancestors who incite mixed emotions. Algerians are still asking who they are.

Some see their country as a Mediterranean society, a rich agglomeration of past cultural deposits. At the base of its cultural geology are the Berbers, whose race is spread throughout North Africa. Over the centuries, their blood has been mixed with successive Phoenician, Roman, Vandal, Byzantine, Arab, Turkish, Jewish, and Spanish migrations, ending with an eclectic mix of "French" colonists drawn from all over Europe. Within this multicultural Algerian house, two invaders stand out today: the Arab occupant and the French ghost. The Arab came to liberate the Berber from the darkness of unbelief, and the Frenchman to uplift the barbarous Arab from sloth and backwardness. Both are entwined in an embrace from which neither can be released, nor wants to be.

France is very much present in spirit. Store signs are still in French after thirty years of Arabization. The currency is the dinar, but merchants quote prices in centimes, as they did before they won independence. The important newspapers are in French. Snack bars are full of croissants and crème-filled napoleons (along with pizza, hamburgers, and *m'hajeb,* a spicy local crêpe). Much of the civil and criminal law is French, grafted with Islamic law. For proponents of a conglomerate Mediterranean identity, the French heritage is part of a messy family history.

Yet the French legacy also arouses powerful love-hate emotions in Algerians. Thus, another view sees Algeria as a Muslim and Arab country, opposing itself to a colonial inheritance associated with inequality and humiliation. But where is the place of the Berber in this monocultural framework? Or the European? And there is an even more difficult question. Who is actually a Muslim? A Muslim, by definition, is one who submits to God. Through submission, a Muslim can find the inner peace that is necessary for harmonious living with one's neighbor. A Muslim nonbeliever is a contradiction in terms. And what about believers who are nonobservant? Are they no longer Muslims? And what degree of observance is necessary to please God? Who can answer for God?

Within this Arabist-Muslim current, the Islamists want Algeria to have not only a Muslim identity but a Muslim society governed by Islamic law. And how otherwise? they would ask. To submit means to follow God's law as revealed to his apostles Abraham, Moses, David, Jesus Christ, and, finally, to Mohammed. But if, as the Koran says, there is to be no compulsion in religion, so how, then, can one assure submission to the law? The Islamists are divided over the methods and interpretations of the law. However, they are united in their belief that a government gets its legitimacy from God, and that justice comes from following God's ordinances.

The American ambassador to Algeria, Cameron Hume, explained this dichotomy between a pluralistic Mediterranean worldview and a monocultural Arab-Muslim one when I visited him at his palatial villa in the American diplomatic compound on the heights of El-Biar. His description of forces in tension offered a tempting way to understand Algerian politics. Between the lines was the implication that the Mediterranean model was pluralistic and tolerant, the Arabist-Muslim one closed, monolithic, and less tolerant.

Yet, like all efforts to tidy up reality into schemas and categories, the analysis seemed flawed by my encounters with real people. There is, for example, Lynda Tamdrari, a radio journalist, comic, and musician. She is in her thirties, and wears stylish sleeveless dresses that come to a halt just above her knees. She is among the one-third of the women on the streets of Algiers who do not cover their heads. Lynda thinks of herself herself as devoutly religious and is scrupulous about fasting during Ramadan. She is an active member of the Francophone Assembly for Culture and Democracy (RCD), whose base is in Berber Kabylia. The party, which regards itself as liberal, is rabidly anti-FIS, and anti-Islamist. The RCD was active behind the scenes in persuading the generals to cancel the national elections in 1992, when it was clear the government would have to share power with a FIS majority. She believes in the separation of church and state and was leaving for Rome to participate in interreligious dialogue, but she is not in favor of any dialogue with the FIS, and she is deeply suspicious of Hamas.

And where does Louisa Hanoune fit in this bipolar picture of Algeria? She is the militant leftist leader of the Algerian Workers Party who defends the FIS and has been outspoken in her opposition to the coup d'etat of 1992 that blocked the impending Islamist victory. "It was a catastrophe," she noted in a long series of interviews published in 1996, like "throwing a match in an oil well. As in all countries, she said, "hatred in Algeria was born of injustice and humiliation." The elections, she insists, were about the reconquest of

Algeria by its own citizens—an overwhelming desire by the electorate to rid itself of thirty years of authoritarian and capricious misrule.

Hanoune is much admired by Islamists and religious Muslims throughout the Arab world. They like her for her integrity and her respect for the right of religious parties to participate in the political process even when she disagrees with their positions. Positing, as many of the liberal intellectuals do, that Algeria is faced with "two visions of society," one democratic the other Islamist, she believes, offers a completely false choice—one that only serves the government's interests. Algerian society, she insists, "is too complicated to be reduced to such simplicities. The struggle has been over power."

It was, she noted, an arbitrary authoritarian state that used religion to shore up its power, a tactic that backfired. "There has never been democracy in Algeria, nor are there any real foundations of a republic to preserve, when the self-proclaimed democratic elite's first response to defending the 'republic' is to call in the army and do to the FIS exactly what they were accusing them of preparing. This avant-garde of Francophones, journalists, doctors, writers argued contemptuously that the Algerians are not mature enough for democracy. They called them illiterates and imbeciles who do not know how to vote. Instead, they turned to those who had been overwhelmingly rejected by the electorate to defend their 'democratic vision.' Democracy is not about the choosing between the good and bad victims of repression, but about the creation of institutions that can guarantee to each the right of expression and necessity to respect the other."

Louisa Hanoune defies all the clichés. She is the only female leader of a political party in the Arab world. She is a militant defender of the rights of women and defends the Islamists. To the Algerian and Muslim masses throughout the Arab world she is a courageous opponent of government injustice.

Then there is Aïssa Benlakhdar. He is the successor to Mohammed Bouslimani, the former president of Irshad wal-Islah, Hamas's philanthropic association. Today, Hamas holds three of the thirty ministries in the government of Abdelaziz Bouteflika. Benlakhdar believes the *sharia* should be used to govern a Muslim society, but he accepts that its interpretation is not easy—which is why there are four schools of law in the Muslim world, all of which borrow from one another. He applauds the fact that *fetwas* in Algeria are no longer issued by a single authoritative mufti, unless the matter concerns a narrow, ritualistic point of law. Society is too complex for broad authoritative rulings to be made by an individual, no matter how wise. The Haut Conseil Islamique (The High Islamic Council), made up of religious and secular authorities, rules on big questions such as abortion or women's rights in divorce and marriage.

Aïssa believes democracy and Islam are compatible. "Just as you in the United States have a written Constitution and you are free to pass laws that do not contravene the Constitution as interpreted by your Supreme Court, so we can have a similar process where laws are voted but would also have to pass the test of constitutionality. Only our Supreme Court would be made up of specialists in religious law. Their constitution would be the Koran, which is a general statement of values and guidelines for living, together with the Sunna and Hadith. The way the Prophet lived his life and the things he said help us interpret the law in everyday life—like your case law." Or, as he might have said in the case of monks, like interpreting the Rule of Saint Benedict, which is based on the life and teachings of Jesus Christ. Aïssa, interestingly, means Jesus in Arabic.

The mural on the cupola inside Notre-Dame d'Afrique seemed apt. I had taken two Algerian acquaintances to see the basilica. Nacer, a young man in his thirties, worked in a government publishing house and had helped me get a taxi one day. Learning that I was an American seemed to strengthen his natural desire to be helpful to a confused foreigner. His friend Mohammed imported pasta-making equipment. The two of them had never been inside the church. Amédée was living next door to the basilica, in the former residence of Cardinal Duval, and he happily gave us a guided tour.

As we looked at the mural, Amédée explained to us that the little boy on the beach with a pail and shovel illustrated a story from the life of Saint Augustine. It showed Saint Augustine watching the child trying to fill with water a hole he had dug in the sand. Saint Augustine is supposed to have said to him, "Don't you know you that you will never be able to fill that hole?" And the boy answered, "I will fill the hole with water before you fill your head with the idea of God."

Outside the basilica, in the bright sunlight, sheep were sleeping on the steps and nibbling blades of grass that had grown up between the stone squares of the esplanade overlooking the Mediterranean. There were the usual policemen stationed around the basilica to discourage terrorists from desecrating the church or attacking visitors. One of them was standing under a palm tree, and he looked particularly friendly.

Nacer proudly introduced me as an American. I asked the policeman about the equipment he was carrying. He had a Beretta side arm, along with an AK-47. His walkie-talkie was made by Motorola and his uniform was the same blue one with the telltale exposed fly zipper worn by the Police Nationale of France. His boots were Algerian, he told me, smiling. He agreed to pose for a picture with Mohammed and Nacer in front of the statue of Cardinal Lavigerie, whose truncated arm stretched forth. A Muslim policeman posing in front of a Christian crusader, wearing a French uniform hung with Italian, Russian, and American hardware, said something to me. The global cop. But can there really be such a thing as a global community? I wondered. The global community is an oxymoron, like a Muslim atheist. Tribes are global now—the tribes of police enforcement, scientists, human rights activists, the international corporations, drug dealers, but do global tribes create a global community?

Communities are supposed to be places of intimacy, warmth, and relationships that sustain. When three people come together in the Lord, the Bible says, there is already a community of faith. In the Middle Ages, monasteries that grew to more than 500 monks would send some off to create new foundations. More than five hundred brothers could no longer be a true community. The globe is too big a place to provide for warmth and intimacy. The more we connect with those far away, the more we seem to disconnect from those closest to us. Will the Internet do on a global scale what the telephone did to the French in Algeria?

When telephones were introduced in Algeria, the French army's Arab Bureau got lazy. The Arab Bureau was responsible for maintaining good relations with the *indigenes* and for knowing what was going on in the villages. Traditionally, this had been done by officers riding their horse into the *bled* for several weeks, traveling the circuit, sipping tea with the local leaders for long hours, and building personal relationships. But the telephone made it possible to do away with long, hot, and dangerous rides into the backcountry, thus weakening the ties that only effort and face-to-face relations can create. It was considered more efficient simply to call, have a little chat on the phone, so officers didn't have to waste all that time.

If the monks in the Middle Ages were right in believing that a community is by definition relatively small, how does a community maintain a sense of identity without becoming inbred and overly cloistered, becoming "navel-gazers," as Bishop Scotto said of the Church when it is deprived of the challenges of coexisting with those of other faiths? And how does a community become open to change and evolution without blurring its identity and loosing sight of what it has that is worth preserving? The monks' abbot general, Bernardo Olivera, had told them to dig deeper into their own identity as Christians in order to follow the path of spiritual sharing and openness. The monks found that their identity as Christians was strengthened, not threatened, by witnessing the message of universal love as practiced by Muslims. Tibhirine had become an open cloister, all-loving and loved by all.

I wandered about the plaza, admiring the view of the Mediterraean from the top of the escarpment that descends to the old Christian cemetery in the former Saint-Eugène quarter. I thought about Duval's deathbed prediction—that Algeria would surprise the world. Algeria certainly had surprised me.

Is not the act of a Muslim government honoring Cardinal Duval and seven "insignificant" Trappist monks with a state funeral the beginning of something new—at least in the eyes of much of the Western world, so accustomed to thinking of Muslims as violent fanatics at war with so-called Western values? Yet what are Western moral values if not Judeo-Christian values, values that were born in the deserts of the Middle East and to which Muslims subscribe?

For those who have grown cynical about Christianity, is it not surprising that Algeria is home to a tiny Christian community giving witness to the message of universal love by performing good works and being true friends to Muslims, unto death? I was astonished when Bishop Teissier told me that President Boumediene had asked him back in the mid-1970s to teach the Koran to the wives of his ministers. What an extraordinary sign of goodwill and faith in a representative of a sister religion. Or was the gesture more of a testimony to Boumediene's belief in the underlying unity of Muslim and Christian values, sincerely practiced, that in the midst of a campaign of Islamization and Arabization he would entrust the forming of Muslim souls to a Catholic priest, and one from a people who had shown Muslims more contempt than love?

A professor at the University of Algiers, who wishes to remain anonymous, predicted after the death of the monks: "One day, those seven monks will be considered saints by Muslims, Christians, and Jews."

Yes, out of all the horror, Algeria may surprise the world.

Afterword

The story of the monks continues to unfold on different fronts. Mohammed was released after eight months of detention, during which time the Trappists continued to pay his salary as *le gardien,* a responsibility he has now resumed. His liberation was celebrated with a huge couscous feast at the monastery with the monks-in-waiting, Bishop Teissier, Gilles Nicolas, Robert Fouquez, numerous neighbors, and his family.

Mohammed's lawyer had convinced the judge of the plausibility of his escape from the terrorists the evening of the kidnapping by producing a witness who had had a similar experience. The witness was among several peasants from the neighborhood whose families were known not to agree with Zitouni's way of fighting and who had been kidnapped two days before the monks were. The hostages were taken to a building in the countryside, where some of them were culled and tortured out of sight, but within earshot of the others. Among those listening to the screams were a father and his son. They decided to escape the next night, but were hunted down. The father was caught and killed, but the son was able to hide and get away. The kidnappers were described as being from outside the area.

The lawyer used this story as evidence that it was possible to elude captors in the night, especially if they were outsiders and thus not familiar with the area. The witness also said that he had heard the voices of the monks, who were held briefly at the same location.

Joining the five monks living in Algiers is a new brother, Jean-Michel, from Notre-Dame de Tamié. They will all need to exercise the virtue of patience, as the prospect of their returning to Tibhirine is now clouded. A local family of four was massacred in the summer of 2000, but by whom and why is not known. The Ministry of the Interior, which is responsible for the security of the monks, cannot say when they will be allowed to reoccupy the monastery. Killing continues in parts of the countryside, much of it viewed by the government as residual banditry. Throughout the years 2000 and 2001, there was a disturbing increase of violent incidents in the regions around Oran, Blida, Medea, and Jijel, where a new group has been formed—the Group Salafist for Preaching and Combat (GSPC), a rival to the GIA. The *concorde civile* continues and the amnesty has been extended. As many as five thousand repentants have turned in their arms since the fall of 1999, when the program was announced.

The new Algerian ambassador posted to Washington, D.C., Driss Jazairi, is the great-great-nephew of Emir Abdelkader, and he wants to make Americans more aware of his famous forebearer.

President Bouteflika visited France in June of 2000 and gave a speech before the French National Assembly. He spoke about Abdelkader, the Church in Algeria, and the legacy of colonialism.

> *The colonialism of the past century opened for us the doors of modernity, but it was a modernity that came into our home like a burglar, a modernity that caused fear, uncertainty, and frustration. And it is true, as well, that modernity discredits itself and denies its own essence when it presents a face that is vicious by its oppression and rejection of others who are different. . . .*
>
> *The modernity to which we aspire, Mr. President, and which for us is imperative to survive is not, as our enemies insinuate, an artificial veneer, or a servile imitation of thought and behavior. . . . To assimilate the scientific spirit and participate in the course of human progress and technological progress—two aspects which for us cannot be dissociated—presupposes the complete awakening of our ability to exercise responsibly our freedom and to reaffirm the role of reason, which is freedom's natural handmaiden.*
>
> *To the Archbishop of Algiers, Monsignor Dupuch, who asked him the reason why he defended the Christians in Damascus in July of 1860, Abdelkader replied, "What I did conformed to the obligations of my faith and my respect for the rights of humanity." Abdelkader had already in his day a very clear and modern notion of the rights of man, which he did not separate from his conception of a humanistic Islam that was open and tolerant.*

As to the importance of international cooperation in fighting terrorism, Bouteflika underlined the dangers of an indifferent attitude in the face of a threat that is not confined within national borders and which had already spilled into France:

> *Such indifference has led to the targeting of intellectuals, government workers, innocent villagers, foreigners, and religious, be they Muslims or Christians, as shown by the assassination of numerous imams, the Bishop of Oran, Monsignor Claverie, the unspeakable massacre of the monks of Tibhirine. . . . Permit me, though, to give particular homage here to the rare self-abnegation of the Church of Algeria, a Church that unflinchingly has proven throughout the worst moments of our torment its mission of human solidarity in my country.*

Appendix A: GIA Communiqué No. 43, Addressed to the French Government*

God says: "Fight against those to whom the Scriptures were given but who believe neither in God nor the Last Day, who do not forbid what God and His apostle have forbidden, and who do not embrace the True Faith, until they submit and pay tribute" (Koran, Repentance: 29). He also says: "Fight all the polytheists as they all fight you and know that God is with those who fear Him" (Repentance: 36).

The first verse concerns the people of the Book, among whom are the Jews and the Christians, and the second concerns all polytheists. God has ordered the believers to kill the infidels, starting with those nearest to them and those who are the most dangerous and harmful to religion and the life of Muslims. God said: "O believers! Fight among the infidels those who do you harm and may they find your resistance firm. Know that God is with those who fear Him" (Repentance: 123).

Based on these teachings, the GIA has killed the unbelievers from all confessions and ordered them all to leave the country. When my brother Saif Allah Dja'far was emir, the GIA gave them a time limit of a month to do so. Thus, he followed the example of God's messenger who had granted a month's reprieve to Bani Nossayr's tribe.

The GIA has deprived them of the peace and safety, which they thought they had. It has authorized the elimination of those who insisted on staying in our country. Some have heeded the order given and others stubbornly remained. That is when the mujahideen began to kill them, either in groups or individually. Others among them have fled. Those who stayed thought their presence here was important in order to fight Islam and the Muslims. Among them are

*Translated into English from the French translation of the Arabic in *L'Express*, May 30, 1996.

politicians, soldiers, evangelists, and many others. God said: "They will not stop fighting you until you convert to their religion, if they are able to" (Koran, The Cow: 217).

The good Lord has helped the mujahideen of the GIA kill a large number of unbelievers, Jews, Christians, polytheists, and atheists. God helped them again, a few days ago, to kidnap seven proselytizing monks in the region of Medea, who are still alive and well. This announcement coming more than twenty days after their kidnapping, clearly shows that the infidel junta can neither protect itself nor others.

During the last few days, especially since the ranks have been purged of sectarians and heretics, the mujahideen have managed to inflict heavy losses among the infidel soldiers, by killing or wounding them, in several areas of the country.

In Laghouat, our brothers the mujahideen have managed to kill over a hundred infidels and take an equal number prisoner. They also shot down a helicopter. It is the third aircraft brought down in the area. In the town of Medea itself, surrounded by infidel soldiers, an ambush was set for one of their groups that came to rescue the monks. Six machine guns were captured and about ten men were killed. The rest turned back, defeated. God said: "If the impious who fight against you take flight, they will find no protectors. The law of God does not change and will not change" (Koran, Al-Fath: 22–23).

Please note that those infidel soldiers, faced with the obvious failure of their attempt at surrounding the whole area where the monks are held, resulting from the actions carried out by our mujahideen brothers, are now turning to artillery attacks and air raids with military planes and helicopters, with the intent, most likely, of killing the monks, since they have lost all hope of recovering them alive. It shows the weakening of their forces. May God be thanked from beginning to end.

The monks arrogantly presume that Sheikh Abou Younes Attia, may God bless his soul, promised to spare their lives and grant them safety. But there is no evidence of this act and it is not credible, as there is no witness to attest to it. Even if he had, such an act would have been wrong as the monks never stopped trying to evangelize

Muslims, to show their religious symbols and solemnly celebrate their holiday.

All of this points to treason, as is demonstrated by the ulema, which has interpreted the conditions defined by the emir of the believers, Omar Ibn al-Khatab (concerning tolerance toward Christians on Islamic land). Even if this promise they refer to is authentic, they have misused it. That is why they have become like those who fight against God's religion. So they deserve the fate of the unbelievers.

Another interpretation is given by the *djaz'arist* heretics. The latter do not consider as legitimate the murder of those unbelievers. They condemn such an act. They say that these men are monks and that monks must not be killed. They are wrong. Everyone knows that the monk who withdraws from the world in order to pray in his cell is called a hermit among Christians. It is the murder of such monks that Abou Bakr has forbidden. But monks who leave their hermitage and mingle with people, and draw them away from the divine path are proselytizing* then their murder becomes sanctioned. This is exactly the case of these captive monks who do not live apart from the rest of the world.

As it is rightful to fight for the religion of God and the Muslims, it is also rightful to treat the monks as one treats the infidels when they are taken in combat as prisoners: murder, slavery, or exchange for Muslim prisoners, according to the law and in accordance with the recommendations published in the first issue of Sheikh Abou Abdallah Ahmed's *Al-Ta'ifa al-Mansoura* (*The Victorious Community*), may God bless his soul.

The GIA believes neither in a dialogue, nor truce, nor reconciliation with the impious ones. For these reasons, we will not engage in a dialogue with this filth and despicable trash. But we are addressing this communiqué to France and to its president, Jacques Chirac. We are telling them: "Your seven monks are still alive, safe and sound."

As it is my duty and that of all Muslims to free our prisoners, in conformity with the Hadith, "Free the suffering," I can imagine

---

*Based on the GIA's peculiar interpretation of Ibn Taymiyya.

freeing our prisoners for yours. We have a full list: First, you must free our brother Abdelhak Layada and then we will name the others, God willing. But we would first like to know your decision.

Lastly, you know that the GIA respects its promises and fulfills them. As an example, we can remind you of the liberation of the Yemeni and Omani ambassadors in exchange for the liberation of the late Sheik Abou Abdallah Ahmed. The other unfortunate example is the case of the Air France airbus hostages, where, as a result of the stubborness and obstinacy of Mitterand and Balladur, tragedy struck. Our brothers slit the throats of quite a few passengers and killed some others.

God willing, we will make good our promises. You have a choice. If you free your prisoners, we will free ours, and if you refuse, we will slit their throats.

May God be praised. . . .

Thursday, April 18, 1996.
The GIA emir, Abou abd al-Rahmen Amin

Appendix B: Glossary

Abbey: a monastery, distinguished from a priory by size; considered more prestigious than a priory

Abaya: a long robe with sleeves, often black, and worn by women with a head scarf

Ad nutum: a temporary appointment, made at the discretion of the abbot of a "mother" monastery, of a superior to a "daughter" monastery whose community is too small (less that six stabilized) to elect its own superior

AIS (Armée Islamique du Salut): the official armed branch of the Islamic Salvation Front (FIS), formed in 1994 to wage war by Islamic rules

Algérie Française: slogan used by the European population who, during the war of independence, wanted French Algeria to remain part of France, a France that stretched from Dunkirk to Tamanrasset

ALN (Armée de Libération Nationale): National Liberation Army; the combat arm of the FLN, it did the actual fighting during the war of independence, and it never numbered much over thirty thousand

Aman: a pledge of safe conduct or security, by which a non-Muslim living in Muslim territory becomes protected in his life and property, usually for a limited period

Berber: original non-Arab inhabitants of the Maghreb whose origins are subject to dispute among specialists; in Algeria, there are four Berber groups—Kabyles, Chaouias, Tuaregs, and M'zabites

Beylek: area administered by the bey, or provincial governor, during the Ottoman Empire

Bled: backcountry and small rural villages

Burnous: a hooded woolen cape, usually black, off-white, or brown

Caliph: the title taken by Mohammed's successors, who functionned as both secular and religious leaders of the Islamic community but were subject to governing in accordance with *sharia,* as interpreted by the ulema (body of Muslims trained to interpret religious law)

Cellérier: person responsible for the material side of monastic life, including finances, personnel needs, and supplies

Coopérant: a French citizen who does national service (for draft-age males;

also as alternative service) abroad as a civilian in the occupations determined by the host country

Da'wa: Islamic missionary work, generally out among Muslims in need of moral and spiritual renewal; religious instruction from the Koran to help guide people on the right path

Dey: Algerian title of the Turkish governor (bey) of Algiers before the French conquest in 1830

DGSE (Direction Générale de la Sécurité Extérieure): French security service responsible for foreign intelligence, falling under the authority of the army

Dhimmi: Muslim juridical term for the rights due Christians and Jews (People of the Book) living in a society governed by Islamic law, where they can practice their religion and hold government (usually administrative) positions under rules that vary from country to country

Divine Office: the name for the canonical hours: Vigils, Lauds, Terce, Sext, None, Vespers, and Compline

Djaz'ara: Algerian Islamic and legalist school of reform that pursues a national, rather than an international, jihad while not rejecting modernity (as opposed to the *salafists*); a practitioner of this is a *djaz'arist*

DST (Direction de la Sécurité du Territoire): French security service responsible for intelligence activity on French territory, accountable to the Ministry of the Interior

Father: an ordained priest; all monks are brothers, but, strictly speaking, only those who are ordained are called father

Fellagha (or *fell*): originally meant brigands, deserters, or fugitives but now means "rebels"; name given to Arab guerrilla fighters during the Algerian war of independence

Fetwa: a decree or ruling of a legal or theological nature, usually issued by a mufti or a religous council; it carries moral authority among the faithful and has legal force in countries where the government adopts the ruling as law

FFS (Front des Forces Socialistes): a Kabyle-based political party lead by Ait Ahmed

FIS (Front Islamique de Salut): the Islamic Salvation Front, a party formed in 1989 whose agenda was the creation of an Islamic state, succeeded in defeating the FLN in the local elections of 1990

Fitna: disturbance, civil discord, divisiveness in the Muslim community; considered a punishment inflicted by God upon the sinful or unrighteous

FLN (Front de Libération Nationale): a broad coalition party formed to unify opposition (or eliminate political rivals) against France during the war of independence; Algerian Liberation Front is the official party

Gandoura: sleeveless ankle-length tunic usually worn by men in the Algerian countryside

GIA (Groupe Islamique Armé): Armed Islamic Group. The most active and indiscriminately violent Islamic opposition group in Algeria; considered responsible for most of the civilian killings after 1993

Gourbi: a traditional adobe-style house seen in the Algerian countryside

Hadith: the body of sayings of the Prophet Mohammed, preserved and passed on in oral and written form as remembered by the men and women called the Companions of the Prophet. It provides guidance on a wide range of subjects of a personal or theological nature; is a part of the Sunna and complement to the Koran, it must be taken into consideration to properly interpret the Koran.

Hamas: newly named Movement for Society and Peace (MSP); an Islamist theocratic party dedicated to peaceful change led by Mahfoud Nahnah; main principles include Islam as the state religion and unifying core of social values, commitment to democracy and free choice, cultural diversity, and promoting Arabic as the national and official language of Algeria.

Haram: forbidden, illicit, against the law of God

Harki: an Algerian soldier who actively fought with the French in Algeria during the war of independence, often as scouts and trackers; considered traitors by the FLN after the war

Haut Comité d'Etat (HCE): High Committee of State, formed as an emergency governing body in January 1992, after the cancellation of the national elections

Hijab: nunlike garb that covers a woman's body, exposing only the face and hands

Hittists: the unemployed, mostly young men who have nothing to do but lean on walls (*hit*) and chat with their friends

Hogra: injustice, arbitrary use of power, contempt for the people

Ijma: Islamic word for consensus

Imam: a Sunni Muslim preacher, spiritual guide, or leader of the official prayer; usually not required to have any special degree or education, other than being respected in his own community and knowledgeable of the Koran

Islam: from Arabic word *salam*—meaning peace, salvation, or submission; Islam means to surrender to the will of God. Islam considers itself a continuation of prior divine revelations made to Jews and Christians. Islam puts special emphasis on the transcendence, oneness, and unity of God, summed up in the Islamic profession of faith: "There is no god but God." Many devout Muslims consider the nation-state as a false idol, hence their desire to restore the *umma*, or the religious community. It teaches that God's revelation occurs through nature, history, and Scripture and that the God of Judaism, Christianity, and Islam is one. Muslims, like Jews and Christians, consider themselves children of Abraham, but they are closest to the Jews in their practices and beliefs

Islamism: a diverse group of ideologies in Islam that promotes the *sharia* (religious law, of which there are four different schools of interpretation) as a comprehensive basis for governing society; maintains that all law ultimately derives from God and a just society can occur only when it is governed according to divine law as interpreted by Islamic legal scholars (now a field of law taught at Harvard and other law schools)

Jamaa (pl. jamaate): name given to small independent Islamic groups

Jamaa al Islamiyya: a *jamaa* of this name claimed responsiblity for the kidnapping of the monks; Its Pakistani namesake (Jama'at-i Islami), founded in 1941, was a nonviolent opposition movement against British rule and provided inspiration to other Islamic groups.

Jihad: literally, "to strive or to struggle in the way of God." The "greater jihad" is the struggle over onesself, to purify one's soul; the "lesser jihad" is the defense of Islam against those who persecute or corrupt Muslims. Though the term Holy War was meant to be understood primarily as a peaceful defense of Islam through *da'wa,* it has been used to refer to violent warfare, as has been exemplified by extremists in their defense of Islam. Some Muslim jurists developed a polarized worldview that divided it into the house of peace and house of war. Muslims, they asserted, had a duty to expand the House of Islam as part of their "civilizing mission." For most Muslims, on a practical daily basis, jihad is the striving to better one's life through service to others and by self-improvement.

Kafir: refers to unbelievers—Jews and Christians—whom Muslims view as having spurned the revelations of the earlier prophets, turned away from the paths of divine righteousness, and covered over the truth by distorting earlier revelations. Muslims believe Jesus was not crucified, but Judas, who was substituted for Christ, although Jesus did ascend to heaven, along with Moses and Mohammed. The word can also apply to apostate Muslims.

Kamis: cotton tunic that has Mao-style collar and reaches to the lower calf; worn often by Islamists and fundamentalists, supposedly replicating the look of the Prophet

Kashabiya: hooded robe made of sheep or camel wool and worn by men on top of regular clothes in winter

Koran: Islam's sacred Scripture; it represents the literal word of God spoken to Mohammed, an uneducated camel driver, in an extremely poetic form of Arabic and transmitted by the Angel Gabriel over a period of twenty-two years. The Koran affirms prior divine revelation and considers as holy books the Torah, the Psalms, and the Gospels, but it adds its own interpretations. Notably, the Koran has Abraham sacrificing Ishmael rather than Isaac, and the Jesus of the Gospels, though born of the Virgin Mary and sinless (and to some Muslims the greatest of God's apostles), is not accepted as the son of God.

Le pouvoir: literally, "the powers that be"; term used to refer to the Algerian government or to the ruling elite

Maghreb: geographical area that comprises all three North African countries: Morocco, Algeria, and Tunisia

Majlis ash shoura: a consultative assembly, meeting, public audience; an institution that often played a major role in Islamic life; in Algeria, the consultative council of the FIS

Maquis: hiding places in the countryside, derived from the French word meaning "scraggy vegetation"; somewhat like sagebrush; term was used in World War II for the wooded areas where French Resistance fighters hid—hence, they were also called *maquisards.*

Marabout: a Muslim hermit or holy man; often venerated by the common people.

MIA (Mouvement Islamique Armé): Armed Islamic Movement; a militant group that started violent actions in 1985 under its leader, Mustafa Bouyali, and carried forward by Abdelkader Chebouti after the elections of 1991 were nullified

Minbar: pulpit in a mosque

Moghazni: Algerian irregulars working with the French army, often assigned to protect SAS officers; looked down upon by *harkis,* who were front-line fighters

Mufti: a state-appointed Muslim theological authority who combines religious, judicial, and civilian responsibilities

Mujahid (pl. mujahideen): a fighter for the faith, one who wages war against the unbeliever; in Algeria, an FLN soldier during the war of independence

OAS (Organisation Armée Secrète): a militant clandestine French group created in February 1961 that refused to accept the notion of an independent Algeria, though interested in some form of confederation

Pied-noir: literally, "black foot" or "black-booted"; name given by the Algerians to the French invaders, who wore black army boots; later, the term was used to designate all the foreigners living in Algeria.

Pillars of Islam:

1. Profession of faith, or shahada: "There is no god but God, and Mohammed is his Messenger."
2. Prayer: to be performed five times a day, according to strict rules,
3. Tithing: paying the *zakat,* a tithe of 2.5 percent, once levied on the well-to-do to help the poor; nowadays, it is considered a voluntary charity and a moral duty of good Muslims.
4. Fasting: during the month of Ramadan (a Muslim must refrain from eating, drinking, smoking, and sexual intercourse from dawn until sunset),
5. Pilgrimage, or Hajj: obligation for all able Muslims who can afford it to go to Mecca at least once in a lifetime

Raï: a modern mix of Western and Arabic music; its themes, usually about sex and drugs, are considered indecent by Islamists; symptomatic of Western vulgarity and degrading influence on Islamic culture.

Ratissage: from French for "raking"; a methodical house-to-house search of an area (including summary executions) employed by the French and later by the Algerians

Repentis: word for opposition groups that laid down their arms after the vote on the *concorde civile* in September 1999

Ribat-es-salaam: means "bond of peace"; name for the semiannual meetings of Christians and Muslims at Tibhirine that began in 1979

Roumi: Arabic term for Romans; came to be used to designate European Christians; in Algeria, it is used with reference to the French.

Salafists: theocrats; in Algeria, they generally rejected participation in the democratic electoral process as being non-Islamic and considered themselves as part of a universal Islamic revolutionary movement

SAS (Section Administrative Spéciale): unit in charge of regrouping Algerians, putting them under military protection during the war of independence

Shahada: profession of faith of the Muslims (see Pillars of Islam)

Sharia: "Koranic law"—a comprehensive law that includes a Muslim's duties to God and to society; it incorporates regulations governing prayer and fasting, as well as family, penal, and international law; it is based upon the Koran, the Sunna, and the work of early Muslim scholars

Sheikh: a respectful name given to the head of a family, clan, or tribe in Arab countries; also one of the higher order of religious persons who preach in mosques

Shiism: one of the two great branches of Islam; it considers Ali, the Prophet Mohammed's son-in-law and fourth *caliph,* as the first imam and rightful successor of Mohammed. It exalts martyrdom and favors a mystical, messianic, and passionate approach to faith. For the Shiites, the mystical role of the imam is reflected in the existence of a religious hierarchy that closely resembles a clergy. Historically, Shiism has maintained that the Muslim clergy should be critics and commentators of those in power, rather than sharing power themselves, which might have a corrupting influence. What has happened in Iran, where tradition has been overturned, is an interesting exception. Contrary to Sunni belief, Shiites consider that prayers conducted by a morally unworthy prayer leader have no value. Shiites regard themselves as the true orthodoxy, even though they represent only 10 to 15 percent of Muslims. They are found mostly in Iran, but also in Iraq, Bahrain, and Oman. Strong minorities exist also in Lebanon, Kuwait, Afghanistan, and Pakistan.

Sobh: first morning prayer for Muslims; occurs at first twilight or when a thread can be seen with the naked eye

Solemn Profession: a monk's definitive vows that include stability, obedience, humility, and charity

Sufism: Muslim mysticism, created in reaction against the growing worldliness of the Islamic community; it emphasizes the inner life of the spirit and moral purification. It began in the eighth century and later developed into a mystical doctrine of seeking communion or even ecstatic union with God. It took several centuries to achieve an acceptable synthesis between moderate Sufism and orthodoxy. Sufi brotherhoods provide not only spiritual education but much-needed humanitarian aid. The term *Sufism* covers a great diversity of historical and geographical backgrounds. The number of Sufis in the world is not really known, since Sufis do not usually advertise themselves as such.

Sunna: refers to the customary behavior, teachings, and practices of the Prophet, which constitute "the Tradition." The character and personality of the Prophet inspired such confidence and commitment among his followers that the practices of the Prophet, or Sunna, became the norm for community life. The Sunna of the Prophet was drawn up and fixed in writing and is as authoritative as the Koran for Muslims, from both a legal and a doctrinal point of view.

Sunnism: one of the two great branches of Islam and considered to be the orthodox one by its followers, who represent from 85 to 90 percent of all Muslims. It accepts the Sunna as an authoritative supplement to the Koran. In terms of worship, Sunnis make a distinction between the function and the character of the person. It has no clergy and no sacraments, but it is heavily ritualistic, particularly in preparation for prayer. Sunnis accept Shiites as Muslims because their doctrine mostly coincides with orthodox Islam, but it rejects their belief in the mystic role of the imam.

Taghout: the devil, evil tyranny, or injustice caused when God's law is transgressed

Takfir wal Hijra: the name of a radical branch of the Muslim Brotherhood; it wanted to wage war against those governments it considered corrupt and unjust. Takfir wal Hijra means "Apostasy and Holy Migration," refering to when the Prophet had to emigrate from Mecca with his followers to go to Medina in 622 when he was persecuted for his faith by the Meccans.

Tamazigh: language and alphabet used by the Berbers

Trabendo: from the Spanish word for contraband; trafficking in illegally imported goods on the black market

Tuareg: nomadic Berber tribes of the Sahara

Umma: the worldwide Muslim community

Wahhabism: from the name of its founder, Abd al-Wahhab; doctrine and practices of the Wahhabis, members of a strict, conservative branch of Islam practiced in, and promoted by, Saudi Arabia

Wilaya: administrative division of the Algerian territory under the authority of a *wali,* who corresponds to a French prefect

Zakat: from Arabic, meaning "to purify"; a religious tithe, one of the five Pillars of Islam, a moral obligation to contribute money to help others

Zouave: from Zouaoua, name of a Kabyle tribe, from which came the first all-Algerian battalion to fight with the French at the time of their conquest of Algeria

Appendix C: Dramatis Personae

KIDNAPPED TRAPPIST MONKS:

BROTHER BRUNO, was born Christian Lemarchand on March 1, 1930, near Paris, the son of an army officer. As a child he grew up in Indochina and Algeria. Ordained as a young man, he later chose a career in education, teaching French literature. He had been a secondary school principal for fifteen years at the time he entered Notre-Dame de Bellefontaine in 1981. In 1989, he transferred to Notre-Dame de l'Atlas at Tibhirine, where he was assigned the job of hotelier. Later, he was assigned to the monastery's annex in Morocco. He had returned to Algeria in March 1996 to take part in the election of a new prior. He was sixty-six when he died.

BROTHER CÉLESTIN, born Célestin Ringeard on July 27, 1933, was raised by his mother after his father died when he was an infant. In 1957, he went to Algeria to do his military service as a medic before becoming a priest in 1960. In Nantes, he worked first as a parish priest until 1975 and then on the street with alcoholics, delinquents, and prostitutes (educateur de rue), until he entered Notre-Dame de Bellefontaine in 1983. From there he transferred to Tibhirine in 1986. He was musically gifted and, for a while, was the cantor for the community. He was sixty-two when he died.

BROTHER CHRISTIAN-MARIE, born Christian de Chergé on January 18, 1937, was the son of a military officer descended from an aristocratic family with a long military history. He did his military service in Algeria as an officer during the war of independence, interrupting his seminary school studies. He was ordained in 1964, then became a chaplain at Sacré-Cœur in Montmartre before deciding to become a Trappist monk in 1968, when he entered Notre-

Dame d'Aiguebelle. He transfered to Tibhirine in 1971; he was elected prior in 1984 and again in 1990. He was fifty-nine when he died.

BROTHER CHRISTOPHE was born Christophe Lebreton on October 11, 1950, to a strongly Catholic family. His father was the director of a livestock breeding center in the Loire Valley. He did his national service as a civilian, working with retarded children in Algiers. In 1974, he decided to enter Notre-Dame de Tamié in the Savoy, from where he went to Tibhirine in 1987. There, he was responsible for the garden and planning the liturgy; he also acted as master of the novices, guiding their spiritual life. He was forty-five when he died.

BROTHER LUC, born Paul Dochier on January 31, 1914, was the son of a shoe manufacturer. He studied medicine in Lyons before entering Notre-Dame d' Aiguebelle in 1941. He arrived at Tibhirine in 1946 to serve the poorest of the French poor, which at the time were French Muslims. He ran the monastery's dispensary and was also the community's cook. He was eighty-two when he died.

BROTHER MICHEL was born Michel Fleury on May 21, 1944, to a Catholic family of modest means. He joined the Communist workers' union as a machinist and later the Prado Association in Marseilles to assist unskilled workers and North African emigrants. In 1980, he became a novice monk at Notre-Dame de Bellefontaine, but the abbey's grandeur made him uncomfortable. In 1984, he went to Tibhirine, where he worked as assistant cook and gardener. He died on his fifty-second birthday.

BROTHER PAUL was born Paul Favre-Miville on April 17, 1939, in the mountains of Savoy, the only son of a blacksmith. He did his military service in Algeria as a paratrooper officer from 1960 to 1961, then returned home to help his father in the family plumbing and heating business. In 1984, he entered Notre-Dame de Tamié, but, seeking greater simplicity in his vocation, he transferred to Tibhirine in 1989. His mechanical ability was invaluable to the monastery where he served as hotelier and was known as the man with "the golden hands." He was fifty-seven when he died.

SURVIVING MONKS:

BROTHER AMÉDÉE, born Jean Noto on October 17, 1920, in Algiers, entered the Order of White Fathers (Pères Blancs), where he showed a strong desire to dedicate himself to working with Muslims. He was eventually advised that for such a calling, a life of prayer, contemplation, and simple manual labor as a Trappist monk might better accomplish his goal. He entered the monastery at Tibhirine in 1946 and was ordained a priest in 1952. Amédée was very close to the local villagers.

BROTHER JEAN-PIERRE was born on February 14, 1924, in the Lorraine, one of six children in a devout Catholic family of flour-mill workers. Following the German invasion of Alsace-Lorraine, the eighteen-year-old Jean-Pierre was drafted into the German army. He escaped being sent to the Russian front due to a false diagnosis of tuberculosis during his military medical examination. After going to Marist schools, he was ordained in 1953, entering Notre-Dame de Timadeuc in Brittany in 1957. Seven years later, in 1964, he and three other monks from Timadeuc responded to a plea from the Bishop of Algiers to supply Notre-Dame de l'Atlas with more monks.

MUSLIMS:

ALI BENHADJ was a primary school teacher of Arabic and a preacher in Algiers when he was arrested in the 1980s for having the wrong political sympathies. In jail, he read Islamic revolutionary writings and became more radical due to the influence of imprisoned militant Islamists. After four years in prison, he continued preaching and attacking government corruption and secularism. He was idolized by much of the unemployed youth. In 1989, he became the vice president of the newly formed Islamic Salvation Front (FIS), which united various militant Islamic organizations.

MOHAMMED BOUDIAF a lawyer with socialist leanings, was one of the original founders of the National Liberation Front (FLN) in 1954. He spent twenty-seven years in exile after being arrested in 1963 by President Ben Bella for opposing the political monopoly of the FLN. In 1992, he was asked by a government in crisis to take over the presidency of his country. Boudiaf was assassinated on June 29, 1992, by one of his security guards.

MOHAMMED BOUSLIMANI was the leader of an Islamic charitable association, Irshad-wal-Islah, and was a widely respected Islamic thinker and activist. He was kidnapped by members of the Armed Islamic Group in November 1993. His captors were seeking the endorsement of a recognized religious leader for their campaign of total war. He refused to associate himself with the tactics of his kidnappers in their war against the government, especially the killing of unarmed civilians. His body was found in January 1994.

IBN TAYMIYYA (1263–1328) was a Muslim theologian whose writings were selectively exploited by certain extremists in Algeria. His doctrines sought to harmonize the role of tradition, reason, and free will and promoted a "conservative reformism." He believed that religion and government needed each other. He believed the power of the government was necessary to remind citizens of their obligations to God and to be attentive to Koranic law. Without submission to the law, including the obligation to govern justly, governments would become tyrannical. Ibn Taymiyya's strict constructionist approach to interpreting the Koran is reflected in the way Islam is practiced in Saudi Arabia today, a country that gave support to the Islamist movements in Algeria.

ABASSI MADANI was a university professor with a Ph.d. in comparative education before he started preaching in the mid-1980s. A disenchanted ex-member of the FLN, he became, along with Ali Benhadj, a cofounder of the FIS in 1989, following massive student riots that launched broad-ranging constitutional reforms, ending the monopoly of political power held by the FLN since 1962.

JAMEL ZITOUNI was a young Algerian "Afghan" who had fought the Soviets. In the fall of 1994, he became supreme emir of the Armed Islamic Group (GIA), one of several armed Islamic opposition groups fighting against the Algerian government. Under his leadership, all restraints on killing civilians were removed, and his holy war was extended to include France. He was reported killed in July 1995, two months after the death of the seven monks.

APPENDIX D: Chronology of Main Events

647 Arabs annex Berber lands of the Maghreb (today Tunisia, Algeria, and Morocco).

1575 Ottoman Turks invade the Maghreb; Algeria becomes Ottoman province.

1830 French land at Sidi-Ferruch, beginning 132 years of occupation.

1843 *Trappists begin construction of first monastery at Staouéli, near Algiers.*

1848 Algeria administered as a French department, becoming an integral part of France.

1865 French citizenship open to Muslims who give up adherence to their religious law.

1868 Monsignor Charles Lavigerie founds missonary order of Pères Blancs.

1904 *Trappists depart Algeria as atmosphere of anticlericalism pervades France.*

1938 *Trappists return to Algeria and establish new monastery at Tibhirine.*

1954 NOVEMBER 1: National Liberation Front (FLN) launches war for independence from France.

1961 FEBRUARY–MAY: OAS organized to continue the fight to keep Algeria French.
APRIL: French generals rebel.

1962 MARCH 18: Accords signed at Evian, granting Algerians the right to vote for independence.
JULY 5: Algeria declares independence.

1963 Ahmed Ben Bella becomes the first president of Algeria. New constitution recognizes Christian holidays, with full pay.

1964 Christian Church of Algeria established under the Ministry of the Interior.
Trappist Abbot General orders closure of monastery at Tibhirine.

1965 Col. Houari Boumediene deposes Ben Bella and becomes new president Second Vatican Council articulates new ecumenical spirit.

1971 *Christian de Chergé arrives at Tibhirine.*

1975 *Threatened closure of monastery by Algerian authorities.*

1976 National Charter proclaims commitment to socialism and Islamic values.

1978 Death of President Houari Boumediene.

1979 FEBRUARY 7: Col. Chadli Bendjedid named president.
MARCH: *First ribat-es-salam takes place at Tibhirine.*

1984 *MARCH: Christian de Chergé elected prior of Notre-Dame de l'Atlas.*

1985–87 Oil prices start to collapse, reducing government spending for social programs.

1988 OCTOBER 4: Students riot in Algiers, government initiates reforms.

1989 FEBRUARY 5: New constitution permits free elections, freedom of the press, and freedom of assembly.
SEPTEMBER 14: Islamic Salvation Front (FIS) gains legal recognition as a party.

1990 MARCH: *Christian de Chergé reelected prior of Notre-Dame de l'Atlas.* JUNE: FIS candidates win first free multiparty municipal elections.

1991 JANUARY: Gulf War begins.
MAY 25: General strike called by the FIS.
DECEMBER 26: FIS wins majority in first legislative elections.

1992 JANUARY 11: State of emergency declared. President Chadli Bendjedid forced to resign.
JANUARY 12: Creation of High Committee of State. Annulment of elections.
JANUARY 14: Mohammed Boudiaf named president of High Committee of State.
JUNE 29: Assassination of President Boudiaf.

1993 OCTOBER 30: GIA issues ultimatum to foreigners to leave Algeria within thirty days.
DECEMBER 15: Assassination of fifteen Croats near Medea.
DECEMBER 25: GIA emir, Sayah Attia, visits monastery.

1994 MAY: AIS formed to fight in Islamically correct way, sparing innocent civilians.
MAY: Brother Henri Vergès and Sister Paul-Hélène Saint-Raymond shot.
SEPTEMBER: Jamel Zitouni becomes supreme emir of the GIA.
OCTOBER: Two Augustinian sisters killed entering a church in Bab-el-qued neighborhood of Algiers.
DECEMBER: Assassination of Pères Blancs in Tizi-Ouzou.

1995 NOVEMBER: Sister Odette Prévost killed; Sister Chantal Galichet wounded.

1996 *MARCH 27: Kidnapping of seven monks at Tibhirine.*
MAY 21: *Death of monks announced* in communiqué 44.
JULY: GIA emir, Djamel Zitouni, killed in ambush.
AUGUST: Assassination of Archbishop of Oran, Pierre Claverie.

NOTES

1. Mourning

This chapter is drawn from articles in the French press, which covered the story very extensively throughout the summer of 1996, although the story was virtually ignored in the United States. *Le Nouvel Observateur, La Croix, Le Monde, Paris Match,* and *L'Express* were particularly useful for describing the funeral at the basilica. There were interesting remarks about the funeral ("It was too grand") in Jean-Luc Barré's *Algerie: L'Espoir Fraternel,* which I also drew upon to descibe the the atmosphere of decay and filth. Abbot Olivera's homily was published in *Jusqu'où Suivre?*—a collection of eyewitness accounts of certain dramatic events preceding, and including, the kidnapping of the monks.

2. Two Mohammeds

For Christian de Chergé's experiences during the Algerian war of independence, I relied heavily on Marie-Christine Ray's excellent biography, *Christian de Chergé, Prieur de Tibhirine.* She draws on interviews with his fellow officers and subsequent correspondence with wartime friends. In addition to her book, I used interviews with members of Christian's family and also benefited from a long discussion with a fellow SAS officer, today a Père Blanc, Jean-Marie Gaudel. The role of the SAS as a kind of pastoral experience for French soldiers is described in Joseph Kraft's *The Struggle for Algeria.*

On the *pied-noir* "character" and the OAS, there are several excellent sources I have used. *Curé Pied-Noir, Evêque Algérien* (conversations with Jean Scotto) is full of firsthand insights. Scotto was a *pied-noir* and had poor working-class *pieds-noirs* in his parish of Bab el Oued in Algiers. He nursed a great bitterness toward the OAS and their scorched-earth policy after March 18, 1962, when the Evian Accord was signed, setting July 5 as the date of the referendum on Algerian independence. *A Savage War of Peace,* by Alistair Horne, is a masterful overall political history of the war, perhaps the best book in English for anyone interested in understanding the war that militarily and politically foreshadowed America's debacle in Vietnam. *L'Algérie des Français* is a very useful collection of short essays edited by Charles-Robert Ageron; it covers Algeria's colonial history, the struggle between the liberal reformers in Paris and the *pieds-noirs* in French Algeria, and the war itself. Perhaps one of the best books in English that treats in depth the period of the OAS is *Wolves in the City,* by Paul Henissart. For the colonial mentality and attitudes toward the Arab, Jules Roy's, *The War in Algeria,* published in 1961, remains the most sad and poignant. Roy was a *pied-noir,* and today he is still an active voice in the ongoing drama of French-Algerian relations.

Le Cardinal Duval, by Marie-Christine Ray, is the most important work in French on the life and thought of Cardinal Duval, presented as a series of interviews with the cardinal. These interviews were first published in 1984, then reedited in 1998, after his death. Other insights into the personality of the cardinal came from members of the Algerian Church and from Jean Scotto's book.

3. Entering the Chain

Again, I have relied heavily on Marie-Christine Ray's biography of Christian de Chergé for the period between the end of the Algerian war of independence and his departure for Tibhirine in 1971. My conversations with Christian's brothers Robert, Hubert, and Henri were also very valuable, as were talks with his mentor in Rome, Father Maurice Borrmans. Madeleine Arcand's *A Century of Hope: A History of the First Houses of the Society of Helpers in the United States Province* is an interesting source of late-nineteenth-century American social history that I suspect has been overlooked by scholars. Christian's great-great-aunt, Mother Marie Saint Bernard and the works of her order in the United States are described in considerable detail in this one-hundreth-anniversary publication issued in 1992 by the Society of Helpers in Chicago. It is an outsiders's view from within the trenches of American poverty.

There are obviously many works on Saint Benedict and the Rule. I have found particularly useful Dom Claude Jean Nesmy's, *St Benoît et la Vie Monastique* and Julian Stead's *Saint Benedict: A Rule for Beginners.* Conversations with older monks at Abbey Bellefontaine and Abbey Aiguebelle provided insight into the changes that have occurred in the order since Vatican II. The history of the Trappists in Algeria was taken from *Collectanea Cisterciensia.* Particularly useful was "Les Monastères Cisterciens d'Algérie," by Claude Garda, which gives an excellent history of the first Trappist presence at Staouéli from 1843 to 1904. The latter was the year the Trappists sold their domains to a Swiss businessman and transferred their community to Maguzzano, Italy, fearing expropriation by the French government. Garda mentions the "bed of cannonballs" that was placed under the first cornerstone of the new monastery at the groundbreaking ceremony where

Gen. Thomas Bugeaud was present. Trappists today are sometimes shocked and disbelieving when told this, yet the story is repeated in *Algeria and Tunis,* a colorful travelogue by Frances Nesbitt, who was also an accomplished watercolorist.

4. Years of Crisis

In the introduction of Robert Masson's *Tibhirine, les Veilleurs de l'Atlas,* Bishop Teissier described the traffic up to the monastery. Marie-Christine Ray's biography of Christian de Chergé was a valuable source of anecdotes and also described his conflicts with his brothers and their doubts about his vocation as a Trappist at Tibhirine. Her book was well received by both the Trappist community and by the de Chergé family, though some monks believe she exaggerated the degree of opposition to Christian's calling, describing it more as "hesitation." Christian de Chergé's article "Prier en Eglise: A l'Ecoute de l'Islam" reveals the depth of his ecumenicism vis-à-vis Islam. In it, he states, "Nothing is more foreign to the Gospels than a sectarianism which is unable to proclaim the faith of the centurion or the charity of the Samaritan as something good in themselves. . . . The Word of God is one . . . but its echo through history and in hearts seeking the straight path is infinitely diverse." (Revue Tychique No. 42)

5. *Ribats*

The minutes of the *ribats* were the primary source for this chapter. Also used were Christian's writings, collected in *Sept Vies pour Dieu et l'Algérie* (edited by Bruno Chenu) Christian's own writings supplant Marie-Christine Ray as a primary source from 1984 on. I also had the benefit of two conversations with Claude Rault, the Père Blanc friend of Christian and founder of the *ribats.*

Sufism is a complex topic and is, by necessity, treated in a cursory manner here. The point of view presented is mainly that of a Catholic, Maurice Borrman's who represents a Christian view that Sufism is something apart from regular Islam. This view would be hotly disputed by many Muslims, certainly by North African ones. Sufism is the heart and soul of Algerian Islam, even if it veers sometimes toward maraboutism. Both maraboutism and Sufism center on a community formed around a spiritual leader and both lay great stress on obedience. Sufis are sometimes thought of as "Islamic monks."

In Algeria, Sufism is the Islam of the countryside. The influence of Sufism is reflected in the nom de guerre of President Boumediene, cobbled from the name of a Spanish Sufi, Abou Mediene (Gallicized version of Abu Madyan), who is considered to be the patron saint of Algeria. Boumediene studied at the ultraorthodox Al-Ahzar Mosque and Islamic Theology Center in Cairo. Abdelkader was a Sufi, and his father was the leader of a Sufi brotherhood.

The description of Sufism used here, aside from that attributed to Professor Borrmans, is based on conversations with a Moroccan Sufi whom I got to know in France. The notion of Sufism as something heterodox is a view closely associated with the stricter Wahabite school, which disapproves of singing, dancing, and having too much fun. In the view of Hossein Nasr, an Iranian Sufi and professor at George Washington University, Sufis are completely orthodox in their commitment to following the rules of external piety, but they also seek a deeper, more esoteric knowledge of the divine.

An excellent book on Sufism is Martin Lings's *A Sufi Saint of the Twentieth Century,* which is about the Algerian sheik Ahmad al-Alawi, founder of the Alawine Sufi brotherhood in Mostaganem, his followers participated in the *ribats* at Tibhirine. Especially interesting is chapter 4, which gives Sheikh Alawi's reply to a critic in Tunis in 1920 who reflected certain puritanical trends in the Ben Badis reformist movement. Whereas he believes Christianity suffers from having its priesthood or spiritual authority marginalized by the laity, Islam, which has no priesthood per se, "does have a large number of very limited individuals who imagine that the whole religion is within their grasp and that anything outside the scope of their meager understanding is outside the pale of Islam itself"—words which might well apply to some Christians.

6. Under the Virgin's Gaze

In this chapter, I drew on conversations with Abbot Jean-Marc Thévenet and Brother Philippe Hémon, both of Notre-Dame de Tamié in Savoy. Hémon wrote an article for *Collectanea Cisterciensia,* "Vers un Dieu en Visagé de Vous," in which he summarizes different impressions from his numerous visits to Tibhirine and gives details of daily life at the monastery. My visits with Elisabeth Bonpain, Christophe's sister, as well as with his mother, Jehanne Lebreton, were rich with information and insights. For the brief sketch of Saint Bernard, I relied on *Christendom and Christianity in the Middle Ages,* by Adriaan Bredero.

7. Revolution

Several interviews informed this chapter: Mireille Duteil, a journalist with *Le Nouvel Observateur;* Ahmed Mahiou a professor of international law at the Center for Arab Studies at the University of Aix-en-Provence who was present at the 1988 riots in Algiers; Séverine Labat, who wrote *Les Islamistes*

Algériens; Francis Ghiles, a British journalist who is part Berber and part Jewish; and Ibrahim Younessi, who spent many hours talking with me about the FIS, of which he was a member.

Among the published materials, I found Pierre Guillard's *Ce Fleuve Qui Nous Sépare* very informative and detailed; it is the source for many of the quotes here that are attributed to Ali Benhadj. Guillard writes the book as a letter from a slightly disappointed admirer, chiding Benhadj for his excesses. It draws on Guillard's own close contacts with other Arab-speaking French journalists who claimed to have been in the mosques when Benhadj preached, as well as on his own extensive time in Algeria. *L'Algérie par Les Islamistes,* by Al Ahnaf, Botiveau, and Frégosi, was very useful. This collection of articles, speeches, interviews, and other writings of the different Islamist leaders gives the reader an undiluted sense of the Islamist message as well as the divergences therein.

It is notable how similar the Islamist criticisms of the secular Muslims governing Algeria today are to the Catholic critique of modern society in the nineteenth century. The pronouncements of Pope Leo XIII (*Rerum Novarum*) and, later, Pius X condemning materialism, "free thinking," democracy, socialism, and growing godlessness wrapped in cult of technical progress divorced from a strong moral anchor reflect themes also echoed by Abdelkader in his *Lettre aux Français* and by others today in the Muslim world. These parallels are readily apparent in *Hitler's Pope,* by John Cornwall, especially his discussion of the modernist crisis in chapter 2.

8. A Country of Orphans

I used several sources for information on President Boudiaf: *La Poudrière Algérienne,* by Pierre Devoluy and Mireille Duteil; *L'Histoire de l Algérie Depuis l' sIndépendance,* by Benjamin Stora; *Une Autre Voix pour l'Algérie,* by Louisa Hanoune; and an interesting conversation with Séverine Labat, who supplied me with the nicknames for Boudiaf. Ryszard Kapuscinski's chapter, "Algeria Hides Its Face," in *The Soccer War* describes the coup d'état that overthrew President Ahmed Ben Bella, one in which Bouteflika played a role.

For information on the metastasizing of the FIS into armed groups, and the culture gap between the older generation of mujahideen (1954–1961) and the young FIS supporters, Luis Martinez's *La Guerre Civile en Algérie* and Mireille Duteil and Pierre Devoluy's *La Poudrière Algérienne* were particularly useful. A small but very telling collection of essays edited by Rémy Leveau, *Algérie dans la Guerre,* has a number of excellent contributions, including one by Martinez, who is an Algerian living in France and doing scholarly research under a pseudonym. These short essays were researched in Algiers in the early 1990s based on interviews with young people in the pro-FIS neighborhoods.

Zamakhshari's commentary about the problems of interpreting the Koran were taken from *Judaism, Christianity and Islam,* by F. E. Peters (vol. 2, chapter 2).

9. A Visit from the Abbot General

Conversations with Abbot General Olivera and the writings of Christian de Chergé found in *Sept Vies pour Dieu et l'Algérie* were the primary sources for the major portion of the chapter: To describe the political events surrounding the strike of May 1991, I drew on books by Pierre Guillard, Séverine Labat, and Ghazi Hidouci, a former Algerian minister of economics (1989–1991). The latter devotes a chapter to the strike in his *La Libération Inachevée.* Another source of information on the strike was Aissa Khelladi, a former captain in the Algerian security services. Khelladi, whose nom de plume is Amine Touati, lives and writes in Paris. His books have attracted attention because of his obvious depth of knowledge. While he castigates the government for its corruption and greed, his agenda is suspect. His book *Algérie: Les Islamistes à l'Assaut du Pouvoir* is very detailed, as is his novel *Peurs et Mensonges,* which captures the atmosphere of fear and intimidation in Algiers.

10. Poyo

For this chapter, I relied on *Sept Vies pour Dieu et l'Algérie* and conversations with Bernardo Olivera and Père François de Sales, the former abbot of Notre-Dame de Tamié, who had been present at Poyo.

11. God Is Great

Sept Vies pour Dieu et l'Algérie, edited by Bruno Chenu, and *Les Martyrs de Tibhirine,* by Mireille Duteil, were the most useful published sources. In addition, I drew upon interviews with some of the monks who had been in the Atlas at the time of the massacre of the Croats. Information about the kidnapping and killing of Mohammed Bouslimani was drawn from material in *L'Innocence Fertile,* by Abdelkader Ferchiche. Ferchiche is a former Algerian journalist who left Algiers after having his family threatened and terrorized in their apartment. His book was the first homage to all the Christians who had stayed on in Algeria and been killed for their commitment to the Algerian people. He includes, as well, the story of Sheikh Bouslimani. Additional details were provided by members of the Hamas party in Algeria

12. Father Christmas

Sept Vies pour Dieu et l'Algérie, Jusqu'ou Suivre? (notes and commentary of Abbot General Bernardo Olivera), and Christan's talk to the Cistercian sisters at Brailmont in Belgium (September 1994) all recount the visit of Attia and his men to the monastery. For information on Sayah Attia, I relied on Algerian newspaper articles in *El Mudjahid* (April 17, 1994), *El Watan* (March 1 and April 17, 1994), *La Liberté* (June 5, 1994). *Algérie Actuelle* (June 1996), cite Bishop Claverie of Oran as saying that Attia had given his *aman* to the monks. Sidi Ali Benhadjar, a former GIA cohort of Sayah Attia and present at the monastery the night of the Christmas visit, says he heard Attia give the *aman*.

13. In God's Hands

Sept Vies pour Dieu et l'Algérie; Le Souffle du Don (Christophe's journal); and conversations with monks and their families provided the basis for this chapter. Robert Masson's *Jusqu'au Bout de la Nuit,* a homage to all the Christian religious killed from 1993 to 1996, gives details on the murder of Henry Vergès and Sister Paul-Hélène, as well as the seventeen others who would die.

14. Descent into Hell

Luis Martinez's *La Guerre Civile en Algérie* (pp. 307, 309) is the source for AIS declarations condemning the GIA for blaspheming Islam, excerpted from collections of letters written by the FIS leadership abroad. The murder of the Pères Blancs at Tizi-Ouzou is described in detail in chapter 1 of Armand Duval's *C'était une Longue Fidélité à l'Algérie et au Rwanda.* The book gives a good overview of the history of the Pères Blancs and postindependence Algeria, though from a completely Catholic perspective.

15. Déjà Vu

Jacques Vergès's *Lettre Ouverte à des Amis Algériens Devenus Tortionnaires,* is a moving personal outcry by a man who had fought against the use of torture by French soldiers during the war of independence. The book illustrates how Algeria has, as a child often does with his parents, adopted the parent's worst as well as best forms of behavior. In this book, the emphasis is clearly on the worst. Not only are former French methods of interrogation widely used in Algeria but many components of Algerian law are taken almost verbatim from the law codes of Vichy France, particularly regarding rights in criminal cases.

Treatment of the *harkis* after independence is a very sore subject in France.

On this topic, I found both Benjamin Stora's *La Gangrène et l'Oubli* (pp. 200, 261) and Jean Mabire's "On les Appelait les *Harkis*" very informative—one historical, the other highly personal. Mabire, a former commander of a *harki* unit, describes the *harkis* as not motivated by ideology or love of France, but by their pay and benefits packet and belief in French military strength. The best *harkis* in his unit, Mabire says, were of peasant stock and retained their ancestral respect for the virtues of strength and justice. The worst were those earlier transplants to the mainland, who came back to fight under the tricolor but who had lost their Muslim identity without yet really becoming French. But the most trustworthy, Mabire says, were those who had deserted the ALN because they could never go back to the other side. He used these men for his personal body guards and as trackers.

In Febuary 2001, the Jospin government designated a national day of recognition for the *harkis*' contributions and loyalty shown to France (exact day still to be determined). French leftists oppose the gesture because it indirectly honors the colonialist legacy.

16. Sorrow and Joy

Details about Paul's family life and personality were provided by his sisters and other members of his family during a visit to Thonon in Savoy. His military career is accounted for in *Debout les Paras* in Military Bulletin no. 160, 1996. Paul's letter to his former abbot at Tamié is included in *Sept Vies pour Dieu et l'Algérie*. Some of the local Muslim personalities are described in Christian's community bulletin of December 1990. Discussions with surviving monks, members of Luc's family, and relatives of Bruno provided important details, as did Christophe's journal, *Le Souffle du Don*.

17. Emptying the Fishbowl

Mireille Duteil's *Les Martrys de Tibhirine,* published only four months after the monks were kidnapped, was a useful source on the role of Sant' Egidio and on the general political situation in France, including the spread of the jihad to the streets of Paris in the summer of 1995. Duteil attributes to Zitouni the initiative for the terror against France, whereas other sources say Mohammed Said, an emir of the jaz'arists who had joined the GIA, was the organizer and Zitouni simply the executor (though he, in fact, killed Said and other *jaz'arists* rivals in the fall of 1995). Revelations in the French press during the winter of 2001 by Algerian military defectors assert that the government security forces were behind the bombings as well as some of the massacres in Algeria. *La Sale Guerre,* by Habib Souadia a former army lieutenant now in exile, has raised a storm because of the author's obvious direct knowledge of certain events and the graphic details he supplies; it has been widely covered in the French press.

As to the character of the Hamas party, conversations with Bishop Teissier and the new Algerian ambassador to the United States, Driss Jazairi (his name means Mr. Driss Algeria), provided useful insights, confirming that this party is for governance by *sharia* but against the use of violence to obtain political ends. Conversations with Luis Martinez, Francis Ghiles, Jacques Loquin, and the former Spanish deputy chief of mission in Algiers, Luis Calvo, were all helpful in portraying the climate in 1995–1996.

El Watan, a generally conservative anti-Islamist newspaper with close ties to military security sources, speculated about the war of the clans Benhadjera versus Baghdadi, the latter considered loyal to Zitouni. There are many theories about the kidnapping, although it is generally assumed that it was ordered by Zitouni, though using a group from outside the region. Often mentioned is the Hattab clan. Sidi Ali Benhadjera, now an ex-member of the GIA, has written a personal memorandum, "L' Affaire de la Mise à Mort des Sept Moines en Algérie," obtained from sources in Algeria. He claims to have been absolutely against doing any harm to the monks. Benhadjera was at odds with Zitouni, whose methods he considered un-Islamic.

Christian's talk on the five pillars of peace can be found in *L'Invincible Espérance,* edited by Bruno Chenu.

The description of the events that took place at the monastery in the early-morning hours of March 27 is contained in different reports provided by Amédée, Jean-Pierre, and Tierry Becker to Bernardo Olivera and published in *Jusqu'où Suivre?* [*How far to go?*].

18. Martyrs of Hope

Following the news of their death, the French press was awash in articles about the kidnapping of the monks. Much of the information is presumed to have come from contacts of journalists within their own intelligence community—information that is not always reliable, for various reasons. *L'Express* (July 25, 1996) carried one of the first broad overviews of the monks' story, beginning with the Christmas break-in by Sayah Attia. That article claimed that Philippe Rondot, former head of the DST, who had gone to Algiers, had been told with great certitude by the DGSE lieutenant colonel at the French embassy that two of the older monks had been released along the road to Annaba (formerly Bône).

Numerous interviews with a retired DGSE officer produced a generally similar rendition as that reported in the press, of Abdullah delivering the cassette to the French embassy. The main detail missing in press stories was

Abdullah saying to his French interlocutors, "we are very upset," and his request for French help in obtaining the monks' release. There is no reason I can think of why this would have been fabricated by the DGSE, as it paints a somewhat more benign picture of Zitouni than the accepted one of a enraged killer with no limits.

Mireille Duteil provides details in *Les Martrys de Tibhirine* on the discontinuation of *El Ansar* and the suspension of support by its various Libyian and Palestinian backers.

Talks with Bernardo Olivera and Armand Veilleux provided additional details about the visit to the morgue to verify the identity of the monks. The heads had presumably been seen earlier by French intelligence so as to inform the Church (Cardinal Lustiger had snuffed out the candles on May 23, the day of the announcement on Radio Medi I) seven days before Algerian authorities publically confirmed their death (May 30). *Jusqu'où Suivre?* also describes many details of the visit of Bernardo Olivera and Armand Veilleux to Algiers for the memorial service at the basilica.

Bishop Teissier kindly provided samples of the hundreds of letters sent to him from ordinary Algerians after the monks' assassination.

19. Postmortem

Descriptions of the departure from Algiers, the convoy to Medea, and burial ceremony at the monastery are drawn from details provided by Christophe's sister Elisabeth Bonpain, as well as by Armand Veilleux and Bernardo Olivera, all of whom were present at the ceremony.

El Watan (April 3, 1996) describes events preceding the kidnapping and the feud between the two clans, Baghdadi and Benhadjera. The author of the article, Salima Tlemçani, entertains no uncertainty about the identity of the kidnappers ("elements of the Benhadjera clan") in her front-page story, presumably because her information was provided by Algerian security forces. Her article, naming Benhadjera clan, is at odds with the testimony of Sidi Ali Benhadjera, himself, who after leaving the GIA, wrote a tract saying that the authors of the kidnapping "have nothing to do with Islam, neither in its words nor beliefs, and desecrate its teachings by their actions and spirit." His tract also confirmed what was widely reported in the press—that there were deep splits within the GIA over Zitouni's aggressive violence against those who disagreed with him or whom he judged a threat. Perhaps Benhadjera's clan was itself divided and he had nothing to do with the action, assuming the *El Watan* article is accurate.

20. A Visit to Algiers

Bishop Claverie apparently had a premonition, reported in a phone call to a friend, that his meeting with the French foreign minister, Hervé de Charette, during his visit could cost him his life, as this would show his sympathy for the enemy (*Le Monde,* June 8, 1998).

An Algerian, Nadia Aïtzia, a lawyer who saw the *repentis* (the repentantones) twice on local TV, told me that they explained their decision to quit the maquis because "the Saudis told them." The Saudi government had been a supporter of the FIS before it was banned in 1992. Afterward, support may have continued through unofficial channels or through private individuals.

SELECTED BIBLIOGRAPHY

BOOKS

Abd El Kader. *Lettre aux Français*. Translated by René R. Khawam. Paris: Editions Phébus, 1997.

Abdelnasser, Walid Mahmoud. *The Islamic Movement in Egypt, Perceptions of International Relations 1967–81*. London and New York: Kegan Paul International, 1994. (Chapters on the development of Al-Ikhwan Al-Muslimun 1954–81, Clandestine Islamic Organizations, Islamic Movement in Egypt 1967–81, Hasan al-Banna, Sayyid Qutb, the Concept of Jihad)

Ageron, Charles-Robert. Edited by. *L'Algérie des Français*. Paris: Editions du Seuil, 1993.

___. *Histoire de l'Algérie Contemporaine, 1830–1999*. Paris: Presses Universitaires de France, 1999.

___. *Histoire de la France Coloniale, Des origines à 1914*. Paris: Colin, 1991. (Period studied: 1870–1914)

Al Ahnaf, Mustafa, Bernard Botiveau, and Franck Frégosi. *L'Algérie par ses Islamistes*. Paris: Editions Karthala, 1991.

Alleg, Henri. *La Question*. Paris: Editions de Minuit, 1961.

Antier, Jean-Jacques. *Charles de Foucauld*. Librairie Académique Perrin, 1997.

___. *Marthe Robin, Le voyage immobile*. Librairie Académique Perrin, nouvelle édition, 1996.

Aouli, Smaïl, Ramdane Redjala, and Philippe Zoummeroff. *Abd el-Kader*. Paris: Editions Fayard, 1994.

Arcand, Madeleine. *A Century of Hope*. Chicago: Society of Helpers, 1992.

Armstrong, Karen. *Muhammed, A Biography of the Prophet*. San Fransisco: Harper, 1992.

Barbour, Nevill, Ed. *A Survey of North West Africa. The Maghrib*. London: Oxford University Press, 1962. (Chapter on Algeria, pp. 201–255)

Barré, Jean-Luc. *Algérie: L'Espoir Fraternel*. Paris: Editions Stock, 1997.

Belvaude, Catherine. *L'Algérie*. Paris: Editions Karthala, 1991.

Benzine, Rachid, and Christian Delorme. *Nous avons tant de choses à nous dire*. Paris: Albin Michel, 1997.

Bessaïh, Boualem. *De L'Émir Abdelkader à l'Imam Chamyl.* Alger: Editions Dahlab, 1997. (Chapters on Abdelkader)

Blunt, Wilfrid. *Desert Hawk. Abd el Kader and the French Conquest of Algeria.* London: Methuen and Co, 1947. (Chapters I, II, III, IV, XIV, XVI, XX, XXI, XXII)

Borgé, Jacques, and Nicolas Viasnoff. *Archives de l'Algérie.* Archives de France, Paris: Editions Michèle Trinckvel, 1995.

Borrmans, Maurice. Editor. *Guidelines for Dialogue between Christians and Muslims.* Interreligious Documents I. New York: Paulist Press, 1981.

Boutaleb, Abdelkader. *L'Émir Abd-el-kader et la Formation de la Nation Algérienne.* Alger: Editions Dahlab, 1990.

Burgat, François. *L'Islamisme au Maghreb.* Paris: Editions Payot et Rivages, 1995.

Camps, Gabriel. *Les Berbères, Mémoire et Identité.* Paris: Editions Errance, 1980. (Introduction, pp. 5–12, Origins, pp. 13–40, Religion, pp. 176–194)

Cassian, John. *Conferences.* New York: Paulist Press, 1985.

Chenu, Bruno. Edited by. *L'Invincible Espérance.* (Letters and communications of Christian de Chergé) Paris: Bayard Editions, Centurion, 1997.

___. Edited by. *Sept Vies pour Dieu et l'Algérie.* (Collection of letters and bulletins of Christian de Chergé and other monks). Paris: Bayard Editions, Centurion, 1996.

Churchill, Charles-Henry. *La Vie d'Abdel Kader.* Translation by Michel Habart. Alger: SNED, 1981.

Claverie, Pierre. *Les Evêques du Maghreb.* Paris: Les Editions du Cerf, 1996.

___. *Lettres et Messages d'Algérie.* Paris: Editions Karthala, 1996.

Cornaton, Michel. *Les Camps de Regroupement de la Guerre d'Algérie.* Paris: Editions L'Harmattan, 1967. Preface by Germaine Tillion. Afterword by Bruno Étienne. (Chapter III)

Devoluy, Pierre, and Mireille Duteil. *La Poudrière Algérienne.* Paris: Editions Calman-Lévy, 1994.

Durand, Joseph. *Itinéraire du Dernier Coopérant Français en Algérie.* Paris: Editions L'Harmattan, 1997.

Duteil, Mireille. *Les Martyrs de Tibhirine.* Turnhout, Belgium: Editions Brepols, 1996.

Duval, Armand. *C'était une Longue Fidélité à l'Algérie et au Rwanda.* Paris: Médiaspaul Editions, 1998.

Esposito, John L. *Islam and Politics.* Syracuse University Press, 1984. (Chapters on Jamaat al-Muslimin, Takfir wal Hijra, and the Muslim Brotherhood)

Étienne, Bruno. *Abdelkader.* Paris: Hachette, 1994.

___. *L'Islamisme Radical.* Paris: Hachette, 1987.

Ferchiche, Abdelkader. *L'Innocence Fertile.* Montélimar: Kader Ferchiche, 1998.

Forestier, Patrick. In collaboration with Ahmed Salam. *Confession d'un Emir du GIA.* Paris: Editions Grasset et Fasquelle, 1999.

Frère Christophe. *Aime Jusqu'au Bout du Feu.* Annecy: Editions Monte-Cristo, 1997.

___. *Le Souffle du Don. Journal de Frère Christophe, Moine de Tibhirine.* Paris: Bayard Editions, Centurion, 1999.

Gacemi, Baya. *Moi, Nadia, Femme d'un Emir du GIA.* Paris: Editions du Seuil, 1998.

Goubert, Pierre. *The Course of French History.* London & New York: Routledge, 1991.

Guerre d'Algérie, 1957: La Bataille d'Alger. Paris: Paris-Match. Collection of articles.

Guide du Jeune Musulman. *Les Piliers de l'Islam.* Paris: Editions Universel, 1997.

Guillard, Pierre. *Ce Fleuve Qui Nous Sépare. Lettre à l'Imam Ali Belhadj.* Paris: Editions Loysel, 1994.

Guitton, René. *Si Nous Nous Taisons.* Le martyre des moines de Tibhirine. Paris: Edition Calman-Levy, 2001.

Hanoune, Louisa. *Une Autre Voix Pour l'Algérie.* Paris: Editions La Découverte, 1996.

Henissart, Paul. *Wolves in the City. The Death of French Algeria.* New York: Simon & Schuster, 1970.

Hidouci, Ghazi. *Algérie. La Libération Inachevée.* Paris: Editions la Découverte, 1995.

Hirtz, Georges. *Islam-Occident, Les Voies du Respect, de l'Entente, de la Concorde.* Paris: Éditions PSR, 1998.

Horne, Alister. *A Savage War of Peace. Algeria 1954–1962.* London: Macmillan, 1977.

Imache, Djedjiga, and Inès Nour. *Algériennes entre Islam et Islamisme.* Avignon: Edisud, 1994.

Julien, Charles-André. *Histoire de l'Afrique du Nord, de la conquête arabe à 1830.* Paris: Payot, 1961. (Chapters on the seventh-century and the Berbers).

Kepel, Gilles. *Jihad. Expansion et Déclin de l'Islamisme.* Paris: NRF, Gallimard, 2000. (Chapters on Algeria).

Khadra, Yasmina. *Morituri.* Paris: Editions Baleine, 1997.

Khelladi, Aïssa. *Peurs et Mensonges.* Paris: Editions du Seuil, 1997.

Kraft, Joseph. *The Struggle for Algeria.* Garden City, NY: Doubleday, 1961.

Labat, Séverine. *Les Islamistes Algériens*. Paris: Editions du Seuil, 1995.

Laoust, Henri. *Islam. Past Influence and Present Challenge*. Edited by A. T. Welch and Pierre Cachia. Edinburgh University Press, 1979. (Chapter: L'Influence de Ibn Taymiyya)

Laroui, Abdallah. *L'histoire du Maghreb, un essai de synthèse*. Paris: François Maspéro, 1970. (Part IV: chap. XIII, XIV, XV)

Lesegretain, Claire. *Les Grands Ordres Religieux, Hier et Aujourd'hui*. Paris: Editions Fayard, 1990. (Chapter on Cistercians and Trappists)

Leveau, Rémy, Ed. *L'Algérie dans la Guerre*. Bruxelles: Éditions Complexe, 1995.

Lings, Martin. *A Sufi Saint for the Twentieth Century*. Cambridge, England: Islamic Texts Society, 1993.

Livre Blanc sur la Répression en Algérie (1991–1994). Comité Algérien des Militants Libres, de la Dignité Humaine et des Droits de l'Homme. Suisse: Editions Hoggar, 1995.

Loquin, Jacques. *L'intégrisme Islamique. Mythe ou Réalité?* Paris: Editions l'Harmattan, 1997.

Louf, André. *La Voie Cistercienne: A l'Ecole de l'Amour*. Paris: Editions Desclée de Brouwer, 1980.

Malti, Djallal. *La Nouvelle Guerre d'Algérie*. Paris: Editions La Découverte, 1999.

Martinez, Luis. *La Guerre Civile en Algérie*. Paris: Editions Karthala, 1998.

Masson, Robert. *Jusqu'au Bout de la Nuit. L'Église d'Algérie* Paris: Les Editions du Cerf, 1998.

___. *Tibhirine. Les Veilleurs de l'Atlas*. Paris: Les Editions du Cerf, 1997.

Mathias, Grégor. *Les Sections Administratives Spécialisées en Algérie, entre idéal et réalité (1955–1962)*. Paris: Editions L'Harmattan, 1998. (Introduction, Chapter: Création des SAS et Formation des Officiers SAS)

Merad, Ali. *L'Islam Contemporain*. Paris: Presses Universitaires de France, 1984.

___. *Le Réformisme Musulman en Algérie de 1925 à 1940. Essai d'histoire religieuse et sociale*. Paris et la Haye: Mouton & Co, 1967. (Introduction, First Part: Chapters II, III; Second Part: Chapters I, IV; Third Part: Chapters III, V; Fourth Part: Chapters I, II, III, VI, VII)

Merton, Thomas. *Spiritual Direction and Meditation*. Collegeville, Min: The Liturgical Press, 1960.

Messaoudi, Khalida. *Une Algérienne Debout*. Entretiens avec Elisabeth Schemla. Paris: Editions J'ai Lu, Flammarion, 1995.

Montagnon, Pierre. *Histoire de l'Algérie, des origines à nos jours*. Paris: Pygmalion, 1998. (Emir Abdelkader, Periods 1871–1880, 1914–1918, 1936–1945, and Chapter XVIII)

Mouilleseaux, Louis. Under the direction of. *Histoire de l'Algérie*. Paris: Editions de Paris, 1962. (Periods 1830–1880 and 1914–1945)

Nasr, Seyyed Hossein. *Ideals and Realities of Islam*. London: Mandala, HarperCollins, 1991.

Nesmy, Dom Claude Jean. *St. Benoît et la Vie Monastique*. Paris: Editions du Seuil, 1959.

Nozière, André. *Les Chrétiens dans la Guerre*. Paris: Editions Cana, 1979.

Olivera, Bernardo. *Jusqu'où Suivre? Les Martyrs de l'Atlas*. Paris: Les Editions du Cerf, 1997.

Peters, F. E. *Judaism, Christianity and Islam*. Vol. 1, 2, 3. Princeton, NJ: Princeton University Press, 1990.

Provost, Lucile. *La Seconde Guerre d'Algérie. Le Quiproquo Franco-Algérien*. Paris: Flammarion, 1996.

Quandt, William B. *Between Ballots and Bullets*. Washington, D.C.: Brookings Institution Press, 1998.

Ray, Marie-Christine. *Le Cardinal Duval*. Paris: Les Editions du Cerf, 1998.

___. *Christian de Chergé, Prieur de Tibhirine*. Paris: Bayard Editions, Centurion, 1998.

Rouadjia, Ahmed. *Les Frères et la Mosquée*. Paris: Editions Karthala, 1990.

Roy, Jules. *The War in Algeria*. New York, NY: Grove Press, 1961.

Ruedy, John. Ed. *Islamism and Secularism in North Africa*. Center for Contemporary Arab Studies, Georgetown University, Washington, D.C.: New York: St. Martin's Press, 1994.

Sagdeev, Roald, and Susan Eisenhower eds. *Islam and Central Asia, an enduring legacy or an evolving threat?* Washington, D.C.: A Center for Political and Strategic Studies Book, 2000.

Saint Bernard. *On the Song of Songs*. London: A. R. Mowbray and Co., 1952.

Schapiro, J. Salwyn. *Anticlericalism, Conflict between Church and State in France, Italy and Spain*. Princeton, NJ: Van Nostrand, 1967. (Chapter on France)

Scotto, Jean. *Curé Pied-Noir, Evêque Algérien*. Paris: Editions Desclée de Brouwer, 1991.

Stead, Julian. Editor. *Saint Benedict: A Rule for Beginners*. Hyde Park, NY: New City Press, 1994.

Stora, Benjamin. *Dictionnaire Biographique de Militants Nationalistes Algériens, 1926–1954*. Paris: Editions L'Harmattan, 1985.

___. *La Gangrène et l'Oubli*. Paris: Editions La Découverte, 1991.

___. *Historie de l'Algérie Coloniale, 1830–1954*. Paris: Editions La Découverte, 1991.

___. *Historie de l'Algérie depuis l'Indépendance*. Paris: Editions La Découverte, 1994.

___. *Histoire de la Guerre d'Algérie*. Paris: Editions La Découverte, 1993.

Talbi, Mohamed. *Plaidoyer pour un Islam Moderne*. Casablanca: Editions Le Fennec, 1998.

Taleb, Ahmed. (aka Ibrahimi, Ahmed Taleb) *Lettres de Prison, 1957–1961*. Alger: SNED, Editions Nationales Algériennes, 1977.

Teissier, Henri, Mgr. *L'Eglise en Islam*. Paris: Editions Le Centurion, 1984. (Chapter I, L'itinéraire spirituel d'un Algérien: Abd-el-Kader)

___. Edited by. *Histoire des Chrétiens d'Afrique du Nord*. Paris: Desclée de Brouwer, 1991. (Chapter 6: *L'Eglise d'Algérie: enracinement, épreuves et conversions, de 1830 à nos jours* by Denis Gonzalez. P. 117–138)

___. *Lettres d'Algérie*. Paris: Bayard Editions-Centurion, 1998.

___. *La Vie Spirituelle*. Paris: les Editions du Cerf. Revue bimestrielle, Oct. 1997. (The entire issue is dedicated to Pierre Claverie on the first anniversary of his death)

Touati, Amine. *Algérie, Les Islamistes à l'Assaut du Pouvoir*. Paris: Editions L'Harmattan, 1995.

Turin, Yvonne. *Affrontements Culturels dans l'Algérie Coloniale. Ecoles, Médecines, Religion, 1830–1880*. Alger: Entreprise Nationale du Livre (ENAL), 1983.

Vatikiotis, P. J. *The History of Egypt from Muhammad Ali to Mubarak*. Baltimore, MD: The Johns Hopkins University Press, 1969.

Vergès Jacques. *Lettre ouverte à des amis algériens devenus tortionnaires*. Paris: Albin Michel, 1993.

Von Graffenried, Michael. *Inside Algeria*. New York: Aperture Foundation, 1998.

Zartman, I. William, M. A. Tessler, J. P. Entelis, R. A. Stone, R. A. Hinnebusch, and S. Akhavi. *Political Elites in Arab North Africa*. New York & London: Longman, 1982.

___, and W. M. Habeeb. Eds. *Polity and Society in Contemporary North Africa*. Boulder, Colorado: Westview Press, 1993.

JOURNALS AND PERIODICALS

Ageron, Charles-Robert. "La prise du pouvoir par le FLN." *L'Histoire*, no 231. Dossier Spécial, April 1999.

Algérie: "Les raisons de la colère." *Les Cahiers de l'Orient*, no. 51. Third Quarter, 1998.

Attaf, Rabha. "L'affaire de Ouargla—Mythe fondateur du discours de l'éradication." Published in *Peuples Méditerranéens*, no. 70–71, First Quarter, 1995.

Attaf, Rabha, and Fausto Giudice. "Algérie: La Grande Peur Bleue. Questions about a faceless war." *Les Cahiers de l'Orient*. First Quarter, 1995.

___. "La Bleuïte, encore et toujours." *Les Cahiers de l'Orient*. First Quarter, 1995.

Benchenane, Mustapha. "L'Armée, Cœur et Axe du pouvoir." Paris: *Autrement 38–82.*

Borrmans, Maurice. "Lavigerie et les Musulmans en Afrique du Nord." *Bulletin de Littérature Ecclésiastique*. Toulouse: Published by the Catholic Institute in Toulouse, January–June 1994.

Burgat, François. "Algérie: L'AIS et le GIA, itinéraires de constitution et relations." *Monde Arabe: Maghreb, Machrek,* no. 149, July–Sept. 1995.

De Chergé, Christian. "L'Algérie devant Dieu." Dissertation written as part of a research project about Algeria by the students of IPEA. Rome: Papal Institute of Arabic Studies, June 1974.

Dumont, Marie. "OAS, La stratégie de la terreur." *L'Histoire,* no. 231. Dossier Spécial, April 1999.

"L'Europe et l'Islam–L'Algérie et la France." *Enquête sur l'Histoire,* no. 15, Winter 96.

Garda, Claude. "Les monastères cisterciens d'Algérie. Notre-Dame de Staouëli-Notre-Dame de l'Atlas." *Collectanea Cisterciensia 58,* 1996. (pp. 201–216)

Gèze, François. "Algérie: pourquoi le silence?" Directeur général des Éditions La Découverte.

Gravrand, Charbel-Henry, ocso. "Mémorial de l'Abbaye d'Aiguebelle, leur maison mère: Aux Frères Moines de N.-D. De L'Atlas." *Collectanea Cisterciensia 58,* 1996. (pp. 336–351)

Harbi, Mohammed. "Le F.L.N., Boumediene, Chadli." Paris: *Autrement,* 38–82.

___. "La Politique Occulte des Clans." Paris: *Autrement,* 38–82.

Hémon, Philippe. "Vers un À-Dieu En-Visagé de Vous." Personal testimony of a monk about his brothers at the monastery of Notre-Dame de l'Atlas. From *Collectanea Cisterciensia,* fasc. 3, 1996.

Henry, Jean-Robert. "France-Algérie: Assumer l'Histoire Commune." *Confluences, Méditerranée. Passions Franco-Algériennes*. Paris: L'Harmattan, no. 19, Fall 1996.

___. "La France au Miroir de l'Algérie." Paris: *La Mémoire. Autrement,* 38–82.

___. "L'identité imaginée par le droit. De l'Algérie coloniale à la construction européenne." *Cartes d'Identité,* Presses de la Fondation Nationale des Sciences Politiques, novembre 1994.

___. "Sur l'Intertextualité des Stéréotypes en Situation Coloniale." *Rives Nord-Méditerranéennes*, no. 10, 1995.

Itinéraires. Algiers: Semestral Review published by Emir Abdelkader Foundation, no. 2, January–June 1998.

Kapil, Arun. "Les Partis Islamistes en Algérie: éléments de présentation." *Monde Arabe: Maghreb, Machrek,* no. 133, Sept. 1991.

Kepel, Gilles. "Aperçus sur l'Idéologie du GIA." *Pouvoirs: l'Algérie,* Paris: 86 Seuil.

Martin, Denis-Constant. "Comment dit-on "nous" en politique?" *Cartes d'Identité,* Presses de la Fondation Nationale des Sciences Politiques, Nov. 1994.

Martinez, René. "Lundi Ier Novembre 1954." Paris: *La Mémoire, Autrement,* 38–82.

Morelle, Chantal, and Maurice Vaïsse. "Histoire secrète des accords d'Evian." *L'Histoire,* no. 231. Dossier spécial, April 1999.

Olivera, Bernardo, Abbot General.

I. "Our Brothers of Atlas, For a faithful reading of the events," May 27, 1996.

II. "Our Brothers of Atlas, Chronicle of the trip to Algeria," June 11, 1996 (part 2).

III. "Our Brothers of Atlas, Radiant witnesses of Hope: Your story and ours," Oct. 12, 1996.

IV. "Our Brothers of Atlas, Keeping their memory alive," May 21, 1997. From Unpublished Letters.

"La Parole aux Algériens." *Confluences, Méditerranée,* no. 25. Paris: Editions L'Harmattan, Spring 1998.

Pennington, Basil. "The Cistercian Martyrs of Algeria, 1996." *Encounter,* published by The Papal Institute of Arab and Islamic Studies in Rome, no. 233, March 1997.

Pervillé, Guy. "Monseigneur Duval, un évêque contesté. Alger 1941–1962." *Autrement,* Collection Mémoires, no. 56, March 1999.

___. "La tragédie des Harkis: Qui est responsable?" *L'Histoire,* no. 231, Dossier Spécial, April 1999.

Ray, Ellen. "Algeria: Theocracy by terror?" *Covert Action Quarterly,* Winter 1999.

Slama, Alain-Gérard. "Oran, 5 Juillet 1962: le massacre oublié." *L'Histoire,* no. 231, Dossier spécial, April 1999.

Stora, Benjamin. "La guerre sans fin." *L'Histoire,* no. 231, Dossier Spécial, April 1999.

Teissier, Henri. "L'Eglise en Islam." Paris: Le Centurion, 1984.

Turquié, Sélim. "La France dite et maudite. L'errance entre deux terres." Paris: *Autrement,* 38–82.

___. "Trucs, Troc, Piston et Système D. Algérie au Jour le Jour." Paris: *Autrement,* 38–82.

"Le Volcan Algérien." *L'Atelier de Géopolitique*, no. 1, Fall 1999.

Winock, Michel. "La France en Algérie: Cent trente ans d'aveuglement." *L'Histoire,* no. 231, Dossier Spécial, April 1999.

INDEX

LaVergne, TN USA
03 April 2011
222651LV00001B/109/P